Israel's Scripture Traditions
and the Synoptic Gospels:
Story Shaping Story

ISRAEL'S SCRIPTURE TRADITIONS

and the

SYNOPTIC GOSPELS

Story Shaping Story

To Bill,

WILLARD M. SWARTLEY

With appreciation for your friendship & scholarship

Willard Swartley

Mar 24, 95

HENDRICKSON PUBLISHERS
P.O. BOX 3473 ■ PEABODY, MA 01961-3473

ISBN 1–56563–001–7

Library of Congress Cataloging-in-Publication Data

Swartley, Willard M., 1936–
    Israel's scripture traditions and the Synoptic Gospels: story
shaping story / Willard M. Swartley.
        p. cm.
    Includes bibliographical references and index.
    ISBN 1–56563–001–7 (pbk.)
    1. Bible. N.T. Gospels—Criticism, interpretation, etc.
    2. Bible. O.T.—Theology. 3. Bible. N.T.—Relation to the Old
Testament. I. Title.
    BS2555.2.S93   1994
    226'.066—dc20   94-25577
                                                               CIP

DEDICATION

To my grandchildren
Kristen Marie
Jeremy Daniel
John Mark
Michael James

Who pass on the story

"God, your praise, like your name
reaches to the ends of the world . . . "

"Then tell the next generation
that God is here
our God and leader
for ever and ever."
(Ps 48:10, 14, JB)

TABLE OF CONTENTS

LIST OF TABLES

ABBREVIATIONS

AB	Anchor Bible
ABD	Anchor Bible Dictionary
AnBib	Analecta biblica
ANETS	Ancient Near Eastern Texts and Studies
ANRW	*Aufstieg und Niedergang der römischen Welt*
ATR	*Anglican Theological Review*
BA	*Biblical Archaeologist*
BBB	Bonner Biblische Beiträge
BJRL	*Bulletin of the John Rylands Library*
BJS	Brown Judaic Studies
BR	*Biblical Research*
BTB	*Biblical Theology Review*
BWANT	Beiträge zur Wissenschaft vom Alten und Neuen Testament
BZ	*Biblische Zeitschrift*
CBA	Catholic Biblical Association
CBQ	*Catholic Bible Quarterly*
CBQMS	Catholic Bible Quarterly Monograph Series
ETL	*Ephmerides theologicae lovanienses*
ExpTim	*Expository Times*
FRLANT	Forschungen zur Religion und Literatur des Alten und Neuen Testaments
FS	Festschrift
GNS	Good News Studies
HBT	*Horizons in Biblical Theology*
HSM	Harvard Semitic Monographs
HTR	*Harvard Theological Review*
IDB	*Interpreter's Dictionary of the Bible*, ed. G. A. Buttrick
Int	*Interpretation*
IrishBibStud	*Irish Biblical Studies*
ISBE	*International Standard Bible Encyclopedia*
JAAR	*Journal of the American Academy of Religion*

JBL	*Journal of Biblical Literature*
JQR	*Jewish Quarterly Review*
JR	*Journal of Religion*
JSNTSS	Journal for the Study of the New Testament, Supplement Series
JSOT	*Journal for the Study of the Old Testament*
JSOTSS	Journal for the Study of the Old Testament, Supplement Series
JTS	*Journal of Theological Studies*
NCB	New Century Bible
Neot	*Neotestamentica*
NovT	*Novum Testamentum*
NovTSup	Novum Testamentum, Supplements
NovTSup n.s.	Novum Testamentum, Supplements, new series
NTS	*New Testament Studies*
OBO	Orbis biblicus et orientalis
OP	Occasional Papers
OTL	Old Testament Library
Persp Rel Stud	*Perspectives in Religious Studies*
PMS	Pickwick Monograph Series
RSR	*Recherches de science religieuse*
SBL	Society of Biblical Literature
SBLDS	Society of Biblical Literature Dissertation Series
SBLMS	Society of Biblical Literature Monograph Series
SBM	Stuttgarter biblische Monographien
SBT	Studies in Biblical Theology
SJT	*Scottish Journal of Theology*
SNTSMS	Society for New Testament Study Monograph Series
SPB	Studia postbiblica
SPS	Studies in Peace and Scripture
TBü	Theologische Bücherei
TLZ	*Theologische Literaturzeitung*
TPINTC	Trinity Press International New Testament Commentary
TR	Text Reader
TU	Texte und Untersuchungen
TZ	*Theologische Zeitschrift*
USQR	*Union Seminary Quarterly Review*
VC	*Vigiliae christianae*
WCC	World Council of Churches
WMANT	Wissenschaftliche Monographien zum Alten und Neuen Testament
ZAW	*Zeitschrift für die alttestamentliche Wissenschaft*
ZNW	*Zeitschrift für die neutestamentliche Wissenschaft*
ZTK	*Zeitschrift für Theologie und Kirche*

PREFACE

"Indeed Christians have always believed we are not saved by a text
or a narrative, but by the life, death, and resurrection of Jesus
Christ in time and space."—Brevard S. Childs[1]

With this point Childs critiques David Kelsey's and Stanley
Hauerwas' genial contributions on narrative, the means whereby
Christian faith best expresses its theology and shapes Christian character. This study, *Israel's Scripture Traditions and the Synoptic Gospels:
Story Shaping Story,* may be similarly criticized. But the other side of
the truth, to counter Childs, is that the Christian faith is passed from
generation to generation by those who "Love to Tell the Story," as the
old gospel song says. Without the story and its telling,[2] we would not
know the saving truth of "the life, death, and resurrection of Jesus
Christ." This work examines the first three Gospels to enable us to
understand more clearly how the biblical story of faith, in its old and
new covenant expressions, is narrated in the Synoptics. It is a biblical
theological study in continuity and transformation.

In 1979 I published *Mark: The Way for All Nations,* a book
that popularized the insights of my doctoral dissertation on "Markan
Structure" completed at Princeton Theological Seminary in 1973. In
these works I undertake a section by section study of Mark with
particular attention to elements of structural cohesion. Stimulated by

---

[1] B. S. Childs, *Biblical Theology of the Old and New Testaments: Theological Reflection on the Christian Bible* (Minneapolis: Augsburg/Fortress, 1992),
665.

[2] Note the development in biblical storytelling: T. Boomershine, *Story
Journey: An Invitation to the Gospel as Storytelling* (Nashville: Abingdon, 1988).

the biblical theological contribution of Bernhard W. Anderson in several Princeton courses, I came to see that Mark utilized Israel's faith story, with its major themes of deliverance from the *sea*, covenant-formation on the *mountain*, testing in the *wilderness*, guidance on the way, and self-identity debates around *temple* and *kingship*. Subsequent years of study have confirmed and extended these insights. Since 1986 a related insight developed and matured: not only is Mark structurally toned by this OT–NT relationship, but the Synoptic Gospels together bear this mark of identity, despite the fact that each manifests its own distinctive structural design, literary purpose, and theological emphases.

During the 1980s I headed up annual June seminar studies consisting of several professors and seminary seniors in an effort to ascertain the relation of peace to central biblical theological streams of thought. In the 1986 seminar an intense discussion of kingship by two OT scholars, Gerald Gerbrandt and Ben Ollenburger, sparked for me a key insight that provided a breakthrough in my developing notions about the Synoptic Gospels. Both persuasively argued the positive function of kingship, with its divine and human aspects, in OT theological expression. Ollenburger further contended that numerous texts distinguish between Yahweh's covenant commitment to Davidic royalty and to Zion, an argument now accessible in his *Zion, the City of the Great King*. In the same seminar we discussed Israel's exodus traditions and their relation to the southern Davidic kingship traditions. The intensity and clarity of the discussion pushed a button of insight in my ongoing quest to understand the Synoptic structural design oriented to Galilee and Jerusalem, a feature many scholars have come to regard as a structural opposition and theological polarity (see ch. 2 below).

Suddenly I articulated the discovery: just as the Synoptics' Galilean sections develop theological emphases associated with Israel's faith traditions that originated in the north, so the Synoptics' Jerusalem sections explicate new theological interpretations of faith traditions more distinctive to Israel's southern religious experiences, namely, temple and kingship. Scholarly testing of this thesis had to wait several years until dedicated sabbatical time, for which I thank the Associated Mennonite Biblical Seminaries, afforded an opportunity to do a thorough study of each Gospel's structure and theological contribution. In 1988–89 I took up the task in the context of the rich resources, both faculty and library, of the Yale Divinity School. I am especially grateful to Brevard Childs, Richard Hays, Susan Garrett, and Paul Minear for the wise counsel and helpful encouragement, with cautions, that each gave to a part or the entire manuscript in its first stages. I also owe a great debt to two of my former AMBS teachers and then later colleagues: Howard H. Charles who taught me the inductive method of biblical study, an empowerment for careful scrutiny of the text, and Millard Lind, from whom I learned much about Israel's exodus and conquest traditions through an OT–NT co-teaching experience from 1978 to 1986 at AMBS. I have also been stimulated by Jacob Enz in his concern for an intracanonical approach to Scripture.

Many other people have contributed to the sharpening of my insight and contribution: my AMBS faculty colleagues who discussed the Mark and Luke sections of ch. 4 and gave helpful critique; Perry Yoder and Jacob Elias, colleagues who read the entire manuscript in its first galley stage and made many helpful suggestions, some of which led me to reassess a given emphasis or consider another view or source; Beth Bontrager and Jewel Gingerich-Longenecker for their significant editorial assistance; Willard Roth and Diane Zaerr who read portions of the manuscript to aid style and readability. Moreover, I thank Chris Marshall (from New Zealand) who, during his sabbatical at AMBS, helped me with both content and literary matters. I thank also my students in my New Testament Theology and Ethics course who gave helpful suggestions, as well as Ashish Chrispal, Dean of Union Biblical Seminary, Pune, India, who during his sabbatical at AMBS gave several helpful suggestions. For the painstaking task of indexing I thank Beth Bontrager for her excellent work in preparing the author and scripture indexes, and Kevin Miller for skillfully assisting me in computer searches to prepare the subject index.

I am also grateful to David M. Scholer for encouraging me in this project and for suggesting Hendrickson Publishers as publisher. Most significant, Patrick H. Alexander, Hendrickson editor, has given me wise counsel and extensive editorial assistance to improve the manuscript.

I express much gratitude to all these helpers. Without them the project would not have achieved its present form.

INTRODUCTION

This study proposes that key Old Testament theological traditions influenced the structure and theology of the Synoptic Gospels. It examines how this occurs in each of the four major sections of the Synoptic Gospels. Israel's major faith traditions, it is argued, afforded a structural framework for the *synoptic* presentation of Jesus as evidenced in the Synoptic Gospels' canonical form. These traditions functioned at both conscious and subconscious levels to provide a pattern by which the early church grasped, interpreted, and presented the synoptic story of Jesus. By utilizing the conceptual and liturgical structures of Israel's faith, the Synoptics offer a unique representation of *Story Shaping Story.*

While acknowledging the distinctives of each Synoptic Gospel, this study proposes new understandings of the common core of the synoptic tradition.[1] New perspectives are offered both on biblical theology in its consideration of the relation between the Testaments and on the origin and function of the Synoptic Gospels.

Pioneering redactional studies of the Synoptic Gospels in the 1950s (Conzelmann on Luke, Marxsen on Mark, and Bornkamm, Barth, and Held on Matthew) accented the diverse theological emphases of each Gospel.[2] As a result of this approach, relatively scant

---

[1] New data for assessing the order of the Gospels' origins may emerge as a side-benefit of this study.

[2] By highlighting the diversity among the Synoptics, these studies might have resulted in the discarding of the synoptic conception. But such has not occurred. The similarity in general content among the Synoptics—at least in the formal sense—as well as the similar order of the canonical form of the synoptic tradition have been apparently sufficiently self-evident that the conception has endured in scholarly work.

attention has been given to the structural and theological patterns that unite the first three Gospels.

Nor have contributions in New Testament theology and ethics addressed adequately the matter of the Synoptics' distinctive structure. They have tended to opt for one of three approaches: to focus on the historical Jesus (Jeremias[3]), to follow a rather standard topical format in presenting the theology of the Synoptics' portrait of Jesus (Ladd,[4] Kümmel,[5] Goppelt[6]), or to describe, first Jesus and then the redactional emphases of the first three Gospels (Schrage,[7] Verhey[8]). While these contributions present themes common to the synoptic tradition—the proclamation of the kingdom of God, the parables of Jesus, christological portrait(s), the love commandment, Jesus and the law—the theologies especially fail to assess the similar and distinctive theological and ethical accents of each of the three Gospels.[9] Thus, a presentation of the Synoptic Gospels' theology and ethics—and the presentation of the story of Jesus—must still come to terms with the narrative unity and similarity of the Synoptics, while at the same time showing the distinctive way in which each Gospel develops a common structural pattern in its presentation of the story of Jesus.[10]

---

[3] J. Jeremias, *New Testament Theology: The Proclamation of Jesus,* trans. J. Bowden (New York: Scribner's, 1971).

[4] G. E. Ladd, *A Theology of the New Testament* (Grand Rapids: Eerdmans, 1974), Part I.

[5] W. G. Kümmel, *The Theology of the New Testament,* trans. J. E. Steely (Nashville/New York: Abingdon, 1973).

[6] L. Goppelt, *Theology of the New Testament,* vol. 1 (Grand Rapids: Eerdmans, 1981).

[7] W. Schrage, *The Ethics of the New Testament,* trans. D. E. Green (Philadelphia: Fortress, 1988). Schrage's approach is to first treat several topics under "Jesus' Eschatological Ethics," then "Ethical Beginnings in the Earliest Congregations," and then "Ethical Accents in the Synoptic Gospels." Here each Gospel is discussed separately.

[8] A. Verhey, *The Great Reversal: Ethics and the New Testament* (Grand Rapids: Eerdmans, 1984). Like Schrage, Verhey presents the ethics of Jesus, the early church, and each Synoptic Gospel separately in three sequential sections.

[9] Ladd gives little attention to how the three Gospels develop these themes with different emphases; he tends to homogenize data from the three to build a discussion around the given theme. Though more critical in the selection and use of data, Goppelt also fails to pick up the different emphases among the Synoptics (see, e.g., his discussion of Jesus' "suspension of the law," 124–27). Do Matthew and Mark, or Luke and Mark, really give the same perspective on Jesus' relation to the law?

[10] Perhaps it is noteworthy that the treatment of each Gospel's distinctiveness has appeared in the ethical treatments (Verhey and Schrage), rather

The recent "Gospel as Story" contributions have enhanced our understanding of the Gospels as distinctive literary works.[11] But these studies have not been analyzed and correlated in order to aid or advance our understanding of the common structure that characterizes and qualifies these Gospels to be a "synoptic" witness to Jesus.[12] For example, one might now compare the settings of each Gospel story as these have been developed by the authors of these several "Story" volumes.

Bo Reicke has proposed that the synoptic content and structure developed in response to catechetical and didactic needs in the early church. He regards the topical groupings with segments on discipleship as support of this theory.[13] His proposal, however, does not consider the potential influence of Old Testament traditions and themes upon the formation and development of these units. Similarly, but with contrasting explanation, C. H. Dodd argued years earlier that the Markan outline—the base or source of the synoptic pattern— originated for and from early church preaching. Its basis was thus kerygmatic. Using an early kerygmatic outline of Jesus' ministry that preserved some chronological and topographical features, but was essentially topical, Mark compromised between a chronological and topical order of events.[14] Dodd's proposal, written twenty years before

---

than the theological. But then these were written later, in the 1980s, which likely accounts for the difference. Verhey handles themes common to the Synoptics by identifying them as teachings of Jesus. These themes are treated first, and then later each of the Synoptics' distinctive emphases are presented. While both sections use some of the same text references, no attention is given to the common synoptic core that mediates the teaching of Jesus distinctively presented by each Gospel.

[11] See, e.g., D. Rhoads and D. Michie, *Mark as Story: An Introduction to the Narrative of a Gospel* (Philadelphia: Fortress, 1982).

[12] Recent studies devoted to the "synoptic problem" have also failed to show the common strands that bind the Synoptics, but have centered rather on the sequence of the origin of the Synoptic Gospels.

[13] B. Reicke, *The Roots of the Synoptic Gospels* (Philadelphia: Fortress, 1986), especially chs. 4–6.

[14] C. H. Dodd, "The Framework of the Gospel Narrative," *ExpTim* 43 (1932), 396–400 = *NTS* 1 (1953), 1–11. Dodd's view suffers from his assumptions that Mark was a collector of what he received: independent pericopes, larger complexes of narrative, and an outline of the whole ministry into which he integrated the independent pericopae and larger complexes. Because the outline was too meager to provide settings for all of the received narrative, he settled for a compromise between a chronological and topical order (p. 400). In view of the later extensive redactional study of the Synoptics, Dodd's proposal now seems "primitive."

his influential *According to the Scriptures*,[15] failed to consider the formative influence of the Old Testament faith-story upon the shape of the pre-Markan outline or the Markan narrative achievement.

While numerous writers have proposed various types of Old Testament influence upon one or all of the Synoptic Gospels (see ch. 1), only those arguing for a lectionary function behind the composition have developed a perception of the origin of the Synoptics that shows Old Testament influence on both the distinctive content and order of the Synoptic Gospels. Here M. D. Goulder's proposals that the Synoptic Gospels were modeled after Jewish lectionaries are noteworthy.[16] But even these give only limited rationale for the sequence of content—since it varies from Gospel to Gospel—and for the function of that content within the larger design of each of the Synoptics. Nor do these proposals explain the distinctive synoptic structure, consisting of Galilean and Jerusalem divisions joined by a Journey section.

This study contributes to this lacuna in synoptic research. It proposes a rationale for the distinctive macro-structure of the Synoptics—as opposed to that of the Johannine and noncanonical Gospels—and shows why particular pericopae are located within the respective main sections of the pattern.[17] By doing so it shows how

---

[15]C. H. Dodd, *According to the Scriptures: The Substructure of New Testament Theology* (London: Nisbet, 1952).

[16]M. D. Goulder, *The Evangelists' Calendar: A Lectionary Explanation of the Development of Scripture* (London: SPCK, 1978), and *Midrash and Lection in Matthew* (London: SPCK, 1974). Unfortunately, E. Richard's extensive report of research on Luke in the 1970s ("Luke—Writer, Theologian, Historian: Research and Orientation of the 1970s," *BTB* 13 [1983], 3–15) omits even passing reference to Goulder's work, which is devoted to the originating impulse behind Luke's Gospel. No mention is made either of J. Drury's *Tradition and Design in Luke's Gospel* (Atlanta: John Knox, 1976), which follows C. F. Evans's earlier proposal that Luke's journey narrative follows the topical sequence of Deuteronomy (pp. 138–64).

Similarly, F. Bovon's extensive history of research fails to mention C. F. Evans's essay and proposal in his review of studies on Luke and OT interpretation (*Luke the Theologian: Thirty-three Years of Research [1950–1983]*, trans. K. McKinney [Allison Park, Penn.: Pickwick, 1978], 78). Nor does he refer to it in his recent essay in discussing Luke's structure ("Studies in Luke–Acts: Retrospect and Prospect," *HTR* 85 [1992], 183–86).

The contributions of Riesenfeld and Gerhardsson have spoken to the origin of the gospel tradition as a whole, but not to the reason or logic of the synoptic pattern as distinct from that in John.

[17]My doctoral study of Mark's structure was the first step in this present effort ("A Study in Markan Structure: The Influence of Israel's Holy

Israel's faith traditions shaped the content and structure of the Synoptics' stories of Jesus.

Chapter 1 locates the study within the context of scholarly work on the Old Testament's influence on the New, especially the Synoptic Gospels. This requires some attention to the relation between the Testaments as well. I then describe my method, which draws on different approaches to the Gospels, but is oriented primarily to what is known as compositional analysis, utilizing both structural and narrative analyses. This approach accords well with Brevard Childs's call for theological reflection on the *canonical* form of the tradition, with awareness of the heritage and journey of those traditions in the faith of the communities which sustained and nurtured them.

Chapter 2 identifies and discusses the four major Old Testament theological traditions which form the heart of this biblical theological approach to the Synoptics. Special attention is also given to the unique Galilee-Jerusalem structure of the synoptic tradition and its significance as understood by various scholars.

Chapters 3–6 show the extent and nature of the influence of four major Old Testament faith traditions upon the structure and theology of the Synoptics. Chapter 3 focuses on the impact of the Old Testament exodus (deliverance and wilderness) and Sinai traditions upon each of the Synoptics. Chapter 4 shows the influence of what Old Testament scholarship calls the "conquest traditions" (including the theme of the "divine warrior"), but which should perhaps be designated differently (see ch. 4, part A). I argue that these traditions played a major and decisive role on the Galilean and journey sections of the Synoptics' presentation of the story of Jesus. Here I show differences as well as similarities. For example, while the exodus traditions are quite formative in each Gospel, the degree and type of influence differs among the Gospels: exodus influence is more prominent in Luke's journey narrative than it is in Matthew's parallel section. Further, the exodus and conquest traditions influenced both the

---

History Upon the Structure of the Gospel of Mark" [Ph.D. diss., Princeton Theological Seminary, 1973]). W. A. Meeks's study, *The Prophet-King: Moses Traditions and the Johannine Christology* (NovTSup n.s. 14; Leiden: E. J. Brill, 1967), represents some elements of this task for John's Gospel. As his study shows, the exodus and kingship traditions are the most influential in the shaping of John's story of Jesus. But it also argues that the Johannine kingship tradition is not Davidic, but is derived from second–first century B.C. Jewish sources that portray Moses as a king. See Appendix I below.

Galilean and journey sections in Luke, whereas in Mark the exodus traditions, in their formative influence, are more focused in the Galilean section; the conquest traditions, in their formative influence, are more focused in the journey (ὁδός) section.

Chapters 5 and 6 demonstrate that the Old Testament temple and kingship traditions played a major and decisive role in the Synoptics' portrait of Jesus' Jerusalem ministry. Here again, both the differences and similarities among the Synoptics will be noted. For example, Mark's use of Israel's temple tradition, and Jesus' relationship to it, differ from Luke's. But in all three Gospels Jesus' relation to the temple reflects temple traditions from the earlier story and plays a major role in the shaping of the prepassion narrative. Chapter 5 also considers wisdom traditions, since they appear to have influenced Matthew's temple section.[18] Chapter 6 shows that kingship traditions significantly shaped the passion narrative.

While this study accents the sequential factor in the relation of the influence of the Old Testament traditions upon specific Synoptic sections, to some extent these traditions are fused with and overlap each other in both the older and newer stories. To be sure, exodus and kingship traditions are foundational to the presentation of the Jesus story in all four Gospels, a point of convergence between the Synoptics and John. With the kingdom of God motif permeating the Synoptics' story, the theme of kingship cannot be restricted to the passion narrative. Even so, the identity of Jesus as King, while anticipated in earlier narratives, becomes a major focus in the passion narrative. Further, granting these features of fusion, some overlapping, and creative artistic interweaving of motifs, the case for a sequential, formative influence (i.e., exodus, conquest, temple, and kingship) upon the structural and theological design of the Synoptics is very strong. Thus, while on the one hand we need to resist the notion that the development of the narrative plot is restricted to the use of only one theme from Israel's tradition history in any given synoptic section, we can also see a substantial *sequential* shaping of the structure and theology of the Synoptics. Further, this feature is distinctive to the Synoptics; it is not present in either John or the noncanonical Gospels.

To assist the reader in locating each part of chapters 3–6 in relation to the whole, and to show the steps in my method and scope

---

[18]This falls within the synoptic section of temple tradition influence, reflecting the priestly and courtly setting where wisdom flourished in Israel's history.

of treatment as well, I portray here in a diagram the sequence of topics to be followed in each chapter, with pagination indicating where each topic begins:

Ch. Sections	3. Exodus	4. Conquest	5. Temple	6. Kingship
Describe Tradition	45	96	154	199
Mark	48	98	157	203
Matthew	61	116	170	215
Luke	74	126	185	232
Continuity and Transformation	91	145	192	247

In light of the findings of chapters 3–6, chapter 7 first synthesizes the findings of the study, summarizing and clarifying the insights. Second, it analyzes briefly the synoptics' hermeneutical use of the OT traditions. Third, it seeks to discern the meaning of the distinctive synoptic design, especially the symbolic roles of Galilee and Jerusalem. Here I set forth an hypothesis that the theological emphases of the Synoptics' Galilean and journey sections correlate with the Old Testament (northern) theological traditions. Similarly, the Synoptic portraits of Jesus' Jerusalem ministry, in both the prepassion and passion phases, correspond to the Old Testament (southern) traditions. I then propose that four major streams of Old Testament tradition, in an overall sequential order, shaped the synoptic pattern of the Gospel tradition. Fourth, inquiring further as to the *why* of this pattern, I address the topic of the Gospels' origins and functions in early Christianity. Because chapters 3–7 argue for a significant correspondence between the Old Testament and New Testament on the "sequential and cumulative action of God"[19] at the point of pattern and emphases, I speak to the relation of this study to Michael Goulder's proposal (and also more recently to Thomas J. Tally's[20]) that the origin of the Synoptics should be sought in the early church's need for lection readings, even an annual cycle of lectionary readings which tell in narrative form the story of Jesus. While this study judges this factor significant, it proposes also other important functions, namely, the transforming of its faith-traditions shared with Judaism as part of its self-understanding in theological identity, and a two-sided apologetic function, both self-defining in relation to Judaism and missional in relation to Gentiles.

---

[19] For this phrasing I am indebted to D. Patrick, *The Rendering of God in the Old Testament* (Philadelphia: Fortress, 1981), 113.

[20] T. J. Tally, *The Origins of the Liturgical Year* (New York: Pueblo, 1986), 231–38.

Two appendixes focus on questions related to the findings of this study. Appendix I examines the study's import for understanding the Synoptics' relationship to John's Gospel. I consider also whether any new light is shed on the relationship of the canonical Gospels to the noncanonical Gospels.

Appendix II seeks to verify the findings of this study through "outside checks." I investigate whether the commonly recognized distinctive Synoptic features show any correlation with this study's proposals regarding the thematic foci of Israel's faith traditions in each of the four respective Synoptic sections. The findings from this investigation generally corroborate the theses developed in this contribution.

1

GETTING ORIENTED

While scholars often distinguish between Jesus, the early church, and the author of the Gospel, this investigation focuses on their final, canonical form. Such an approach fuses Jesus, the early church, and the Gospel writer into a final portrait. Historical research assumes that within this fusion the earlier contributions shaped the latter. Because the author is responsible for the last phase of the canonical form, the usual referent in the discussion will be to the author. Not only did Jesus' deeds and words and the early church's missional and catechetical needs shape the Synoptics' story of Jesus, but Israel's faith traditions influenced the story as well. Further, this study seeks to understand the significance of this distinctive Synoptic structure for the confessional self-identity of both the early church and those of us who seek to shape our lives by these scriptural witnesses.

Peter Stuhlmacher has recently stressed that the earliest Christian reflection on Jesus appealed to the Old Testament in order to understand its nascent faith. He rightly argues that the church's earliest kerygma looked to the Old Testament to interpret the meaning of Jesus for faith. The story of Jesus begins even prior to the kerygma in its dependence upon Old Testament traditions for explication. As Stuhlmacher puts it:

> It is not only that the biblical canon forces on us the theological question of how and for what reasons the New Testament, which begins with the Gospels' narrative about Jesus, remains dependent on the Old Testament. It is also that even initial formulations of the kerygma implicitly and explicitly refer to the Old Testament, in order that, starting there, they can make it possible to understand and hear who Jesus was and what he became for faith.[1]

---

[1] P. Stuhlmacher, "Jesus as Reconciler. Reflections on the Problem of

Citing Lohse and Goppelt in support, Stuhlmacher maintains, as the following section depicts, that the early church understood the significance of Jesus' life, death, and resurrection through
the help of Old Testament Scripture.[2]

SEEING THE CONTEXT

The scholarly literature of the past forty years on the New
Testament's use of the Old Testament, or put conversely, the Old
Testament's influence upon the New, may be classified into three types
of studies, as follows:

1. *The use of key OT texts (Dodd, Lindars, Juel) or key themes
(Piper, Mauser, Hobbs).*[3] In an effort to provide a more satisfactory
account than that of Rendell Harris's *Testimonies* on the New Testament's use of the Old,[4] C. H. Dodd proposes that some fifteen pas-

---

Portraying Jesus within the Framework of a Biblical Theology of the New
Testament," in *Reconciliation, Law & Righteousness: Essays in Biblical Theology,*
trans. E. R. Kaling (Philadelphia: Fortress, 1986), 3.

[2] For an excellent account of how the early Christians arrived at their
initial confessional understandings of Jesus, see L. T. Johnson, *The Writings of
the New Testament: An Interpretation* (Philadelphia: Fortress, 1986), 87–111.

[3] Outside the scope of this work are the many studies of the use of Old
Testament quotations in specific parts of the Synoptic Gospels or in one Gospel
as a whole. Most notable here are K. Stendahl, *The School of St. Matthew and Its
Use of the Old Testament* (2d ed.; Philadelphia: Fortress, 1968); R. H. Gundry,
The Use of the Old Testament in St. Matthew's Gospel (NovTSup 18; Leiden: E. J.
Brill, 1967); A. Suhl, *Die Funktion der alttestamentlichen Zitate und Anspiel-
ungen im Markusevangeliums* (Gütersloh: Gerd Mohn, 1965); on selected key
quotations, J. Marcus, *The Way of the Lord: Christological Exegesis of the Old
Testament in the Gospel of Mark* (Louisville, Ky.: Westminster/John Knox, 1992);
D. J. Moo, *The Old Testament in the Gospel Passion Narratives* (Sheffield: Al-
mond, 1983); R. T. France, *Jesus and the Old Testament: His Application of Old
Testament Passages to Himself and His Mission* (Downers Grove, Ill.: InterVar-
sity, 1971). For general study of the New Testament's use of the Old see R. N.
Longenecker, *Biblical Exegesis in the Apostolic Period* (Grand Rapids: Eerdmans,
1975); C. K. Barrett, "The Interpretation of the Old Testament in the New," in
D. McKim, ed., *The Authoritative Word: Essays on the Nature of Scripture* (Grand
Rapids: Eerdmans, 1983), 37–58; E. E. Ellis, "How the New Testament Uses the
Old," in *Prophecy and Hermeneutic in Early Christianity* (Grand Rapids: Eerdmans, 1978), 147–72. For a history of research see E. E. Ellis, *The Old Testament
in Early Christianity* (Grand Rapids: Baker, 1992), 53–74.

[4] R. Harris, *Testimonies I and II* (Cambridge: Cambridge University,
1916 and 1920).

sages in the Old Testament functioned crucially for the early church in its perception and proclamation of Jesus' life, death, resurrection, and exaltation.[5] That these texts are foundational is attested by their frequency throughout the New Testament. Dodd also contends that they function not only as proof texts but as pointers to a larger passage, whose meaning influenced the entire argument.[6] Grouping these texts under three main headings—apocalyptic-eschatological, New Israel, and Servant of the Lord and Righteous Sufferer,[7] Dodd argues that the early church utilized these passages to formulate its understanding of its place in God's eschatological drama, its self-identity, and its christological conceptions of Jesus. This achievement formed the substructure of all Christian theology.[8]

Barnabas Lindars slices the pie differently, using most of the same but also many texts other than those identified by Dodd.[9] Stressing that the early church often modified Old Testament texts and shifted their application, Lindars carefully examines four thematic clusters of New Testament uses of the Old: texts relating to Jesus' resurrection,[10] texts that aid in developing a passion apologetic,[11] texts interpreting the events of Jesus' ministry as "Christus Revelatus,"[12] and texts addressing questions of Jesus' birth and lineage.[13] Lindars also considers Paul's use of Old Testament quotations and the church's use of Scripture more broadly.[14] The most striking fea-

---

[5] These texts are Ps 2:7; 8:4–6; 110:1; 118:22–23; Isa 6:9–10; 53:1; 40:3–5; 28:16; Gen 12:3; Jer 31:31–34; Joel 2:28–32; Zech 9:9; Hab 2:3–4; Isa 61:1–2; Deut 18:15,19. C. H. Dodd, *According to the Scriptures: The Substructure of New Testament Theology* (London: Nisbet, 1952), 31–57.

[6] Ibid., 126.

[7] Ibid., 62–103.

[8] Ibid., 111–27.

[9] B. Lindars *New Testament Apologetic* (London: SCM, 1961).

[10] Here Lindars shows how the logic of the early church proceeded along the lines that the grave could not contain Jesus (Acts 2:24 using Ps 116); that resurrection comprises exaltation (in which Ps 110:1 is joined to Ps 8:7 in 1 Cor 15:25; Eph 1:22; Heb 2:5–8); and that the outpouring of the Spirit results in gifts that empower for ministry (Ps 68:19 as used in Acts 2 and Eph 4:8–11).

[11] Here Isa 53, the passion Psalms, and Zech 9 and 14 are crucial.

[12] The dominant Synoptic texts are Ps 2:7; Isa 42:1; 61:1; Ps 78:2; Isa 6:9f.; Ps 8:3; 118:22 with Isa 28:16 (linked also to Dan 2:34 in Luke 20:18).

[13] Mic 5:1; Isa 8:23–9:1; 9:5; 11:1, 10; Deut 18:15, 19; 2 Sam 7:14; Isa 7:14; Num 24:17; Isa 60:1 are cited and discussed to show how these shaped the early church's developing Christology.

[14] For extended study of Paul's use of Scripture, see E. Earle Ellis, *Paul's Use of Old Testament* (Edinburgh: Oliver and Boyd, 1957 [repr. Grand Rapids:

ture of this process was the early church's explication of Jesus' messiahship in the form of apologetic against Jewish unbelief: "Unbelief is a factor which demands attention in the earliest stage of the apologetic."[15]

Donald Juel refocuses the investigation of Jesus' messianic identity so that Jesus as the *crucified* Messiah becomes the foremost issue in the early church's *Messianic Exegesis*. As Juel puts it: "the beginnings of Christian reflection can be traced to interpretations of Israel's Scriptures, and the major focus of that scriptural interpretation was Jesus, the crucified and risen Messiah."[16] Acknowledging his debt to Nils Dahl's *The Crucified Messiah*, Juel argues that the core issue of earliest post-Easter Christian belief was the church's struggle to understand how one crucified as "King of the Jews," a messianic pretender, was indeed the fulfillment of Israel's royal messianic hope. Making sense of the salvation events accomplished in Israel's midst and seeking to understand the gospel of the crucified Messiah preceded all apologetic agenda.[17] Hence, Juel begins with the Old Testament royal messianic traditions, specifically with 2 Samuel 7:14 and its impact upon later Hebrew Scripture and post-biblical Judaism. The Synoptics' use of Psalm 2:7 and Isaiah 42:1 are viewed against this context of question and inquiry. Similarly, Juel contends that Psalms 22, 31, and 69 were utilized from the very beginning of post-Easter Christian faith as royal messianic psalms because their themes and images enabled those first believers to grasp the meaning of and confess belief in the suffering, crucified Messiah. He identifies several verbal links between these psalms and Psalm 89 to argue for their inherent royal function.[18] Juel then treats sequentially the influence of

---

Baker, 1981]). Note also R. B. Hays's recent study, *The Echoes of Scripture in the Letters of Paul* (New Haven: Yale, 1989).

[15]Lindars, *New Testament Apologetic*, 285–86.

[16]D. Juel, *Messianic Exegesis: Christological Interpretation of the Old Testament in Early Christianity* (Philadelphia: Fortress, 1988), 1. As this title suggests, Juel holds that the early Christian use of Scripture was primarily christological in focus. However, Hays's *Echoes of Scripture* argues that Paul's hermeneutic was ecclesiological in focus; it was motivated by and directed to the fact of the new peoplehood, marked certainly by their Christ identity. In my judgment, these two emphases qualify each other; they are not alternatives, but two dimensions of early Christian experience.

[17]Juel, *Messianic Exegesis*, 60.

[18]This strategy is dubious, in my judgment, and leads Juel to a position less ambiguous than that of the Gospel narrative. When the royalty appeal is made that clear and strong, the irony of the Gospels' passion narratives loses its force. Jesus' royalty was acclaimed not simply and explicitly on the

Isaiah 53 (Servant) and Psalm 110 (ruling Messiah) upon early Christian christological reflection, and subsequently considers the influence of the Daniel 7:13 Son of humanity tradition. In all these perceptions—and later Christian appropriations of them—the paradox, indeed scandal, of the crucified Messiah remains central.[19]

Another spate of contributions has focused on the influence of specific themes from Israel's salvation history. In several articles in the 1950s Otto Piper argued for exodus influence in Mark and the New Testament more broadly, but he never followed up his provocative suggestions with substantial demonstration of how his insights might be fleshed out in close study of the Gospels, even though he proposed that this influence had something to do with the origin of the Gospel pattern.[20] The studies of John Bowman and E. C. Hobbs identified numerous specific instances of exodus influence upon Mark's Gospel.[21] Complementing these is Ulrich Mauser's insightful contribution showing the influence of the wilderness theme in Mark.[22] The Dodd, Lindars, and Juel contributions also show that certain Old Testament themes (especially the kingship and servant traditions) shaped the early Christian understandings of Jesus.[23] While these writings anticipate some of the findings of this study, several restrict their work to Mark and none have correlated their theses with the structure of the synoptic pattern.

2. *Focus on salvation-history and ecclesial identity (von Rad, Gese, Dahl).* A major current in biblical studies since the 1920s has

---

terms of Psalm 89, but always with a challenge to qualify and transform the tradition, as ch. 6 will show.

[19] Juel, *Messianic Exegesis*, 119–79.

[20] O. A. Piper, "God's Good News: The Passion Story According to Mark," *Int* 9 (1955), 165–82; "Unchanging Promises: Exodus in the New Testament," *Int* 11 (1957), 3–22; "The Origin of the Gospel Pattern," *JBL* 78 (1959), 115–24.

[21] J. Bowman, *The Gospel of Mark: The New Christian Jewish Passover Haggadah* (SPB 8; Leiden: E. J. Brill, 1965) and E. C. Hobbs, "The Gospel of Mark and the Exodus" (Ph.D. diss.; University of Chicago, 1958).

[22] U. Mauser, *Christ in the Wilderness: The Wilderness Theme in the Second Gospel and its Basis in the Biblical Tradition* (London: SCM, 1963). Note also a similar type of analysis in Paul S. Minear's commentary on Mark 3:13–19, in that the appointment of the Twelve on a mountain is explicated against the background of the Lord "creating Jacob and forming Israel" and the significance of the mountain as a place of sacred revelation (*Saint Mark* [LBC; London: SCM and Nashville: Abingdon, 1962], 65).

[23] See also D. M. Hay, *Glory at the Right Hand: Psalm 110 in Early Christianity* (SBLMS 18; Nashville/New York: Abingdon, 1973).

been the effort to identify and understand the nature of the relationship between the Testaments, specifically the relationship of the early
Christian believers and their writings to the Hebrew Scripture.[24] Reventlow has outlined and discussed the range of efforts to resolve this
enigma.[25] Of the various proposals, those of Gerhard von Rad and
Hartmut Gese are most fruitful, in my judgment, and illumine the
findings of this study.

As specific emphases within the salvation historical and typological understandings of the relationship between the Testaments
in Reventlow's treatment, von Rad stresses the process of tradition
history in which "new interpretations regularly relate the old traditions to the present" and the typological character of the Testaments'
relationship, whereby "typology is a means of discovering structural
analogies between saving events attested by both Testaments."[26] Utilizing von Rad's understandings, E. Earle Ellis describes this process
as it bears upon foundational motifs, many of which will be developed
in this study: "The first aspect of the process is evident in the way in
which the prophets 'placed the new historical acts of God ... in exactly
the same category as the old basic events of the canonical history': a
new creation, a new Exodus, a new covenant, a new Davidic kingdom,
a new Zion or temple." This process, Ellis contends, continues into
the New Testament.[27] J. A. Baker's understanding of typology is simi-

---

[24]Two essay collections are representative: B. W. Anderson, ed., *The
Old Testament and the Christian Faith: A Theological Discussion* (New York:
Harper & Row, 1963); C. Westermann, ed., *Essays on Old Testament Hermeneu-
tics* (Richmond, Va.: John Knox, 1963). See also J. Barr, *Old and New in Inter-
pretation: A Study of the Two Testaments* (New York: Harper & Row, 1966); F. F.
Bruce, *This is That: The New Testament Development of Some Old Testament
Themes* (Exeter: Paternoster, 1978); and the extensive bibliographies in H. G.
Reventlow, *Problems of Biblical Theology in the Twentieth Century*, trans. J.
Bowden (Philadelphia: Fortress, 1986).

[25]Reventlow, *Problems*.

[26]Ibid., 12, 25. Oscar Cullmann's approach is similar: "each time
corrections of the interpretation of past saving events *are undertaken in the light
of new events*" (*Salvation in History* [New York: Harper & Row, 1967], 88).
Cullmann's understanding of the relation between the event and interpretation
differs from von Rad's. Cullmann emphasizes the role the event plays for the
receiver of revelation (91); von Rad regards the decisive events in history as the
object of Israel's faith (*Old Testament Theology*, trans. D. Stalker [Edinburgh:
Oliver and Boyd, 1962], 1.120).

[27]E. E. Ellis, "The Old Testament Canon in the Early Church," in
Mikra: Text, Translation, Reading and Interpretation, ed. M. J. Mulder and H.
Sysling (Philadelphia: Fortress, 1988), 687.

lar: "it is 'not a method of exegesis or interpretation but the study of historical and theological correspondences between different parts of God's activity among his people.' "[28]

Hartmut Gese extends and modifies von Rad's emphases so that the process of reinterpreting the tradition as witnessed by the canon forms the heart of his emphasis. The canon provides "a conclusion and a boundary" to the tradition history process "because the New Testament claims that the history of revelation attained its goal in the death and resurrection of Jesus."[29] Within the Old Testament, both Sinai and Zion are major interpretive centers, and these bear significantly upon New Testament emphases.[30] Seeking to avoid any identification of this biblical theological enterprise with an investigation into the development of concepts, H.-J. Kraus cautions against orienting these Old and New relationships to *conceptions* and prefers to speak of *themes*: "a search is to be made by 'themes' for connections . . . between texts with related themes."[31]

Congruent with these endeavors are Nils Dahl's insights in *Das Volk Gottes*. As the subtitle indicates,[32] Dahl's study is concerned with the ecclesial self-identity of early Christian believers, especially in relation to Israel as the people of God. Devoting the first half of his work to the major perceptions or notions (*Gedanken*) in Israel's self-identity, Dahl then seeks for the basic images of self-identity in the New Testament writings. The portrayals of the two peoples share major identity perceptions and conceptions. In the Synoptics the place of Jesus' followers corresponds roughly with the place of Israel, so that tension emerges between Jesus' followers and the synagogue. Jesus' followers are not called the "new Israel," as Paul later designates them (Gal 6:16), but they are described as the sheep of the true Shepherd who is both Son of God and King of Israel.[33] Jesus' followers, who are designated disciples (μαθηταί) or Christians, (χριστιανοί) continue their characteristic self-identification as the people of God, λαός (θεοῦ).[34] The church also takes on new identity-conceptions, espe-

[28]Reventlow, *Problems*, 31.
[29]H. Gese, *Essays on Biblical Theology*, trans. Keith Crim (Minneapolis: Augsburg, 1981), 32.
[30]Reventlow, *Problems*, 149–51.
[31]Ibid., 159–60.
[32]N. Dahl, *Das Volk Gottes: Eine Untersuchung zum Kirchenbewusstsein des Urchristentums* (Oslo: I Kommisjon hos Jacob Dybwad, 1941).
[33]Ibid., 173–74.
[34]Ibid., 203.

cially "body of Christ" and "temple of the Holy Spirit," which leads
Dahl to speak of its trinitarian self-identity.[35] Similarly to Kraus, Dahl
distinguishes his study from any history of ideas or motif research. He
is concerned with the appearance in time and history of a people and
their self-identity in relation to Israel. Many of the old self-concep-
tions in motifs and themes continue, but the essentially new is that
God's promises to Israel were fulfilled in Jesus, and the end-time
people of God have appeared.[36] The most striking distinctive feature
of the Christian community's religious identity lies in the difference
between Israel's strong monotheistic conception of God and the trinitarian view of God that emerged in the early Christian communities.[37]

The relevance of this second type of study for this present
volume consists in its emphasis on the continuity and discontinuity
of the older and newer stories of faith. This study shows that early
Christian understandings of Jesus reflect, at a fundamental level,
motifs and structures of thought that testify to Christian self-identification with Israel. Israel's story shapes the Christian story, despite
the presence of strong tension and conflict that in turn modifies and
transforms the older story. The process of tradition history, interpreting new events in light of the older events, joins itself to the quest for
self-definition: how do we as God's new people comprehend and
express, defend and proclaim, God's revelation of salvation and judgment in Jesus, of whose story we are witnesses?

3. *A liturgical function (Daube, Bowman, Goulder) or a literary-
structural paradigm (Evans and Moessner for Luke's journey narrative*[38]
and Derrett and Roth for Mark). In a 1958 essay, "The Earliest Structure of the Gospels," David Daube argued that the structure of the
Gospel narratives has been decisively influenced by the expositions
of the Passover eve liturgy.[39] His most convincing support is the
structural correspondence between the series of four questions in

---

[35]Ibid., 278.

[36]Another contribution which develops similarities and unity in
God's saving work with his people, Old and New, is P. Minear's *The Eyes of Faith:
A Study in the Biblical Point of View* (Philadelphia: Westminster, 1946).

[37]Ibid., 277–78.

[38]John Drury echoes aspects of Goulder's liturgical emphases and
argues also for the imprint of Deuteronomy upon Luke's journey narrative, but
in a more flexible way than Evans and Moessner. He includes influence also
from the Elisha narrative and shows other OT influences upon other parts of
the Gospel, especially chs. 1–2 (*Tradition*, 46–71, 138–64).

[39]D. Daube, "The Earliest Structure of the Gospels," *NTS* 5 (1958),
174–87.

Mark 12:13–37 and the four questions of the Passover liturgy. He shows not only the general structural parallel but the matching character of the questions to the four types of sons identified in the Haggadah liturgy. This means "that the immediate stimulus comes neither from the Old Testament nor from some ordinary rabbinic source, but from the Haggadah."[40]

John Bowman has argued similarly for the origins of the Gospel of Mark: "Mark is a new Haggadah for the yearly celebration of the new Christian Passover and memorial of the Lord's crucifixion. There would be a need for such a service in the early church."[41] Bowman devotes a lengthy discussion to midrashic materials and holds that Mark must be understood against that background.[42] Bowman also connects events in the Markan text to specific events in the Old Testament, such as the feedings of the multitudes in Mark 6–8 to Exodus 12. He suggests many parallels, such as: Jesus' baptism parallels Moses' call; John the Baptist parallels Aaron; the healing of the woman with the flow of blood inversely parallels the plague of blood on Egypt.[43] Mark is "a triumphant epic story of deliverance which as it ascends to its climax in Jerusalem bursts one by one the bonds that enshackled His people." Functioning as a new Passover Haggadah, Mark's Gospel "is the story of deliverance proclaimed."[44]

While Bowman's thesis focuses on Mark, Michael Goulder develops the theory that both Matthew and Luke were written to provide year-long lectionaries for the Christian believers. Mark's Gospel, however, provided only a half-year lectionary—a point which contradicts Philip Carrington's lectionary theory of Mark based on his analysis of the forty-eight divisions in Codex Vaticanus. Goulder investigates the Jewish lectionaries and proposes a list of annual readings for Torah, the Histories or Isaiah or The Twelve (one of these cycles each year on a triennial calendar presumably), and the Writings or Ben-Sira or the Chronicler (idem). He then proposes as a parallel to these Old Testament cycles a year-long text cycle of readings from the New Testament epistles, Matthew, and Luke respectively, with a half-year cycle from Mark.[45]

---

[40] Ibid., 186.
[41] Bowman, *Mark,* 158.
[42] Ibid., 31–89 and 125, n. 1.
[43] Ibid., 105–15, 147.
[44] Ibid., 158, 315.
[45] The theory and evidence for this is developed throughout the book; the summary of readings is on p. 307, fold-out sheet Table VIII (*Calendar*).

Aware of the boldness of his hypothesis, Goulder introduces his work with a plea for openness to consider a novel theory regarding synoptic origins: "could it be that the Gospels are in the order in which we have them because they provided lessons for a whole primitive Christian Year, partly Jewish in its background, but reaching its climax each year at Passover and Easter?" Noting that each Synoptic closes with an apocalyptic discourse, a passion narrative, and resurrection story, he queries, "could it be that all three were written as a series of 'readings' for a succession of Saturday nights and festivals running up to Easter?"[46] Goulder's strongest and clearest evidence, in my judgment, lies in his correlation of longer Gospel sections with feast weeks in the annual cycle, like Matthew 5–7 for Pentecost, a parallel to the Jewish Feast of Weeks that celebrates the giving of the Torah on Mount Sinai, and the Harvest parables (Matt 13) at the time of the Jewish Feast of Tabernacles (a harvest festival).

While these hypotheses of Daube, Bowman, and Goulder—which have not been widely accepted by New Testament scholarship—explain in part the selection of content and its order in the Synoptics, they supply no rationale for this content appearing *in this order within the distinctive Synoptic structure*, a structure that differs notably from John's or the non-canonical Gospels'. Here lies a deficiency in the lectionary theory that gives one pause. For if the distinctive structure is not accounted for, can Goulder's explanation of the order of the pericopes—which indeed varies among the three Gospels—be convincingly maintained?

Converging with Goulder only in part, C. F. Evans and David P. Moessner have proposed that Luke's journey narrative is modeled after Deuteronomy. Goulder correlates these readings with the synagogue Torah readings for months 9–11 and identifies numerous corresponding themes.[47] C. F. Evans had earlier proposed and identified specific textual correspondences for the whole of Luke's journey narrative and Deuteronomy.[48] For Evans, the parallel had significance in that it afforded a structural model, for both Deuteronomy and Luke 9:51–19:44 are set within a journey framework. In this way Evans contributes an explanation for one major section in the synoptic structural design, but only for Luke (see ch. 4 and especially Table III for more on Evans). Goulder notes Evans's work, but he explains the

[46]Goulder, *Calendar*, ix.

[47]Ibid., 95–104.

[48]C. F. Evans, "The Central Section of Luke's Gospel," in *Studies in the Gospels*, ed. D. E. Nineham (Oxford: Blackwell, 1955, 1967), 37–53.

correspondence not in terms of structural similarity (journey settings), but by their parallel functions in the annual cycle of readings.
He then accounts for the disparity in that Luke uses nine chapters
(9–18) in only *three* months as compared to his earlier use of nine
chapters (1–9) in *eight* months. This happens, he says, to prepare the
catechumens for baptism which comes at Easter and to bring to a
climax the twelfth month of readings consisting of the entire passion
narrative. The journey narrative, with its concentration on discipleship, thus provides three readings per week to meet the church's
catechetical needs. Just as Deuteronomy is catechetical in its design,
so also is Luke's journey narrative. "The church took over Deuteronomy as the basis for its catechesis."[49]

David P. Moessner's recent study also argues that Luke
modeled his journey narrative on Deuteronomy.[50] Unconvinced by
Evans's proposal,[51] Moessner seeks to establish the connection on
foundational thematic similarities: the journey setting, Jesus as a journeying banquet guest/rejected prophet combined with themes of eating and rejoicing before the Lord, the unbelief and obstinacy of the
people to acknowledge both Moses and Jesus as God's sent prophets,
and the specific Lukan connection: Jesus a prophet like Moses (Acts
3:22).[52] Moessner also theorizes that the Lukan journey narrative represents eyewitness tradition with distinct northern affinities, a Stephen-
Philip theological circle and Samaritan setting.[53] Like Moses, Jesus
lived and died for his people—a death precipitated by the people's
stubbornness—"because God so willed that the Exodus redemption
led by Moses be consummated in the Exodus of the Prophet who, like
Moses, must suffer and die to effect new deliverance for the people."[54]
Evans's and Moessner's contributions contain much solid evidence
and will be considered further in chapter 4 of this study.

---

[49]Goulder, *Calendar*, 90–94 (quotation on 94).

[50]D. P. Moessner, *Lord of the Banquet: The Literary and Theological
Significance of the Lukan Travel Narrative* (Minneapolis: Augsburg/Fortress,
1989).

[51]Ibid., 44, n. 123.

[52]Ibid., 84–187. See especially 174ff. for an attempt to integrate these
themes. Moessner's thesis is weakened, in my judgment, because Luke 11:37–54
is the only text which explicitly joins the two themes of journeying guest and
rejected prophet, the two motifs he regards as central to this section. And there
it is the Pharisee who throws the banquet! Moessner's diagram (176) shows how
he must choose different texts and hook them together to make his point.

[53]Ibid., 318–22.

[54]Ibid., 323.

Several scholars have advanced theories of influence of specific Old Testament structural paradigms upon the formation of Mark's Gospel. Duncan Derrett has attempted to show that the Moses-Joshua narrative lies behind Mark 1–12, and that Mark crafted each pericope to match a prototype from the older narrative:

> Mark 1–12 is written to parallel, and to comment upon, Exodus, Numbers and Joshua, concentrating on details in broad sequence, but ignoring episodes and material which, as they stand, are repugnant to the Gospel. . . . Genesis and Deuteronomy loom in the background, taken more or less for granted.[55]

Derrett also holds that this Markan use of the Old Testament followed the homiletic hermeneutic of early Judaism. Hence each "section of Mark is a preacher's prompt; the whole a homiletic mnemonic continuum."[56]

Indeed, some of Derrett's evidence is convincing. Providing a broader framework and specific rationale for Derrett's connections, this study argues that not only Mark but the Synoptic structural pattern was influenced by Israel's major faith traditions. Indeed, the Galilean and journey sections of this design echo theological motifs from the Moses to Joshua corpus.

Wolfgang Roth, however, contends that a better and more convincing structural paradigm is "the Elijah/Elisha Narrative [for it provides a] conceptual and narrative model for Mk."[57] Roth presents a variety of evidence for his theory: the similar number of sixteen miracles in the Elisha cycle and Mark up to the exclamation in 7:37, "He has done all things well"[58] (later Markan miracles are treated under the "duplicating" motif to match Elisha's relation to Elijah);[59]

---

[55]J. D. M. Derrett, *The Making of Mark: The Scriptural Bases of the Earliest Gospel* (Shipston-on-Stour: Drinkwater, 1985), 24.

[56]Derrett, *Making*, 24 (see discussion on pp. 24–37).

[57]W. Roth, *Hebrew Gospel: Cracking the Code of Mark* (Oak Park, Ill.: Meyer-Stone Books, 1988), 19.

[58]Ibid., 5–8.

[59]This represents the unsatisfactory nature of much of Roth's evidence. Other than the feeding in 8:1–9 the miracles can hardly be regarded as duplicates; 8:21–26 is the first healing of a blind person. Roth counts and identifies eight miracles in Mark after 7:37 and parallels them to Elijah's eight, noting that this model is more important than a full duplication of another sixteen (16–17). But if the Elijah-Elisha narrative is really the paradigm, why not present Jesus' miracles in the same Elijah-Elisha sequence since he also argues for the John the Baptist-Jesus sequence paralleling that of Elijah-Elisha? Also his counting is open to dispute. It is at variance with that of A. M. Farrer,

the analogical progression in 2 Kings 2–13 and Mark 1:9–11:33 in which the commissioning of the prophet leads in both cases to "setting in order the affairs of the temple";[60] Elijah's commissioning of Elisha as parallel to the John-Jesus sequence in Mark 1:14–15 and background for the logic of the authority debate in 11:27–33, a sequel to the temple episode; and, among *many* others, a four-sectional outline—quite arbitrary in my judgment—of both the Elijah-Elisha narrative and Mark's Gospel.[61]

While each of these proposed links of the whole or a part of the Synoptics' content to portions of the Old Testament may be flawed on crucial points for lack of solid evidence, the fundamental notion of certain imitative literary relationships can hardly be dismissed.[62] The findings of this study will construct an overall understanding of the Synoptics' structural design that explains why such connections can be seen. These connections as theories of compositional motivation are generally not persuasive, but the reason for such correspondences lies at a deeper level, namely, the larger picture of story shaping story.

FINDING A METHOD AND THEOLOGICAL PERSPECTIVE

While drawing upon the contributions of New Testament scholarship broadly, this study has for its methodological home the convergence of three current emphases: canon criticism, tradition history in the sense of "streams of tradition" (see below and ch. 2), and compositional-narrative analysis. It utilizes, therefore, the in-

---

who argued unpersuasively that a "twelve-plus-one" cycle of miracles—and disciples as well—connects Mark's structure to the OT tribal count (*St. Matthew and St. Mark*, 2d ed. [Philadelphia: Westminster, 1966], 98, 206).

[60]Roth, *Hebrew Gospel*, 9.

[61]Ibid., 24–25. I know of no literary narrative or structural studies which support Roth's sectional divisions for Mark: 1:1–13; 1:14–7:37; 8:1–15:39; 15:40–16:8. The break between 7:37 and 8:1 violates numerous textual literary codes and clues, as most commentaries will point out.

[62]The Lukan journey narrative's dependence upon Deuteronomy is certainly the more convincing of these. Derrett's proposals on Mark are in a general way persuasive, but not his pericope-for-pericope connections. This study seeks perspectives from broader considerations—faith tradition-history and theological motifs—that explain why these types of connections can be seen, but are not convincing as theories of literary models. For a wider discussion of literary models at work in Mark, see V. K. Robbins, *Jesus the Teacher: A Socio-Rhetorical Interpretation of Mark* (Philadelphia: Fortress, 1984).

sights of tradition history in that it seeks to demonstrate the formative influence that major Old Testament faith traditions had upon the canonical shape of the synoptic tradition. Since this study makes its original contribution in the Synoptics it will simply draw upon scholarly work already done on Israel's faith traditions.

This study is oriented to compositional-narrative criticism because its understanding of the Synoptic Gospels has been informed by perceptions derived from structural studies that have utilized both compositional and narrative analyses. Without the many redactional studies that have so greatly enriched our understanding of the Synoptic Gospels, the younger methods of compositional, structuralist, and narrative analyses would likely have been less fruitful. Indeed, these various approaches can and should be used as complementary components of the literary paradigm for study of Scripture.

The process and results of this study depend upon two factors of methodological and theological significance. The first is the interaction between the canonical form of Scripture and the tradition-bearing communities of faith within which Scripture acquired its canonical form. The second is the interaction between compositional-narrative analysis, as a method of study, and the theological significance of the structure of Scripture's canonical form, especially in the Synoptic Gospels.

Canonical Form and Tradition History

Brevard Childs has called attention to the scriptural significance of the final canonical form. While Childs's contribution contains numerous emphases, I identify three crucial to this study.

1. Specific traditions were remembered, passed on, valued and treasured as formative impulses within the development of what later became canon. As Childs puts it,

> [I]t is crucial to see that the issue of canon turns on the authoritative role played by particular traditions for a community of faith and practice. . . . There is an organic continuity in the historical process of the development of an established canon of sacred writings from the earliest stages of the New Testament to the final canonical stabilization of its scope.[63]

---

[63]B. S. Childs, *The New Testament as Canon: An Introduction* (Philadelphia: Fortress, 1984), 21.

This present study, however, does not focus on the process from "the earliest stages of the New Testament to the final canonical stabilization," but rather emphasizes how Old Testament theological traditions influenced that process as seen from and in the final form. In this respect the study tilts in the direction of Childs's emphases, rather than Sanders's. Sanders's interest, leaning to the hermeneutical side and stressing the process by which canon is formed, welcomes the designation, "canon criticism," whereas Childs cautions against it, for to think that our hermeneutic is derivative from the canon process itself is to put ourselves into the canon-making mode, rather than to accept canonical form and content as the basis of the church's authority for thought and life.[64] Childs's primary concern is that biblical scholarship pay more attention to the canonical form of Scripture and recognize there its source of authority for shaping the church's beliefs and action.

However, James A. Sanders has written similarly to Childs regarding the role of the tradition-journey within the canonical process, but with stress on its significance for the exegesis and hermeneutic we employ in our endeavors to understand the text:

> A major exercise in canonical criticism is locating and identifying two types of "precursor" material in the biblical passage being studied: the community traditions being called upon or reflected in the passage; and the international wisdom traditions being called upon or being reflected in the passage. In other words, one searches for the homegrown traditions and the borrowed ones. This is a first step . . . [after preliminary exegetical work has been done]. The next step is to discern the hermeneutics by which those identified traditions function in the passage, how they were adapted, represented, and resignified.[65]

Using Sanders's metaphor, this study focuses on the "homegrown traditions" in the Synoptic Gospels, those which the communities of faith in the New Testament-making era brought with them from their heritage in God's covenant relationship with Israel. Likewise, reflecting Childs's emphasis, it shows that these traditions have decisively shaped the Synoptics' presentation of Jesus. Further, it concentrates not on the Gospels' use of Old Testament quotations or allusions—a significant and widely recognized task for New Testa-

---

[64]See ch. 7 of this study (pp. 289–91 and nn. 65–70) for a fuller discussion of these issues and their bearing upon this study.

[65]J. A. Sanders, *Canon and Community: A Guide to Canonical Criticism* (Philadelphia: Fortress, 1984), 47.

ment scholarship as noted above—but on the very *Gestalt* or structural form of the Synoptic Gospels. It examines the structural design of the Synoptics in order to grasp how they were shaped by major OT traditions which, when utilized to explicate the meaning of the Jesus event, gave the community its faith-identity.[66] Without the new faith-identity created by Jesus, however, the Gospels would not have come to be.

2. The portraits of Jesus in the Synoptic Gospels were shaped by the Jesus traditions present in the early church and by earlier traditions of faith which gave rise to the canonical form of the literature of the Hebrew Bible. Childs enunciates this principle with regard to the shaping of the New Testament canon,[67] but its logic extends also to the traditions of faith which the communities inherited as legacy from Israel's faith experience:

> Far from being objective conduits of received tradition, the tradents, authors, and redactors of the New Testament effected a massive construal of the material by the very process of selecting, shaping and transmitting it. At the heart of the process lay a dialectical move in which the tradents of the developing New Testament were themselves being shaped by the content of the material which they in turn were transmitting, selecting, and forming into a scriptural norm.[68]

Walter Rast demonstrates this in textual study. After showing the influence of the exodus tradition throughout the Hebrew Scripture, he says in his "Method and Theology" reflections:

> Old Testament theology arises from Israel's own way of receiving and responding to the words and deeds of God. This process, by which older themes about the ways of God with Israel are taken up and seen in new

---

[66]Odil Hannes Steck's proposal that we think in terms of "streams of tradition" describes well the approach of this study. He too says that we must think more broadly than textual use but also the way in which expansive conceptual emphases, recurring over a period of time, have not only influenced the content but also molded the shape of a writing. As examples, he cites the wisdom and Jerusalem cult traditions. See his provocative and helpful essay, "Theological Streams of Tradition," in *Tradition and Theology in the Old Testament*, ed. D. A. Knight (Philadelphia: Fortress, 1977), 183–214 (197–98 for above specifically).

[67]Hartmut Gese makes the same point in discussing the development of tradition in the OT and its bearing upon final form. He speaks first of "formation of a totality" or "growth toward a whole," and then says, "Canonization is the final result in the formation of tradition." See his essay, "Tradition and Biblical Theology," in *Tradition and Theology*, ed. D. Knight, 301–26 (315–17 for these phrases).

[68]Childs, *Canon*, 22.

ways at a later time, points the way to understanding the Old Testament's own confessions of God.[69]

Similarly, in introducing his study of the Sinai to Zion traditions, Hartmut Gese proposes that the Testaments are connected by the τέλος of the tradition-content of the Old Testament. He regards New Testament theology, even Christology specifically, to be the manifestation (*Geschehen*) of the theology of the Hebrew Scripture. The New Testament is not simply an addition to, but also contains, the theology of the first Testament. Thus, the revelatory process is ontological, in which the death and resurrection of Jesus is its culmination.[70]

The work of Foster R. McCurley[71] shows how several basic religious conceptions (order versus chaos, divine and human sexuality, and sacred mountain) underwent massive transformation, though always with elements of continuity. It illustrates the impact of tradition-bearing and tradition-forming dialectic upon a given conception over a long period of time. It illustrates also the twofold influence noted by Sanders: that both the homegrown and the borrowed influences are significant, and that conflicting elements within the dialectical process are forged into some sort of resolution that in turn shapes the community's ongoing faith identity.[72]

3. The meaning of a given piece of canonical literature, and certainly the canon as a whole, transcends its original, specific, historical significance. This point is not a whistle to throw off controls upon

---

[69]W. E. Rast, *Tradition History and the Old Testament* (Philadelphia: Fortress, 1972), 72.

[70]H. Gese, *Vom Sinai zum Zion* (Munich: Chr. Kaiser, 1974), 30.

[71]F. R. McCurley, *Ancient Myths and Biblical Faith: Scriptural Transformations* (Philadelphia: Fortress, 1983).

[72]In his massive study, *The Great Code: The Bible and Literature* (New York/London: Harcourt Brace Jovanovich, 1982), Northrop Frye represents in bold and macro-thematic strokes the threads of continuity and sense of canonical completion that potentially emerge from intracanonical reflection. It shows that the functions of bearing and transforming tradition proceed in dynamic dialectical relationship. While Frye's proposals go beyond the limits of usual New Testament narrative analyses, it is difficult to deny the observations he makes in the texts, once we grant that the meaning of the text cannot be limited to authorial intention or the original historical situation. Frye takes this point of view, arising from the "new criticism" of the 1930s and his own use of myth criticism. While agreeing with this point in part, I think we need to be more expansive in our view of authorial intent, not limiting such to a given point in the consciousness of the author at the moment of writing, but recognizing the author as bearer of tradition and meaning which extends beyond that time and situation. The author self-consciously stands in the service of greater meaning.

historical and literary methods. But it does acknowledge that the tradition-bearing and tradition-forming task of the community of faith, though dependent upon the canon as pruning norm upon acceptable limits of diversity,[73] continues beyond the canon. Nor does holding that the meaning of the text transcends that of the historical event out of which it arose mean that the interpreter creates the meaning of the text.[74] The text, precisely because it belongs to a particular tradition-bearing stream, remains at the center of exegesis and hermeneutics. The task of the interpreter is to grasp the meaning of the text in its canonical form, accepting the paradox that knowledge of the historical exigencies that occasioned the text and its pre-canonical trajectory will illumine its meaning, while its ongoing meaning as literary narrative in canonical function transcends the original historical meaning of the event or word.[75]

Narrative Analysis and the Theological Significance of Structure

Utilizing contributions from numerous scholars in the compositional-narrative analysis of the Synoptics and offering insights of its own, this study seeks to grasp the overall structure of each Gospel

---

[73]For development and elaboration of this twofold function of the canon, see J. H. Yoder, "The Authority of the Canon," 265–90, and W. M. Swartley, "Beyond the Historical-Critical Method," 246–48, both in *Essays on Biblical Interpretation: Anabaptist-Mennonite Perspectives*, ed. W. M. Swartley (Elkhart, Ind.: Institute of Mennonite Studies, 1984).

[74]Mary Ann Tolbert rightly says that "meaning occurs in the interaction of text and reader." The text "provides structures and clues to guide the reader," while the reader must fill in the gaps and blanks. The reader is "both controlled by the text and free of it, for the text creates a role for the reader, but each reader fulfills that role differently, depending on historical or individual circumstances" (*Sowing the Gospel: Mark's World in Literary-Historical Perspective* [Minneapolis: Augsburg/Fortress, 1989], 52). Although the reader should give priority to the text's intended meaning(s), in my judgment, the history of interpretation shows how greatly the individual, historical, and cultural circumstances affect interpretation (see W. M. Swartley, *Slavery, Sabbath, War and Women: Case Issues in Biblical Interpretation* [Scottdale, Penn.: Herald, 1983]).

[75]This aspect of the point is put well by Childs:
"[T]he function of canonical shaping was often precisely to loosen the text from any one given historical setting, and to transcend the original addressee. The very fact that the canonical editors tended to hide their own footprints, largely concealing their own historical identity, offers a warrant against this model of historical reconstruction" (*Canon*, 23).
Childs then disagrees with Barr, Dunn, and Brown who link "the canonical level of the text" with "a specific historical level of the initial collectors of the tradition."

and to show how that structure carries specific narrative emphases. While narrative analysis is now widely recognized to be well suited to the study of the Gospels,[76] the distinctive aspect of the present study is its demonstration that major Old Testament theological traditions influenced the composition and narrative form of the Synoptic Gospels as literary creations. It shares with numerous recent studies (see especially Rhoads, Culpepper, Tannehill, and Tolbert) a primary commitment to narrative criticism,[77] in which meaning is perceived by analyzing the narrative world of the text.

But this method must not be orphaned from its parents, the historical-critical method and tradition-history. Narratives too have homes; their full potential of meaning and significance can be grasped by seeing them not only as meaning-bearing entities in their own right, but also as social, historical, and biological personalities shaped by particular genes and environment. Thus, in the study of narrative, questions about parents, sibling relational factors, and children contribute to our understanding of the full meaning of the narrative. Accordingly, this study unapologetically draws upon tradition-historical and environmental studies of biblical texts, even though its primary focus is upon the narrative of the Synoptic Gospels. It also seeks to wed the study of Gospel narrative with that of the community's faith traditions, transmitted by the community in both oral and written form over many centuries. In biblical narrative the river of tradition runs deep, serving as a well-spring of refreshment for each new generation.

By combining the methods of tradition-history and compositional analysis, this study demonstrates the type of insights that arise from sustained effort to pursue the significance of intertextuality

---

[76]A. Wilder articulated this point some years ago in *Early Christian Rhetoric: The Language of the Gospel* (New York: Harper & Row, 1964), xxv. See also J. Donahue's recent statement in *The Gospel in Parable: Metaphor, Narrative, and Theology in the Synoptic Gospels* (Philadelphia: Fortress, 1988), 25.

[77]For a description of narrative criticism, see D. Rhoads, "Narrative Criticism and the Gospel of Mark," *JAAR* 50 (1982), 411–34; Tolbert, *Sowing*, 90–108; S. D. Moore, *Literary Criticism and the Gospels: The Theoretical Challenge* (New Haven, Conn.: Yale University, 1989), 41–68; and more broadly: M. Bal, *Narratology: Introduction to the Theory of Narrative* (Toronto: University of Toronto, 1985); W. C. Booth, *The Rhetoric of Fiction*, 2d ed. (Chicago: University of Chicago, 1983); S. Chatman, *Story and Discourse: Narrative Structure in Fiction and Film* (Ithaca, N.Y.: Cornell University, 1980). For three representative applications to Gospel studies see Rhoads and Michie, *Mark as Story*; R. C. Tannehill, *The Narrative Unity of Luke–Acts: A Literary Interpretation*, vol. 1 (Philadelphia: Fortress, 1986); R. A. Culpepper, *Anatomy of the Fourth Gospel* (Philadelphia: Fortress, 1983).

(see Kort below) and intratextuality, whereby meaning is conveyed by the particular language that is used, and the tradition it represents.[78] Wesley A. Kort has shown that narrative analysis may mean at least one of four different literary methods: myth criticism, structural analysis (and here he means structuralist),[79] critical hermeneutics (a label which seems to me to be unsatisfactory for the work of Gadamer and Ricoeur), and composition criticism. He illustrates the last type by the works of Robert Alter, *The Art of Biblical Narrative*, and Frank Kermode, *The Genesis of Secrecy*.[80] The emphases of composition criticism, as Kort describes them, mesh well with those of this study, especially on the following points: the principle of material selection, the blending of author and artistry which often means the

---

[78]While *intertextual* denotes the method of this study, the commitment of time and energy this study requires on the part of writer and reader is one of *intratextual* stance; the immersion of one's thought and life in biblical narrative, images and symbolic meaning structures. On the latter, see G. A. Lindbeck, *The Nature of Doctrine: Religion and Theology in a Postliberal Age* (Philadelphia: Westminster, 1984), 113–24.

[79]Structural(ist) studies may generate insights useful to compositional analysis, as E. S. Malbon's works on Mark have demonstrated. Two of her earlier articles, "Galilee and Jerusalem: History and Literature in Marcan Interpretation," *CBQ* 442 (1982), 242–55, and "The Jesus of Mark and the Sea of Galilee," *JBL* 103 (1984), 363–77, show fruitful use of structuralist method in text analysis. Her more comprehensive application of structuralist method to Mark in *Narrative Space and Mythic Meaning in Mark* (San Francisco: Harper & Row, 1986) demonstrates how structure, when analyzed and exposed, discloses meaning. The results of her investigations generally concur with the insights of compositional analysis employed in this study.

Her article on "Structuralism, Hermeneutics, and Contextual Meaning," *JBL* 51/2 (1983), 207–20, also shows how those doing textual exegesis by either the structuralist or hermeneutical methods may be closer to each other than to those interested in other goals (i.e., philosophy or theory) within the same disciplinary methodology. In contrast to Malbon's work, C. W. Hedrick's essay represents an inadequate use of structuralist analysis ("What Is a Gospel? Geography, Time, and Narrative Structure," *Persp Rel Stud* 10 [March 1983], 255–68). Limiting his analysis to the formal considerations of temporal and spatial "markers" in Mark, he fails to consider the structural significance of other recurring motifs or themes. By overemphasizing geographical and temporal "markers," he makes arrival in Judea (10:1) structurally determinative and thus discounts the important thrice-recurring passion predictions and seven strategically placed uses of ὁδός throughout 8:27–10:52.

Hence, we must consider not only which method is employed, but how comprehensively that method is applied.

[80]W. A. Kort, *Story, Text, and Scripture: Literary Interests in Biblical Narrative* (University Park, Penn./London: Penn State University, 1988), 50–96.

concealment of the author, and the view that "the author's intention [is] to create in the narrative a sense of greater meaning than what is immediately available . . . [i.e.,] to write a narrative that will be laden with inexhaustible, elusive meaning."[81]

In his attempt to define narrative unity among the Gospels, Roland Frye looks for the central event, the denouement, in each Gospel narrative.[82] Strikingly, he finds this to be the same in each of the Synoptics, even though they differ in their selection and organization of individual pericopae. These turn out to be different in specific content, *but* the functional significance of each in relation to the total story, the entire Gospel, is strikingly similar. He then examines the temptation narratives in Matthew and Luke and shows again, despite differing redactional interests, that the function of that narrative and the larger Gospel stories is remarkably alike. In a similar way, Israel's basic traditions of faith play comparable structural and meaning-bearing roles in the Synoptics, even though each one develops different dimensions of meaning and significance from those traditions.

Narrative Analysis and Tradition History

Not only is canonical form related to the process and fruit of tradition-history and not only does narrative analysis show the significance of structure for ascertaining the religious or theological meaning of canonical texts, but narrative analysis itself invites reflection upon the significance of traditions in the narratives. This study provides an extended illustration of the intrinsic relation between narrative analysis and tradition history. It shows that while narrative analysis explicates the meaning of the structure, the traditions behind the structure determine to a great extent the religious meaning of the text. This religious meaning may be variously denoted as the scriptural, canonical, or theological meaning. Use of these terms

---

[81]Kort, *Story*, 86, 90, 94 (quotation on last page). Kort's categorization, while helpful, also has its limitations, for the emphases and procedures of these four categories are not necessarily mutually exclusive. Elements of myth analysis may be incorporated into compositional criticism; the same is true for structural(ist) analysis and critical hermeneutics. But the latter is more a philosophy of texts and language, than it is a method of interpretation. The reasons for Kort's own preference for textuality (chs. 4–5) over narrativity merit our attention; this study represents a blend of both, however.

[82]"The Jesus of the Gospels: Approaches Through Narrative Structure," in *From Faith to Faith: Essays in Honor of Donald G. Miller*, ed. D. Y. Hadidian (PMS 31; Pittsburgh: Pickwick, 1979), 75–89.

entails the concept of authority, and thus points to the way the text functions in forming and shaping faith in the communities of believers who then and now invest their lives in the claims of the texts.[83] The narrative thus witnesses to the community's identity and also further develops the community's identity in both its faith-understanding and self-definition. In this process narrative produces and conveys religious meaning, thus functioning as *scripture*. When narrative functions in this way it gains status as canon, by providing authority for life.[84] In this process the particular structure of a narrative stands in the service of faith. The structure draws upon the faith traditions of the people from whom the narrative arises and in turn further forms the people's faith. Thus there is a sequential dependence of *scripture* on narrative, narrative on structure, and structure on faith traditions which in turn are developed from the religious experiences of the people who *own*, i.e., claim, and live by that narrative as *scripture*.

Narrative analysis and tradition history are to be viewed thus as complementary, not competing, methodologies; the choice between viewing texts as windows and viewing them as mirrors has been misconceived. Werner Kelber rightly calls for fresh hermeneutical assessment of the role of tradition in the task of narrative analysis. He observes that the narrativity of the canonical Gospels sets them off in form and genre from the so-called noncanonical Gospels, a point which this study speaks to in its concluding remarks. Moreover, he notes that narrativity requires utilization of tradition, and thus:

> To say that the Gospels work out of and respond to tradition is to suggest the possibility of understanding the study of narrativity and

---

[83]W. R. Farmer's work on the development of the canon bears this out in a singular and impressive way. See *Jesus and the Gospel: Tradition, Scripture, and Canon* (Philadelphia: Fortress, 1982), 165–221; Farmer and D. M. Farkasfalvy, *The Formation of the New Testament Canon: An Ecumenical Approach* (New York/Ramsey/Toronto: Paulist, 1985), 9–40.

[84]Two discussions of the religious and/or scriptural meaning of texts are especially insightful and provocative: In *Biblical Interpretation of the Bible* (New York: Oxford University, 1988) R. Morgan, with J. Barton, calls attention to the religious meaning of biblical texts, as distinct from the historical or literary meanings (21–43). W. C. Smith suggests that the historical study of the Bible is the pre-scriptural phase and the newly acclaimed literary method is a post-scriptural phase. In neither approach does Scripture "serve as a transcendent luminosity . . . . we scholars do not in fact understand what scripture is. We do not know how to treat a text as scripture" ("Scripture as Form and Concept: Their Emergence for the Western World," in *Rethinking Scripture*, ed. Miriam Levering [Albany, N.Y.: State University, 1989], 45–46).

tradition historical analysis as mutually enriching and corrective enterprises.[85]

This study assumes and demonstrates that the two enterprises are interwoven: narrativity requires tradition.[86] As a narrative discloses its full meaning, it prompts questions that often receive answers only from an understanding of traditions behind the text. For this reason the task of compositional analysis, as a significant component of narrative analysis, invites intertextual and intratextual study.[87] Gospel study must utilize methods that affirm both narrativity and tradition as intrinsic components of the genre that we call "Gospel."[88] As scholarship continues to develop and refine its methodological approaches, both the academy and the church will be enriched by forging a method that simultaneously attends to both features of the canonical Gospels' genre: narrativity and tradition-bearing witness.[89]

This contribution is thus dedicated to both the religious quest of persons seeking to understand the Christian faith, as witnessed to by the Synoptics, and the formation of the identity of Christian communities that treasure Scripture in its canonical form as empowerment for thought and life.

---

[85]W. H. Kelber, "Narrative as Interpretation and Interpretation of Narrative: Hermeneutical Reflections on the Gospels," *Semeia* 39 (1987), 107–33; quote on 124–25. While Kelber uses the term "tradition" to refer to that received from Jesus and the early church, the same point applies to what Jesus and the early church received from OT faith, the focus of this study.

[86]Several general literary contributions have made this the starting point of their reflections. J. Hollander proposes five types of intertextual echo: acoustical, allegorical, schematic, metaphorical, and metaleptic (*The Figure of Echo: A Mode of Allusion in Milton and After* [Berkeley: University of California, 1981]). Of these descriptions, the schematic represents the way the Synoptics echoed the major OT traditions, according to my view. T. M. Greene identifies and discusses four types of intertextual relationships that a literary work might bear to its predecessor: imitative, eclectic, heuristic, and dialectical (*The Light in Troy: Imitation and Discovery in Renaissance Poetry* [New Haven, Conn.: Yale University, 1982], 38–46). While elements of all these are present in the Synoptics' use of Israel's theological traditions, I do not see that any one of these types fits well the intertextual phenomenon of this study.

[87]See n. 78.

[88]This is true for the canonical Gospels, but it may not apply to all the noncanonical Gospels. See Appendix I.

[89]This point of view is in keeping with Hans Gadamer's understanding of meaning and hermeneutical theory, as well as recent trends in theology and ethics; see Lindbeck, 82–84, and Stanley Hauerwas, *The Peaceable Kingdom* (Notre Dame/London: University of Notre Dame, 1983), esp. 29ff.

2

THE BASIC COMPONENTS

Three interacting components lie at the heart of this study: Old Testament faith traditions, the content of the Synoptic Gospels, and the distinctive common structure of the Synoptics—that which marks them as *syn-optic*, as distinct from John's Gospel and the non-canonical Gospels. This chapter identifies and describes the Old Testament faith traditions that are shown in chapters 3–6 to be influential in shaping the Synoptics' story of Jesus. It also identifies the distinctive content of the Synoptics and then examines the distinctive Synoptic structure.

OLD TESTAMENT FAITH TRADITIONS

Chapters 3–6 will show that four of Israel's faith traditions played major roles in shaping the structure and thematic accents of the Synoptics' story of Jesus. It is striking that these same four faith traditions appear in one of Israel's earliest poetic articulations of faith, in the famous Song of the Sea in Exodus 15:1–18. This recital of God's saving deeds on behalf of Israel mentions the same four themes of divine redemptive activity that shape the Synoptic story: exodus, way-conquest, temple, and kingship.[1] The Song of the Sea falls readily into the four-point outline:

---

[1] I am indebted to Walter Brueggemann for alerting me to this text and its parallel to the Synoptic structural sequence.

The Lord's Salvation at the Sea	1a–12
The Lord Leads the Conquest	13–16
The Lord Brings Them to His Sanctuary	17
The Lord Will Reign For Ever and Ever	18

In this hymnic burst of praise, the sea-event, unlike Sinai or wilderness, receives sole focus within the exodus traditions. As Childs says, "Ex. 15 reflects a poetic tradition of the event at the sea, which . . . has been transmitted within the larger framework of the exodus and conquest traditions."[2] Childs also notes many connections in linguistic imagery and emphasis to numerous psalms. This confirms Kapelrud's insights that the psalms were the great melting pot of Israel's traditions: they produce "a final picture of Israelite Judean religion . . . taken over by Judaism and Christianity."[3] Kapelrud stresses the interacting formative roles of cult and tradition, and indeed Exodus 15:1–18 is a poetic hymn of worship.

While the sea miracle and the conquest are the primary events celebrated in this hymn of praise—and Yahweh is the sole actor and subject of these events—the mention of Yahweh's sanctuary[4] and his eternal kingship is the more striking because of the likely early date.[5] Israel's cultic legacy witnesses clearly to the prominent role that these four streams of tradition had within the worshiping community, even at an early date.[6] In his analysis of Exodus 15 together with

---

[2] B. S. Childs, *Exodus: A Commentary* (London: SCM, 1974), 245.

[3] A. S. Kapelrud, "Tradition and Worship: The Role of the Cult in Tradition Formation and Transmission," in *Tradition and Theology in the Old Testament*, ed. D. Knight (Philadelphia: Fortress, 1977), 121.

[4] Martin Noth, however, takes the position that "sanctuary" in 17b designates "not a single holy place, but the whole land, as the possession of Yahweh" (*Exodus: A Commentary* [OTL; Philadelphia: Fortress, 1962], 126). Even so, the structure of thought is such that later use of the hymn would surely pour into the phrase, the temple on Mount Zion.

[5] This pattern likely reflects influence of the Baal and other ancient Near Eastern myths. In the Psalms as a whole—in the many Zion and kingship psalms—the temple and Zion emphases occupy more space than the exodus and conquest themes.

[6] While the emphases here and in the fourfold structural outline for the synoptic traditions have similarities to George Ernest Wright's theology of a recital of God's acts in history in *God Who Acts: Biblical Theology as Recital* (SBT 8; London: SCM, 1952), and Paul Minear's (*The Eyes of Faith*), some of the fundamental categories are quite different. Instead of emphasizing God's revelation in history, this study speaks of traditions in Scripture (*word* is more the focus than history), and instead of making "recital" the genre of faith's

Psalm 24, Frank Cross has identified what he calls the "ritual conquest" as "a basic ingredient of certain cultic traditions in old Israel."[7]
The imagery of Yahweh Seba'ot and mighty Warrior (*gibbôr milḥa-
mâh*) occurs within numerous early poetic hymns celebrating Israel's
exodus-conquest (Deut 33:2–3; Judg 5:4–5; Ps 68: 8–9). While these
hymns reflect numerous cosmic images ("from heaven fought the
stars"), this poetry predates the "creation-kingship" motifs popularized during the monarchy and in later apocalyptic literature.[8] Further, Cross claims that the exodus-conquest poetry had its home in
the Gilgal cultus, which celebrated specifically the Lord's coming from
Sinai into his holy place (Ps 68:18; Exod 15:13). Joshua 3–5, Cross
contends, preserves cultic traditions derived from a spring festival
celebrating the exodus-conquest event. In this festival, six components may be reconstituted: sanctifying the people, as for holy war or
approaching a sanctuary (3:5); bearing the ark of the covenant in
solemn procession; reenacting the crossing of the Jordan, a replay of
the Red Sea miracle (4:21–24); erecting at the Gilgal sanctuary twelve
stones for a memorial; recalling a circumcision etiology (5:2–8); and
rehearsing the appearance of the angelic captain of Yahweh's war.[9]

---

confession, it examines major sections of biblical narrative, i.e., entire Gospels.
This study bears affinities also to Gerhard von Rad's emphasis on faith traditions, but sees no need to stress discontinuity between Israel's faith and its
history, as von Rad does in his *Theology*, 1.116–21.

   [7] F. M. Cross, Jr., "The Divine Warrior in Israel's Early Cult," in *Biblical
Motifs: Origins and Transformations*, ed. A. Altmann (Cambridge, Mass.: Harvard University, 1966), 24–25.

   [8] Cross suggests a twelfth-century date for Exod 15 ("Divine Warrior,"
22). He apparently dates the other texts cited above from about the same period
(25). For extended analysis of Ps 68 and its early depiction of this Yahweh
Seba'ot tradition, see P. D. Miller, Jr., *The Divine Warrior in Early Israel* (HSM
5; Cambridge, Mass.: Harvard University, 1975). See also M. C. Lind's treatment
of Exod 15 and Judg 5 in *Yahweh Is a Warrior* (Scottdale, Penn.: Herald, 1980),
46–89. B. S. Childs notes the differing views of scholars on dating in his
commentary, *Exodus*, 245–47.

   [9] Cross, "Divine Warrior," 27. It is possible to see somewhat parallel
motifs in the Synoptics "Galilee-to-Jerusalem" section: (1) Jesus' call to take up
the cross and give one's life for the gospel; (2) Jesus' leading the disciples as in
a sacred procession, teaching the way of discipleship; (3) the Transfiguration
and exorcism as pointing to post-resurrection power—thus the big, ultimate
barrier broken by God's feat in Jesus; (4) promising the twelve disciples seats of
conquest and judgment (only in Matt 19:27 and Luke 18:30; cf. Mark 10:28–30);
(5) drinking the cup of suffering; and (6) Jesus' appearing as the One who gives
his life a ransom for many, followed by the opened eyes of blind Bartimaeus
who follows Jesus on the way. That Jericho functions prominently in both

Cross contends that this tradition was joined with the southern kingship-royal cult tradition, thus blending the "cultus of the league and the cultus of the kingdom." In both traditions the ideology of divine warfare and the presence of a divine sanctuary figured prominently, though the inauguration of a temple into the cultic ceremony reflects Canaanite influence.[10] In the monarchy the league traditions were more and more suppressed and the traditions of God's covenant with David and Zion gained ascendancy. In Second Isaiah, however, the exodus-conquest and second exodus-second conquest reemerge as vital elements of both God's kingship and God's reclaiming of Zion and its people for the sake of the world (Isa 40:3–6; 51:9–11; 35:8–10; 25:6–8; 55:1–5; and most notably, 52:7–12).[11] In these texts two strands of tradition are wedded: "one derived from the ritual Conquest, [and] one from the procession of the Ark to Zion and the manifestation of Yahweh's kingship."[12] Later prophetic eschatology, even as expressed in Qumran's War Scroll, continues to blend and echo in various patterns these two traditions.[13]

Old Testament scholarship, however, has more recently cautioned against sharply dichotomizing between northern and southern theological traditions. After noting L. Rost's position of assigning the Sinaitic and Davidic covenant theologies to the north and south respectively,[14] and N. Poulssen's view that the rise of the alien institutions of temple and kingship "had the effect of suppressing the ancient Mosaic tradition,"[15] B. W. Anderson says, "the separation of covenant theologies on the basis of geography is undoubtedly an oversimplification."[16] Anderson then draws on Cross's work above to observe that the theme of Yahweh as divine Warrior is common to

---

stories is also striking. Some of these connections are more fanciful than others. Perhaps this "hermeneutical event" belongs solely to my/our minds as readers, and cannot be said to be part of the author's or text's hermeneutical event at all.

[10]Cross, "Divine Warrior," 28.

[11]Ibid., 28–29.

[12]Ibid., 30.

[13]Ibid. Similarly, of the four traditions forming the core of this study, exodus and kingship are the most prominent traditions influencing the Synoptics.

[14]L. Rost, "Sinaibund und Davidsbund," *TLZ* 72 (1947), cols. 129–34.

[15]N. Poulssen, *König und Tempel im Glaubenszeugnis des Alten Testamentes* (SBM 3; Stuttgart: Katholisches Bibelwerk, 1967).

[16]B. W. Anderson, "Exodus and Covenant Theology in Second Isaiah and Prophetic Tradition," in *Magnalia Dei: The Mighty Acts of God*, ed. F. M. Cross, W. E. Lemke, and P. D. Miller, Jr. (New York: Doubleday, 1976), 345.

both the exodus and Zion traditions. Further, David's escorting of the sacred Ark into Jerusalem shows the fusion of the northern traditions into the south's symbols and theology of divine presence. The fusion of the traditions occurred before the work of the Deuteronomist, contra Rost.[17]

Jon Levenson descriptively reviews the evidence for what he designates as the earlier scholarly "majority opinion" which argued for distinctive northern and southern components of tradition.[18] Levenson contends that those theological emphases held to be "northern" (outlying shrine centers critical of Zion's centralized cult and view of kingship) can also be shown to have existed in the south, and that those held to be "southern" (e.g., the dynastic view of kingship) can be shown to have been present in the north. Hosea 3:5 shows pro-Davidic affinities within an avowed antimonarchical book; Micah 6:1–8 shows Sinaitic covenant tradition within a southern prophetic book; and Psalm 97, an explicit Zion psalm, reflects the theophanic language of Sinai. He proposes, rather, that the distinction is not basically geographical, but *social*: "It pits city against countryside, rather than Judah (south) against Israel (north)."[19] Levenson's primary thesis, however, does not deny the distinctiveness of the Sinai and Zion traditions, but shows that they are not inherently opposed to each other. Rather, the Zion literature took over Sinai traditions. As he puts it, " . . . even in demonstrably southern literature, the Mosaic/ Sinaitic and the Davidic/Zionistic orientations could coexist peacefully."[20] He does not deny the distinctiveness of traditions with northern (and earlier) origin and those of southern (and later) origin; instead he denies the incompatibility of those distinctive traditions. He opposes those views that assume a "purism" in northern and southern dichotomy. Levenson rightly accents the intermingling and fusion of Israel's varied traditions (earlier and later, northern and southern) into a sufficiently common strand that the continuing southern kingdom readily confesses the Sinai covenant legacy as its own. In this respect, his alternative "city vs. country" proposal is an "aside" which actually threatens—in the same way the geographical purism does—the main thesis of his book.

---

[17] Anderson, "Exodus and Covenant," 345–46.

[18] J. D. Levenson, *Sinai and Zion: An Entry into the Jewish Bible* (San Francisco: Harper & Row, 1985), 188–92. In view of Anderson's essay, it may be questioned just how extensive this "majority opinion" was.

[19] Ibid., 192ff. with quotation on p. 200.

[20] Ibid., 194.

Levenson's treatment of Israel's faith traditions, representing broader trends in Old Testament scholarship,[21] is thus a welcomed corrective to an earlier, overrefined dichotomy. But neither this corrective nor Anderson's caveats undermine the distinctiveness of the traditions or the notion of northern (which is "country" sociologically) and southern (also defined by its center as "city" sociologically) settings which gave rise to complementary sets of traditions. Indeed, the exodus-Sinai and conquest traditions developed in premonarchical Israel and were nurtured in the north before there ever was a Zion. The discrete identities of the different traditions, and the recognition that they had separate, distinctive histories of origin, including geographical referent points, are necessary presuppositions against which both Anderson's cautions and Levenson's correctives make sense. The mention of cultic shrines at Bethel and Gilgal, as in Amos 5:4–5 and Hosea 8:11–14; 9:15; 10:5, is, as Levenson notes, poor evidence that here the Mosaic Sinai traditions were preserved, since indeed the prophets attack the syncretism which is idolatry.[22] Nonetheless, these texts testify to the existence of northern cultic shrines (note also Shiloh, 1 Sam 3:19–4:22; Jer 7:12), whose origins predated the rise of Zion. Similarly, it is clear that the temple and kingship traditions which developed during the monarchy or even earlier (see n. 5 above), had an original southern (city) setting and were in various ways promulgated throughout Israel. Granting Kapelrud's point that Israel's cultic life was the grand melting point of Israel's faith traditions and Levenson's critique of geographical "purism," it still must be noted that many psalms nonetheless reflect orientation to one or the other set of traditions, exodus-Sinai and conquest or Zion's temple and kingship. For the former ("northern"), see Psalms 75, 77, 78, 80, 81, 105, 106, 114, 136; for the latter ("southern"), see Psalms 20, 46, 48, 76, 84, 87, 89, 97, 99, 101, 132. Psalms 72, 74, and 114 show both sets of traditions. Levenson's insight, that on occasion the two sets of tradition are fused with the effect that the two correct each other, is instructive. Of Jeremiah 7:1–15 and Psalm 50 he says, "In Jeremiah 7, Sinai demolishes the hubris of Zion; in Psalm 50, Zion demolishes the hubris of Sinai."[23] That these respective sets of traditions were blended together in complementary, and sometimes critiquing, relationship is a significant precursor for the Synoptics' story of Jesus.

---

[21] See H. Gese's *Vom Sinai zum Zion* and the essays in *Tradition and Theology in the Old Testament.*

[22] Levenson, *Sinai and Zion*, 192.

[23] Ibid., 209.

That Second Isaiah played a major role in revitalizing and
blending these traditions is significant for our study, for Second Isaiah
not only shows extensive incorporation of the exodus traditions into
his strong Zion theology,[24] but in keeping with the cosmic claims of
Zion's theology, Isaiah directs the vision of God's goal for Israel
toward the horizon that includes the whole world (42:6; 49:6–7;
52:7–10; passim). As Anderson puts it, Second Isaiah

> is a debtor to the Israelite sacred story . . . found classically in the
> Pentateuch, to the prophets who preceded him, to wisdom circles, to the
> liturgical traditions of the Psalter, and to the royal theology of Zion. In
> his prophecy all of the traditions of Israel came together and, under
> the alchemy of his poetic and theological insight, were given a new
> synthesis.[25]

Second Isaiah's contribution is essential for this study of the Synoptics' structure and theology, because the Synoptic structure is not
simply "Galilee-Jerusalem," but "Galilee-Jerusalem-Return to Galilee" (in Mark and Matthew). The return to Galilee functions in such
a way as to match structurally and in significance Isaiah's call for

---

[24]See B. C. Ollenburger, *Zion, the City of the Great King* (Sheffield:
JSOT, 1987) for the central place and function of Zion theology in Second
Isaiah. For the incorporation of exodus motifs into this Zion theology see B. W.
Anderson, "Exodus Typology in Second Isaiah," in *Israel's Prophetic Heritage:
Essays in Honor of J. Muilenberg*, ed. B. W. Anderson and W. Harrelson (New
York: Harper & Row, 1962), 177–95. The themes and motifs may be summarized
as follows:

1. 40:3–5	The way in the wilderness is to be prepared.
2. 40:17–20	Yahweh transforms the wilderness.
3. 42:14–16	Yahweh provides a way that is not known.
4. 43:1–3	Yahweh protects Israel through waters and fire.
5. 43:14–21	Yahweh does a *new* thing—making a way in the wilderness.
6. 48:20–21	Water flows from the rock as the people return.
7. 49:8–12	The desert and mountains become highways by which are bubbling springs of water, with Israel again entering the land of promise.
8. 51:9–10	As in the old exodus *and* creation Yahweh will make a way through the sea.
9. 52:11–12	Yahweh will lead his people in the new exodus.
10. 55:12–13	Israel "shall go out in joy . . . and peace."

[25]Anderson, "Exodus and Covenant," 340. Anderson's essay seeks to
explain Second Isaiah's omission of the Sinaitic covenant when he draws so
heavily upon the exodus traditions and in view of the fact that the Sinai
covenant event was firmly secured in the sacred story by Second Isaiah's time.

God's salvation to encompass the whole earth. Hence, Isaiah's use of both the older and younger faith traditions of Israel sets a structural model for the Synoptics' story of Jesus.

Each of the next four chapters begins by describing the content, scope and emphases of each of Israel's four faith traditions crucial to this study. Two comments are necessary to anticipate those discussions. In order to reflect the original distinctness and later canonical fusion of the exodus and Sinai traditions,[26] the terms exodus and Sinai (or exodus-Sinai) designate the Old Testament tradition(s) considered in chapter 3. Just as these traditions have separate but linked identities in Israel's faith story,[27] so also they have distinct and complementary identities in their influence upon the Synoptics.

THE DISTINCTIVE STRUCTURE: GALILEE–JERUSALEM

The common structure of each Synoptic Gospel consists of a Galilean section, a Journey to Jerusalem section, and a Jerusalem section.[28] The efforts to understand why the Synoptics present Jesus' ministry within the distinctive "Galilee-journey-Jerusalem" structure have been many. Since John gives a historically more plausible outline of Jesus' movements between Jerusalem and Galilee—showing three

---

[26]G. von Rad, *The Problem of the Hexateuch and other Essays*, trans. E. W. Trueman Dicken (New York: McGraw Hill, 1966), 53–54.

[27]Von Rad credits the fusion of the two traditions to the Yahwist and then observes that, due to the Yahwist's Hexateuchal incorporation of the Sinai tradition into the exodus-settlement traditions (see the latter Ps 106 and Neh 9 recitals), "the simple soteriological conception of the Settlement tradition . . . is now coloured by the divine self-revelation of Mt. Sinai." The God of "redemptive activity" is the God who calls humans to obedience. Von Rad regards this blending of the two traditions as defining fundamentally the two "propositions of the whole message of the Bible: Law and Gospel" (*The Problem*, 54). I contest this formulation and suggest that the fundamental definition is that of Gospel as both Liberation and Law. Von Rad's thesis on the incorporation of Sinai into the exodus traditions needs critical testing. The Exodus narrative testifies to an inherent unity of these two themes.

[28]Within this common design there is also variation. Luke's Journey section is longer than the other two, and Matthew's Galilean section is comparably longer than Luke's and Mark's. Outside this common structure, differences appear at both the beginnings and endings, though all have a brief Judean section at the beginning. Matthew and Luke contain their own distinctive birth narratives, and Luke diverges from Matthew and Mark in ending his Gospel not with a return to Galilee, but with waiting in Jerusalem for the unfolding drama of his second volume.

trips north and south—the synoptic portrait begs for some explanation, theological or otherwise.

Most scholars have sought for answers in the arena of literary style combined with theological purpose, though two exceptions to this may be noted: the liturgical view (which is also theological in a specialized way), and here M. D. Goulder's work is most important; and the effort to understand the structure within a structuralist mythical grid, as Elizabeth Struthers Malbon has done.

Aside from these efforts, the theological explanations consist of essentially three types, all with a common base of agreement. They agree that Galilee-Jerusalem represents a polarity: Galilee represents the land of reception, Jerusalem the place of rejection (this of course is basic to Malbon's structural analysis as well). They disagree, however, in the significance of Galilee.

1. Ernst Lohmeyer, followed by Willi Marxsen, developed the view that in Mark Galilee denotes the place of eschatological fulfillment and the origin of Galilean Christianity, the originating impulse of the Gospel of Mark. As Lohmeyer puts it: "For St. Mark 'Galilee is the holy land of the Gospel, the place of its eschatological fulfillment . . . Jerusalem is the city of deadly enmity to Jesus, of sin, and of death.' "[29] In Galilee Jesus proclaimed the coming of the kingdom. Similarly, the disciples are instructed to go to Galilee (14:28; 16:7) for the eschatological consummation of the kingdom. By making this its climax, Mark's Gospel signals to the Christian community of his time intensified hope for imminent eschatological consummation. Marxsen takes the cryptic line in Mark 13:14, "let the reader understand," as an awakening call to those who have fled Jerusalem and located in Pella. This command to go to Galilee both justifies their new location and beckons them to await the imminent parousia.[30]

Werner Kelber also basically follows this view but adds new features: the eschatological function of Galilee represents in Mark "a new time and new place," in opposition to the long-standing messianic hopes of Judaism. Indeed, the Old Testament Zion tradition clearly denoted Jerusalem as the place for eschatological fulfillment.

---

[29]E. Lohmeyer, *Galiläa und Jerusalem* (Göttingen: Vandenhoeck & Ruprecht, 1936), 26, 34, trans. L. E. Elliott-Binns in his book, *Galilean Christianity* (SBT 16; London: SCM, 1956), 35.

[30]W. Marxsen, *Mark the Evangelist: Studies on the Redaction History of the Gospel*, trans. R. A. Harrisville et al. (Nashville/New York: Abingdon, 1969), 175–76. Critics of Marxsen's thesis have rightly pointed out that technically Pella is not in Galilee, but in Decapolis.

The Gospel of Mark thus introduces a new stage in the eschatological hope: consummation will take place in a new place and a new time which is about to come. "Galilee is the New Jerusalem because this is where in the time of Mark the authentic future lies."[31]

Elliott-Binns' study, *Galilean Christianity*,[32] representing a variant emphasis, argues against the above assumption that Galilean Christianity is linked with a Gentile church population. He argues instead for a largely Christian Jewish population, which played a major role in all early Palestinian Christianity. He notes, for example, that James, the brother of Jesus and a Galilean, took up the leadership of the Jerusalem church after the death of the apostle James.

2. Lightfoot[33] (whose view changed after hearing T. W. Manson lecture on the topic), Boobyer,[34] Evans,[35] and Burkill[36] (as well as many others) have argued that Galilee represents the place of call to mission, and specifically the call to Gentile mission. The Isaiah phrase "Galilee of the Gentiles" (Matt 4:15) is determinative for this view. The term links Jesus and the church: as Galilee was literally the place of Jesus' kingdom proclamation and ministry, so Galilee will be where Jesus will send his disciples into all the world, as Matthew explicitly declares. These writers make no necessary association between this use in the Gospel and the identification of the Gospel with some form of early Galilean Christianity.

The strength of this view over the former is that Mark and Matthew agree on the textual and symbolic significance of Galilee. Or put conversely, the weakness of the first view in connecting Galilee in Mark to the parousia is that none of the other canonical testimonies concur; Mark thus stands against the larger tradition. Matthew clearly identifies the risen Jesus' return to Galilee as culminating in the commissioning of the disciples to go in mission to the nations, the Gentiles. The Luke–Acts account of Jesus' ascension and his eventual

---

[31]W. Kelber, *The Kingdom in Mark: A New Place and New Time* (Philadelphia: Fortress, 1974), 136–47 (quotation on p. 139).

[32]See n. 29.

[33]R. H. Lightfoot, *The Gospel Message of St. Mark* (Oxford: Oxford University, 1950), 106–16. This corrects his earlier position in *Locality and Doctrine in the Gospels* (London: Hodder & Stoughton, 1938), 62–67.

[34]Boobyer, "Galilee and Galileans, 334–38.

[35]C. F. Evans, "I Will Go Before You Into Galilee," *JTS* n.s. 5 (1954), 3–18.

[36]T. A. Burkill, *Mysterious Revelation: An Examination of the Philosophy of St. Mark's Gospel* (Ithaca, N.Y.: Cornell University, 1963), 252–57.

return in like manner (the parousia presumably) is located in Judea, on Mount Olivet, a sabbath day's journey outside Jerusalem (Acts 1:10–12).

3. The third view, proposed by Norman Perrin and developed further by Lloyd Gaston, combines the two views above. Perrin and Gaston agree that the Gentile mission is not to be substituted for the parousia in Mark but that it is rather the locale and context for the parousia.[37] Thus, Galilee in Mark 16:7 connects the Gentile mission and the parousia, as does Mark 13:10. The themes of mission and parousia must be interlinked in Mark also with the resurrection and the implied rebuilding of the temple.[38] The "going before you to Galilee" is "after I am raised up." Both the resurrection and the promised rebuilding of the temple are linked by "three days" (8:31; 9:31; 10:33; 14:58). Hence the "return to Galilee" brings to a climax several Gospel themes: Jesus' resurrection, the rebuilding of the temple, the mission to the Gentiles (13:10; 14:9), and the expected parousia (13:10). All are linked together by Mark's literary motifs of "three days" and the promised post-resurrection appearance in Galilee. The mission to the Gentiles is the locus and means of new temple worship. The old ναός with its separating curtain(s) is gone; the new ναός is erected precisely where Gentile and Jew are one in missional discipleship and eschatological hope. The return to Galilee, as Galilee itself, then, has in Mark as its *ultimate* symbolic function the call to anticipate the parousia. But "on the way," both the worldwide mission and the new ναός worship, embracing both Jew and Gentile and rising precisely in the setting of the mission itself, are essential precursors of the parousia. These emphases, through text-narrative analysis, are developed more fully in chapter 5 of this study.

Elizabeth Struthers Malbon's structuralist study of the Markan Galilee-Jerusalem geo-space seeks to separate narrative function from theological significance, at least initially, for purposes of clearer analysis. Her study highlights the polar opposition between Galilee and Jerusalem.[39] Her analysis concludes that in Mark the tradition of

---

[37] For Perrin, see H. D. Betz, ed., *Christology and a Modern Pilgrimage: A Discussion with Norman Perrin* (Claremont, Calif.: The New Testament Colloquium, 1971), 43; Lloyd Gaston, *No Stone Upon Another: Studies in the Significance of the Fall of Jerusalem in the Synoptic Gospels* (NovTSup 23; Leiden: E. J. Brill, 1970), 474–75.

[38] I have developed this in an essay, "Temple and Nations in Mark 11–16," presented at the 1976 Annual Society of Biblical Literature. See *SBL Abstracts* (Missoula, Mont.: Scholars, 1976), no. 262.

[39] See p. 28, n. 79.

expected eschatological consummation in Jerusalem is broken; there is a dramatic reversal of expectations. The long-held Old Testament tradition of Yahweh's dwelling in Zion and bringing security to his people from Zion undergoes a reversal; the eschatological blessings will come now in Galilee. Malbon's structural perception is correct, and the reversal theme is well put. But it need not be limited to eschatological hope, for the Zion tradition also includes the Torah going out from Jerusalem to all nations (Isa 2:4), which is already in Mark's time the means of bringing šālôm to the nations. The Gentile mission, with its miracle of uniting former enemies into one body in Christ, is the fulfillment of this vision, the making of a Pax Christi.

This survey of the scholarly work on Galilee-Jerusalem structure has focused primarily on its significance in Mark. It has offered the possibility that the significance of this structure in Mark may be different from that in Matthew. However, if the emphases of position 2 above are followed, that difference is negligible. In either position the function of Galilee is strongly positive, compared to Jerusalem's function. In light of the discussion above focusing on Israel's theological traditions, the significance of Mark's and Matthew's geo-spatial narrative structure calls for a recognition and an analysis of the apparent transformation of Israel's traditions. Does Zion's *shekinah* glory shift to Galilee? Does it journey as a pilgrim to the nations and there proclaim the gospel of God's reign? And how does Luke fit with this paradigm, when he has Jesus commanding the disciples to tarry in Jerusalem until they receive the Holy Spirit? Might there be evidence in the very structural design of the Synoptics for Donald Goergen's suggestion: "Jesus seems to have spiritually identified more with the wilderness, Moses-prophet, exodus traditions than the Jerusalem, David-Messiah, Zion traditions"?[40]

These are the questions that need resolution in any attempt to correlate the structure and theology of the Synoptics with Israel's major traditions of faith. In chapter 7 I synthesize my findings and put them into dialogue with Sean Freyne's recent study, *Galilee, Jesus and the Gospels*, in order to clarify and to resolve the significance of the Synoptics' geographical structure in relation to their overall literary designs and theological intentions.

---

[40]D. Goergen, *The Mission and Ministry of Jesus* (Wilmington, Del.: Michael Glazier, 1986), 1.157.

3

🐚

THE FORMATIVE INFLUENCE OF
OLD TESTAMENT EXODUS AND SINAI
TRADITIONS ON THE SYNOPTIC
GALILEAN NARRATIVE

The exodus and Sinai traditions functioned crucially in the Synoptics' presentation of the Galilean phase of Jesus' ministry. To demonstrate this, the first section defines briefly what is meant by Israel's exodus and Sinai traditions. Then, since each of the Synoptics develops its narrative of Jesus' deeds and words differently, subsequent sections treat each Gospel separately (sections 2–4 in each chapter) in order to show how each reflects the influence of exodus and Sinai traditions in its presentation of Jesus' Galilean ministry. The fifth section examines the continuity and discontinuity in the traditions. Chapters 4–6 will also follow this fivefold procedure to demonstrate the influence of the way-conquest, temple, and kingship traditions respectively upon each of the Synoptic Gospels.

The continuity and discontinuity also reveals significant transformations of thought which reflect the particular emphases of the respective Gospel. These emphases, while rooted in Jesus and the early church's catechesis, arise from the authorial purpose interacting with the needs of the church communities to which the Gospels are addressed. Thus each Gospel has both a theological and pastoral goal, for not only does the Gospel present the story of Jesus as a biblical-theological achievement, but it does so within the context of the particular needs of specific communities of faith. These pastoral and missional challenges stamp each Gospel with distinctive characteristics: Mark bears a kerygmatic tone; Matthew, a catechetical style; and Luke, several dimensions of apologetic purpose.

I examine the Gospels in the sequence Mark, Matthew, Luke because the majority of New Testament scholars continues to hold to Markan priority. While frequently comparing the emphases of the three Gospels, this study seeks to avoid the common but dubious method of ascertaining a Gospel's redactional emphasis via a given theory of literary dependence. The basic theses of this study, therefore, are not dependent upon any one order of Gospel origins. The commentary treats each Gospel in its own narrative right. The rationale for this decision is twofold: (1) narrative analysis is better served by unhooking the investigation from the laborious and precarious effort to distinguish between traditional material and redactional additions (since selectivity of traditional material significantly affects authorial purpose also); and (2) the results of this investigation, standing free of any one theory of Gospel origins, can lead to new reflections on the order of the Gospel origins, since it will be natural to ask which Gospel's theological emphases or structural design most likely gave rise to the others. Except for some remarks in Appendix I, these matters lie outside the scope of this study.

THE EXODUS AND SINAI TRADITIONS

Exodus 1–15 is the foundational scriptural text that describes Israel's deliverance from bondage in Egypt. In this narrative both *deliverance* (Exod 3:8) and *salvation* (Exod 14:13; 15:2) are primary emphases. In Israel's memory and celebration of the exodus, God's power and will, despite human resistance and unbelief, predominate. Because the event testifies to God's faithfulness to the divine promise to the patriarchs, it assures Israel of God's providence; as a symbol of hope, it foreshadows events to come.[1]

Michael Fishbane traces the journey and power of the exodus motif throughout the Hebrew Scripture. He notes its connection to the conquest, and that these two separate events of redemption often fuse in Israel's poetic-liturgical expression:

---

[1]M. Fishbane, "Exodus 1–4: The Prologue to the Exodus Cycle," in *Text and Texture: Close Readings of Selected Biblical Texts* (New York: Schocken Books, 1979), 64–65. J. S. Croatto focuses on the exodus tradition and its significance for liberating justice in his *Exodus: A Hermeneutics of Freedom*, trans. Salvator Attanasio (Maryknoll, N.Y.: Orbis, 1981). He also shows how this motif plays a central role in the prophets, Jesus, and Paul.

> The sea looked and fled
>   Jordan turned back (Ps 114:3).

These twin motifs of redemption appear not only in Israel's poetic liturgy (the worship of the Psalms), but also in the prophetic oracles of hope for the future (in Hosea, Jeremiah, and Isaiah).[2]

Israel's wilderness experience is linked to the exodus motif as well (Hos 2:16–17; Isa 48:20–21).[3] This wilderness tradition includes God's guidance and testing of Israel, Israel's rebellion, and God's gift of manna. In Exodus these wilderness themes occur both before and after the Mount Sinai encounter, and the theme dominates the book of Numbers.[4] In Psalm 78 (see vv. 13–31) Israel's deliverance from bondage, its rebellion in the wilderness, and God's guidance and provision of bread from heaven are all intertwined. Deliverance and wilderness are also tightly linked in v. 52, summarizing the leitmotifs of the chapter:

> Then he led out his people like sheep,
>   and guided them in the wilderness like a flock.[5]

This parallelism clearly unites the wilderness experience with the exodus events.

Another event associated with the exodus traditions is God's giving of the law to Israel on Mount Sinai. This tradition includes God's making a covenant with Israel (Exod 19:3–8) and the giving of the Decalog as a constituent part of that covenant (Exod 20:1–17). In the tradition history, therefore, Mount Sinai includes covenant and law; indeed, theologically they are inseparably one.[6] The Sinai tradi-

---

[2]Fishbane, "The 'Exodus' Motif: The Paradigm of Historical Renewal," in *Text and Texture*, 121–40. In his ground-breaking study of the pentateuchal traditions, Noth regards these as the two basic complementary themes and designates them: "Guidance out of Egypt" and "Guidance to the Arable Land" (M. Noth, *A History of Pentateuchal Traditions*, trans. B. W. Anderson [Englewood Cliffs, N.J.: Prentice-Hall, Inc., 1972], 47–54).

[3]Fishbane, "Exodus," 125, 134, and Noth, *History*, 58–59, who holds this to be a contribution of the *southern* tribes.

[4]See here the excellent study of G. W. Coats, *Rebellion in the Wilderness: The Murmuring Motif in the Wilderness Tradition of the Old Testament* (Nashville: Abingdon, 1968).

[5]Psalms 105 and 106 also fuse both the conquest and the exodus-wilderness events; the latter accents Israel's rebellion in the wilderness.

[6]See here the significant work done on the covenant form with its structural similarity to the Hittite suzerainty treaties: K. Baltzer, *The Covenant Formulary* (Philadelphia: Fortress, 1971); G. E. Mendenhall, "Ancient Oriental

tion, which had apparently independent origins since it is not mentioned in early faith recitals (Pss 78, 105, 136), was later joined to the exodus traditions (Neh 9) and is a constituent part of the narrative in Exodus 1–24. In the recital of Nehemiah 9, Ezra's prayer of repentance narrating God's gracious acts for Israel mentions "right ordinances and true laws, good statutes and commandments" given on Mount Sinai as part of the wilderness experience (vv. 12–15). In yet a later recital, the sermon of defense before the Sanhedrin, Stephen likewise mentions God's gift of living oracles on Mount Sinai to the congregation in the wilderness (Acts 7:38). Thus, by the time the Synoptic Gospels were written, precedent for blending the exodus, wilderness, and Sinai traditions together clearly exists.[7]

As discussed earlier, the exodus and Sinai traditions are sometimes fused with the way-conquest traditions (see Fishbane above and Childs in ch. 2). Hence, a case can be made for regarding exodus-Sinai and conquest traditions as one interwoven complex of memory in Israel's faith recitals and celebrations. This parallels a point (to be developed in chapter 5) that the temple and kingship traditions overlap and are fused with each other, both in Israel's story and in the Synoptics' story of Jesus. Viewed from this perspective, this study then concerns itself with the influence of two major complexes of traditions, exodus-conquest and temple-kingship, upon the shape of the Synoptic Gospels. But even though these sets of traditions overlap and are fused in both canons of Scripture, thematic and motif distinctions are evident. Even in the narration of the stories, both Old and New, a significant degree of both separateness and sequential emphasis is also present. In the older story, in Israel's primary history, Exodus 23:20 marks the transition from the exodus to the way-conquest narratives:

> I am going to send an angel in front of you,
>   to guard you on the way
> and to bring you to the place that I have prepared.

This theme continues in Numbers and Deuteronomy and culminates in Joshua with Israel's possession of the land, regarded as a gift from God.

---

and Biblical Law," *BA* 17 (1954), 26–46, and "Covenant Forms in Israelite Tradition," *BA* 17 (1954), 50–76; D. J. McCarthy, *Treaty and Covenant*, 2d ed. (AnBib 21A; Rome: Pontifical Institute, 1978).

[7]Since exodus is the foundational event, the term exodus is often used in biblical scholarship, and sometimes in this study also, to denote this entire stream of emphasis.

Similarly, in the Synoptics' story the beginning of the journey narrative marks the shift from a primary focus on exodus-wilderness themes to way-conquest themes. However, the Transfiguration event, in its strong echoing of Mount Sinai events, exemplifies the overlap of the two traditions. In Matthew and Mark the Transfiguration is located near the beginning of the Journey narrative, matching the placement of the Sinai event in Exodus 24 and 34, in the early part of the way-to-the-land section. But Luke places the Transfiguration in his exodus section, before his Journey narrative begins (9:51). As chapter 4 will discuss, Luke does this in order to accentuate the exodus theme and correlate Jesus' "exodus" with his liberating ministry of releasing the oppressed, thus echoing God's work in Israel's exodus.

In summary then, it is important to recognize both the overlapping and fusion of the exodus and conquest traditions *and* the distinction between the two. This distinction applies to themes or motifs within the two traditions and to the narrative sections in which these are developed, in the Exodus-Joshua story of Israel[8] and the Synoptics' story of Jesus.

MARK

1. *Content and Structure of Mark's Galilean Section*

The Galilean section of Mark's Gospel begins at 1:14 with Jesus entering Galilee and proclaiming the gospel of God; it ends at 8:27 with Jesus' leading his disciples "on-the-way" to Caesarea Philippi. The content of this section is as follows:

Call of four disciples (1:16–20)
One day of activity in/around Capernaum (1:21–45)
Conflict with religious leaders (2:1–3:6), followed by summary
    paragraph (3:7–12)
Appointing twelve and defining the power and people of the
    kingdom (3:13–35)
Teaching in parables (4:1–34)
Four miracle stories (4:35–5:43), with a thematic summary (6:1–6)
Sending out the Twelve, occasioning flashback on John (6:7–30)
Jesus feeds the multitudes twice, with contrasting responses to his
    ministry in ch. 7 (6:30–8:26)[9]

---

[8]As an overture to the story, Genesis frequently anticipates both traditions.

[9]These divisions and description of content depend upon the analysis

Numerous studies of Mark's Gospel identify discipleship as one of Mark's major themes.[10] Further, many commentators divide the book into six major sections, with 1:16–3:12, 3:13–6:6a, and 6:6b–8:26(30) constituting the first three main sections.[11] This structure highlights the theme of discipleship, since the beginning of each section shows Jesus' progressive work with his disciples: call of four, choosing of twelve, sending out of twelve. A point less widely noticed is the respective topographical location of the sequence: sea (1:16–20), mountain (3:13–19), and then gathering the sent-out ones into a wilderness place (ἔρημος τόπος, mentioned three times in 6:31–35). Paralleled by neither Matthew nor Luke, this is uniquely Mark's compositional design.[12] But the common synoptic tradition of Jesus' ministry in Galilee, with its concentration on exodus themes, prompted Mark to develop this exodus-Sinai-wilderness set of traditions into his topographical sequence of sea, mountain, and wilderness that now functions as narrative frames for his emphasis on discipleship.[13] In

---

of the Gospel's structure in my book, *Mark: The Way for All Nations*, 2d ed. (Scottdale, Penn.: Herald, 1981), chs. 2–6. This depends in turn upon my doctoral dissertation ("Markan Structure").

[10]See ch. 4, n. 4 below, for the more accessible sources. These contributions and others are taken into account in the recent study by C. C. Black, *The Disciples according to Mark: Markan Redaction in Current Debate* (JSNTSS 27; Sheffield: Sheffield Academic, 1989). Chs. 2–5 of Black's study present the differing interpretations of the role of the disciples in Mark. Chs. 5–6 show the inadequacy of current redactional approaches, in that scholars work with different methodological assumptions and different ways of reading the text. Ch. 7 seeks to rehabilitate the redactional-critical method, and ch. 8 formulates a method for studying Mark.

[11]For the widespread agreement of commentators on this issue, see Swartley, "Markan Structure," 39–53.

[12]My earlier studies (*Mark* and "Markan Structure") develop this point. The sequence of Israel's deliverance from the *sea*, receiving the Torah-Covenant for the Twelve tribes on the *mountain*, and living on manna in the *wilderness*, appears to have influenced Mark's shaping of his Gospel. See Swartley, "Markan Structure," 205–22.

[13]O. A. Piper has argued that, while Mark accented certain exodus motifs, the origin of the synoptic pattern was influenced by these motifs, and this in turn derived from Jesus' self-consciousness during his earthly ministry ("God's Good News," 165–82; "Unchanging Promises," 3–22; "Origin of the Gospel Pattern," 115–24). Piper did not correlate his insights with the structure of the Gospels or with Mark specifically, which I sought to do in my dissertation. This study will show some modification of the views developed in my dissertation, and it works with the entire synoptic tradition in its canonical form, not only Mark's Gospel.

The influence of the exodus on Mark's Gospel has been developed

the Nehemiah 9 and Acts 7 recitals, the thematic sequence of emphases matches the exodus-Sinai-wilderness order. This is striking since
the narrative in Israel's story, according to Exodus and Numbers, has
wilderness themes both before and after Sinai. Mark's order reflects
the sequence of the recitals of his time.

2. Liberation in Mark

a. Mark 1:16—3:12. This section begins with Jesus' call of
four disciples from the sea and contains two series of stories which are
essentially liberational. Werner Thissen demonstrates the permeating
emphasis of liberation in each of the five stories in 2:1–3:6.[14] He also
shows how this segment relates to the preceding one, namely, by
answering questions raised by Jesus' liberating deeds[15] in the earlier
unit, 1:21ff.[16]

Jesus' liberating events in this segment are:

> forgiving sins (2:1–12)
> calling Levi the tax collector to be a disciple (2:13–15)
> eating with sinners and tax collectors (2:15–17)
> not fasting according to custom (2:18–21)
> breaking the sabbath for life-giving causes, i.e., providing food
>   for his hungry disciples (2:22–28)
> healing a man's withered hand (3:1–6).

These liberating actions put Jesus in direct conflict with the religious
leaders, toning the early narrative with the shadow of his death (3:6).
But if this segment answers the former segment, as Thissen suggests,

---

most extensively by E. C. Hobbs in his unpublished doctoral dissertation,
"Gospel of Mark," 34–55.

[14]W. Thissen, *Erzählung der Befreiung: Eine exegetische Untersuchung
zu Mk 2,1–3,6* (Echter Verlag, 1976). The book as a whole develops this point.

[15]Thissen has also persuasively argued that the stories of this unit
show the authentic historical Jesus. This is what Jesus did, and this is what
shaped the traditions of Jesus and the communities formed by those traditions
(*Erzählung der Befreiung*, 245–55). Thissen uses a variety of criteria to determine authenticity, more than merely Bultmann's double-sided exclusion principle (232–38), but he does cite a confirming sentiment even from Bultmann,
who lists as characteristic of the historical Jesus: exorcisms, breaking sabbath
commandments, relaxing purity practices, polemic against Jewish legalities,
fellowship with ostracized persons such as tax collectors and harlots, and
concern for women and children. Indeed, he was not an ascetic like John the
Baptist (254, n. 92; from R. Bultmann's *Das Verhältnis der urchristlichen Christusbotschaft zum historischen Jesus* [Heidelberg, 1960], 11).

[16]Thissen, *Erzählung der Befreiung*, 260–321.

then 1:21ff. is also liberational. Mark's frontispiece for Jesus' public ministry is an exorcism in the synagogue (1:21–28).[17] True to Mark's overall portrait of Jesus' kingdom power pushing back the darkness, Jesus confronts at the outset of his public career the demons and the Satanic power they represent. This generates a shock-wave of questions revolving around the issue of Jesus' authority (1:27–28)— another of Mark's recurring themes (4:41; 11:28ff.). The exorcism is followed by Jesus' healing of Peter's mother-in-law from fever and illness (1:29–31). Finally, verses 32–34 are a Markan summary that reports Jesus' evening activity on the same day and highlights his healings of many sick people and his deliverance of many from demons.

The section of 1:21–3:6 may thus be aptly titled "Liberation from Bondage." With the exception of 1:35–39, this theme embraces all the stories.[18] Exorcisms and healings are two of the most prominent types of Jesus' liberating actions. Jesus' first public action was an exorcism (1:21–28; see also his summaries in 1:32–34; 3:7–12). This experience, while common in the first-century world, has been marginalized from our modern consciousness—or its authenticity has been disputed—since such experience does not fit our modern world view of reason and scientific method.[19] Following the exorcism are four stories of healing: Peter's mother-in-law (1:29–31); the leper (1:40–45); the paralytic (2:1–12); and the man with a withered hand (3:1–6). Healing emphases also occur in the two summarizing paragraphs (1:32–34; 3:7–12) that mention driving out demons as well (in the latter text it is implied; see also 1:39).

---

[17]H. C. Kee seeks to identify a communal setting for such emphases: "If one seeks for a *Sitz im Leben* for such a collection, the first in the series gives us a clue: it is a community in which Jesus is regarded as an agent who has come in the end time to defeat the powers of Satan" (*Community of the New Age: Studies in Mark's Gospel* [Philadelphia: Westminster, 1977], 36).

[18]This pericope links Jesus to the source of his transcendent power, enunciated at his baptism and in the wilderness temptation in Mark's prologue (1:1–13). For an excellent discussion of the importance of Jesus' dependence upon this transcendent power, see M. J. Borg, *Jesus, A New Vision: Spirit, Culture and the Life of Discipleship* (San Francisco: Harper & Row, 1987), 39–75.

[19]See Borg, *Jesus, A New Vision*, 60–65; G. H. Twelftree, *Christ Triumphant: Exorcism Then and Now* (London: Hodder and Stoughton, 1985); W. Wink, *Unmasking the Powers: The Invisible Forces That Determine Human Existence* (Philadelphia: Fortress, 1986), 43–50; M. S. Peck, *People of the Lie: The Hope for Healing Human Evil* (New York: Simon and Schuster, 1983); W. M. Swartley, ed., *Essays on Spiritual Bondage and Deliverance* (*OP* 11; Elkhart, Ind.: Institute of Mennonite Studies, 1988).

Jesus' third type of liberating action is his disregard of class and social status codes. He calls Levi, a tax collector, to follow him and he then eats with tax collectors and sinners. Jesus thus breaks the bondage of human alienation that arises from class partitioning in social structure.

Fourth, by choosing not to fast because it is time to celebrate the dawning of the kingdom, Jesus paves a new path of freedom in religious ritual, replacing the ascetic practice of John's disciples with celebration.

Climactically, Jesus' fifth type of liberating action threatens another strand of contemporary Jewish identity, that defined by sabbath *halakah*. From the viewpoint of the Pharisees,[20] Jesus broke the sabbath law itself, twice in this section (2:23–28; 3:1–6), and no offense could be greater. But from Jesus' view it was liberation on a most crucial point, for it raised the fundamental issue of the sabbath's purpose, bringing to the fore the exodus memory itself: does celebrating the sabbath mean keeping laws or liberating from bondage? Jesus' incisive declaration (2:27) and question (3:4) bring this issue squarely into focus. The exodus traditions of the sabbath are clear on this matter, for the sabbath was instituted to mark a new time for the redeemed (Exod 12) and was to be observed as a divine gift celebrating both humanitarian equality (masters and servants rest alike) and freedom from bondage (Deut 5:12–15). Jesus reaffirmed these sabbath purposes.

b. Mark 3:13–6:6a. The second section of Jesus' Galilean ministry in Mark (3:13ff.) begins with Sinai themes associated with the exodus tradition. Jesus' making (ἐποίησεν, in 3:14 and 16[21]) of the Twelve on the mountain echoes Moses' constituting Israel with twelve pillars corresponding to the twelve tribes of Israel (Exod 24:4),[22] and the Beelzebul controversy that immediately follows parallels Moses'

---

[20]For discussion of the Pharisees' identity of the *halakah's* authority with that of the Torah, see L. Goppelt, *Theology of the New Testament* (Grand Rapids: Eerdmans, 1981), 1.87–91.

[21]I accept the longer reading in v. 16 with its strong MS support: ℵ B C* Δ 565. Mark is quite intentional here: Jesus *made* Twelve.

[22]Paul Minear says of this Markan text: "The place of the disciples' commissioning was significant—a mountain. In ancient oriental thought heaven and earth came nearest to each other on a mountain-top. The mountain was the place most appropriate for especially sacred revelations (9:2; 13:3), for significant appointments, for bestowals of grace and power. This was no routine rendezvous. . . . 'He appointed Twelve.' The number was intentional. Jesus wanted new representatives of the twelve tribes of Israel" (*Saint Mark*, 65).

confronting the peoples' idolatry in their worship of the golden calf.[23] Then in the next pericope Jesus defines membership in the new community: "Whoever does the will of God is my brother, and sister, and mother." Jesus' earthly family pales in significance when set beside the new kingdom family, a reality similar to the defining of the covenant community in Israel (Exod 19:3–5).

The parables of the kingdom (4:1–34) also fit typologically into this Sinai complex in that they portray the distinctive character of the new kingdom and its people. Just as the Sinai covenant was given as invitation and identity for those called to be a "kingdom of priests," so here Jesus sets forth the nature of the new kingdom. From the perspective of *seeing*, it is mysterious—at the moment, hardly visible. But to ears of understanding (which even the disciples don't have, v. 13), the seed now being sown will germinate, sprout and, in some cases, bring forth abundant fruit. The crucial identity feature for those in whom it will grow and flourish is that they truly *hear* the kingdom call (varied forms of the verb ἀκούω occur 13 times in 4:3–33). The parables in Mark then echo in function but not in type, God's formation of a covenant-Torah relationship with Israel. The parables of the kingdom promise a (re)new(ed) peoplehood, the shape of which is yet to be seen.[24]

The seed image, which also unites the parable segment, occurs in three of the four parable units; indeed, what the sower sows is the word (λόγος, v. 14). The term "the word" (τὸν λόγον) occurs in each of the four descriptions of both the soils and (no) fruit. From the standpoint of the hearer, response to the *word* is crucial. Accordingly, Jesus is portrayed as both proclaimer and teacher of the *word*.[25] This,

---

[23]This association depends upon the biblical view that idolatry was inspired by demon power (Deut 32:17; Ps 106:37 and 96:5 [LXX]; Bar 4:7). See also Paul's argument in 1 Cor 10:6–22.

[24]Mark's editorial work on the parables already alludes to the inclusion of Gentiles. At two places this shows through: in his distinctive use of ἐκεῖνοι (the more distant demonstrative pronoun) to designate those who hear and bear (much) fruit (v. 20) and his distinctive wording in v. 32, ὑπὸ τὴν σκιὰν αὐτοῦ τὰ πετεινὰ τοῦ οὐρανοῦ κατασκηνοῦν. Of the OT "great tree" texts possibly alluded to, Dan 4:21; Jer 17:23; and Ezek 31:6, only the latter in its third strophe (LXX), has both "shade" (σκία) and "dwell" (though a different word, κατῴκησεν). Its noun, "all nations" (πᾶν πλῆθος ἐθνῶν), seems to lie behind Mark's "birds" (πετεινά). Mark's μεῖζον πάντων may also echo Ezekiel's πᾶν πλῆθος.

[25]The portrait of Jesus as Teacher in Mark has been argued also on different grounds by R. Meye and V. Robbins: R. Meye, *Jesus and the Twelve* (Grand Rapids: Eerdmans, 1968) and Robbins, *Jesus the Teacher*.

too, is an exodus image, reflecting Moses as giver and teacher of Torah.[26] Thissen has also shown how Mark weaves into his portrait of Jesus the image of teacher. At three different places and in various types of material Mark drops into an otherwise continuous flow of thought the phrase, "And Jesus was speaking the word to them" (Mark 2:2; 4:33; 8:32). The key words are τὸν λόγον ἐλάλει. It occurs at the beginning of the conflict stories, at the end of the parables, and between Peter's confession and Peter's and Jesus' rebuking of each other (8:32 occurs at the beginning of the journey section; the word boldly [παρρησία] may indicate a new phase in the Jesus-disciple relationship). When the recurrence of this phrase is assessed in relation to Mark's emphasis on Jesus teaching (διδάσκω) in 1:22—where Jesus is initially introduced—and as one who teaches with authority (1:27–28; cf. 4:1–2; 9:31), it is clear that this is a vital point to Mark.

Thissen argues that this "speaking the word" is Mark's verb that matches his distinctive use of the noun "gospel" (εὐαγγέλιον). Indeed, the latter is used twice in Mark's keynote introduction of Jesus' appearance in Galilee: he comes preaching the gospel/εὐαγγέλιον of the kingdom of God.[27] This may be the case, but if this is true then it would seem that his verb for preaching (κηρύσσω) and its several uses should also come into focus (1:38, 39, 45; 6:12). All these verses are Markan summaries, and thus they depict Mark's interest in Jesus' portrait.[28]

---

[26]In 1:44 and 7:10, in the Galilean section, Mark refers to Moses as Torah-giver and teacher. But none of the teaching is located on a mountain and none echoes specific themes of Moses' teaching in any explicit way. Perhaps Mark intends to present Jesus as Teacher-Deliverer in 1:21–28 and then again in 4:1–5:43, by putting segments of teaching and deliverance back to back. But there appear to be no clear textual markers for this, unless one regards the strange expression of Jesus sitting on the sea in a boat to teach (4:1) as such a marker. But this is unlikely.

[27]Thissen, Erzählung der Befreiung, 322–30.

[28]Thissen's interest in this point is twofold; it shows how Mark stitched together the pre-Pauline εὐαγγέλιον tradition with Jesus as teacher, thus connecting the kerygma with this new phenomenon called a Gospel, and second, how in so doing Mark creates a "narrative theology" or "theological narrative" (Erzählung der Befreiung, 330). Thissen's insights are helpful in showing how Mark binds the kerygma of the passion and resurrection, which Paul preached, with the earthly words and deeds of Jesus. But this in itself does not provide the literary criteria by which to judge the Gospel to be a theological narrative. It may contribute to that, but other factors must come into focus in order to see its narrative quality. See D. Rhoads and D. Michie, Mark as Story.

The series of miracles in 4:35–5:43 shifts the narrative away from the Teacher portrait of Jesus and resumes the exodus theme of liberation from bondage, intensifying the note already struck in the first section (1:16–3:6). Numerous writers have noted that Jesus' rebuke (ἐπετίμησεν) of the sea (v. 39) stands in the tradition of the divine fight against the sea chaos in both exodus and creation.[29] The sea, here in its chaos, is viewed as part of the demonic power which the kingdom's power breaks and conquers. This is followed immediately by Jesus' exorcism of the Gerasene demoniac, from whom he casts a legion of demons. The next two healing narratives highlight Jesus' power to release the afflicted from incurable illness and even death. With this series of stories, culminating in the raising of Jairus' twelve-year-old daughter, the Gospel's narrative reaches its initial crest, anticipating Jesus' own resurrection and victory over all the powers of evil.

As Kathleen M. Fischer and Urban C. von Walde note in their study of this miracle catena, Mark chooses these four miracles in order to show forth God's mighty power in Jesus' ministry. In the stilling of the storm "Jesus is acting in ways similar to Yahweh in re-creating the harmony of the universe in reclaiming it from Satan." In the exorcism Jesus manifests the divine power over personal possession by Satan. In the healing of the woman's incurable illness and in the raising of Jairus' daughter "the ultimate affliction of evil upon the world . . . is conquered." Further, they observe that

> the miracles are not simply demonstrations of divine power but are exorcisms, the means by which, in Mark's apocalyptic world-view, God's sovereignty over Satan reasserts itself. And this sovereignty controls all areas of life. Thus Mark presents a Jesus who has power greater than any human malady, a power from God which exerts itself to right the order of creation by expelling and controlling Satan's grip over man and the world.[30]

Jesus' mission to liberate from bondage is comprehensive and complete. But the depth of its meaning remains a mystery, waiting

---

[29]McCurley, *Ancient Myths and Biblical Realities*, 58–61; T. Fawcett, *Hebrew Myth and Christian Gospel* (London: SCM, 1973), 88–90; T. N. D. Mettinger, "Fighting the Powers of Chaos and Hell—Towards a Biblical Portrait of God," *ST* 39 (1985), 36; H. C. Kee, "The Terminology of Mark's Exorcism Stories," *NTS* 14 (1968–69), 232–46; and *Miracle in the Early Christian World* (New Haven/London: Yale University, 1983), 151–65.

[30]K. M. Fisher and U. C. von Walde, "The Miracles of Mark 4:35–5:43: Their Meaning and Function in the Gospel Framework," *BTB* 11 (1981), 15.

to be unveiled. The concluding paragraph (6:1–6), accenting the rejection of Jesus by the people of his home town because of their unbelief, strikes the antagonist chord of the narrative plot that will expose the necessity of gaining final triumph only through suffering. This theme will be discussed in chapter 4's treatment of 8:27–10:52.

Until now we have drawn an analogy between Mark's portrait of Jesus as Liberator and the work of Moses. But the theology of the exodus affirms not Moses, but Yahweh as the actual Liberator, indeed as the Warrior who has triumphed gloriously (Exod 15:1–3). Just as Yahweh-Warrior conquered through miracles ("Pharaoh's chariots and his host he cast into the sea . . . Thou didst blow with thy wind, and the sea covered them; . . . " [vv. 4a, 10a]), so Jesus is depicted by Mark as God's Warrior, attacking Satan's stronghold through his exorcisms as well as his healings. Jesus' method of subduing the enemy stands fully within the divine warfare miracle tradition:[31] *the word (of God) in and through Jesus is the power that smites the demons.* The exodus type behind Jesus' work is thus not Moses, but Yahweh. Hence, the push-and-pull of the narrative—"who then is this?" (4:41; 6:2)— is to see who Jesus really is, the Son of God (1:11; 9:7; 15:39), which until now has been a secret to all humans in the narrative.[32]

James M. Robinson has argued that Mark depicts Jesus' ministry as "a cosmic struggle in history to inaugurate the eschatological reign of God."[33] Robinson rightly observes that the verbal exchanges between Jesus and the demons consist not of conversation, but of hostile shouts and orders. The demons' recognition of Jesus' divine power by calling him "Holy One of God"(1:24), "Son of God" (3:11), "Son of the Most High God" (5:7), are but seductive attempts by the demons "to gain power over Jesus by using his secret, spirit-world name."[34] Jesus consistently silences them, for there is no common ground between the two opposing powers. Rather, a sharp contrast emerges: the demons are violent and destructive, seeking injury and

---

[31]M. C. Lind's *Yahweh Is a Warrior* is the best exposition of Yahweh's warfare as essentially miraculous. True, many deviations from this model, set forth in Exod 14:14, occur within Israel's history, but this does not change the essential nature of Yahweh's warfare.

[32]F. J. Matera describes well this Markan literary feature: "the reader enters the world of Mark's story with a knowledge that the characters within the narrative struggle to attain: Jesus is the Son of God" (*Passion Narratives and Gospel Theologies* [Maryknoll, New York: Paulist, 1986], 52).

[33]J. M. Robinson, *The Problem of History in Mark* (SBT 21; London: SCM, 1957), 38.

[34]Robinson, *Problem of History*, 36–37.

death of the human person; Jesus' actions are liberating, restoring the human to tranquillity and communion with self and others. Hence in these confrontations, history discloses the cosmic struggle of "Son of God *versus* demon, Holy Spirit *versus* unclean spirit." Jesus' function, says Robinson, is "to enter this struggle on behalf of the true destiny of mankind and with his heavenly power . . . carry through to the victory, and to the life and communion that it brings."[35] Indeed, this depiction of Jesus' ministry in Mark strikes the liberational chord at its deepest level.

Foster R. McCurley contributes larger biblical-theological dimensions to this topic. McCurley describes a long trajectory that embraces God's triumph over primeval chaos, God's victory over chaos (and bondage) through Yahweh as Warrior and King in Israel's history, and Jesus as "The Son of God Versus Chaos."[36] His portrait of Jesus' ministry fits well with that above.[37] McCurley considers Jesus' rebuke of the sea chaos (Mark 4:35–41) to parallel Yahweh's rebuke of Satan (Zech 3) and God's earlier creation rebuke of primeval chaos (as in Ps 18:15c). In rebuking and exorcising demons Jesus carries forward God's purpose, establishing sovereignty through victory over evil (cf. Pss 76:5–6; 80:16; 104:7 for the Lord's rebuke and victory over the enemy).[38] This portrait of Jesus extends God's liberating actions in Hebrew Scripture.[39]

---

[35]Ibid., 39, 42.

[36]McCurley, *Ancient Myths*, 12–71.

[37]It fits well with Mark and Luke, but not Matthew, in my judgment. Matthew does not accent either the historical or cosmic battle between Jesus and demonic powers in the way Mark and Luke do.

[38]McCurley, *Ancient Myths*, 46–52. This theme of Jesus as holy warrior has been most fully developed in a recent study by P. D. Bender, "The Holy War Trajectory in the Synoptic Gospels and the Pauline Writings" (M.A. thesis, Associated Mennonite Biblical Seminaries, 1987).

[39]It fits, on the one hand, with the recital of God's acts of salvation which free from oppression (see Wright, *God Who Acts*, 35–58]); it fits also with J. D. Levenson's work, which views God's acts of victory over evil to be clustered around primordial time and end-time, since the Gospels present Jesus as bringing the eschatological victory of the kingdom in his own life and death. The language itself is used, as Levenson shows, by Israel to call God forth, on the basis of the primordial victory, to act in Israel's history and thus show divine victory over foes that threaten God's sovereignty (*Creation and the Persistence of Evil* [San Francisco: Harper & Row, 1988], 11–25, 50). In my judgment, Levenson unnecessarily separates his view from the Yahweh as Warrior tradition. That tradition does not view God as continually acting in history, as he suggests (50 and 163, n. 7), but rather identifies specific times and events in which God is shown to vanquish evil.

Within this context of seeing Jesus' ministry as God's war against evil, Mark's prominent emphasis on "Do not fear, only believe" (Mark 5:36) is immediately noteworthy. It stands in the tradition of the "fear not" (*'al tîrā'*) divine warfare oracles, which figure prominently in Hebrew Scripture.[40] The call to trust in Yahweh for defense is also a major feature of the Zion theology of Isaiah and the royal psalms.[41] Two recent doctoral dissertations on Mark enhance our understanding of these themes in Mark. Using narrative criticism, Christopher D. Marshall demonstrates that Mark's call to faith functions as a prominent narrative strand.[42] Herbert L. Swartz examines how Mark's fear and amazement vocabulary opposes the call to faith; fear and amazement are unwanted substitutes for and opponents of faith.[43] While neither of these writers correlates his work with Old Testament oracles of divine warfare, their composite contribution makes possible a new understanding of Mark: the call not to fear, but only to believe, reflects Israel's tradition of accenting the appropriate human role in God's fight against evil. Indeed, Mark's enigmatic

---

[40]E. W. Conrad, *Fear Not Warrior: A Study of 'al tira' Pericopes in the Hebrew Scriptures* (BJS 75; Chico, Calif.: Scholars, 1985). Conrad has shown the pervasiveness of this formula in much of the Hebrew Bible. Unfortunately, he did not include the Psalms; had he done so, the connection between God's cosmogonic victory in creation and Yahweh's victory in divine warfare would become more evident and would provide a basis to sustain the critique of Levenson in the above note. These comments prompt a methodological issue: did Yahweh's victories in history provide the basis for the cosmogonic theology of triumph or vice versa? Even though many texts present the primordial victory as the basis for assuring historical triumph, Israel's course of theological reflection likely developed in the opposite sequence.

[41]Ollenburger, *Zion,* shows by his study of numerous royal psalms and the Isaianic Zion theology that Yahweh calls Israel to humble trust in and reliance on divine protection and security. Zion theology thus repudiates Israel's proud, boastful military alliances.

[42]C. D. Marshall, *Faith as a Theme in Mark's Narrative* (SNTSMS 64; Cambridge: Cambridge University, 1989). Marshall shows convincingly that the call to faith permeates the first eleven chapters, while unbelief functions as a foil to accent faith: "The element of belief and unbelief plays an important role in shaping how Mark tells his story" (226).

[43]H. L. Swartz, "Fear and Amazement Responses: A Key to the Concept of Faith in the Gospel of Mark" (Th.D. diss., Toronto School of Theology, 1988). Swartz shows a distinctive narrative emphasis on this theme in Mark; the feature is not only a matter of proportional quantitative uses over Matthew and Luke, but is firmly rooted in Mark's style and theology (291). Swartz thus sees 16:8 as the intended narrative climax which, in light of the theme developed through the narrative, calls the reader to not let trembling, amazement and fear stifle faith (254–75).

narrative calls the reader to *understand*. When, however, it appears that Peter in his confession understands that Jesus is the Messiah, he is rebuked. The way of Jesus' triumph over evil through suffering must yet be learned. This learning, rooted in faith, stands against fear, amazement, and trembling. But for the disciples this learning must await Jesus' own victory over evil.

c. Mark 6:6b—8:30. Mark's third section begins with the sending out of the Twelve (6:7–13), which may echo the exodus story of the twelve sent out to the promised land. But here the mission is totally positive in that the Twelve did as Jesus instructed them. Nonetheless, a period of wilderness experiences follows, in which the disciples are led to an initial stage of perceiving Jesus' identity through the miracles of the loaves. After the first feeding, followed by the disciples' fear and amazement at Jesus' ghostly appearance on the sea during their boat ride, the narrator explains their fear: "for they did not understand about the loaves, for their hearts were hardened." Indeed, this theme echoes Israel's inability to grasp God's providing presence in the wilderness, even refusing to understand his miraculous power when manifested.[44] But Mark gives the disciples little hint as to what they should have understood, although this understanding is essential.[45] Subsequently, after the second feeding, on the boat ride the disciples discuss the problem of having only one loaf of bread (the term διαλογίζομαι may also mean "argue" or "dispute," with shades of complaint and murmur, cf. 2:8). An intense round of questions occurs (8:17–21), again focusing on the question, "Do you not yet understand?"[46]

---

[44]The murmuring motif punctuates Israel's wanderings, as Ps 78 shows. The murmuring, as interpreted in the several recensions of the stories, is represented as a failure to perceive God's provision (see, e.g., Num 11 and 20). See also Coats's treatment of the rebellion/murmuring theme in *Rebellion in the Wilderness*.

[45]Q. Quesnell's study of Mark through the lens of this verse is excellent. It shows how Mark entraps the reader into the narrative and gives hints here and there to unravel the mystery, which, though, as F. Kermode maintains, is never completely resolved: Q. Quesnell, *The Mind of St. Mark: Interpretation and Method Through the Exegesis of Mark 6:52* (AnBib 38; Rome: Pontifical Biblical Institute, 1969) and F. Kermode, *The Genesis of Secrecy: On the Interpretation of Narrative* (Cambridge, Mass.: Harvard University, 1979), 56–72.

[46]For exposition of this section and reporting of scholarly work on it, see S. Masuda, "The Good News of the Miracle of the Bread: The Tradition and Its Markan Redaction," *NTS* 28 (April 1982), 191–219. Giving special attention to the role of the reader in understanding this narrative are two helpful studies: R. Fowler, *Loaves and Fishes* (Chico, Calif.: Scholars, 1981) and J. Bassler, "The

While this section utilizes aspects of the exodus-wilderness tradition, it also transforms elements of that tradition. For while Israel acted exclusively in relation to its neighbors, Jesus finds reception in Tyre and Sidon. The Syro-Phoenician woman (7:24–30) emerges as a type of appropriate faith response. She begs for the bread (ἄρτος appears in v. 27!) which the Jewish leaders refused because of bondage to their customs (7:2, 5). Further, the healing of the mute and deaf man (7:31–37) is located in outsider/Gentile land area; it leads to a crescendo of praise, even signaling messianic disclosure (7:37 echoes Isa 35). The second feeding also occurs in Gentile area. These positive Gentile responses contrast sharply to the negative responses of the insiders (7:1–23; 8:10–12). Further, the two-pattern—two feedings, two boat rides, and two contrasting responses in chapter 7—prepares for the two-touch cure of the blind man (8:22–26), likely symbolic of Jesus' double ministry to Jews and Gentiles. All this is prerequisite to the unveiling of Jesus' messianic identity at Caesarea Philippi, located on Israel's northernmost border.[47] At the most distant point from Israel's center of religious, political, and military power (Jerusalem), Jesus prompts Peter's confession. Furthermore, this occurs only after Gentiles have been healed and fed by Jesus. But Peter's response to Jesus' teaching about suffering shows he did not understand Jesus' messiahship on Jesus' terms or the nature of the kingdom Jesus proclaimed, or certainly the significance of such a location for this breakthrough.

Structurally, Peter's confession occurs at the end of the wilderness section and at the beginning of Mark's "on-the-way" section (see ch. 4). In terms of theological tradition history, it introduces a transformational perspective to both Israel's wilderness and conquest traditions. The first of these points will be explicated at the end of this chapter; the second, at the end of the next chapter.

Parable of the Loaves," *JR* 66 (1986), 157–72. See also my own treatment of the section, *Mark*, ch. 6, and "Markan Structure," 86–91, 198–202.

[47]Swartley, *Mark*, 112–21; W. Kelber, *The Kingdom in Mark*, 48–65, and *Mark's Story of Jesus* (Philadelphia: Fortress, 1979), ch. 2 ; E. Malbon, "The Jesus of Mark and the Sea of Galilee," *JBL* 103 (1984), 363–77. A number of scholars have also seen corresponding significance in the two series of numbers connected with the two feedings: five and twelve on the west side feeding symbolic of disclosure to the Jews, and four and seven with the east side feeding symbolic of disclosure to the Gentiles. That Jesus makes a point of the numbers on the boat ride (8:17–21) and of the understanding they are to prompt seems to confirm this perception. See Masuda, "Good News," 204–6, and Swartley, *Mark*, 127–30.

MATTHEW

1. Content and Structure of Matthew's Galilean Section

The Galilean section of Jesus' ministry in Matthew begins in 4:12 or 17 and concludes prior to Peter's confession at 16:12 or after the confession at 16:20. Evidence supporting the earlier points for the beginning and ending includes: Jesus' location in Galilee already in 4:12–16 (this is noted with eschatological-theological significance) and in 16:13 the extension of Jesus' journey beyond Galilee, to Caesarea Philippi, to an area called Gaulanitis. Further, the Matthean phrase, "district of Caesarea Philippi," suggests that Jesus and his disciples have left Galilee. Arguments for the later beginning and ending are the structural markers that are crucial to Matthew's overall design. Both 4:17 and 16:21 begin with the phrase, "From that time Jesus began ... " (ἀπὸ τότε ἤρξατο ὁ Ἰησοῦς). Jack Dean Kingsbury argues persuasively that this phrase is Matthew's structural marker that introduces, respectively, Jesus' Galilean and Perean-Jerusalem ministries.[48] And indeed, Jesus' public ministry is not mentioned until 4:17; similarly, not until 16:21 does the narrative state that it is necessary for Jesus to go to Jerusalem (δεῖ αὐτὸν εἰς Ἱροσόλυμα ἀπελθεῖν). Thus, while the 4:17 and 16:20 divisional limits are the more persuasive, the double emphasis on Galilee in 4:12–16, both in descriptive narrative and in an Isaianic quotation, must not be overlooked. The phrase "Galilee of the Gentiles" contributes an important interpretive perspective to Jesus' entire Galilean ministry.

The content of Matthew's Galilean section consists of three extended discourses, each followed by narrative sections recounting Jesus' deeds and general itinerary. The Sermon on the Mount (chs. 5–7) is followed by a narrative section of ten miracles (chs. 8–9). The Missionary discourse (ch. 10) is followed by narratives focusing on Jesus' identity and the consequent mounting tension between Jesus and the Jewish leaders. In this context 12:15–18 quotes Isaiah 42:1–2, signaling Jesus' turn to the Gentiles and thus abrogating the bold declaration of 10:5, "Go nowhere except to the house of Israel." The Parables discourse (ch. 13) then has Jesus directing his word to his disciples.

---

[48]J. D. Kingsbury, *Matthew: Structure, Christology, Kingdom* (Philadelphia: Fortress, 1975), 7–37. Kingsbury argues that 4:12–16 belongs to the earlier section in that 4:13–14 matches 2:23, and thus marks the conclusion of Jesus' early journeying. It concludes the former section and sets the stage for the Galilean ministry, which begins in 4:17 (p. 16).

This is followed by the content of Mark 6:30–8:26, which depicts first a Jewish ministry that contrasts to a subsequent Gentile area ministry. In its presentation of the deeds of Jesus, Matthew's Galilean section resembles Mark's Galilean section. Thus, in regard to the liberating emphases of Jesus' ministry, the points made for Mark apply here as well; however, this is true only in regard to the content of the synoptic tradition, not to Matthew's use of it. The striking feature of Matthew's use of these stories is the way they serve catechetical purposes, reflecting and instructing his church communities in areas of Christology, discipleship, and mission.[49] Matthew' s three major discourses develop further this distinctive narrative intention.

2. The Exodus Tradition

The influence of the exodus traditions upon Matthew's Galilean section has long been a matter of scholarly debate. The liberational exodus motifs are indeed prominent in Matthew's earlier infancy narrative. The naming of the baby *Jesus*, "for he will save his people from their sins" (1:21), fuses exodus (salvation) and conquest (Jesus = Joshua) traditions, a fusion common to earlier faith expressions. Herod's killing of the male babies in an attempt to destroy Jesus (2:16–18) recalls Pharaoh's edict that all male babies be killed, including Moses (Exod 1:16). Both Jesus and Moses were forced to flee to survive; when Jesus later departed from Egypt, he fulfilled a prophetic word reflecting the exodus tradition: "Out of Egypt I have called my son" (2:15c from Hosea 11:1). John the Baptist's preaching in the wilderness (3:1) echoes the exodus' wilderness call to true faith, through repentance of sin. Similarly, Jesus' temptations (4:1–13) show three motifs of the exodus tradition: the wilderness setting, fasting for forty days and nights (Exod 24:18; 34:28), and the testing of obedience.[50]

---

[49]Heinz Joachim Held emphasizes both the christological function and the call to faith and discipleship emphases of the miracle stories in Matthew. See "Matthew as Interpreter of the Miracle Stories" in *Tradition and Interpretation in Matthew*, ed. G. Bornkamm, G. Barth, and H. J. Held (Philadelphia: Westminster, 1963), 168–206 and 246–259. R. H. Gundry sees Matthew's use of the miracle catenae in chs. 8–9 as underscoring the authority of Jesus. See his *Matthew: A Commentary on Literary and Theological Art* (Grand Rapids: Eerdmans, 1982), 137–80.
[50]B. Nolan, however, says that the exodus archetype is not really as much in evidence as is the "sure oath to David" (*The Royal Son of God: The Christology of Matthew 1–2 in the Setting of the Gospel* [OBO 23; Göttingen: Vandenhoeck & Ruprecht, 1979], 36–38).

Perhaps Matthew has set his typological calendar one step forward, putting exodus motifs into his infancy-preparation section and then developing another theme in his Galilean section, even though the stories of the synoptic tradition he uses are thoroughly liberational. While indeed the exodus symbolism is not as extensive in Matthew's Galilean section as has sometimes been assumed, the larger umbrella of exodus traditions, especially the Sinai tradition, shapes his story of Jesus, in both structure and theological emphasis. Nor is the liberating aspect of the exodus absent; it shows itself in several structurally significant ways.

a. Matthew's summaries. Casting an interpretive hue over his long Galilean section, Matthew's summaries highlight the liberational dimension of Jesus' ministry. Three similar formulations arch over the narrative—occurring roughly at the beginning, midpoint, and end of the section: 4:23–25; 9:35–36; and 15:29–31. These summaries thus punctuate Matthew's entire Galilean section. The first two use the same three phrases to summarize Jesus' ministry: "teaching in their synagogues," "proclaiming the good news of the kingdom," and "curing every disease and every sickness among the people." All three summaries state that great crowds came to Jesus; the first and last note the scope of Jesus' healings: "all the sick, those who were afflicted with various diseases and pains, demoniacs, epileptics, and paralytics" (4:24) and "the lame, the maimed, the blind, the mute, and many others" (15:30). Matthew intends to present Jesus as a healer; he heals every type of disease. Matthew makes this obvious by concluding his first segment of three healings (8:1–16) with the prophetic text, "He took our infirmities and bore our diseases" (8:17). Terence L. Donaldson also aptly argues that the first and last of these summaries function as inclusios for Jesus' Galilean ministry. Both are located on *mountains*, a setting uniquely Matthean.[51] Thus, the mountain location and the liberational emphases summarizing Jesus' ministry echo the Sinai and exodus traditions.

b. Positive Gentile responses. Matthew contains several additional exodus-echoes in his Galilean section. His first summary's list of diseases, appearing early in the Gospel, ends with the unexpected note: "his fame spread throughout all Syria, and they brought him all the sick . . . " (4:24a). Verse 25 then mentions all major parts of Israel

---

[51] T. L. Donaldson, *Jesus on the Mountain: A Study in Matthean Theology* (JSNTSS 8; Sheffield: JSOT, 1985), 113, 119. Note also that the crowds of 4:23–25 are joined to the Sermon discourse on the mountain.

as places from which his follower-crowds came: Galilee, Decapolis, Jerusalem, Judea, and from beyond the Jordan. And indeed, like Syria, the Decapolis and beyond the Jordan signify that his ministry of liberation was not confined to Jews, but included Gentiles also. Matthew highlights this point by giving narrative prominence to the healing of the Capernaum centurion (8:5–13), a story not in Mark. The liberation punch line appears in vv. 10ff.: " 'Truly, I tell you, in no one in Israel have I found such faith.' " A general statement follows that both includes Gentiles in the messianic banquet with Abraham, Isaac and Jacob and pronounces a harsh word of judgment upon the "heirs of the kingdom."

Matthew's incorporation of a beyond-Israel stance emerges also in the structure of his single, lengthy ten-miracle catena (chs. 8–9).[52] Mark's miracles appear in three separate segments (Mark 1:21–45; 2:1–3:6; 4:35–43). Matthew's structural prioritization of the Gentiles' and Israel's responses in 8:10–13 parallels the marvelling crowds' equally telling exclamation at the catena's conclusion: " 'Never has anything like this been seen in Israel' " (9:33b). Superficially, this suggests a miracle occurring outside Israel, but the text gives no evidence of this.[53] Rather, *Matthew has a Gentile choir singing refrains of praise for Jesus' ministry.* Matthew's final summary for the Galilean section repeats this technique and point, ending with the phrase: "And they praised the God of Israel" (15:31c). This summary does not specify that the crowds included Gentiles but the phrase, "God of Israel," implies speech from the Gentile perspective, as did 9:33b. Further, 4:24–25 has already shown that Matthew includes Gentiles in the crowds.

The mid-section of the Galilean ministry also bears on this discussion. The second summary statement—emphasizing Jesus' healings of many brought by the crowds—leads into the mission discourse of chapter 10, but does so through emphasis on Jesus' great compas-

---

[52]These are also interspersed with two units of teaching emphasizing discipleship (8:18–22 and 9:9–18). The storm at sea, a miracle story, is transformed into a pericope on discipleship also. See Held, "Matthew as Interpreter," 248, and P. F. Ellis, *Matthew: His Mind and His Message* (Collegeville, Minn.: Liturgical, 1974), 42.

[53]The double statement of a report going throughout all that district (vv. 26 and 31) seems to imply that the healing of the two blind men occurred in a different district than did the healing of Jairus' daughter, thus possibly in Gentile area. If that is so, Matthew uses this last miracle to get to the same point. From a narrative point of view, the location makes no difference, for the refrain's function is clear.

OLD TESTAMENT EXODUS AND SINAI TRADITIONS

sion upon the crowds, for they were as sheep without a shepherd. Twelve were selected (10:1–4)[54] and sent out to "Go nowhere among the Gentiles, and enter no town of the Samaritans, but go rather to the lost sheep of the house of Israel" (10:5–6). By contrast, however, the Gospel ends with Jesus sending his disciples to "all the nations."

Granted, chapter 10 indicates that Jesus' mission was first and foremost to bring renewal to Israel, but Jesus' ministry, as presented in Matthew, is never *limited* to Israel. Two distinctive narrative features aid our understanding of Matthew's view and emphasis on this matter which appears to be a logical contradiction. Dorothy J. Weaver calls attention to the first feature: Jesus' missionary discourse does not tell us that the disciples actually went out or returned from a journey. Though they are now under a "Sent Commission," the fulfillment of their commission stays open literarily through 11:2—28:16–20.[55] Rather, 11:1 focuses on Jesus' own action; the reader can only infer the action of the disciples from the action of Jesus: "he went on from there to proclaim and teach in their cities." Hence the narrator continues to have the reader identify with the words and actions of Jesus, not the disciples' action. The disciples' going out is delayed until the reader is also called to go in 28:16–20. By delaying "the fulfillment of Jesus' commission from within the text (11:1) to a point beyond its boundaries (beyond 28:20)," Matthew's story "elicits the positive response of the implied reader to the challenge set forth in 10:5b–42 and reissued in 28:18–20."[56] One major implication of Weaver's insights is that the mission to "Israel only" does not stand separate from the mission to all the world. While in the narrative they are distinct, the narrative also delays fulfillment of the first so that the two are ultimately conjoined into one. By this narrative technique Matthew maintains both the Jewish priority and the Gentile certainty.

The second feature expressing Matthew's distinctive view appears in the dramatic turnabout in 12:15–21. Here, after strong negative responses from Jewish leaders to Jesus' two sabbath viola-

---

[54]Here Matthew combines their appointment and sending, which in Mark occur separately (3:13–19; 6:7–13).

[55]D. J. Weaver, *Matthew's Missionary Discourse: A Literary-Critical Analysis* (JSNTSS 38; Sheffield: JSOT, 1990), 124–53. Just as Peter Ellis shows that Matt 5–7 "is funneled through 28.16–20 to become the standard of Christian existence for the ongoing community—both Jewish and Gentile—of Matthew's day" (*Matthew*, 121), so Weaver has shown that Matt 10—with its limited mission to Israel—must also be funneled through 28:16–20.

[56]Weaver, *Missionary Discourse*, 153.

tions, Matthew has Jesus withdraw, presumably to a Gentile area, since the text quotes Isaiah 42:1–4 to declare that Jesus' mission includes "proclaim[ing] justice to the Gentiles" for "in his name will the Gentiles hope." Matthew uses the quotation to indicate to the reader that the 10:5 command is eclipsed by Jesus' own intentions. But again the narrative does not portray Jesus going immediately into Gentile areas. Rather, he disputes with Pharisees (12:24ff.). Not until 15:21–38 does Jesus' action demonstrate his commitment to the Gentiles. But the narrative, by quoting Isaiah in 12:15–21, paves the way for this action.

Why this extensive Matthean emphasis on Gentile interests in Jesus' Galilean ministry? Is it apologetic, as some have argued? That is, does it proffer a theological rationale for Matthew's community to engage in mission to the Gentiles, rather than turn inward as a survivor remnant community after the fall of Jerusalem, as post-exilic Israel did? Perhaps, and perhaps Kingsbury is also correct when he regards Galilee in Matthew as the place where mission, first to Israel and then to the Gentiles, takes place, although that sequential order is not programmatically supported by Matthew's representation of Jesus' own ministry.[57]

Another proposal is that Matthew is showing that the oft repeated exodus theme, "that the Egyptians may know that I am the Lord," has now come to fulfillment. *In the Galilean ministry of Jesus all come to praise the God of Israel!* When seen in this larger dimension, the assessment of the parallel between Matthew's ten miracles in chapters 8–9 and the ten plagues in Exodus must be assessed more positively than Davies and others have judged,[58] since their function in the text correlates directly with a larger leitmotif of both Exodus and Matthew. Matthew's achievement then is to utilize the exodus plague tradition to show its fulfilled missional intention—*in Jesus.* It is no longer judgment upon the pagans, but salvation and blessing for the pagans (echo Gen 12:3). Conversely and sadly, because Israel's (not Pharaoh's) hardness of heart leads many of them to unbelief and rejection of Jesus, God's judgment falls upon Israel. This explains well Jesus' excoriation of an unreceptive Israel, especially in 8:11–13; 11:20–24; and 12:38–42. In each of these texts Israel's response is contrasted to that of the Gentiles. In the last text Jesus appeals to the

---

[57]Kingsbury, *Matthew*, 24.

[58]W. D. Davies, *The Setting of the Sermon on the Mount* (Cambridge: Cambridge University, 1964), 86–93. However, the view that these ten miracles echo an exodus motif continues to be held by numerous writers.

"sign of Jonah," an ironic reminder that Gentiles repent when given the prophetic word of correction. The mission only to Israel, then, in chapter 10, doesn't so much emphasize a *heilsgeschichtliche* sequence, but rather clarifies Israel's spurned opportunity. The statement, "I was sent only to the lost sheep of the house of Israel," in the healing of the Canaanite (rather than Mark's Syro-Phoenician) woman's daughter (15:24), testifies again, in ironic twist, to the double-sidedness of Jesus' ministry, as witnessed by Matthew.

c. *Jesus' command to love the enemy.* In the above analysis the Gentiles are viewed positively in their response to Jesus. But in several passages in the Sermon on the Mount, the term Gentiles is used to depict behavior that contrasts to the conduct Jesus espouses (5:47b; 6:7, 32; and likely 7:6; cf. later negative portraits in 18:17; 20:19, 25; 24:9). Further, the enemy that Jesus commands to love and the evil one that Jesus instructs not to resist are likely Gentiles. Thus in view of the strong narrative concern that both Jews and Gentiles are recipients of Jesus' ministry, these commands provide another perspective to the exodus motifs noted in a. and b. above. Does the term enemies include or primarily denote Gentiles? If so, what is the significance of this command to love the enemy? Does it have any bearing on this analysis of the larger profile of the Gentiles in Matthew's Galilean section?

Scholars debate various issues in the exegesis of 5:38–48, among which is the identification of the enemy (political, religious, or personal) and the interplay between this effort and the supposed life-setting of the teaching. Richard A. Horsley argues that " 'love your enemies' pertains neither to external, political enemies nor to the question of non-violence or non-resistance."[59] Following Tannehill, Horsley considers 5:39–42 as "focal instances," and he identifies the life-setting to be local socio-economic relationships within village life. The instruction was addressed to "people caught in . . . severe economic circumstances"; however, "love your enemy" hardly had the wealthy ruling elite in mind.[60] While these "focal instances" might have wider referents, "love your enemies" "apparently referred to persecutors outside the religious community, but still in the local

---

[59]R. A. Horsley, "Ethics and Exegesis: 'Love Your Enemies' and the Doctrine of Non-Violence," *JAAR* 54 (1986), 3. Article also in *The Love of Enemy and Nonretaliation in the New Testament*, ed. W. M. Swartley (Louisville: Westminster/John Knox, 1992), 72.

[60]R. A. Horsley, *Jesus and the Spiral of Violence: Popular Jewish Resistance in Roman Palestine* (San Francisco: Harper & Row, 1987), 262–69.

residential community—and certainly not the national or political enemies (Romans)."[61] In this identification of the "enemies," no correlation can be made to the above query about how this command relates to the portrayal of Gentiles elsewhere in Matthew's Galilean section, since the enemies are local compatriots who compete for economic survival.

Walter Wink regards Horsley's reconstruction of the socio-economic setting for Jesus' teaching as correct, but additionally holds that such peasant life included the reality of the Roman occupation. Indebtedness was the most serious socio-economic problem of Jesus' Galilean setting. Jesus addressed the poor who "share a rankling hatred for a system that subjects them to humiliation by stripping them of their lands, their goods, finally even their outer garment."[62] Addressed to people under Roman occupation, all five "instances" point Jesus' hearers to a new way of response that disarms the enmity. Jesus commands a nonviolent shock-tactic that exposes the indignity of the oppression. By seizing initiative in the situation, both the dignity of oppressed one is restored and the enemy relationship is simultaneously disarmed. Thus Jesus sets forth a "way of fighting evil with all one's power without being transformed into the very evil we fight."[63] Although Wink does not explicitly link his exegesis of 5:38–42 to the love of enemy command in 5:43, his later response to Horsley affirms "that Jesus taught love of enemies in reference to Romans and their puppets."[64] Jesus' radical "third way" expresses love for the enemy by seeking to transform the relationship so that dehumanization of both the oppressor and oppressed, aggressor and victim, comes to an end.[65] In Wink's analysis, the enemies to be loved are predomi-

---

[61] Horsley, "Ethics," 24, also in *The Love of Enemy*, ed. W. Swartley, 93. Horsley argues against using the Zealots as a foil for understanding Jesus' love of enemy command. Following Morton Smith, Horsley argues that a Zealot party did not exist until A.D. 66.

[62] W. Wink, "Neither Passivity nor Violence: Jesus' Third Way," *SBL 1988 Seminar Papers* (Atlanta: Scholars, 1988), 214. Also in his revised version of this essay, in *The Love of Enemy*, ed. W. Swartley, 107.

[63] Wink, "Neither Passivity or Violence," in *SBL Papers*, 223; in *The Love of Enemy*, ed. W. Swartley, 117.

[64] Wink, "Counterresponse to Richard Horsley," in *The Love of Enemy*, ed. W. Swartley, 134.

[65] Horsley appears to restrict the enemy command from application to the real enemies, although his application of the teaching to conflict situations among village factions is not to be avoided either. In contrast, Wink leaves the scope of application open, to wherever enemy relations exist—socio-economic, racial, political, or personal.

nantly Gentiles. Since Wink contends that Jesus prescribes a tactic intended to disarm the enmity and put the human relationship on a new basis, this response toward Gentile oppressors readily harmonizes with Matthew's favorable portrait of their response to Jesus noted above.

Examining the same texts at the level of the Matthean narrative, Dorothy Jean Weaver understands Jesus' commands to not resist the evil one and to love the enemy to refer to those who revile (5:11), persecute (5:11, 44), say evil things (5:11), and tell lies about the disciples (5:11). The referents include also the adversary (5:25), the 'council' (5:22), the judge (5:25), and the court assistant (5:25). These "are the 'evil one' (τῷ πονηρῷ; 5:39a) and 'the enemies' (τοὺς ἐχθρούς; 5:44)."[66] In Matthew's setting all these people were likely part of the Gentile world, though Jewish persecution can not be completely ruled out as a possibility. For Weaver's reconstruction, as well as Wink's, the love of enemy command is a significant aspect of Matthew's depiction of the Gentiles. But how does this relate to any echo of the exodus faith-tradition?

Since Torah law calls for kindness and help to the enemy in need (Exod 23:4–5; Deut 22:1–4), Jesus' love command is not altogether novel, as William Klassen has shown.[67] But when viewed specifically within the exodus and conquest traditions, transformation is apparent. In Jesus' and Matthew's social worlds, enmity between Jews and Gentiles was not only socio-racial, but also political (Wink) and religious (Weaver). Thus, the mixed Jewish and Gentile crowds depicted in Matthew's Galilean narrative as well as Jesus' response to the centurion (8:4–13) exemplify Matthew's own appropriation of Jesus' love of enemy command (see also 15:21ff.).[68]

---

[66]D. J. Weaver, "Transforming Nonresistance: From *Lex Talionis* to 'Do Not Resist the Evil One,' " in *The Love of Enemy and Nonretaliation in the New Testament*, ed. W. Swartley (Louisville: Westminster/John Knox, 1992), 49.

[67]W. Klassen, *Love of Enemies* (Philadelphia: Fortress, 1984), 12–66. Not all of Klassen's cited texts refer to love of enemies. Most speak of nonretaliation and some of loving response when wronged by a brother (59). See also his essay, "The Novel Element in the Love Commandment of Jesus," in *The New Way of Jesus*, ed. William Klassen (Newton, Kans.: Faith and Life, 1980), 100–114. See p. 112, n. 5, in Klassen's "Novel Element" essay for sources which discuss the degree of newness in Jesus' love command. But again, this is not the same as love of enemy.

[68]I hold that the Sermon on the Mount is an integral part of Matthew's narrative and theology. Hans D. Betz' proposal that the Sermon is an earlier literary document (an *epitome*) composed in the milieu of Palestinian Jewish Christianity around A.D. 45 with different theological features from the Gospel precludes the task undertaken here. See H. D. Betz, "The Sermon on the Mount: In Defense of an Hypothesis," *BibRes* 36 (1991), 74–80.

How then does Matthew's portrait of the Gentiles compare to the exodus portrait of the non-Jews, the Egyptians? The relation is one of both continuity and reversal. In Israel's earlier story, a crucial leitmotif appears throughout Exodus: "that the Egyptians might know that the Lord is God." The purpose of the plagues is to bring both the Israelites and the Egyptians to know that the Lord is God. In Matthew's narrative design, the Gentile choir of people praising the God of Israel is most important. These matching narrative emphases manifest strong continuity, in a missional goal to bring the *outsiders* to a knowledge of the God of Israel. Further, Matthew alone oddly identifies the Syro-Phoenician woman as a *Canaanite* and explicitly correlates her request with Jesus' mission of being sent only to lost sheep of the house of Israel (15:24). But this Canaanite is not put off; Jesus receives her and heals her daughter. Finally, in Matthew, Jesus commends her for her great faith, as he did the centurion in ch. 8.

This strong positive portrait of Jesus' response to the Gentiles by Matthew carries an element of reversal of the exodus tradition, in respect to the plight of the Egyptians in the earlier story. Egyptians and Canaanites were vanquished and destroyed. But, in Matthew 2 Egypt aids Jesus' safety and mission. In Matthew, the Gentiles and Canaanites are not destroyed (cf. Matt 15:22), but are commended for their positive responses to Jesus. If they are encountered as "enemy," due to political oppression or religious persecution, they are to not be resisted, but to be loved. In this respect, a transformation of almost paradigmatic proportion occurs.

3. Pentateuchal and Sinaitic Influences

Bacon's thesis that Matthew modeled his Gospel on the Pentateuch by structuring it into five major narratives-plus-discourses, each ending with a standard formula, "And (it happened) when Jesus finished these sayings" (7:28; 11:1; 13:53; 19:1; 26:1), must also be reconsidered as an echo of older story. Though Kingsbury argues against this fivefold division as the primary structure of the Gospel,[69] Gundry aptly suggests that this pattern[70] and the 1:1; 4:17; 16:21 structure proposed by Kingsbury, and possibly other structural fea-

---

[69]Kingsbury, *Matthew*, 7.

[70]Regarding the fivefold division, Gundry (*Matthew*, 10–11), cites also the fivefold division of the Psalms, the Megilloth, the Maccabean history by Jason of Cyrene, *1 Enoch*, the original Perekim that made up *Pirke Aboth* and Papias' "Expositions of the Lord's oracles."

tures as well, should be considered in any exposition of the Gospel. Gundry further observes that "we look in vain for similarities in the contents of Moses' five books and Jesus' five discourses."[71] Similarity in the content does not exist when one, for example, puts Genesis beside Matthew 5:1–7:29, or Exodus beside Matthew 10ff. Granted, the antitheses in the Sermon on the Mount draw from different parts of the Pentateuch. But, beyond these "You have heard" citations,[72] the influence of the Pentateuch upon *the content* of the Sermon on the Mount or the rest of Matthew is not prominent. While it cannot be denied that the five-book design of the Pentateuch has influenced the structure of Matthew, that factor is not crucial for grasping Matthew's distinctive theological use of the exodus traditions. Too much has been made of the structure and not enough of the influence of traditions within the Pentateuch. Matthew's structure, as Ellis notes, is multidimensional, utilizing a variety of compositional techniques: chiasm, symmetry, and concentric design.[73] Once this point is grasped, it is appropriate to regard Matthew's fivefold narrative-discourse structure as a Pentateuchal echo, but not as the key to his use of Israel's traditions nor his theological intentions.

Jesus' declaration in 5:17, "I have not come to abolish the law and the prophets . . . but to fulfill them," enunciates Matthew's Pentateuch-Torah intention. He presents Jesus as one who fulfills the Torah (and the prophets), and whose teachings are new Torah instruction both for the original followers of Jesus and for the church of Matthew's time. Jesus' exposition of God's Torah enables his followers to live by "the greater righteousness" that Jesus actualized by inaugurating the kingdom. Through the power and authority of Jesus in his many liberating deeds, the disciples acclaim Jesus as *Lord* (8:25; 9:28;

---

[71]Ibid.

[72]The two commandments from the Exod 20/Deut 5 Decalogue (in 5:21, 27) refer to the divorce law of Deut 24 (in v. 31), the law against swearing falsely found in Lev 19:12, Num 30:2, Deut 23:21 (in v. 33), citation of the *lex talionis* from the Covenant Code in Exod 21:23–24 and in Lev 24:19–20, Deut 19:21 (in v. 38), and the citation of the command to "love your neighbor" from the Holiness Code in Lev 19:18 (in 5:43). In these, transformation of the tradition is prominent, although the attribution of "hate your enemy" (5:43b) is nowhere to be found in the "Books of Moses." On this latter point, see P. Lapide, *The Sermon on the Mount: Utopia or Program for Action?* trans. Arlene Swidler (Maryknoll, N.Y.: Orbis, 1986), 85–95.

[73]See Ellis, *Matthew*, 10–25. Ellis's concentric thesis, that the discourses emanate from the basic themes of 28:16–20 (19–22), is not as convincing as his chiastic analysis (10).

cf. 8:21; 9:38). While deliverance from bondage is an assumed part of the story, the emphasis falls on the Sinai–Torah part of the exodus tradition. Jesus is the authoritative Teacher and Lord of the community whose Sermon on the Mount is "A Pattern for Life"[74] both for Jesus' first followers and for Matthew's church members. Matthew narrates Jesus' mission instructions so that the Twelve, Matthew's church, and today's ideal readers are the recipients. Matthew's parables of the kingdom blend Jesus' twofold coming: bringing the kingdom in his Galilean ministry and consummating it with final judgment in his coming parousia (this latter theme occurs already in the parables of ch. 13).

In addition to the earlier exodus echo that all might know and praise the God of Israel, and this Sinai echo, to present Jesus as the fulfillment of Moses as mediator of God's Torah,[75] Donaldson has identified a third narrative feature that reflects the Sinai tradition, namely, employing mountains as literary settings. The entire Galilean section is framed by two mountains, quite likely Matthew's own contribution to the tradition.[76]

Donaldson recognizes but downplays the Mount Sinai typology behind 5:1 in order to argue for the more primary significance of Mount Zion's typology, focusing on the eschatological gathering of God's people. His choice of one over the other, however, is questionable. His earlier analysis of mountain traditions in the Hebrew Scriptures acknowledged a convergence of Sinai and Zion around the new law theme: "Thus, just as the final redemption is often pictured as a new

---

[74]From A. M. Hunter, *A Pattern for Life: An Exposition of the Sermon on the Mount, Its Making, Its Exegesis, and Its Meaning*, rev. ed. (Philadelphia: Westminster, 1962).

[75]Ellis (*Matthew*) sums up well Matthew's portrait of Jesus' relation to the law. Jesus' position is enhanced without diminishing Moses, for "the law holds" (to borrow A. Verhey's term, *The Great Reversal: Ethics and the New Testament* [Grand Rapids: Eerdmans, 1984], 83). Ellis notes four ways Matthew instructed his community on this relationship:

(1) the superiority of the New Law over against the Old Law championed by the Pharisees; (2) the superiority of Jesus over against Moses; (3) the superiority of Christian discipleship over against the discipleship of the Old Law as expounded by the Pharisees; and (4) the necessity for Christians as true disciples of Jesus to *do* the law and to do *all* the law (36).

[76]Donaldson notes that Matthew may be dependent upon Mark 3:13a for the mountain setting for the Sermon, but then also says that Matthew's use of it is distinctive (*Mountain*, 110–11), the key point to be made. Mark uses the mountain for a different event, the selection of the Twelve.

Exodus, so eschatological Zion, the goal of this Exodus, stands in these passages [Isa 2:2; Jer 31:31–34; Ezek 40ff.] as a new Sinai. In the future Zion will be the place where the law is heard."[77] Indeed, the two themes are intertwined. As will also be seen in Luke's use of the exodus tradition, Matthew incorporates the exodus tradition within the Zion tradition.

Hence, both traditions throw light on the significance of the Sermon's mountain location. Reflecting Sinai, the Sermon on the Mount is "the messianic interpretation of the Torah for the community." Fulfilling the Zion imagery, it is "the eschatological gathering of the people of God."[78] With Jesus taking Moses' own prophetic role in the Torah, the Sermon claims Jesus to be the fulfillment of the prophetic oracle: "The Lord your God will raise up for you a prophet like me from among your own people" (Deut 18:15). As Donaldson perceives, Jesus' gathering the crowds (ὄχλοι) on the mountain in 15:29–31 represents the final scene of Jesus' Galilean ministry to the crowd. Indeed, this scene strikes again the note of the eschatological gathering of the peoples. In addition, Jesus' feeding of the 4,000 reflects the new exodus-Zion theme of the eschatological banquet (Isa 25:6–10). In Matthew's narrative movement, the Gentiles' feasting on the messianic eschatological bread is God's antiphonal response to the acclaim, "They praised the God of Israel."

Then, after a brief contrasting response by the Pharisees and Sadducees, testing (πειράζοντες) Jesus for a sign, to which Jesus allows only the "sign of Jonah," the curtain falls on Jesus' public ministry in Galilee. In the subsequent boat ride Jesus' quizzing of the disciples as to their understanding of the feedings is, unlike Mark, only a warning to beware of the leaven, i.e., the teaching of the Pharisees and Sadducees.

In accord with his earlier exclamation in 14:33, "Truly, you are the Son of God" (14:33), Peter then confesses Jesus to be the Christ, *the Son of the living God*. Serving as both climax to the Galilean section and transition to the Gospel's next section, this declaration of Jesus' divine Sonship advances a theme sounded earlier in Matthew's infancy and preparation narrative. But now Jesus' own people's response to his Galilean ministry extends a darkening shadow over the exodus miracle: "Out of Egypt have I called my Son" (Matt 2:15 quoting Hos 11:1). In their separate but connected histories, both sons, Israel and now Jesus, would learn yet of the refiner's fire.

---

[77]Ibid., 46.
[78]Ibid., 115, 119.

LUKE

1. Content of Luke's Galilean Section

Luke's Galilean section begins with Jesus' opening address in the Nazareth synagogue (4:16) and ends at 9:50, before Jesus set "his face to go to Jerusalem" (9:51). Like Matthew, Luke's infancy and preparation narratives resonate with exodus imagery. Luke portrays Jesus' birth as God's salvation, redemption for both Israel and the Gentiles (1:47, 69, 77, 79; 2:11, 30–32; 3:6). This salvation brings *peace* as its gift (1:79; 2:14), but a peace that turns the existing social order upside-down (1:51–53):

> He has shown strength with his arm,
>   he has scattered the proud in the thoughts of their hearts,
> he has brought down the powerful from their thrones,
>   and lifted up the lowly;
> he has filled the hungry with good things,
>   and sent the rich away empty.

Luke's exodus imagery thus begins before the Galilean section and continues later in the narrative, even into his second volume, Acts, where Peter expressly identifies Jesus with the prophet to be raised up in the same way God raised up Moses (3:22). Many scholarly contributions identify exodus influence in the journey narrative, but fail to note such in the Galilean section. This study rectifies that omission by demonstrating that exodus themes permeate the Galilean section.

Charles Talbert's analysis of the Galilean section presents a series of parallel correspondences, beginning after Luke's frontispiece of the Nazareth encounter (4:16–30):

1. Jesus encounters and exorcises demons	4:31–41 and 8:26–39
2. Jesus in a boat: nature miracles	5:1–11 and 8:22–25
3. With Pharisees, controversy over forgiveness of sins	5:17–26 and 7:36–50
4. Jesus, unlike John, eating and drinking	5:27–6:5 and 7:31–35
5. Jesus with the Twelve, teaching crowds	6:12–16 and 8:1–3
6. Jesus teaches multitudes, stresses "hearing and doing"	6:17–49; 8:4–8, 16–20[79]

---

[79]C. Talbert, *Literary Patterns, Theological Themes, and the Genre of Luke–Acts* (Missoula, Mont.: Scholars, 1974), 40.

As Talbert notes, the second set of texts does not follow the Gospel's sequential order. While this point to some extent weakens his thesis regarding Luke's architectonic design, the recurring pattern of doublets or duality in Luke is unmistakably present here and elsewhere.[80] These doublets show the Lukan emphases: battle against the demons, power over the sea (though 5:1–11 has more to do with discipleship than sea chaos), forgiveness of sins, celebration of the kingdom time, the Twelve as the nucleus of the emerging Jesus community, and learning the way of God's kingdom.

Talbert's analysis, however, also obscures much of the content of this Galilean section in that a single episode in an entire segment represents the whole. Many of the segments are remarkably similar in form and order to those in Mark. They are interchanged with Luke's additional material through chapter 8, shared sometimes with Matthew (i.e., Q, for those who hold this view). A listing of Luke's segments in Table I at the end of the chapter shows their order of occurrence, content, and their similarity to or difference from Mark.

The last segment (9:18–50) of Luke's Galilean section includes Markan and Matthean journey narrative. Luke advances this material in order to clear the narrative deck for a new beginning at 9:51. Also, in this unique pattern, Luke does not locate Peter's confession at Caesarea Philippi. Hence, by virtue of his "Great Omission," which included Jesus' journey to Tyre and Sidon and into the Decapolis, Luke crafts a narrative in which Jesus does not travel outside Galilee. Even Jesus' mission to the Gerasene is depicted in relation to Galilee, ἀντιπέρα Galilee (8:26). Only at 9:51, where the journey begins by going through a Samaritan village, does Jesus finally leave Galilee.

2. Luke's Exodus Theology

Luke's inclusion of 9:18–50 in the Galilean section, though creating disagreement on the limits of the Galilean ministry,[81] yields evidence that exodus theology explicitly shapes Jesus' Galilean ministry in the Synoptics. This segment includes the transfiguration. Luke introduces into the transfiguration narrative the very word "exodus,"

---

[80]See F. Neirynck's study concerning how extensive the art of duality is in Luke, arising possibly from the effort to certify with two or three witnesses: *Duality in Mark: Contributions to the Study of the Markan Redaction* (Louvain: Leuven University, 1972).

[81]This difference in Luke's relocating of material is minor actually when compared to the amount of material he locates in the journey section, which in Matthew or Mark was located in the Galilean section.

translated "departure" by both RSV and NRSV (9:31). Even though the implied emphasis falls upon joining the word to some future experience in the phrase, "about to fulfill (ἤμελλεν πληροῦν) at Jerusalem," the word "fulfill" indicates completion of action already begun. This beginning is Jesus' Galilean ministry, clearly introduced by the liberational tone and content of Luke's frontispiece for the Galilean ministry in 4:16–19. Hence, Luke presents an "exodus" narrative inclusio for the Galilean ministry, which in turn clarifies how Luke has shaped Jesus' Galilean ministry through exodus eyes of faith.[82]

Much of the literature that recognizes exodus themes in Luke focuses either on Jesus' death as his "exodus"; or his death, resurrection and/or ascension as fulfilling his "exodus"; or links the exodus theme with the journey narrative.[83] These studies rarely show, however, that exodus themes also accent Luke's story of Jesus' Galilean ministry. In addition to Luke's exodus inclusio for the Galilean narrative, five other features show Luke's toning of the Galilean section with exodus emphases.

a. *Jesus contextualizes Jubilee: Luke 4:16–19 fulfills Isaiah 61:1–2a.* By citing Isaiah 61:1–2a in 4:18–19 as the frontispiece for Jesus' public ministry, Luke introduces Jesus' ministry with a strong liberational tone. In terms of tradition-history, Luke is utilizing exodus theology as it was earlier used by Second (Third) Isaiah.[84] A fivefold portrait of liberation emerges in this reading from Isaiah:

a To *preach good news* to the poor,
  b To proclaim *release* to the captives,
    c And recovery of *sight* to the blind,
  b′ To send forth the *oppressed in release,*
a′ To proclaim the *acceptable year* of the Lord.[85]

---

[82]By this I do not say that Luke used Mark and Matthew. Rather, the Jesus tradition as used by all three had already been so understood. By treating each Gospel separately in this chapter, I seek to show *how* each author shaped the exodus grasp of Jesus' Galilean ministry. Indeed, we cannot disprove the good possibility that Jesus designed his ministry in this way.

[83]S. H. Ringe recounts some of these studies, and also proposes exodus influence on the journey section: *Jesus, Liberation, and the Biblical Jubilee* (Philadelphia: Fortress, 1985).

[84]For an overall discussion see B. W. Anderson's article, "Exodus Typology in Second Isaiah." For specific use of this text as exodus tradition in Isaiah, see D. L. Tiede, *Prophecy and History in Luke–Acts* (Philadelphia: Fortress, 1980), 44.

[85]This chiastic format follows in part Tiede's analysis, though he extends it to the whole passage (Tiede, *Prophecy and History*, 35).

This quotation, however, is not a pure use of Isaiah 61:1–2a. The second strophe of Isaiah 61:1 is omitted ("to bind up the broken-hearted") and in its place, as Luke's fourth strophe, is a line from Isaiah 58:6, "to set free the oppressed." This use of Isaiah 58:6 suggests that Luke wants to highlight the freeing of people from oppression. This theme represents one aspect of Luke's contextualization of Jubilee, i.e., appropriating the OT Jubilee prescriptions into issues and needs of contemporary cultural relevancy. This is carried forward by his portrait of Jesus' proclaiming the gospel of salvation and peace and in his many stories of Jesus' liberating people from Satan's bondage. Jesus' healings and exorcisms (see part c below) and Luke's summary of Jesus' ministry in Acts 10:38, "he went about doing good and healing all that were oppressed of the devil," are evidence for a liberation theme in the Gospel.

As Susan Garrett proposes, Isaiah 58:6 also expresses Luke's overall emphasis and tones his use of Isaiah 61:1–2a. Thus, Jesus was anointed with the Spirit of God in order that he might "loosen the bonds of wickedness, undo the bands of the coercing yoke, send the oppressed into freedom, and break apart every unjust contract."[86] Luke's narrative strategy is to testify through many stories of liberation that Jesus' gospel of the kingdom of God frees people from oppression of all kinds. It is the gospel of "our God reigns" in Jesus! Isaiah 52:7, from which this exclamation is drawn, also shaped Luke's story (see ch. 4).

Luke's use of Isaiah 61:1–2a has been widely associated with the notion that Luke's Jesus proclaims Jubilee, and that his ministry should be seen in that perspective.[87] By inserting a line from Isaiah 58:6 Luke is able to repeat ἄφεσις (release) in b and b', which suggests

---

[86]S. R. Garrett, *The Demise of the Devil: Magic and the Demonic in Luke–Acts* (Minneapolis: Augsburg/Fortress, 1989), 71–72. Garrett proposes that the term, "bond of iniquity," used for Simon Magus in Acts 8:23, is an allusion to Isa 58:6. See also her connection of the term, "gall of bitterness," to the LXX of Deut 29:17 (MT: v. 18) which speaks of "a curse against those who disobey the covenant by committing idolatry" (138). As the subtitle of her book indicates, Luke emphasizes the gospel's encounter of the demonic and magic, and shows its victory over it.

[87]J. H. Yoder, *The Politics of Jesus* (Grand Rapids: Eerdmans, 1972), chs. 2–3; R. B. Sloan, *The Favorable Year of the Lord: A Study of Jubilary Theology in the Gospel of Luke* (Austin, Tex.: Schola, 1977); D. Blosser, "Jesus and Jubilee, Luke 4:16–30: The Year of Jubilee and Its Significance in Luke," (Ph.D. diss., University of St. Andrews, 1979); S. H. Ringe, *Jesus, Liberation, and the Biblical Jubilee* (Philadelphia: Fortress, 1985).

his intention to connect this inauguration address with Jubilee, since ἄφεσις is used in the LXX in Leviticus 25 and 27 to translate *yôbēl*, the horn blast announcing Jubilee.[88] But the specific concerns of the Jubilee Year are not developed literally in Luke's Gospel. Except for his emphasis on forgiving debts,[89] he does not take up the other Jubilean prescriptions—the releasing of slaves, land lying fallow, and the redistribution of land (Lev 25; Deut 15). Even on the topic of debts, Luke's version of the Lord's Prayer (11:4) ironically uses "sins"(ἁμαρτίας) in the first half of the couplet instead of "debts"(ὀφειλήματα) as does Matthew 6:12 (the second half is τοῖς ὀφειλέταις, a noun in Matthew, and παντὶ ὀφείλοντι, a participle in Luke).

But this does not mean that Luke is not a jubilean Gospel. Rather, Luke contextualizes Jubilee, presenting a strong prophetic and revolutionary portrait of Jesus' ministry: Jesus announces blessing and good news to the poor, issues warnings and even condemnation to the rich, fellowships with tax collectors and sinners, shows women in favorable narrative roles, and breaks racial and national boundaries through the gospel's advance (in Acts especially, but also in the Gospel by destroying the barrier between Jews and Samaritans). Each of these points merits attention, for in these we grasp Luke's portrait of Jesus as Herald of Jubilee.

(1) *Blessing to the poor; woe to the rich.* By privileging the narrative position of Jesus' Isaiah reading, Luke accentuates this jubilean motif. Jesus' first action as specified in the reading is that of "proclaiming the gospel to the poor" (εὐαγγελίσασθαι πτωχοῖς). This same note, already struck in the Magnificat (1:51–53), will reach its crescendo in Luke's journey narrative and remain central throughout Luke–Acts. It occurs also in Luke's Galilean section twice after the Nazareth reading: once in hortatory form (6:20–21, 24–25)—with sharp emphasis—and once in narrative comment (8:1–3).

Luke's Sermon on the Plain first promises: "Blessed are you who are poor, for yours is the kingdom of God," and then pronounces a matching woe: "Woe to you who are rich, for you have received your consolation." The women's sharing of their means to support the Jesus movement (8:1–3) shows radical mutuality of economic resources, a model which marks the moral ethos of Luke's Jesus and his

---

[88]Most overlook this connection. See R. Bultmann, *TDNT*, 1.510.

[89]Yoder stresses this aspect of Jesus' ministry as the inauguration of Jubilee (*Politics*, 34–37, 66–74). The point is part of his concern for the poor. See W. Stegemann and L. Schottroff, *Jesus and the Hope of the Poor* (Maryknoll: Orbis, 1986).

early followers. These emphases reflect Luke's interpretation of jubilean prescriptions in a Christian context; they are not a literal enactment of Jubilee. "Blessing to the poor and woe to the rich" announces the eschatological reversal of the reign of God.[90] Luke's economic model is even more radical than literal Jubilee; it puts all wealth *all the time* at the disposal of kingdom work. As early Acts shows, the believers sold their possessions, gave their resources to meet community needs, and did not regard anything as their own (Acts 2:44–45; 5:1–11). This clearly moves beyond the prescriptions of Old Testament Jubilee.

(2) *Jesus' fellowship with tax collectors and sinners.* While this theme is a characteristic feature of the synoptic tradition and not unique to Luke's portrait of Jesus (see ch. 2 above), Luke does emphasizes this aspect of Jesus' ministry. In the Galilean section Luke includes, in addition to the triple tradition appearing in 5:29–32, a saying that expresses the people's rejection of Jesus because he associates with the wrong crowd: "you say, 'Look, a glutton and a drunkard, a friend of tax collectors and sinners!' " (7:34/Matt 11:19). Immediately Luke follows with the story of Jesus and the sinful woman (7:36–50) in which his conduct threatens the boundaries of the prevailing socio-religious order in several ways: association—indeed friendship—with these ostracized groups, sharing table fellowship with them, and forgiving the sins of ritually unclean persons. Welcoming sinners to table fellowship was, as Goppelt notes, both a mediation of divine forgiveness to the sinners and a restoration of them into the community of God's kingdom, proleptic of the last meal and later participation in the Lord's Supper.[91] By calling Levi, a tax collector, into his circle of disciples, Jesus further violated purity boundaries and likely incited questions about his political alignment.

(3) *Women in favorable narrative roles.* This feature, extending throughout both Lukan volumes, appears already in the birth

---

[90]J. Elias, in his doctoral dissertation ("The Beginning of Jesus' Ministry in the Gospel of Luke," Toronto School of Theology, 1978), argues that Jubilee is not a redactional emphasis of Luke, but that eschatological reversal is. Rather, in my judgment, the latter is utilized to show the shape of Luke's contextualized version of Jubilee. In this respect, Blosser disagrees with Sloan's view that Jubilee in Luke is to be understood metaphorically and eschatologically. Blosser rightly argues that the call is for the present; it is the ethical response of the present community of the kingdom.

[91]Goppelt, *Theology*, 131, 216–17. See also D. E. Smith, "Table Fellowship as a Literary Motif in the Gospel of Luke," *JBL* 106 (Dec. 1987), 613–38. Smith takes the view that the "poor" in Luke are blended into the outcast "tax collector and sinner" category in Luke (636). This point needs closer study.

narratives. In the Galilean section women also emerge in favorable narrative roles: the widow of Zarephath, Sidon, whose reception of God's prophet, Elijah, is exemplary (4:25–26); Simon's mother-in-law who, after being healed by Jesus, serves (διακονέω) them (4:38–39); the Nain widow, for whom Jesus has compassion as she grieves for her only son, then dead, and whom Jesus raises (7:11–17); the sinful, forgiven woman, who dares to wash Jesus' feet with her tears of brokenness and thus receives new life (7:36–50); the women from Galilee who follow Jesus (8:1–3); the courageous woman whose faith in Jesus heals her continuous flow of blood (8:42b–48); and Jairus' dead daughter whom Jesus resurrects (8:40–42a, 49–56). These women function in positive narrative roles; all testify to Jesus' liberating ministry, either as its recipients or as supporters. That women figure so prominently in the narrative is liberational as well, for Jesus is breaking the culturally enforced gender boundaries that prevailed in Galilean Judaism. Furthermore, such models encourage women in Luke's churches to participate in Christ's continuing ministry.[92]

(4) *Breaking racial and national boundaries.* Although signals of universal salvation are present already in Luke's birth and preparation narratives, in the Galilean section Jesus confines his travels to Galilee. This does not mean, however, that his ministry is confined to the Jews (4:25–27). The summary statement in 6:17 indicates that "the multitude of people" to whom the Sermon on the Plain is addressed includes people from Tyre and Sidon. The faith of the centurion whose slave Jesus healed surpasses that of any in Israel (7:1–10). But in both these cases the Gentile world comes into Israel. Luke's great mission story of Jesus' disciples going out into all the world to proclaim the gospel happens later.[93]

While the four sub-points above denote specific features of Luke's contextualizing of Jubilee, the following emphases are also part of Luke's larger Jubilean theology and gospel proclamation.

---

[92]For a description of the roles of women in the Jewish, Greek and Roman worlds, see E. and F. Stagg, *Women in the World of Jesus* (Philadelphia: Westminster, 1978), 13–100, and B. Witherington III, *Women and the Genesis of Christianity* (Cambridge: Cambridge University, 1990), 1–28. The Roman world welcomed a significantly wider cultural involvement by women than did the Jewish world. For a description of Luke's portrait of the roles of women, see M. J. Selvidge, *Daughters of Jerusalem* (Scottdale, Penn., and Kitchener, Ont.: Herald, 1987), 89–131. For a critical sociological analysis of the functions of women in Jesus' ministry, see S. Heine, *Women and Early Christianity: A Reappraisal* (Minneapolis: Augsburg, 1988), 60–62.
[93]This is the simplest explanation for Luke's Great Omission.

b. Jesus comes "to proclaim good news." A key term (and a Lukan favorite) in Jesus' Nazareth sermon is "to proclaim good news" (εὐαγγελίζω, 4:17). The word already occurs in Luke's opening chapters (1:19; 2:10; 3:18) and four times in the Galilean section (4:43; 7:22; 8:1; 9:6). All these uses are uniquely Lukan and have no parallels in Mark and Matthew. The term occurs twice later in Luke and many times in Acts.[94] It fits into Luke's semantic world of salvation (σωτηρία, 1:69, 71, 77; 19:9, and σωτήριον, 2:20; 3:6), to save (σῴζω, 8:12, 36, 50; 9:24, 56; 13:23), Savior (σωτήρ, 1:47; 2:11), and Luke's recurring use of the word "peace" (εἰρήνη, fourteen times in the Gospel).[95] All three terms, proclaim good news, salvation, and peace, are linked in various texts with "kingdom of God," so that Luke's view of "gospelizing the kingdom of God" (a literal translation of εὐαγγελίζεσθαι τὴν βασιλεία τοῦ θεοῦ in 4:43; 8:1; 16:16; Acts 8:12) is bringing to people *salvation* and *peace. Gospel* and *salvation* are linked in 2:10–11, 20; *gospel* and *peace* in 2:10, 14, and Acts 10:36. Luke 10:1–12 strategically links *peace* and *kingdom.* By juxtaposing these terms Luke clearly draws on Second Isaiah's use of the exodus tradition and its combination of these terms with Zion imagery and theology (see Isa 40:1–9; 52:7–10). Luke draws on Isaiah 61:1–2a to denote the nature of Jesus' ministry, and he also develops his portrait of Jesus' ministry in accordance with the prophetic oracle of Isaiah 52:7:

> How beautiful upon the mountains
>   are the feet of the one who announces gospel (*mᵉḇaśśēr*),
> who proclaims (*maśᵉmîaʿ*) peace (*šālôm*),
> who announces the good gospel (*mᵉḇaśśēr ṭôḇ*).
> who proclaims (*maśᵉmîaʿ*) salvation (*yᵉśûʿâ*),
>   saying to Zion, "Your God reigns (*mālaḵ 'Elohayiḵ*)."

The Septuagint's translation of Isaiah's *mᵉḇaśśēr . . . šālôm* as εὐαγγελιζομένου . . . εἰρήνης is certainly the background for Luke's description of Jesus' ministry in Acts 10:36 as εὐαγγελιζόμενος εἰρήνην (so also the Pauline use in Eph 2:17). The Aramaic Targum translates the last phrase of Isa 52:7, "Your God reigns" (LXX: βασιλεύσει σου ὁ

---

[94]Luke 16:16; 20:1; Acts 5:42; 8:4, 12, 25, 40 (clearly a narrative theme unifying the story of the gospel's spread to Samaria); 10:36 (a key summary text); 11:20; 13:32; 14:7, 15, 21; 15:25; 16:10; 17:18.

[95]See W. M. Swartley, "Politics and Peace (*Eirene*) in Luke's Gospel," in *Political Issues in Luke–Acts,* ed. R. J. Cassidy and P. J. Scharper (Maryknoll, N.Y.: Orbis, 1983), 25–29.

θεός) as "the kingdom of your God will be revealed."[96] Since Jesus heard Aramaic in the synagogue, it is likely that this and other similar texts occasioned his use of "kingdom of God" in his preaching. Luke combines the *good news* of the kingdom with salvation and peace.

The four uses of εὐαγγελίζω in the Galilean section merit brief examination:

4:43. "I must proclaim the good news (εὐαγγελίσασθαι) of the kingdom of God to the other cities also; for I was sent for this purpose." When compared to Mark's "in order that I might preach (κηρύξω) there also" in 1:38 and Matthew's lack of a parallel (4:23 can hardly be regarded as such), Luke's intention shines clearly. This explicit statement of Jesus' mission connects solidly with his larger narrative emphasis. Jesus' mission is to proclaim the good news and thus fulfill the vision of Isaiah 52:7. Jesus brings *gospel,* liberation for the captive, and peace!

A connection between this text and 4:18 is made not only by the use of εὐαγγελίζω, but also by the use of ἀποστέλλω in both texts. Luke ends 4:43 with "for I was sent for this purpose" (ὅτι ἐπὶ τοῦτο ἀπεστάλην), which includes the same declaration as in 4:18, "I have been sent (ἀπέσταλκεν)." Here lies Luke's perspective on Jesus' mission: Jesus was sent with an official commission from God, just as the disciples will later be sent as apostles. Under Jesus' commission εὐαγγελίζω and ἀποστέλλω blend together to show the divine authority and mandate by which Jesus undertakes his mission of liberation.

7:22. When John's disciples ask, "Are you the one who is to come, or are we to wait for another?" (7:19), Jesus answers: "Go and tell John what you have seen and heard: the blind receive their sight, the lame walk, the lepers are cleansed, the deaf hear, the dead are raised, the poor have good news brought to them." The last phrase (also in Matt 11:5) is again a form of εὐαγγελίζω. It connects Jesus' mission to the Nazareth declaration and at the same time strikes the chord of prophetic messianic fulfillment, for the list of Jesus' deeds echoes Isaiah 35 and 61. These prophetic texts celebrate Israel's return

---

[96]See B. Chilton, *A Galilean Rabbi and His Bible: Jesus' Use of the Interpreted Scripture of His Time* (Wilmington, Del.: M. Glazier, 1984), 59. Chilton cites four texts in Isaiah where the Targum uses the phrase "kingdom of God" (24:23; 31:4; 40:9; 52:7). The phrase appears in four other Targum texts also: Zech 14:9; Obad 21; Ezek 7:7(10); Mic 4:7b–8. See Chilton's essay, "REGNUM DEI DEUS EST," *SJT* 31 (1978), 261–70; also in *Targumic Approaches to the Gospels: Essays in the Mutual Definition of Judaism and Christianity* (Lanham/New York/London: University Press of America, 1986), 99–105.

from captivity and utilize exodus themes of liberation to describe the new experience.[97] In this crucial text Jesus' mission is identified as fulfilling the messianic servant mission outlined in Isaiah 35 and 61:1–2a. These deeds distinguish Jesus' mission from other types of messianic hope and from John's preparatory work. This exchange between John and Jesus comes immediately after two important miracles in Luke's narrative: the healing of the centurion's son and the raising of the Nain widow's son (the latter is unique to Luke). By identifying his deeds with these signs of Isaiah's messianic hope, Jesus answers the first half of John's query with an implied yes.

8:1 Jesus travels "on through cities and villages, proclaiming and bringing the good news of the kingdom of God." Like 4:43, this verse summarizes a span of Jesus' activity. It uses two somewhat redundant words, to preach (κηρύσσω) and to proclaim good news (εὐαγγελίζω)[98] to continue the εὐαγγελίζω thread of emphasis. The additional phrase, "The twelve were with him," connects to the following two verses which indicate that some women also follow him. These women, having experienced personal transformation and liberation, as implied in v. 2, and having become vital members of the new kingdom, devote their resources to the welfare of this new emerging community.

9:6 "they departed and went through the villages, bringing the good news (εὐαγγελιζόμενοι) and curing diseases everywhere." Here the Twelve take up the mission of Jesus; the verb εὐαγγελίζω describes their activity. Proleptically, here and in the mission of the Seventy in Luke 10, Jesus' messianic liberation moves into another stage in which his followers take up his work. But in Luke's subsequent uses of εὐαγγελίζω (16:16; 20:1) only Jesus is subject of the action.

---

[97]See Anderson, n. 84 above, and W. E. Rast, *Tradition History*, 61–68. Though placed in the First Isaiah corpus, ch. 35 certainly belongs to the Second Isaiah tradition; the same applies to 61:1–3 occurring in Third Isaiah. Scholarship is rightly challenging the First/Second/Third division on the basis of narrative analysis. See C. R. Seitz for a review of various positions and his own thesis that chs. 36–39 are pivotally related to both First and Second Isaiah and the development of the entire Isaiah tradition (*Zion's Final Destiny: the Development of the Book of Isaiah: A Reassessment of Isaiah 36–39* [Minneapolis: Augsburg/Fortress, 1991], esp. 30–35, 205–8).

[98]Matthew's close parallel, placed elsewhere in the order of the narrative, at 9:35 before the sending out of the Twelve, has κηρύσσων τὸ εὐαγγέλιον τῆς βασιλείας. Like Mark, Matthew uses the noun, εὐαγγέλιον, a few times, though for Mark it is a leitmotif. See chs. 4–6 for discussion of Mark's use.

(Later on, in Acts the apostles pick up and carry forward the εὐαγ-γελιζόμενος mission.)

Luke's use of εὐαγγελίζω to denote the liberational essence of Jesus' mission is thus concentrated in the Galilean section (16:16 retrospectively describes the whole of his ministry while 20:1 is a general statement). The Nazareth manifesto is an overture to this narrative feature. Luke portrays Jesus' liberation as embracing human reality holistically: personal transformation, social transformation, and a new politics which neither courts nor counters Rome.[99] The social and political dimensions of transformation and liberation are less obvious in the Galilean section than the personal dimensions. But the immediate follow-up to the Nazareth sermon shows, as does 7:1–10, that the social dimension is also evident. The receptivity to the gospel by the outsiders in these two pericopes anticipates Luke's larger story.[100]

Luke's focus on liberation and transformation at the personal level is reinforced by the fact that *all* the healing stories in Matthew and Mark (except for those in Luke's Great Omission) appear in Luke. In addition, Luke includes the raising of the widow's son at Nain. Each of these stories—from healing the leper to raising the widow's son—exemplifies the exodus theme of liberation. In addition, Luke's special story of Jesus' forgiveness of the sins of the sinful woman (7:36–50) emphasizes the depth of his liberating proclamation. At the cost of offending his host, Simon the Pharisee, Jesus accepts this woman of the city, likely a prostitute, and responds to her brokenness of life with deep and transforming compassion. Jesus violates the socio-religious codes and seriously damages his reputation in the eyes of the "righteous." But the personal transformation which the woman experienced is invaluable. The prominence of these themes puts into ironic key the query whether this one is really a prophet (v. 39). But most important, Jesus forgives the woman her sins (v. 42, 47–49). This joyful theme of liberation joins those noted above; Jesus is the Savior who brings good news in deeds of transformation. This woman is transformed and receives Jesus' word of *salvation* and *peace* (v. 50)!

---

[99] Swartley, "Politics and Peace," 35–37.

[100] L. C. Crockett has persuasively shown that Luke 4:25–27 was constructed in such a way as to anticipate the Gentile mission: "Luke 4:25–27 and Jewish-Gentile Relations in Luke–Acts," *JBL* (1969), 177–83. The theme of Jesus as the rejected prophet is also anticipated in this narrative (vv. 23–24, and 28–30).

c. Jesus reclaims people from the power of Satan. For Luke, forgiveness of sins involves not only personal transformation, but also freedom from Satan's bondage (Acts 26:18). Luke accentuates this by narrating many stories of Jesus' freeing people from demonic oppression. This emphasis permeates Luke's two-volume narrative, even framing the mission of the early church outside Palestine with narrative inclusios around this theme (Acts 8 and 19). Paul's encounters with Elymas in Acts 13 and the itinerant Jewish exorcists in Acts 19 produce a similar inclusio for Paul's mission. The Pauline mission narrative in Acts ends with the gospel's triumph over magic (19:18–41), an expression of the demonic.[101]

In Luke's Galilean section, as well as in the journey narrative, Luke emphasizes that Jesus delivers humans from demonic power. While it is commonly thought that of the Synoptic writers Mark gives the most prominence to this theme, that opinion must be revised. For, in both the Galilean and journey sections Luke highlights this theme more than Mark. In Luke and Acts, the freeing of people from the power of Satan and the grip of demons demonstrates first and foremost that the gospel is the power of God and that the bondage of the fallen world is coming to an end! The following seven points are the evidence:

(1) Talbert's structural analysis of chs. 4–8 puts a doublet of exorcisms at the head of Luke's duality structure in the Galilean section. Luke's (4:31–37) and Mark's (1:21–28) accounts of Jesus' exorcism in the synagogue are very similar (Matthew lacks a parallel). In both Luke and Mark the story introduces Jesus' public deeds; however, Luke connects the emphasis on authority (ἐξουσία) directly with the exorcism (v. 36), whereas Mark connects it with Jesus' teaching.

(2) Luke includes two features not found in Mark and Matthew. Preceding Jesus' statement to John's inquiry about his eschatological identity (7:22), Luke indicates that "Jesus had just cured many people of diseases and plagues and evil spirits" (v. 21). Luke thus informs the reader that John's disciples saw what Jesus was doing and, just in case the description in verse 22 is not plain enough, Luke includes exorcisms to strengthen the evidence that identifies Jesus with "the one who is to come."

---

[101] See Garrett, *Demise of the Devil,* for a thorough presentation of the narrative function of the gospel's encounter with the demonic and magic throughout Luke–Acts.

A second "Lukan special" occurs in 8:2–3 where the women who followed Jesus, Mary Magdalene, Joanna, Susanna, and many others (ἕτεραι) are introduced as those healed from evil spirits and diseases. The text specifies that seven demons had gone out of Mary Magdalene.[102]

(3) Luke's summary that Jesus healed those troubled by unclean spirits (6:18) has a parallel only in Matthew (4:23).

(4) The triple tradition agrees that when Jesus sent out the Twelve he gave them authority over the demons, and that casting out demons was part of the proclamation of God's kingdom coming into human midst (9:1ff.//Mark 6:7–12//Matt 10:1). But whereas Mark and Matthew put the Beelzebul controversy in the Galilean section, Luke puts it in his journey narrative, a strategic placement, as discussed in the next chapter.

(5) The story of the Gerasene demoniac differs only negligibly among the Synoptics (Luke 8:22ff. and par.). Matthew is the shortest, omitting the details of the demons' power over the man. While Mark's account is the longest, most of his longer form does not deal with the exorcism proper, but serves to presage the mission to the Gentiles.[103]

(6) Luke puts the story of Jesus' healing a boy possessed by an evil spirit (9:37–43a), a sequel to the transfiguration, within his Galilean section. His account exceeds Matthew's, but is shorter than Mark's at two points: a dialogue with the father and a description of the final exorcistic action. Only by its close association with the transfiguration included in Luke's Galilean section can Luke's account be said to have special bearing upon Luke's exodus liberation theme. Luke concludes with a liturgical refrain of praise: "And all were astonished at the greatness (majesty, RSV) of God." Since Luke lacks the pericope on the necessary sufferings of the Son of humanity (see Mark

---

[102] The use of ἕτεραι for others, instead of ἄλλοι, would seem to suggest that the other women were not recipients of the same type of healing. But those who experienced Jesus' liberation from demonic bondage are those named; these carry the lead roles later in the narrative. With our modern feminist consciousness we are prone to react negatively to this narrative and the preceding one about a woman prostitute. But we do so at the cost of silencing an emphasis close to the heart of Luke's Gospel; those who know and love Jesus best are those delivered and forgiven, and women model that role in Luke's narrative.

[103] See R. Pesch, "The Markan Version of the Healing of the Gerasene Demoniac," *Ecumenical Review* 23 (1971), 349–76. Mark emphasizes Decapolis, which Luke avoids, as the place where the man preached what Jesus did.

9:9–13), the refrain recalls the transfiguration as well; the continuity of the two stories evokes awe and wonder at God's glory and power. (7) The section ends with an account of the exorcist who used Jesus' name but did not follow Jesus (9:49–50). Jesus answers his disciples, "Do not stop him; for whoever is not against you is for you." By concluding the Galilean section with this incident, Luke highlights the theme of Jesus' liberating people from Satan's power; even the person exorcising in Jesus' name supports the kingdom mission.[104]

d. Exodus echoes in the Transfiguration. Three points of interest converge in the transfiguration: the distinctive Lukan use of the word "exodus," the abundant imagery which reflects Moses' ascent of the mountain in Exodus 24, and Luke's inclusion of this in the Galilean section.

First, as Joseph Fitzmyer notes regarding Luke's use of "exodus": "the very word echoes the Exodus of Israel from Egypt to its promised land, its land of destiny."[105] In her analysis of Luke's use of *exodus* in the transfiguration, Sharon H. Ringe connects the exodus motif of liberation to Jubilee. While arguing that *exodus* in 9:31 refers primarily to Jesus' Journey to Jerusalem, she also links it to 4:16–19: "Liberation themes are present . . . in Luke's highlighting of Jesus' role as herald of God's reign, and of the proclamation of a Jubilee at its near boundary."[106] Garrett, in "Exodus from Bondage," reviews and assesses previous works which hypothesize different meanings for Luke's use of "exodus."[107] These hypotheses include Jindrich Mánek's view that it provides Luke a literary paradigm in which Jesus' departure from earthly Jerusalem to heavenly Jerusalem corresponds to Israel's exodus from Egypt, and in which the various elements of the Exodus account have antitypological counterparts in Luke's passion story. Alternately, David Moessner theorizes that in Luke, Jesus' journey to the "promised land" is a new exodus which "recapitulates in close literary detail the exodus of Moses as portrayed in Deuteronomy."[108] For Sharon H. Ringe the exodus from Egypt is a theological

---

[104] This saying seems to make the opposite point of the story in Acts 19 where the seven sons of Sceva attempt to use the name of Jesus to exorcise but are overcome themselves by the demons. The two events must assume different motives on the part of those employing the name of Jesus.

[105] Joseph A. Fitzmyer, *The Gospel According to Luke I–IX*, vol. 1 (AB 28; Garden City, N.Y.: Doubleday, 1981), 794.

[106] Ringe, "Luke 9:28–36," 96.

[107] S. R. Garrett, "Exodus from Bondage: Luke 9:31 and Acts 12:1–24," *CBQ* 52 (1990), 657.

[108] Garrett, "Exodus," 657–58 and D. P. Moessner, "Luke 9:1–50:

paradigm which denotes Jesus as a journeyer whose work releases the oppressed from what she identifies as "systems, rules and patterns of indebtedness." But Garrett thinks Ringe too easily demythologizes Luke's view of bondage. Rather, says Garrett, Luke uses exodus as a theological paradigm: "the first exodus prefigures the deliverance from bondage [to Satan] that Luke portrays as constitutive of Jesus' earthly ministry and post-resurrection lordship."[109]

This view of exodus as deliverance from bondage, as Garrett describes, discloses how essential the exodus tradition is to Luke's work. Once this is recognized, then the contextualized forms of Jubilee noted above also function as essential ingredients of Luke's liberational presentation of Jesus. Luke's liberation is rooted firmly in Jesus as Savior, whose proclamation and deeds of the kingdom (εὐαγγελίζω) freed people from bondage to the powers of evil that crippled and bound them. By breaking that bondage, says Luke, Jesus begins a new world in which women and men alike follow Jesus, in which the rich sell their possessions and give to the poor, in which a Samaritan is a true neighbor to the Jew, and in which a new people of "The Way" emerge, including women and men of all races and nations.

Second, numerous articles have listed parallels between the transfiguration and Moses' ascent of the mountain. Luke's special points have been noted as well.[110] This exodus imagery identifies Jesus as one who, like Moses, receives direction from God for the people. In the transfiguration God confirms Jesus as the royal servant of justice to the nations and also as a prophet like Moses, since the voice from heaven speaks phrases from Psalm 2:7; Isaiah 42:1; and Deuteronomy 18:15–18. The voice also confirms Peter's confession (9:20). The typological connection between Jesus and Moses thus centers on Jesus as the one divinely authorized to guide and lead the new community, a function further developed in Luke's Journey narrative. As an inclusio around the transfiguration and exorcism, Luke portrays Jesus speaking twice of his necessary suffering and death, calling his disciples to deny self, take up the cross, and change their notions of greatness (9:23–26 and 43b–48). This emphasis, central in the Journey narrative, anticipates the next section.

Luke's Preview of the Journey of the Prophet Like Moses of Deuteronomy," *JBL* 102 (1983), 575–605, and *Banquet*, 45–69.

[109] Garrett, "Exodus," 658–59. Garrett documents her thesis by appeal mostly to texts in Luke's journey narrative and in Acts, but the case could be made from each major section of Luke's two-volume work.

[110] Moessner, "Luke 9:1–50," 588–92; *Banquet*, 60–64.

Third, by including this segment in his Galilean narrative—
with the transfiguration at its center and the specific mention of
exodus—Luke develops his story of Jesus so that the liberational
power of the exodus decisively shapes the Galilean narrative of Jesus'
ministry. The exodus liberational motif thus frames the beginning
(4:16–19) and ending (9:18–50) of Jesus' Galilean ministry.

    e. Jesus the prophet like Moses. While this point is explicit in
Acts 3:22, Luke 4:24 and Luke 7 anticipate it.[111] In 4:24 Jesus implies
that he is a prophet: "no prophet is acceptable in his own country."
Then in chapter 7 the word προφήτης occurs four times, progressively
unfolding Jesus' identity as a prophet (vv. 16, 26a, 26b, 39). First, the
crowd that witnessed Jesus' raising of the Nain widow's son exclaims,
" 'A great prophet has arisen among us!' and 'God has looked favor-
ably on his people!' " Second, after answering John's messengers and
after their departure, Jesus addresses the crowds concerning John,
asking, " 'What then did you go out to see? A prophet? Yes I tell you,
and more than a prophet.' " Then Jesus quotes the messenger/way text
of Malachi 3:1/Exodus 23:20 and declares that "no one is greater than
John; yet the least in the kingdom of God is greater than he." The
people, of course, understood that Jesus had come preaching the
advent of God's reign. The implication is clear: John was the greatest
in his era, but the antitype/fulfillment of Israel's hopes is present in
Jesus. Hence, "The law and the prophets were in effect until John;
since then the good news of the kingdom of God is proclaimed, and
every one tries to enter it by force" (16:16). Finally, Luke's use of
prophet in chapter 7 seals Jesus' prophetic identity with a twist of
irony: "If this man were a prophet, he would have known who and
what kind of woman this is who is touching him—that she is a
sinner."

    The use of "prophet" in 4:24, common to the synoptic tradi-
tion, occurs here in Luke's distinctive opening manifesto. This use
anticipates the theme of the rejected prophet (see esp. 13:33 and Acts
7). In Luke 9, when the disciples report on what the people say
regarding Jesus' identity, Luke uses the distinctive phrase "old prophets" (vv. 8, 19). Apparently he wants to be clear that the people's
understanding continues along the lines of old-era thinking. In this
way Luke sharply distinguishes between the time of "the law and the

---

[111] G. Nebe's recent study, *Prophetisch Züge im Bild Jesu bei Lukas*
(BWANT 7/7; Stuttgart/Berlin/Köln: W. Kohlhammer, 1989) examines Luke's
extensive portrait of Jesus as prophet.

prophets" as time *before* and the time of Jesus' kingdom proclamation
as time *now* (16:16).

Paul Minear, in his excellent essay, "Jesus as a Prophet Like
Moses," contrasts Jesus' role to that of John, the greatest of the "old"
prophets:

> Until John, [people] were captive to demons and sickness; since John,
> they have been freed. . . .
> Until John, the baptism of repentance for the forgiveness of sins;
> since John, Jesus' baptism by the Spirit enabled him to forgive
> sins. . . .
> Until John, disciples shared in the baptism of repentance;
> since John, disciples were enlisted in a vocation of fishing. . . .
> Until John, the summons to repentance;
> since John, unconditional fellowship with forgiven sinners. . . .
> Until John, sorrow; since John, dancing. . . .
> Until John, the Law and the Prophets;
> since John, the kingdom of God is preached. . . .
> Until John, the Law and the Prophets;
> since John, a radical reinterpretation of Scripture.[112]

Luke's depiction of Jesus as "the prophet like Moses," but
indeed greater than Moses, is highlighted by his transfiguration account, wherein Jesus speaks with Moses and Elijah concerning his
exodus and its fulfillment in Jerusalem. This distinctive Lukan feature,
combined with the heavenly voice certifying Jesus as the prophet like
Moses, shows major exodus influence in Luke's Galilean section.[113]

Noting the extensive traditions in "the synagogue traditions
of Luke's own day" concerning the expectation of a coming prophet
like Moses, Minear says, "When Luke asserted that God had fulfilled
his promise to Moses by raising up a prophet like unto him, he tapped
a huge reservoir of latent images, expressive of Israel's strongest
memories and most vital hopes."[114] Drawing upon the extensive
imagery of Israel's exodus experiences, Luke portrays Jesus in accord

---

[112] P. Minear, *To Heal and To Reveal: The Prophetic Vocation According
to Luke* (New York: Seabury, 1976), 113–16.

[113] Both P. Minear and D. Tiede, in assessing the christological significance of Jesus as prophet in Luke, come to the conclusion that Cullmann
had not given sufficient christological import to this title. See Minear, ibid.,
102–8; Tiede, *Prophecy and History*, 44–58.

[114] Minear, ibid., 108. Minear here draws on W. A. Meeks's important
study, *The Prophet-King*.

with Rabbi Berekiah's dictum of messianic hope, "As the first redeemer was, so shall the latter redeemer be."[115]

EXODUS TRADITIONS:
CONTINUITY AND TRANSFORMATION

This chapter has demonstrated the extensive influence of the
exodus and Sinai traditions upon the Synoptics' portrait of Jesus'
Galilean ministry. In Matthew and Luke the exodus influence leaves a
strong imprint upon the birth narratives as well. Luke stretches the
weight of the exodus tradition across his two-volume narrative. Keller
and Keller have expressed well the parallelism:

> The expected prophet, the second Moses and second Savior of his
> people, is persecuted as a small child by a wicked king, is again called by
> God out of Egypt, gathers his people in the wilderness, proclaims from
> the mountain the law of a new covenant, repeats the miraculous feed-
> ings which belonged to Israel's primeval period during the first journey
> through the wilderness, and recapitulates and surpasses the miraculous
> signs of [Moses, and also] the ancient prophets Elijah and Elisha.[116]

To summarize the findings of this chapter, four major emphases in the exodus and Sinai traditions influence the structure and
accent of Jesus' Galilean ministry in the Synoptics. The first and major
stream of exodus tradition is deliverance from bondage, a liberational
focus in all three Gospels. This figures prominently in Jesus' exorcisms, healings, forgiving of sins, and breaking of racial, gender,
socio-economic, and political barriers erected by cultural and religious sanctions and reinforced further by unclean taboo. Matthew
emphasizes this point by identifying Jesus' healing ministry with the
words of "the prophet Isaiah, 'He took our infirmities and bore our
diseases' " (8:17), and by bringing the ten-miracle catena to a climax
by the crowds' choric, "Never has anything like this been seen in
Israel" (9:33). Both Mark and Luke highlight Jesus' exorcisms as signs
of Jesus' claim to be the Bringer of the kingdom of God. In Luke,
salvation and peace are the fruit of the gospel's liberating power. Also
in Luke, the liberating power of the gospel expresses the Jubilee vision,
which had its origin in Israel's exodus experience (the sabbath of Exod
16 and the sabbatical-Jubilee prescriptions in Lev 25 and Deut 15).

---

[115] Cited by Minear, ibid., 108.
[116] E. Keller and M.-L. Keller, *Miracles in Dispute* (Philadelphia: Fortress, 1968), 222 (quoted by Minear, ibid., 102).

In Mark a second stream of exodus tradition connects to this liberation emphasis, that of Yahweh as Warrior. Jesus subdues the powers of chaos and evil. Satan, the demons, the sea chaos, and even Peter's misguided view of Jesus' messiahship ultimately surrender and yield to the Spirit-empowered rebuke and exorcistic commands of the anointed Son (1:11), whose secret identity is disclosed through acts of divine power.

A third strand of exodus traditions appears in the Synoptics' use of the wilderness motif, with its themes of God's giving manna from heaven, the people's unbelief and rebellion against God, and God's testing, disciplining, and guiding of the people. Emphasis on the wilderness as the locale of God's self-disclosure through the giving of the manna appears most prominently in Mark 6:30–8:21 (in Matthew and Luke the temptation narratives, located prior to the Galilean section, show God's sustaining power for Jesus in the wilderness). Furthermore, in Mark the feedings in the wilderness disclose Jesus' eschatological identity; the disciples' responses are tests of their perception and faith.[117]

Finally, the Synoptics utilize the Sinai traditions to portray Jesus as one like and surpassing Moses. In Mark, Jesus' making of the Twelve on the mountain echoes Moses' representing Israel with twelve pillars at the foot of Mount Sinai. Mark's portrait of Jesus as the authoritative teacher of the word may also be viewed as a Moses-Sinai influence (1:22, 27–28; ch. 4). His three editorial comments that Jesus was teaching the word (2:2; 4:33; 8:32) strengthen this point. In Matthew, Jesus gives Torah-instruction which surpasses what "you have heard" in the rabbinic *halakah* of the Torah. Jesus' teaching in the Sermon presents the true meaning of the Torah; it is the way of "the greater righteousness" that marks the children of the kingdom. Not only does the Sermon appear as God's renewed Torah, given on the mountain as was the law delivered to Moses, but Matthew's entire Galilean section bears a catechetical accent. Thus Matthew draws heavily upon the Sinai tradition. Luke's contribution identifies Jesus as the prophet like Moses. While stating this in 13:33; 16:16; and Acts 3:22, Luke punctuates the Galilean narrative with this emphasis also: in the Nazareth synagogue episode (4:24), through the stages of the

---

[117] While not noted in the study as such, in Matthew Jesus' indictments upon "this evil and adulterous generation" (ch. 12 especially) echo the rebellion/unbelief theme of Israel in the wilderness. Both Mark and Luke also connect the wilderness with the theme of divine guidance and sustenance; it is the place where Jesus retreats to pray (Mark 1:35; Luke 5:16).

narrative in chapter 7, and in the specific mention of Jesus' *exodus* in the transfiguration where Jesus' *glory* illuminates the figures of Moses and Elijah.

To what extent is there continuity in and/or transformation of the Synoptics' use of these exodus-Sinai traditions? To use Kelber's phrase, they function in a new place and a new time.[118] Jesus and the disciples were not rescued from Egypt, they did not ascend Sinai, nor did they wander forty years in the wilderness. Nonetheless, the memories and confessional identity derived from that earlier history provide the experiential and conceptual resources for grasping and communicating the story of Jesus. Continuity and transformation occur simultaneously at many levels of meaning. For Mark and Luke, Jesus' release of people from the bondages of disease, illness and death functions as the counterpart to God's deliverance of Israel from the oppression of slavery in Egypt. For Matthew, Jesus' Sermon on the Mount is a new Sinai-Zion, a people-creating event. And for Mark, the feedings and the boat rides manifest God's revelational faithfulness and test the disciples' grasp of God's divine presence in Jesus. For Luke, Jesus' prophetic role, fulfilling that of Moses, calls believers to live by the words and deeds of Jesus. The law prepared, but Jesus fulfills. His bringing of the gospel of the kingdom establishes a new reality which embraces their lives, providing a new ethos, vision, and empowerment.

And finally, the most striking transformation, indeed nigh reversal, occurs in Jesus' relation to non-Israelites. In the Moses story, the people of other nations threatened Israel's survival, and were therefore viewed as the enemy from whose oppression God delivered Israel or as those over whom God would give victory if they interfered with or obstructed Israel's wilderness life and journey toward the land of promise. But in each of the Gospels the non-Israelites, the Gentiles, are not only recipients, but exemplary models of receiving God's grace, healing, and blessing through Jesus. In both Matthew and Luke, Jesus commands his hearers to love their enemies, to bless those who persecute them, and thus be called God's children.[119] This major transformation, already anticipated in the universal setting of the canon's prologue (Gen 1—11), the promise to Abraham (Gen 12:3)

---

[118] Kelber, *The Kingdom in Mark*, 138–44.
[119] H. Windisch has given an excellent exposition of Matt 5:9, 43ff. viewed within the context of Israel's ethics: "Friedensbringer—Gottessöhne: Eine religionsgeschichtliche Interpretation der 7. Seligpreisung," *ZNW* 24 (1925), 240–60.

and in Second Isaiah's use of exodus imagery to reaffirm Israel's call
(42:1–6; 49:5–6), recurs in other sections of the Synoptics, and thus
continues to disclose major transformation in Israel's traditions of
faith.

Table I: Luke's Galilean Content Compared to Mark's

Segments		In Mark	Not in Mark
4:31–44	Day's work in Capernaum	x	
5:1–11	Simon's catch and call		x
5:12–6:11	Five conflict stories, plus healing of leper	x	
6:12–49	Choosing of Twelve followed by Sermon on Plain		x
7:1–8:3	Heals centurion's slave; raises Nain widow's son; John's question, "Are you he who is to come?"; Jesus and the sinful woman; women followers; Focus: Jesus, a prophet or more?		x
8:4–21	Jesus teaches in parables (but lacks the last two in Mark and has Mark 3:31–35 par. at end)	x	
8:22–56	Jesus' four mighty works (calms sea; heals Gerasene demoniac; heals woman with hemorrhage; raises Jairus' daughter)	x	
9:1–17	Jesus sends out Twelve; Herod's question; Feeding of 5,000 ("Luke's Great Omission")	x	
9:18–50	Peter's confession; suffering of Son of humanity; Self-denial; transfiguration; exorcism; second passion prediction; argument over who is the greatest; disciples' intolerance of exorcism[120]	x	

---

[120] The segments in ch. 9 go beyond Talbert's scope of analysis here, though elsewhere he shows parallel correspondence between Luke 9 and 22:7–23:16 and three parallels between Luke 9 and Acts 1 (Talbert, *Literary Patterns*, 26–27, 61). Talbert borrows the latter from J. G. Davies, "The Prefiguration of the Ascension in the Third Gospel," *JTS* n.s. 6 (1955), 229–33. Talbert notes Lukan alterations from Mark in these pericopes (9:28–36; 9:1–6; 1:11–17) which reflect adjustment to emphases in the parallels in Acts (61–62).

4

THE FORMATIVE INFLUENCE OF THE OLD TESTAMENT WAY-CONQUEST (AND EXODUS) TRADITIONS ON THE SYNOPTIC JOURNEY NARRATIVE

The influence of the Old Testament conquest traditions on the gospel tradition has been seldom noticed, though the impact of the exodus and Sinai traditions has been frequently recognized. This chapter seeks to show that conquest traditions have been especially formative upon the transitional Galilee to Jerusalem section of the synoptic tradition. Again, because each of the Synoptics utilizes this tradition uniquely, developing a distinctive point of view, each Gospel receives separate analysis. The chapter concludes with an assessment of elements of continuity and transformation.

As this chapter title indicates, the influence of exodus traditions also continues in the shaping of the middle section of the synoptic tradition. This occurs for two reasons. First, in the Old Testament the two traditions are fused and often overlap in Israel's faith recitals (see chs. 2–3 above). Several features bind the two traditions together. The pattern of Yahweh's warfare on behalf of Israel, established at the exodus, continues into the conquest narrative and is foundational to both the exodus and conquest traditions.[1] It fuses with the kingship tradition as well, as Cross points out (see ch. 2).

---

[1] The literature on this theme is vast; see especially Lind, *Yahweh Is A Warrior;* Miller, *Divine Warrior,* and "God the Warrior," *Int* 19 (1965), 35–46; P. C. Craigie, "Yahweh Is a Man of War," *SJT* 22 (1969), 183–88; G. E. Wright, *The Old Testament and Theology* (New York: Harper & Row, 1969), ch. 3; W. Janzen, *Still in the Image: Essays in Biblical Theology and Anthropology* (Newton, Kans.: Faith and Life, 1982), 173–211.

God's promise to send an angel before Israel to lead them on the way (peaceably?) into the promised land bridges the exodus and conquest traditions (see Exod 23:20 and 33:2). Second, just as the traditions overlap in Israel's story, so also do they overlap in the Synoptics' story of Jesus. In the gospel story, the traditions blend readily into a common meaning. Liberation from the bondages of sin, devil, and injustice is similar to the conquest of a foe. To illustrate this, Luke continues to tell of exorcisms in the Journey narrative. These may be viewed as conquest stories, but they also exemplify the exodus theme of deliverance from bondage.

Despite these overlapping factors, the central section of all three Gospels distinctly highlights themes and motifs that are part of Israel's conquest narrative. In Mark and Luke the imagery and emphases are unique and striking; they do not occur in the other sections of their Gospels. While Matthew's use of Israel's way-conquest motifs is less evident, his conceptual emphases nevertheless correspond to those of the older story.

Before examining the Gospels, we need a brief description of the conquest tradition(s) of Israel's faith story.

ISRAEL'S WAY-CONQUEST TRADITION(S)

While the term conquest is commonly used in Hebrew Bible scholarship to denote Israel's gaining possession of the land of Canaan, the term itself has no Hebrew text support.[2] The much-used term *yāraš* is regularly translated *to possess* or *to occupy*. As Israel's confessions affirm, the emphasis falls on inheriting the land or receiving it as a gift from Yahweh.

---

[2] A check in Young's *Concordance* reveals the deficiency. I have considered dispensing with the word in this study, but I chose to retain it in order to sustain the connection to OT biblical theological scholarship. Three different scholarly views have been proposed: the traditional view of a combination of military-miracle Yahweh war campaigns as narrated in Joshua 1–11, the view that speaks of exodus tribes joining tribes that never went to Egypt and thus a peaceable settlement in the land (M. Noth and A. Alt), and the view which holds that Israel came into the land during a fortuitous (tenth generation) time, aiding a peasant revolt against the wealthy oppressive city-states (George Mendenhall and Norman Gottwald). Whichever view is held, the main biblical accent is that the land is God's gift to Israel; Israel inherits the land as a fulfillment of promise.

The components of this tradition are God's promise to lead Israel and to give them the land, including the promise to send an angel before them to guard them on the way, and God's miracle-type battles to drive out the enemy nations. While the exodus and conquest traditions overlap and fuse in Israel's recitals of its faith story, Exodus 23:20 serves well as a textual marker for the narrative transition, as noted in ch. 2. Subsequent narrative in Exodus is not always identified with the forward look to the land, but it appears that the canonical compilers intended that it be viewed that way. For example, the giving of the tables of the law in Exodus 34 calls for the ark, which in turn calls for the tabernacle. Above all stands Yahweh's name, and his glory appears at the tent of meeting; Yahweh goes before the people in the cloud by day and the fire by night. This entire portrait reveals God as with the people, moving toward the land of promise.

Deuteronomy portrays Israel's face set toward the land of promise. God's provisions for the covenant people, whether Decalogue, sabbath, sabbatical, Jubilee, regulations for sacrifice, rules for war, or blessings and curses, are all given through the binoculars of faith that sights the promised land. In this context, the so-called conquest tradition may be more aptly designated as "way-to-the-land" tradition. The fulfillment of promise consistently empowers the journey. The emphasis falls on God's leading the people, the people's disobedience and their often recalcitrant spirit (especially in Numbers), and God's steadfast love that outlasts the people's disobedience and rebellion. The conquest is not an end in itself. As Joshua 24 indicates, each generation must acknowledge the land as a gift and answer the integral question: will you serve Yahweh God or the idols of the nations round about you? This choice of loyalty perpetuates the conquest tradition.

The "Yahweh War" component, present in all four major traditions in this study,[3] must also be explicated at several levels. On

---

[3] That Yahweh as Warrior is interconnected to, even lies at the heart of, other traditions such as exodus and kingship, is persuasively argued by Cross, "Divine Warrior," 11–31. L. J. Greenspoon ("The Origin of the Idea of Resurrection," in *Traditions in Transformation: Turning Points in Biblical Faith*, ed. B. Halpern and J. D. Levenson [Winona Lake: Eisenbrauns, 1981], 247–321) contends that Yahweh's holy warfare gives rise to the belief in resurrection in Israel, of which Dan 12:2 is the endpoint, not the beginning (see Deut 32:39; 1 Sam 2:6 for earlier indications). This view, developed with no mention of M. Dahood and his contention that belief in resurrection has a significant place in the Psalms (M. Dahood, *Psalms* [AB; Garden City, N.Y.: Doubleday, 1966]), certainly needs critical assessment. If correct, it provides another element of

one level, the tradition consists simply of war stories, battles in which
Israel often wins and sometimes loses. On another level, the tradition
tells a story of God manifesting divine sovereignty over the covenant
people through both salvation and judgment; wins and losses result from
the people's obedience or disobedience respectively. And at a still deeper
level, the tradition testifies to Israel's reliance on the Lord: will the people
trust the Lord God to provide the way to the fulfillment of the divine
promise? This third level is at the heart of the way-conquest tradition, as
Israel's numerous faith recitals testify (Josh 24; Pss 78; 106; Acts 7).

MARK

More recent Markan scholarship recognizes that Mark crafts
his middle section purposefully. In the absence of geographical designations, another kind of topographical feature, the way/ὁδός, provides settings for the events and teachings.[4] Few scholars, however,
note the relationship between Mark's use of ὁδός in this section (as
well as in 1:2–3) and the function of ὁδός in Israel's first story of
instruction and guidance.[5] The evidence for the impact of the con-

---

continuity between Israel's faith and the Gospels: Warrior-suffering Messiah/
dying King-Resurrected One is a dominant christological portrait of Jesus in
the Synoptics.
    [4]The more accessible treatments of this are W. H. Kelber, *Mark's Story
of Jesus*, 43–56; Swartley, *Mark*, 137–59; E. Best, *Following Jesus: Discipleship in
the Gospel of Mark* (JSNTSS 4; Sheffield: University of Sheffield, 1981), 15–145;
D. M. Sweetland, *Our Journey With Jesus: Discipleship According to Mark* (GNS
22; Wilmington, Del.: Michael Glazier, 1987), 51–69. Best shows the connection
between the 'way' motif and discipleship throughout the Gospel, as do also A.
Stock, *Call to Discipleship: A Literary Study of Mark's Gospel* (GNS 1; Wilmington, Del.: Michael Glazier, 1982) and J. R. Donahue in a brief excellent essay:
The Theology and Setting of Discipleship in the Gospel of Mark (Milwaukee, Wis.:
Marquette University, 1983).
    [5]W. H. Kelber has recognized this connection in several of his writ-
ings; it is most clearly enunciated in his dissertation: "Kingdom and Parousia
in the Gospel of Mark" (Ph.D. diss.: University of Chicago, 1970), 109ff. Kelber's
insight depends, at least in part, on H. Windisch's earlier connection between
Mark's use of "entering into the kingdom of God" and the LXX Deuteronomic
formula of "entering into the land:" "Die Sprüche vom Eingehen in das Reich
Gottes," *ZNW* 27 (1928), 163–92. For additional treatment of the topic see W.
M. Swartley, "The Structural Function of the Term 'Way' (ὁδός) in Mark's
Gospel," in *The New Way of Jesus*, ed. W. Klassen (FS Howard H. Charles;
Newton, Kans.: Faith and Life, 1980), 68–80, and "Markan Structure, 75–86,
163–90.

quest traditions upon Mark's composition of his journey narrative is threefold: Mark's use of ὁδός in relation to this section's content; other features showing conquest (exodus) influences upon this section; and Mark's theological achievement utilizing the conquest traditions.

1. Mark's Use of ὁδός and the Content of 8:27–10:52

The three most prominent emphases of this section are Jesus' messianic identity, especially the Son of humanity (υἱὸς τοῦ ἀν-θρώπου)[6] who must suffer; the recurring passion-resurrection predictions; and the subsequent recurring teaching on discipleship. These interlink tightly in three separate and structurally parallel segments (8:31–38; 9:31–41 or 50; 10:32–45). Christological declarations identifying Jesus with royal messianic hope frame the section: "Messiah" in 8:29 and "Son of David" in 10:47–48.[7] But these declarations are qualified, even controlled, by Jesus' identification of himself as the Son of humanity (8:31; 9:12, 31; 10:32) for whom it is necessary (δεῖ) to suffer and die (8:31; 9:12). But still further, even above these self-designations, towering over them from the high mountain of the Transfiguration, a heavenly voice speaks: "This is my beloved Son; hear him" (9:7). Together with the heavenly voice at Jesus' baptism, "You are my beloved Son, with whom I am well pleased," and the Gentile soldier's confession at the cross in 15:39, "Truly this man was the Son of God," the Transfiguration voice functions as the ultimate christological truth in Mark. Unlike the narrative tension between Messiah and Son of humanity (8:29–33), a paradoxical complementary relationship exists between Son of God and Son of humanity.[8] As

---

[6]Following the suggested translation of F. W. Danker in his review of J. A. Fitzmyer's AB commentary on Luke 1–9 (*Int* 37 [1983], 298), I capitalize *Son* to denote Jesus' special self-consciousness about the uniqueness of his person and mission, and leave *humanity* lower case in order to show the potentially corporate reference (cf. Dan 7:13–14 with 7:27). For recent and discerning views on this much discussed title see B. Lindars, *Jesus, Son of Man: A Fresh Examination of the Son of Man Sayings in the Gospels* (Grand Rapids: Eerdmans, 1983) and the good survey by Goergen, *Mission and Ministry of Jesus* 1.180–204.

[7]Some Markan scholars consider this section to begin with 8:22–26, in which case the frame is two narratives depicting Jesus' healing of blindness. It is difficult to judge on this matter, for these two receptions of sight function well as the climactic emphases of the two sections as well: 8:22–26 for 6:7–8:26 and 10:46–52 for 8:27–10:52.

[8]J. D. Kingsbury, *The Christology of Mark's Gospel* (Philadelphia: Fortress, 1983), 148–50. R. C. Tannehill has shown the dominant narrative role

the Son of humanity fulfills his mission in suffering and death he is confessed as Son of God.

The following pattern reveals the content and purposeful structuring of the section:

Passion-Resurrection Announcement	Disciples Don't Understand	Teaching on Discipleship
1. 8:31	8:32–33	8:34–38
2. 9:31	9:32–34	9:35–50
3. 10:32–34	10:35–41	10:38–45

Each of these three cycles follows the same sequence, and each is connected to Mark's use of ὁδός as the literary frame for this section. The phrase, "whoever will come after me (ὀπίσω μου)" in 8:34 connects the teaching and the cycle back to 8:27 where Jesus is introduced as going "on the way" (ἐν τῇ ὁδῷ).[9] In the center of the second cycle (9:33–34), the phrase ἐν τῇ ὁδῷ occurs twice. The third cycle begins with the phrase, "As Jesus was going on the way (ἐν τῇ ὁδῷ)" (10:32).

Mark uses ὁδός seven times in this section: 8:27; 9:33, 34; 10:17, 32, 46, 52. Matthew has two parallel uses, and Luke only one.[10] Outside 8:27–10:52 and 1:2, 3, Mark also uses ὁδός seven times (2:23; 4:4, 15; 6:8; 8:3; 11:8; 12:14). But here, six have parallels in Matthew, and five occur in Luke.[11] This contrast in usage within and outside this section—only 1:7 or 2:7 for Mark's central section and 5:7 or 6:7 in parallels to Mark—alerts us to a unique Markan use in 8:27–10:52.[12] Mark's seven uses of ὁδός in 8:27–10:52 are also strategically

of Son of God: "The Gospel of Mark as Narrative Christology," *Semeia* 16 (Missoula, Mont.: Scholars, 1980), 57–96. For earlier contributions, see Norman Perrin, "The Creative Use of the Son of Man Traditions by Mark," *USQR* 23 (1967–68), 357–65; P. Vielhauer, "Erwägungen zur Christologie des Markusevangeliums," in *Aufsätze zum Neuen Testament* (TBü 31; Munich: Chr. Kaiser, 1965), 199–214.

[9]N. Perrin, "The Literary Gattung 'Gospel'—Some Considerations," *ExpTim* 82 (1970), 6.

[10]Matthew also has ἐν τῇ ὁδῷ in 20:17b, which roughly, but not precisely, parallels Mark 10:32. Both Matthew (20:30) and Luke (18:35) use the phrase "beside the way" (παρὰ τὴν ὁδόν) in Mark 10:46c.

[11]A sixth (Mark 8:3) occurs within the scope of Luke's great omission and thus has a parallel only in Matthew. Further, Mark's awkward expression, "to make a way" (ὁδὸν ποιεῖν in 2:23) has no parallel.

[12]It also argues against the view that ὁδός is *always* redactional in Mark as proposed by J. Schreiber, *Theologie des Vertrauens: Eine redaktionsgeschichtliche Untersuchung des Markusevangeliums* (Hamburg: Furche-Verlag,

placed. Occurring first in 8:27, the beginning verse of the section, ἐν τῇ ὁδῷ frames Jesus' question about his identity. The same phrase also closes the section (10:52). Mark's preceding section, devoted to the themes of *bread* and *understanding* (6:7–8:21), similarly closes with the section's key term, *understanding* (συνίετε, the last word in 8:21),[13] highlighting the occurrence of ἐν τῇ ὁδῷ at the end of 10:52 even more strongly. Similarly, in Mark 9:33 and 34 the same phrase occurs twice, urging the reader to note that the dispute about greatness took place "on the way."[14] Mark's use of ὁδός functions throughout the

---

1967). Using a structuralist methodology to study Mark's spatial terminology, Malbon in *Narrative Space and Mythic Meaning in Mark* notes the concentration of ὁδός in 8:27–10:52, which she argues "represents the final mediation of the topographical suborder of Mark's Gospel" (104, see also 154). Since she examines only those uses of ὁδός which denote spatial reference, she uses only four texts outside 8:27–10:52 and 1:2–3; 2:23; 6:8; 8:3 and 11:8 (53). The three other uses are 4:4, 15; 12:14. She includes Mark's use of προάγειν for spatial travel imagery and thus has the way motif reappear as the final mediation of the Gospel via προάγειν in 14:28 and 16:7 (165–68).

[13]Verses 22–26 of ch. 8 are probably best regarded as a transitional paragraph between the two sections: A. Stock, "Hinge Transitions in Mark's Gospel," *BTB* 15 (1985), 29. The healing of the blind man by a double touch appears to symbolize the disciples' unfolding messianic understanding pressured by the two bread-feedings and two boat rides (6:30–8:21; N.B. 6:52 and 8:14–21). Hence, the blind man's *seeing*, in Mark's narrative world, symbolizes the dawning awareness of Jesus' messianic identity (8:27–30). But, ironically, Peter and the disciples do not yet see all things clearly. Bartimaeus' opened *seeing* eyes may symbolize that point, occurring at the end of Jesus' hard teachings on discipleship (10:46–52). If that is the case, it supports those who argue that the disciples in Mark are regarded at times in positive as well as negative light: see Robert C. Tannehill, "The Disciples in Mark: The Function of a Narrative Role," *JR* 57 (1977), 386–405, and the summary of the debate in Sweetland, *Journey with Jesus*, 70–84.

[14]These four texts (8:27; 9:33, 34; 10:52) are Mark's most distinctive uses of ἐν τῇ ὁδῷ. Its crucial use in 10:52 puts the blind man "on the way" now following Jesus with opened eyes. This use appears to contrast the phrase in 10:46c where the blind man is sitting "beside the way" (παρὰ τὴν ὁδόν), a phrase likely traditional since it reappears in both Matthew and Luke. In 10:32 ἐν τῇ ὁδῷ (par. Matt 20:17b) denotes the road leading to Jerusalem, a use likely present in the tradition which Mark readily incorporates. In 10:17 the rich man is portrayed as running "into the way" (εἰς ὁδόν) of Jesus. He meets Jesus, learns the cost of discipleship, but does not follow "in the way." It appears probable that Mark consciously portrays the 'way' as the intersecting point, not the path, where Jesus and the rich man met and parted. In this view, εἰς ὁδόν is the abortive form of ἐν τῇ ὁδῷ. It is the point of inquiry about discipleship, but not the path of following Jesus. Similarly, in 10:46c, παρὰ τὴν ὁδόν ("beside the way"), is where the blind sit.

section as a topographical frame for Jesus' teachings on his future as
"Son of humanity" and on the costly discipleship for his followers,[15]
thus uniting Christology and discipleship.[16] Furthermore, the three
ὁδός cycles function also as interchanging segments for the remaining
content of the section:

1. 8:27–38   First ὁδός-Son of humanity/passion/discipleship cycle

2. 9:1–29   Transfiguration followed by an exorcism

3. 9:30–50   Second ὁδός-Son of humanity/passion/discipleship cycle

4. 10:1–31   Teaching on divorce and riches

5. 10:32–45   Third ὁδός-Son of humanity/passion/discipleship cycle

The final paragraph (10:46–52) shows a blind man, calling to
Jesus as "Son of David" for help from "beside the way" (παρὰ τὴν
ὁδόν). Receiving his sight, he then follows Jesus "on the way" (ἐν τῇ
ὁδῷ). In Mark's narrative world, the goal of Jesus' journey has been
achieved: true sight is seeing the real Jesus, the suffering Son of
humanity, and following him *on the way*.[17]

2. Further Evidence of Conquest (Exodus) Influence

Three additional lines of evidence confirm this proposal that
this section of Mark's Gospel bears the imprint of Israel's way-conquest tradition(s). First, Mark 9:1–29 and 10:1–31 contain specific

---

[15]Mark consistently uses the imperfect verb to describe the activity
which took place ἐν τῇ ὁδῷ. In the first three texts (8:27; 9:33, 34), Jesus was
questioning the disciples, denoted by the verb ἐπηρώτα. In 10:32, 52, Mark
connects ὁδός with the imperfect "was following" (ἠκολούθει) in 10:52 and
"following" (ἀκολουθοῦντες) in 10:32 occurring with imperfect verbs. In both
cases, Matthew uses the simple aorist instead of Mark's imperfect. This consistent and distinctive Markan use of the imperfect tense further advances the
argument that Mark handles with care the phrase ἐν τῇ ὁδῷ. The action "in
the way" begins with *questioning* and ends with *following*. In both cases there is
continuing action in past time, a *process* both for Jesus and the disciples.

[16]In 9:33, 34 ἐν τῇ ὁδῷ links the passion prediction and the teaching
on discipleship. In 10:32 ἐν τῇ ὁδῷ introduces the passion statement. In both
8:27 and 10:46, 52 the phrase is directly related to the christological declarations. See above for the link between Messiahship in 8:27–29 and discipleship
in 8:34–37.

[17]See note 9 above. It could be argued that the "way" theme continues
in 11:8. But the character relationships as well as the setting, now Jerusalem,
have significantly changed. Further, it occurs in the triple tradition (Matt
21:8/Luke 19:36). Most striking, while both Matthew and Luke read ἐν τῇ ὁδῷ,
Mark has εἰς τὴν ὁδόν, distinguishing it from the former section.

allusions to events in Israel's Sinai and way-conquest narrative. Second, Mark's sudden prophecy-toned opening (1:2–3), citing and linking several OT ὁδός passages, anticipates his unique use of ὁδός in his journey narrative. In the earlier story these texts functioned as Israel's Magna Carta, announcing the entrance into (Exod 23:20) and return to (Isa 40:3) the promised land.[18] Third, Jesus' self-identification as "Son of humanity" suggests a connection to the "divine warrior" motif in Israel and in the wider ancient Near East.

   a. *Connections between 9:1–29; 10:1–29 and Israel's Sinai and land-entrance experiences.* The transfiguration imagery in 9:2–8 reflects widely recognized allusions to the Sinai/Moses event in Exodus 24.[19] J. A. Ziesler identifies the main connections:[20] the *location on the mountain* (Mark 9:2; Exod 24:12, 15), after *six days* (Mark 9:2; Exod 24:16); both Jesus and Moses take along three named persons up the mountain (Mark 9:2; Exod 24:1, 9);[21] in both cases a voice speaks from the cloud overshadowing the mountain (Mark 9:6; Exod 24:16); and both mention building tents or a tabernacle (Mark 9:5; Exod 25:9). To Ziesler's list can be added the glistening countenance of both Jesus and Moses (Mark 9:2, 3; Exod 34:29–35)[22] and the temporal detail, implicit in Mark and explicit in Exodus, that the voice from the cloud spoke on the "seventh day" (Mark 9:2, 7; Exod 24:16). As Edward C. Hobbs suggests, the story of Jesus' exorcising the demon from the

---

   [18]As Best notes, this is the only formal quotation from the Hebrew Scripture in Mark's entire Gospel (E. Best, "Discipleship in Mark: Mark viii.22–x.52," *SJT* 23 [1970], 326).

   [19]The transfiguration has been understood in various ways: as a displaced post-resurrection narrative (Bultmann), an event best understood in relation to the Feast of Tabernacles occurring at that time in Jesus' ministry (Riesenfeld, Goulder, Ringe, et al.), a key event linking the Gospels' depiction of Jesus with the enthronement of the king (Riesenfeld, Daniélou, and Schreiber), or a combination of the above. For a discussion of these positions, see Donaldson, *Jesus on the Mountain*, 136–48. See also the recent study by W. R. Stegner whose emphasis on the Gospel's use of Israel's traditions matches mine in many respects (*Narrative Theology in Early Jewish Christianity* [Louisville, Ky.: Westminster/John Knox, 1989], 83–104, and the bibliographical summary in W. L. Liefeld, "Theological Motifs in the Transfiguration Narrative," in *New Dimensions in New Testament Study*, ed. R. N. Longenecker and M. Tenney (Grand Rapids: Zondervan, 1974), 162, n. 3.

   [20]J. A. Ziesler, "The Transfiguration Story and the Markan Soteriology," *ExpTim* 81 (1970): 263–68.

   [21]With Moses are also seventy elders (24:1, 9). According to v. 2 Moses only was to "come near to the Lord" while the others worshipped from afar.

   [22]This point comes in the story of Moses' second ascent, but belongs to the Sinai tradition history.

epileptic boy appears as a sequel to the transfiguration just as Moses'
encountering idolatrous Israel—and physically exorcising the idols
from the camp—follows his experience on the mountain.[23] Both
Moses and Jesus descend from the mountain to face the unbelief of
the people[24] (Exod 32:9; 34:9 and Mark 9:19, "O faithless generation"
[ὦ γενεὰ ἄπιστος]).

Another connection between these two sections is the literary framework enclosing the transfiguration story in Mark and the
Mount Sinai events in Exodus. Mark 9:1–29 is placed between two
ὁδός-framed segments (see above and 8:27, 34; 9:33, 34). Also, an
entrance-formula, "entering into the kingdom of God," begins the
segment in 9:1 and recurs three times at the end of the following
ὁδός-cycle (9:43, 45, 47). Similarly, Exodus 24–32 is framed by Israel's
land entrance formulas (Exod 23:23–33; 33:1–3).[25] As Kelber observes, Mark associates his redactional use of ὁδός with another
prominent redactional theme, "entrance into the kingdom of God."
This phrase recurs in 9:47; 10:15, 23, 24, 25, with variant forms in 9:1,
43, 45; 10:14.[26] Guided by a proposal made years ago by Hans Windisch,[27] Kelber argues that Mark's formula is derived from the Septuagint's Deuteronomic phrase of "entering into the land" (Deut 1:8;
4:1; 6:18; 16:20):

> . . . the Markan entrance formula is ultimately derived from a transla-
> tion of Deuteronomy's entrance tradition into an eschatological key.
> Modeled after Israel's first entrance, the present journey into the King-
> dom constitutes a second entry into the Promised Land.[28]

---

[23]Hobbs, "Gospel of Mark," 45–46.

[24]While the structure of the story would attribute the "unbelief" to
the disciples, the use of the term γενεά seems to designate the people as a whole.
This ambiguity may indeed result from the intention of the narrator to echo
Israel's exodus, "way-conquest," story.

[25]In Moses' second ascent the word about driving out the nations
practicing idolatry occurs already on the mountain (34:11–16).

[26]On the basis of the threefold occurrence of (entering) the kingdom
of God in 9:42–50, one might argue for beginning the 10:1–31 segment earlier
or for making a separate segment for 9:38–50. The connection of vv. 33–37 to
38–42 by the recurrence of "in my name" and the focus on "little ones" in 43–48
argue for keeping it all together. Further, the ending exhortation, "be at peace
with one another" (v. 50), is the final answer to the rivalry among the disciples
over who is the greatest.

[27]Windisch, "Die Sprüche, 163–92.

[28]Kelber, "Kingdom and Parousia", 109. In his book, *The Kingdom in
Mark*, Kelber reiterates these points (67–85), but in weakened form since his
emphasis now falls upon imminent parousia expectations and a Galilean Chris-

This correlation between Mark's "entrance into the kingdom" and Deuteronomy's "entrance into the land" heightens the significance of the Transfiguration narrative's allusions to the Mount Sinai event and sheds new light on the enigmatic phrase in 9:1 as well: "Truly I tell you, there are some standing here who will not taste death until they see that the kingdom of God has come with power." When "see the kingdom of God" substitutes for the older story's "see the land," this statement echoes Israel's earlier experience in which only a few members of that generation lived to see the Promised Land.[29] Since for Mark the return to Galilee after the resurrection reestablishes the Galilean proclamation of the kingdom gospel—now with power (cf. Matt 28:16–20)—Bultmann's view that the transfiguration is a displaced post-resurrection narrative (see note 19) gains logical foundation; it fails to grasp, however, the narrative purpose of the event, both in its proleptic function and as an echo of the way/Sinai/entrance traditions. Indeed, as Liefeld concludes, the purpose of the event in its narrative setting is to designate Jesus as "Son of God with power" (cf. Rom 1:4).[30] For Mark, however, such a declaration is too bold without carefully structuring it within another reality, the necessary suffering of the Son of humanity who comes in glory (8:38), bringing the kingdom with power (9:1–9). On both sides of the disclosure of "glory and power" is another inclusio: Jesus' certain suffering and death (8:31–37 and 9:10–13). This point receives more text space than the other. That Elijah is mentioned before Moses in 9:4 is best explained by the prominence given to Elijah in Mark 9:11–13: 9:4 anticipates 9:11–13, verses that underscore the necessity of Jesus' suffering. As the larger section makes clear, Jesus' victory is achieved only through suffering. The christological climax in 15:33–39 makes the same point. For Mark any theology of glory, victory, or conquest is inseparable from a *theologia crucis.*

Some features of 10:1–29 may also hark back to Israel's way-to-the-land experiences. Since it is difficult to understand how the controversy on divorce and remarriage (10:2–12) fits into this section's organization, Hobbs suggests that Moses' discourse on divorce in Deuteronomy 24 provides a structural model. The location of the controversy, "the region of Judea and beyond the Jordan" (10:1) matches Israel's location for Moses' farewell sermon (Deut 1:1–5).[31]

tianity polemic against Jerusalem Christianity.
[29]Kelber, "Kingdom and Parousia," 140.
[30]Liefeld, "Theological Motifs," 179.
[31]Hobbs, "Gospel of Mark," 47–48.

Perhaps even Mark's phrase, ἐκεῖθεν ἀναστάς (10:1, cf. 7:24), alludes to Israel's somewhat aimless but certainly progressive movement toward the east side of the Jordan and into Canaan (cf. Num 23). Other features of 8:27–10:52 recall Israel's way-conquest narrative as well. Kelber and Luz both observe that Mark has numerous redactional uses of ἐξέρχεσθαι ("to go out"/"depart") and εἰσέρχεσθαι ("to come in"/"enter"), imagery derived from Israel's exodus- and entrance-motifs. Kelber identifies nineteen such instances of ἐξέρχεσθαι and eighteen of εἰσέρχεσθαι.[32] Moreover, Mark's ἐν τῇ ὁδῷ section *ends* with Jesus' arrival at Jericho in much the same way that Israel's journey from the wilderness to Canaan climaxed at Jericho (Josh 5:10–15). Mark alone among the synoptics has the distinctive phrase in 10:46a, "And he came into Jericho."[33]

    b. Mark's opening ὁδός *prophecy texts.* Given the above features that connect Mark's journey narrative to Israel's way-conquest tradition, it comes as no surprise that his use of several ὁδός prophecy texts in 1:2–3 anticipates his use of ὁδός in 8:27–10:52. The text quoted from Exodus is God's pledge to Israel: "Behold, I send an angel before you, to guard you on the way and to bring you to the place which I have prepared" (RSV, Exod 23:20). After the title (1:1), Mark cites three Old Testament passages, which only he joins together:

See, I am sending my messenger ahead of you,	Exod 23:20
who will prepare your *way*	Mal 3:1
the voice of one crying out in the wilderness:	Isa 40:3
"Prepare the *way* of the Lord,	
make his paths straight" (italics mine).	

    Two of the OT texts employ ὁδός. The one, Exodus 23:20, is combined with Malachi 3:1; the second is Isaiah 40:3.[34] These three

    [32]"Kingdom and Parousia," 108ff., and *The Kingdom in Mark*, 68; Ulrich Luz, "Das Geheimnis Motiv und die Markinische Christologie" (*ZNW* 56, 1965), 15. Kelber's count (in *The Kingdom in Mark*, 68) includes redactional uses throughout the entire Gospel. Hence the point is not as strong as it first appears.
    [33]Both Hobbs and Austin M. Farrer have recognized this point: Hobbs, "Gospel of Mark," 47–48, and Farrer, *St. Matthew and St. Mark*, 193–94.
    [34]My study of the textual sources of these quotations shows the first to be closest to Targum Onkelos, next closest to the MT of Exodus 23:20 for Mark 1:2b and Malachi 3:1 for 2c. I suggest the source to be a Greek translation

OT texts stand within a deep stream of theological traditions. By its placement at the end of the Book of the Covenant and by its referring specifically to the conquest, the Exodus text underscores both the sanctity of Yahweh's covenant and the prerogative and promise to provide *the way* for the people to fulfill the covenant in the land. Subsequent verses reaffirm the presence of Yahweh's "leading angel" and promise other divine tactics for conquest (i.e., terror, panic, and hornets).[35] The Malachi text is associated with the Lord's coming to purify the temple, a theme fulfilled in Mark in the section immediately following this ὁδός section.

For numerous groups in Israel the Isaiah text historically transmits eschatological hope from one generation to another. In Qumran it supports the sect's decision to begin a purified community waiting *in the desert = wilderness* (*miḏbār*) (1QS 8:12b–16; 9:18c-21). McCasland notes that the term "way," *derek* (ὁδός), denoting study of and faithfulness to the Torah, occurs 33 times in the Manual of Discipline.[36] For them, "wilderness and way" represent their eschatological identity; they live *in the wilderness* to study the *way of Torah.* Thus they prepare the way for the messiah's coming.[37] Mark's ὁδός section comes immediately after his wilderness (ἔρημος) section, reflecting exactly the order of Isaiah 40:3. Similarly, his temple section follows immediately the ὁδός section—replicating the sequence of the larger Malachi 3 text.[38] While scholarship generally has regarded these quotations as introducing only the ministry of John the Baptist, these insights argue for another (the minority) point of view: these two Old Testament quotations signal major themes of the Gospel as a whole, and, together with verse 1, introduce not only John's ministry, but the entire Gospel, as several scholars note. Eduard Schweizer puts the point sharply:

> If we wish to discern what it is that Mark is trying to say, we must observe the way he uses his material. He places these two Old Testament cita-

---

of a Targum. In any event Mark put in *your*/σου for *my*/μου in the last phrase. But the 1:3 quotation from Isaiah is closest to the LXX. Hence it is hard to declare with assurance which textual source Mark used. See Swartley, "Markan Structure," 142, 252–62.

[35]Noth, *Exodus*, 192–93.

[36]V. McCasland, "The Way," *JBL* 77 (1958), 224–25.

[37]In some Qumran texts two Messiahs are expected, a royal and a priestly, thus reflecting the postexilic leadership of Zerubbabel and Joshua.

[38]Much more could be said about the tradition-history of these Old Testament texts. See Swartley, "Markan Structure," 141–62, 252–62.

tions at the beginning so that although they refer directly only to 1:4–8, they still function as a preface to the whole book and introduce everything that follows as the fulfillment of all God's dealings with Israel.[39]

Ernest Best, Ulrich Luz, Paul Minear, and Johannes Schreiber have also connected 1:2–3 with the ὁδός-emphasis of 8:27–10:52.[40] Building upon and advancing beyond these insights, we suggest that this combined Exodus/Isaiah/Malachi quotation anticipates the three sectional sequence of 6:7–8:22 (wilderness/bread), 8:27–10:52 (way/ὁδός), and 11–13 (15) (temple/ἱερόν-ναός). These themes, as literary frames for their respective sections, carry significant theological freight as well.

These two connected ὁδός-quotations confirm Mark's special interest in ὁδός. In both Exodus 23:20 and Isaiah 40:3 "the way" leads to the promised land. Mark patterns his ὁδός in 1:2–3; 8:27–10:52 after the ὁδός of the Old Testament that took the Israelites from Mount Sinai to the promised land.[41] In Mark the promised land is the kingdom of God.

[39]E. Schweizer, *The Good News According to Mark*, trans. D. H. Madvig (Richmond, Va.: John Knox, 1970), 29. J. Bowman has said the same: *Mark*, 11. For a review and assessment of different positions, see R. Guelich, " 'The Beginning of the Gospel': Mark 1:1–15," *BR* 27 (1982), 5–15.

[40]Best, "Discipleship in Mark," 326–329; Luz, "Das Geheimnismotiv," 24–25; Minear, *Saint Mark*, 92; Schreiber, whose view differs in that he regards the whole of Mark as one grand ὁδός processional to Jesus' enthronement, *Vertrauens*, 191–93. A. M. Ambrozic has also noted the programmatic function of 1:2–3 (*The Hidden Kingdom* [CBQMS 2; Washington, D.C.: CBA of America, 1972], 19–20). See also E. Haenchen, *Der Weg Jesu* (Berlin: de Gruyter, 1968).

[41]Ernest Best has summed up well these insights:

> In our section this sense of motion is brought out by the phrase "on the way"; it is found at the beginning of the incident of Peter's confession (8:27); it comes at the end of the second prediction of the Passion when the question of greatness arises (9:33); when Jesus makes the third prediction they are "on the way" going up to Jerusalem (10:32); lastly when Bartimaeus receives his sight it is said that he follows him "on the way" (10:52). If we go back to the beginning of the Gospel and the only formal quotation of Scripture that Mark makes in the whole Gospel we find it again:
>
> "Behold, I send my messenger before thy face,
> who shall prepare thy *way;*
> the voice of one crying in the wilderness:
> Prepare the *way* of the Lord,
> make his paths straight."
>
> Mark's Gospel is the gospel of the Way. It is a way in which Jesus, the Lord, goes and it is a way to which he calls his followers ("Discipleship in Mark: Mark viii.22-x," *SJT* 23 [1970], 326–27).

c. Jesus, Son of Humanity, Divine Warrior. In the narrative linkage between Mark 8:29 where Peter confesses Jesus to be Messiah and 8:31 where Jesus discloses his identity as suffering Son of humanity, Mark interrelates Messiah and Son of humanity. The threefold emphasis on "rebuking" indicates tension between these titles, despite Jack Dean Kingsbury's argument to the contrary.[42] In his article, "The Divine Warrior in the Gospel of Mark,"[43] Bruce A. Stevens argues that Jesus' use of the Son of humanity title recalls an ancient and pervasive divine warrior tradition. He briefly examines the "divine warrior" myth in Canaanite epic, noting the relation there between the high god 'El and the Warrior god Ba'al who defeats Mot (death) and receives from 'El an everlasting kingdom. He then observes a structural parallel in Hebrew thought where Yahweh triumphed over Pharaoh and the gods of Egypt. The scripts are similar, with one essential difference: "The warrior's battle was in history and this broke the a-historical nature of the myth."[44] Stevens also traces the connection in Israel's Scripture between Yahweh as warrior and Yahweh as king. After examining the divine warrior motifs in Jewish apocalyptic literature, he proposes that in Daniel 7:9–14, 27, the "Ancient of Days" is reminiscent of the patriarchal 'El. Further, the "one like the Son of humanity" recalls the triumphant warrior who overcomes the enemy (death) and receives an everlasting kingdom. The "Son of humanity" figure connects also to the corporate "saints of the Most High" (7:27) who suffer in order to gain the victory (7:21; cf. 1:1–20; 3:1–30; 6:6–24). Since divine warrior imagery is associated with the Man in 4 Ezra 13:2–4 and eschatological suffering must precede the coming of the Messiah (2 Bar 27:1–15; 1 Enoch 47) and the coming of the Man (1QH 3:4), including the death of the Messiah in 4 Ezra 7:29, Stevens proposes that Mark 8:29–31 intends to disclose and portray Jesus as the divine warrior.

This tradition illumines the necessity (δεῖ) of the Son of humanity's suffering. Mark puts Messiah and Son of humanity in parallel and connects both to a divinely willed pattern of suffering, death, and resurrection. Drawing upon the apocalyptic genre, Mark

---

[42]Kingsbury holds that the nub of the dispute between Peter and Jesus is on the role of the Messiah-Son of humanity, not on some inherent opposing meanings latent in the titles themselves. See ch. 6, pp. 202–3, for my extensive discussion of this issue.

[43]B. Stevens, "The Divine Warrior in the Gospel of Mark," *BZ* 31 (1987), 101–9.

[44]Ibid., 103.

associates the suffering Messiah, Son of humanity with the victorious divine warrior traditions. Jesus' exorcisms manifest the work of the divine warrior; later, he confidently declares the ultimate triumph of the Son of humanity: "you will see the Son of Man seated at the right hand of the Power, and 'coming with the clouds of heaven'" (14:62).[45] While some may dispute Stevens's joining the Son of humanity and Messiah traditions via the motif of suffering, and may question whether such a conception was part of the theological legacy accessible to Mark, a narrative analysis confirms Stevens's synthesis. The tension arising from the threefold rebuke (see analysis below) results from the fact that other streams of tradition stressed that the Messiah would destroy Israel's enemies (Ps Sol 17:23–42; Pal Targ on Gen 49:11, TJ2 & Neophiti I). The conflict between Peter and Jesus hinges on the selection and interpretation of the traditions, specifically, on the necessity of suffering in this victory.[46] Jesus and Mark may or may not have known the texts cited in Stevens's analysis, but one or both apparently knew the traditions associated with the messianic hope quite thoroughly. Thus the Gospel blends divine warrior-Messiah and Son of humanity into a theological unity, with new coherence within one narrative, in which suffering is the means to victory.

This connection between the Mark 8:29–31 definition of the Messiah's-Son of humanity's work—an emphasis reiterated through Mark 10:45—and the divine warrior motif is an essential and indispensable feature of Mark's ὁδός theology. The emphasis given to Jesus' self-identity and his mission in this section links the Christology of the narrative to the divine warrior motif in Israel's way-conquest faith traditions. Joel Marcus perceives this feature of Mark's use of ὁδός, arguing that the Deutero-Isaian use of the Exodus ὁδός traditions lies behind Mark's use of ὁδός in 1:2–3 and 8:27–52. In Deutero-Isaiah ἀναβαίνει (go up) and ὁδός link the theological traditions of festal procession to the holy city and divine warfare. In Mark, the way is the way to victory that the Lord leads; the disciples follow. The ὁδός of the journey section is not a "human way *to* the βασιλεία but rather . . . God's way, which is his βασιλεία, his own extension of kingly power."[47] "For those with eyes to see (see 4:9, 23), the fearful trek of

---

[45]Ibid.,103–9.

[46]Even those traditions which speak of destroying the enemies often speak of God's doing it without Israel's sword and bow, with the breath of his mouth. The real issue lies in the acceptance of suffering as a way to victory.

[47]J. Marcus, *Way of the Lord*, 33. Marcus makes his point in dispute with Kelber's and Swartley's emphases on ὁδός signifying the way of disciple-

the befuddled, bedraggled little band of disciples *is* the return to Zion, and Jesus' suffering and death . . . *are* the prophesied apocalyptic victory of the divine warrior."[48] Both the first disciples and the readers of Mark's Gospel recognize, therefore, that despite their trials, sufferings, and failures in faith, the "journey up to Jerusalem was the victory march of the divine warrior, casting down every obstacle as he made his triumphant way to Zion, causing the blind to see and the desert to bloom about him (see 6:39; 8:22–26; 10:45–52)."[49] By uniting Son of humanity and divine Warrior, and integrating both thoroughly into the prominent passion predictions and ὁδός framing of this section, Mark forges a distinctive theology: God's victory path for Jesus is through the cross; those who enter God's kingdom must *follow* this suffering Jesus.

3. Mark's Theological Achievement and the Way-Conquest Influence

The theological significance of Mark's weaving Jesus' announced passion and resurrection into the recurring exodus and way-conquest motifs is far-reaching. Many scholars recognize that Mark's ὁδός is indeed the *way* of suffering. Ὁδός in 8:27–10:52 marks not only Jesus' journey to Jerusalem, but also both the *way* of Jesus in his passion and the *way* of disciples who follow him. For all, the ὁδός means suffering.[50] Konrad Weiss[51] and Quentin Quesnell[52] note that 8:27–10:52 concentrates on Jesus' *teaching* on discipleship, in that in this section a much higher percentage of content is teaching than elsewhere in Mark. Weiss and Karl-Georg Reploh further propose that Mark's redactional use of ὁδός is a hermeneutical tool whereby Mark contemporizes Jesus' past history so that Mark's readers hear the call to follow on this way. In this later view, ὁδός leads from Jesus' own

---

ship that leads to the kingdom of God. Actually, both are correct. *Jesus* leads the way and the kingdom is *God's* reign, but the call for disciples to follow Jesus to the kingdom is unmistakably a major accent of Mark's journey narrative.

[48] Marcus, *Way of the Lord*, 36.

[49] Ibid., 37.

[50] Luz, "Das Geheimnismotiv," 24–25; Schweizer, *Good News*, 216, 221–22, 385; Perrin, "Literary Gattung," 6; Best, "Discipleship in Mark," 323–37, hold that ὁδός accentuates the theme of suffering. For a summary of differing interpretations of ὁδός see Swartley, "Structural Function," 77–79.

[51] K. Weiss, "Ekklesiologie, Tradition, und Geschichte in der Jüngerunterweisung Mark viii:27–x:52," in *Der historische Jesu und der kerygmatische Christus*, ed. H. Ristow and K. Matthiae (Berlin: Evangelische Verlagsanstalt, 1960), 412–38. Weiss says, "das Ganze ist Jüngerunterweisung" (419).

[52] Q. Quesnell, *The Mind of St. Mark*, 129.

history to the suffering experience of Christians in Mark's community in the late sixties A.D.[53] Indeed, a closer look at the three passion-and-discipleship-cycles discloses Mark's teaching on necessary suffering that embraces Jesus, his first followers, and those addressed by the narrative. These emphases are essential elements in Jesus' way-conquest theology à la Mark.

In the first cycle Jesus, as the suffering Son of humanity-Messiah, rebukes the disciples for their too eager acclaim of Peter's confession that Jesus is Messiah (ἐπιτιμάω is used already in 8:30). In v. 32 Peter rebukes Jesus for speaking about suffering. Then in v. 33 Jesus sternly rebukes Peter. Two opposing views of messiahship lock horns in this passage. Peter's view reflects the Maccabean model, in which the Messiah will crush the power of the enemy nations.[54] Jesus' view is the way of the suffering Son of humanity. The call to take up the cross means nothing less than willingness to die, to be crucified, for the sake of Jesus' gospel (v. 38), i.e. the kingdom he proclaims. It means losing one's life, being unashamed of Jesus' gospel despite the threat of death (vv. 34–38).

A second confrontation between Jesus and his disciples appears in 9:33–34 where the disciples quarrel over who is the greatest. Here the disciples probably imagine themselves as part of a new ruling government of Palestine, and thus rankle about the ranking of each in the new administration. Jesus responds by calling the disciples to value children, and receive them in "my name." Ranked at the bottom of the social order, the child in Jesus' upside down value system merits care and love. Harsh words of judgment fall on those who cause "one of these little ones who believe in me to sin." The cause of offense to the "little one" or to one's own spiritual welfare must be purged to

---

[53]Weiss, "Ekklesiologie," 425, and K.-G. Reploh, *Markus—Lehrer der Gemeinde: Eine redaktionsgeschichtliche Studie zu den Jüngerperikopen des Markusevangeliums* (SBM 9; Stuttgart: Katholisches Bibelwerk, 1969), 96, 107, 141, 222, 226.

[54]It is striking that the various conceptualizations of evil in and behind biblical thought link war and military weapons to evil itself: in the "Watchers Myth" Asael (Azazel) gives to humans the knowledge of weapons for war (*1 Enoch* 8:1, *OTP*, 1.16); in Genesis 6 the *nephilim* that come from the union of gods and humans are Israel's later giant military foes; in the Isa 14 and Ezek 28 arrogant-king traditions, which provide much of the later imagery for the devil, the kings are dethroned because of oppressive military power and self-deification; in the early *satan* tradition, Satan incites David to take a census for military enlistment. For extensive treatment of the origins of the conceptions of evil reflected in scripture see Neil Forsyth, *The Old Enemy: Satan and the Combat Myth* (Princeton, N.J.: Princeton University, 1987), 44–191.

enter the kingdom of God (v. 47; cf. "life" in vv. 43, 45). Drawing on the imagery of well-prepared salted sacrifices (Lev 2:13), Jesus calls for the self to be purified of evil and ambitious desires, and for his followers to desire to live peaceably with one another (vv. 49–50). This contrasts to the segment's opening portrait of the disciples' disputing with one another over who is the greatest. To walk in the way of Jesus means giving up rivalry over greatness and passionately desiring relationships that do not offend others, but rather yield the fruit of peace.

In the third round of discussion in 10:37, James and John ask for the top seats of power in the coming kingdom: one on the right and one on the left. Jesus' response discloses more fully his messianic mission's transformation of conquest theology. Jesus promises them that they will share in the cup he will drink (see Mark 14:36) and the baptism with which he will be baptized, but that their request is not his to grant. The other ten are indignant, presumably because of James' and John's greedy grasp for power. Then Jesus, calling them together, spoke words that summarize his kingdom way:

"You know that among the Gentiles those whom they recognize as their rulers (RSV, to rule/ἄρχω) lord (κατακυριεύουσιν) it over them, and their great ones (μεγάλοι) are tyrants (RSV, exercise authority/ κατεξουσιάζουσιν) over them. But it is not so among you; but whoever wishes to become great (μέγας) among you must be your servant (διάκονος), and whoever wishes to be first among you must be slave (δοῦλος) of all. For the Son of Man came not to be served but to serve (διακονέω), and to give his life a ransom for many (λύτρον ἀντὶ πολλῶν) (10:42–45).

The verbal and grammatical links between these sentences are crucial. The first sentence speaks of political power and rule, denoted by verb forms of "to lord" (κατακυριεύω) and "to exercise authority" (κατεξουσιάζω); both verbs carry overtones of oppressive rule. Those who so rule are called *great people*. The second sentence is hooked to the first by the word *great*, and the word *great* is sharply redefined: to be great is to be servant. This point is reinforced by restatement, using the image of *first* (πρῶτος), which here means "the head of things." In other words, the head must be the slave of all. The second and third sentences are joined by the connective *For* (γάρ), used with the intensive καί, which here is best translated *also* (as in RSV). This puts the way of the Son of humanity and the way of his disciples into parallel relationship. The service (διακονέω) of the Son of humanity matches and is the foundation for the service of the disciples (who are called to be διάκονοι). Jesus and the disciples are indissolubly linked in this new version of greatness, which is indeed a new ὁδός-conquest theology of thought and action. For the Son of humanity, this life-giving service has ultimate benefit: a ransom for many. Whether this should be considered part of the parallel structure between Jesus and the disciples is debatable. While most of the belabored exegesis of this saying lies outside the scope of this study,[55] the essential point is that Jesus' giving his life as a ransom benefits the many. And although the element of substitution is present,[56] the overall context demands a strong emphasis on the binding relationship between the Redeemer and the redeemed. The redeemed, i.e., the followers of Jesus, are linked to Jesus, to the servant-head who leads the ransomed into servant-living. Certainly this was one of Mark's primary aims in writing the Gospel:

---

[55]M. Hooker has argued that the phrase λύτρον ἀντὶ πολλῶν does not have Isaiah 53:12 as its background: M. Hooker, *The Son of Man in Mark* (Montreal: McGill University, 1967). If, however, we focus on Mark's portrait of Jesus as servant of justice akin to the servant in Isaiah 41–61, then the assessment of the textual similarity needs reappraisal. Hooker's scope of considerations is too narrow and is not oriented sufficiently to the larger role of the servant in Isaiah. The vicarious suffering of 53:12 is not the starting point for the servant's role; the servant's role begins with faithfully proclaiming God's justice and salvation to Israel and the nations (42:1–6; 49:1–7). Mark portrays Jesus' mission precisely in those perspectives.

The Maccabean martyr theology (see 2 Macc. 7; 4 Macc. 6 and 21) is also pertinent. In accepting torture and death, Eleazar says, "Make my blood their purification and take my life as a ransom for theirs" (4 Macc. 6:29; *OTP*, 1.552). Similarly, "let our punishment be a satisfaction on their behalf" (v. 28). For analysis of impact on NT views of atonement, see S. K. Williams, *Jesus' Death As Saving Event: The Background and Origin of a Concept* (HTR Diss. 2; Chico, Calif.: Scholars, 1975), 76–90, 165–202, 230–34; J. Pobee, *Persecution and Martyrdom in the Theology of Paul* (JSNTSS 6; Sheffield: JSOT Press, 1985), 13–46.

Further, does ἀντί mean *instead* (hardly in 1 Cor. 11:15 and Matt. 5:38) or *face to face*, its root meaning? If the latter, then rather than emphasizing substitutionary atonement, followers are linked to Jesus as representative head (see V. Taylor, *The Atonement in New Testament Teaching* [London: Epworth, 1945], 182–96). The person ransomed is bound to the Ransomer, as disciple and servant. This view fits well Mark's logic: Christology forms the basis of discipleship. Nonetheless, it is *Jesus* who gains the victory *for us* (*extra nos*); we participate in his victory (see T. N. Finger, *Christian Theology: An Eschatological Approach* [Scottdale, Penn.: Herald, 1985], 1.303–48).

[56]J. R. W. Stott cites Mark 10:45, and the similar phrase in 1 Tim 2:6, for support of the substitutionary view of the atonement (*The Cross of Christ* [Downers Grove: InterVarsity, 1986], 146–48, 177–79). But Mark 10:42–45 connects discipleship and atonement: Jesus' self-giving life and death function prototypically for discipleship. Goppelt has commendably emphasized this interconnection (*Theology*, 1.194–99).

to set forth Jesus' life, death and resurrection as a call to and an empowerment for faithful discipleship.

This final teaching on the way (ἐν τῇ ὁδῷ), set within the conquest (exodus) imagery of the Old Testament, leaves no doubt that Jesus is presenting a countermodel of greatness for the ordering of social and political relationships. If entering and living within the kingdom are guided by this new empowering imagery, which subverts prevailing empire images, then the "way-conquest" tradition has been transformed. The divine warrior/Son of humanity/Messiah attains the victory through suffering and death, and thereby ransoms many. The inclusio images of Jesus' teaching in this section, *cross* (8:34) and *giving his life as a ransom* (10:45), link the disciples to Jesus in a follower-leader relationship so that Jesus' life and work as Warrior, true Human, and Ruler are the foundation for discipleship.

Mark's servant Jesus does not avoid the fight against evil. Cross-bearing and servanthood are not substitutes for the task of overcoming evil. Rather, God's victory comes in a most unsuspecting way: the way of self-denial, humble service and the very giving of one's life for others.[57] This is the *way of Jesus. And there is also the resurrection*, a vital part of every passion prediction on the way. Jesus' ὁδός is not simply a way to death, but also a way to God's victory.[58] Jesus' death, as a "ransom for (ἀντί) many," assures this victory. For Jesus and his disciples the way of faithful warfare was and is that of humble service, even unto death.[59] God vindicates the faithful.

---

[57]This accords with atonement theories that emphasize Jesus' humiliation and death as tricking the devil (cf. 1 Cor 2:6–8).

[58]Here Malbon's inclusion of προάγειν in Mark 14:28 and 16:7 with ὁδός is strategic, for it enables us to see that the finale of the story is victory beyond death (*Narrative Space and Mythic Meaning*, 70–71, 166–168).

[59]This raises the question whether this means that Jesus' followers should seek suffering, as evidence of their Christian identity, a view that appears in second-century martyr literature, especially Ignatius, who passionately desires martyrdom (Ign. *Rom* 4:1–2; 5:1–3) so that he will be worthy to attain God. But even here, a close study indicates that his worthiness and assurance of true martyrdom are intertwined with the unity of the church over which he was bishop (W. M. Swartley, "The Imitatio Christi in the Ignatian Letters," *VC* 27 [1973], 98–103). D. Patte's exposition of 1 Thess 1:6–7 contends that Paul assured the Thessalonian believers of their own Christ-identity by means of their suffering (D. Patte, *Paul's Faith and the Power of the Gospel: A Structural Introduction to the Pauline Letters* [Philadelphia: Fortress, 1983], 134–40).

For theological perspective to this issue, the sequence of the Markan narrative sections is important. In the Galilean ministry Jesus proclaims the gospel of the kingdom of God. This leads to the clash with the religious leaders.

MATTHEW

1. Content and Structure

Matthew's central section begins at 16:13 and ends at 20:34. Virtually all the content found in Mark appears in Matthew, and in the same order. But Matthew has additional content. Peter's confession that Jesus is "the Christ" includes "Son of the living God." Most significant for this are Jesus' subsequent words:

> Blessed are you, Simon Bar-Jona. For flesh and blood has not revealed this to you, but my Father who is in heaven. And I tell you, you are Peter, and on this rock I will build my church, and the powers of death (gates of Hades) shall not prevail against it. I will give you the keys of the kingdom of heaven, and whatever you bind on earth shall be bound in heaven, and whatever you loose on earth shall be loosed in heaven.[60]

Even though Matthew utilizes the synoptic passion predictions that emphasize the way of the suffering Son of humanity, his literary achievement effects a new narrative. Matthew's sectional structure is as follows:

16:13–20   Peter's confession and Jesus' founding the church.

16:21–17:23 Teaching on discipleship framed by passion-resurrections predictions[61] as an inclusio for this segment that includes the transfiguration and subsequent exorcism.

17:24–18:35 Status, conduct, and responsibilities for life in the kingdom.

19:1–20:16 Costly demands and kingdom reversals.

In this respect, suffering is a consequence of gospel mission. Kingdom witness provokes suffering, a consequence and condition of gospel witness. As the African proverb puts it: "Those who would give light must endure burning."

[60] Matthew also has an additional lengthy section, 17:24–18:35, that shares with Mark only the first nine verses of chapter 18 (except v. 7 on offenses). Similarly, the parable of the laborers in the vineyard in 20:1–16, illustrating that "the last will be first, and the first last" (19:30; 20:16), is not in Mark. Other differences include: the disciples' failed exorcism focuses almost entirely on Jesus' call of the disciples to faith (the faith of the father is absent altogether); an additional teaching about eunuchs being eunuchs for the sake of the kingdom comes at the end of the divorce pericope (19:12); and an additional verse about the Twelve sitting on twelve thrones judging the twelve tribes of Israel appears in the teaching following Jesus' encounter with the rich man (19:28). Many other more minor but significant differences occur as well.

[61] In the first passion prediction "he," referring to Christ, substitutes for "Son of humanity" (16:21). The second cycle is expanded by the long section of 17:24–18:35 so that the overall structure of the section is different.

20:17–34 Third passion-resurrection prediction and teaching on discipleship, with the finale of two blind men receiving
their sight from Jesus *the Lord.*

Matthew's explicit use of the older story appears in his transfiguration account, which accentuates the Moses and Mount Sinai
imagery: Moses' name comes before Elijah's; Jesus' face *shines like the
sun* (cf. Exod 33:29–35); the cloud is a *bright* cloud which echoes the
shekinah glory; and the Son is *one with whom I am well pleased,*
echoing the servant of Isaiah 42:4 who is destined to bring Yahweh's
law to the nations.[62] As Donaldson observes, however, all Moses
typology, heightened though it be, "is absorbed into and transcended
by the Son-Christology." Indeed, Peter's speech is interrupted (17:5, ἔτι
αὐτοῦ λαλοῦντες) by the bright cloud and voice from the cloud.[63] The
voice confirms Peter's confession: "Christ, Son of the living God."
Further, for Matthew the mountain location carries additional meaning, for it ties the event to the beginning and end of Jesus' ministry:
the Mount of Temptation, where Jesus' rule over the kingdoms of the
world—the last temptation—is a contest between God and the devil,
and the Mount of Commissioning, where Jesus exclaims in triumph,
"All authority in heaven and on earth has been given to me." Standing
in the middle of these two moments and mountains is the Transfiguration moment and mountain. It proleptically signals the final
victory and enthronement of the royal Son.[64]

Beyond this loud echo of Sinai imagery, Matthew, differing
from Mark and Luke, lacks explicit reference to the way-conquest
motifs of the older story. Its conceptual emphases, however, are strikingly analogous to the conquest. Indeed, Matthew crafts a narrative
that zeroes in on *that which he and his community deem essential for
both foundational and continuing victory in the life of the church.* This
he does with astounding power and scope. Five features of his achievement toward this end are discernible:

(a) Jesus is portrayed in full christological portrait, which
throughout the narrative breathes assurance of power for victory now
(16:16–19) and certain triumph "in the new world, when the Son of
humanity shall sit on his glorious throne" (19:28).

(b) Jesus will build his church, the church is given authority,
and the powers of Hades shall not prevail against it.

[62]W. D. Davies, *Setting*, 51–52.
[63]Donaldson, *Jesus on the Mountain*, 148, 150.
[64]I am indebted to Donaldson for this synthesis (*Jesus on the Mountain*, 152–56).

(c) The sons of the kingdom are free from the powers, but voluntarily subordinate themselves.

(d) Every member of the kingdom bears responsibility to keep every member in and all sin and evil out of the community.

(e) Victory comes through costly discipleship, servanthood, and surprise reversals.

2. Matthew's Narrative Achievement

Matthew's Jesus assures victory, and that is foundational for the church's victory. In the design of the section the church's victory depends upon Jesus' victory and Jesus' authority in the community. As Daniel Patte puts it, the disciples "do not yet know how they as disciples should relate to the presence of evil (cf. 13:1–53). It is this fundamental change of perspective that Matthew hopes to achieve by means of the last part of the Gospel."[65]

a. Full christological portrait. Jesus emerges in the narrative as "Son of (the living) God" (16:16) as anticipated in 14:33. With a background in 2 Samuel 7:14 and Psalm 2, the ascription carries divine authority and power. In Peter's confession, it is *revealed* by "my Father who is in heaven." Any lingering doubts about divine credentialing vanish completely with the confirming "voice from the cloud, . . . 'This is my beloved Son, with whom I am well pleased; listen to him' " (17:5). The "tax and fish" story's comic relief to Jesus' second passion prediction underscores Jesus' Sonship—he is the son of the king of the temple (17:24). Then in a most serious mood Jesus as Son sets out "the will of my Father who is in heaven" (18:14) regarding offenses that cause "little ones" to fall away and sins within that destroy vitality and victory in the community; Jesus' appeal is to "my Father" (18:10, 19, 35).

Joining this narrative perspective of Jesus' authoritative Sonship is his *authority* as "Lord." Both a petitioner for help (17:15) and Peter as foremost disciple (18:21) address Jesus as "Lord." The narra-

---

[65]D. Patte, *The Gospel According to Matthew: A Structural Commentary on Matthew's Faith* (Philadelphia: Fortress, 1987), 244. By "last part" Patte means the third part of Matthew, following Kingsbury's divisions. In a footnote Patte says that Kingsbury, however, fails to see this fundamental rhetorical purpose in the last part of the Gospel (258, n. 1). Jesus' teaching on this matter occurs in this transitional (Galilee to Jerusalem) section; Jesus' own demonstration of it occurs in the pre-passion and passion sections in Jerusalem.

tive ends with two blind men crying out three times to Jesus as *Lord* for mercy and sight (20:30, 31, 33).

While Matthew is clear that the Son of humanity must suffer, be put to death, and be raised again (17:9, 12, 22; 20:18, 28), he speaks also of Jesus' future role as Son of humanity in eschatological judgment. Of Matthew's three distinctive Son of humanity sayings (16:27; 16:28; 19:28), the third most clearly discloses Matthew's conquest emphasis: "Truly, I say to you, in the new world, when the Son of man shall sit on his glorious throne, you who have followed me will also sit on twelve thrones, judging the twelve tribes of Israel." The present life of the church community stands under the shadow of eschatological judgment. In turn, the eschatological judgment of the Son of humanity, in which the church participates, warrants the church's present accountability in mediating salvation in Jesus Christ and implementing discipline, both denoted by the charge "to bind and loose."

Accordingly, the One confessed to be the Christ, and who also accepts the confession (16:16, 20), holds full authority over the present and the future as Son of God, Lord, and Son of humanity. While the power of the victory of the cross and resurrection shines through the narrative in this full christological portrait, the appropriation of this victory for the disciples and Matthew's community shapes Jesus' didactic interaction with his disciples. Gaining victory is assured; maintaining victory is prescribed.

b. The Church's authority and the Gates of Hades. Matthew declares victory for Jesus and the church by emphasizing Jesus' authority and extending that authority to Peter and the church. P. Ellis suggests that Matthew's structure is such that the final authoritative portrait of Jesus in 28:16–20 has impact upon the whole Gospel in widening concentric circles.[66] His point is especially evident in 16:16–19, for these verses anticipate the final trumpet blast of victory, "All authority in heaven and on earth has been given to me" (28:18). Six narrative statements contribute to the authority of "the Christ" and the church: the Christ is the "Son of the living God"; the confession is not of flesh and blood, but a revelation of the Father; Jesus will build his church on "this rock," Peter and his confession; the powers of Hades shall not prevail against it; "I will give you the keys of the kingdom of heaven," and "whatever you bind on earth shall be bound in heaven, and whatever you loose on earth shall be loosed in heaven."

---

[66]P. Ellis, *Matthew*, 20–25.

Exegetical commentary on these points differs considerably, especially
in relation to Peter's role as rock and the ongoing consequence of his role
in the community.[67] But the underlying point, for whatever position
taken on that matter, is that Jesus confers upon Peter and the church
the authority which God delegated to Jesus as the Christ (28:18).
According to 18:18, the binding and loosing authority is given to all the
disciples, which Matthew's readers understand as embracing themselves.

The crucial points for grasping Matthew's conquest theology
in these declarations are: First, the source of Peter's revelation is
divine disclosure; it is not of human origin, nor can it be understood
by human thinking (vv. 22–23). Jesus' rebuke connects the confession
to the forthcoming passion sayings, thus integrating the authority
given in this text with the way of suffering and death. Likewise, "Son
of the living God" connects the confession to the heavenly voice at the
Transfiguration.

Second, anchored upon Peter's confession of faith stands the
church.[68] It will not be prevented in its authority and power by the
gates of Hades itself. As Patte notes, this may mean that "the church
will conquer the realm of Hades or the church will resist the attack
from the realm of Hades."[69] Patte opts for the former since the
metaphor "gates" is not offensive but defensive; the defensive gates
cannot withstand the conquering power of the church, even over the
realm of the dead. The powers of evil—even those in Hades—must
submit to the authority of Jesus, the Christ and Son of the living God.
Jesus' earlier exorcisms and his conferring this authority to his disciples (10:1) testify to this power.

---

[67]J. P. Meier identifies the foundation rock with Peter; "Firmly
founded on Peter, his church will never be shaken by the assaults of the nether
world" (J. P. Meier, *The Vision of Matthew: Christ, Church, and Morality in the
First Gospel* [New York et al.: Paulist, 1979], 113). Schweizer concurs: "The 'rock'
is Peter himself, not his confession" (*Good News*, 341). But Gundry argues that
Πέτρος is not πέτρα. Rather, πέτρα, the "rock," consists of Jesus' teaching; " '*this*
rock' echoes '*these* my words' " of 7:24, upon which foundation disciples are to
build (*Matthew: A Commentary*, 334).

[68]For a parallel Schweizer notes, "A Jewish saying that calls Abraham
a rock on which God will build the world contains the Greek word πέτρα, and
may therefore be an echo of our saying or a polemical countersaying" (*Good
News*, 342).

[69]Patte, *Matthew*, 232–33. In the Old Testament Yahweh has the
authority to bring back from the dead as in Isa 38:10,17–18; Wis 16:13 (Meier,
Vision, 112). Gundry cites numerous texts where "Gates of Hades" stands for
death (*Matthew: A Commentary*, 332–33).

This bold declaration that the church is founded upon the rock with power over Hades voices Matthew's conquest theology. The powers to be conquered are not, as in the first story, some group of pagan people, even though they be idolatrous (cf. Deut 18:9–14).[70] The understanding of who the "enemy" is has shifted radically. People as such are no longer to be conquered and destroyed. Rather, evil powers in the spiritual realm are identified as the opponents of Jesus and his followers. But not even the headquarters of these powers will prevail against the church as it carries forward its heavenly mandate. Having authority over Hades—the realm of the dead—may also include Jesus' own descent into Hades to announce salvation to the spirits in prison (1 Pet 3:19).

Third, the conferred authority to bind and loose has two levels of meaning. First, in light of intertestamental literature and Jesus' own exorcisms, it designates the authority to bind the powers of Satan and loose people bound by demonic powers.[71] This includes the authority to loose people from sin in the mediation of forgiveness to the repentant (18:15–35; cf. Acts 5:1–11 for the negative side of this power). Second, this authority to bind and loose denotes the task of moral discernment, i.e., declaring what is binding in the law and what may be relaxed.[72] While the halakic meaning accords with Matthew's

---

[70]The rationale for such destruction was that pagan idolatry was empowered by demons (Deut 32:17; Pss 96:5; 106:37).

[71]J. E. Toews, "Jesus Christ the Convenor of the Church," in *Jesus Christ and the Mission of the Church*, ed. E. Waltner (Newton, Kans.: Faith and Life, 1990), 39; R. H. Hiers, " 'Binding and Loosing': The Matthean Authorizations," *JBL* 104 (1985), 233–50. Contra J. D. M. Derrett's view that "bind" means to forbid certain acts and "loose" means to permit certain acts, Herbert W. Basser argues similarly to Toews and Hiers, saying that the better understanding of Matthew's phrase is to take "bind" to mean "to put into chains" and "loose" to mean "to set free" ("Derrett's 'Binding' Reopened," *JBL* 104 [1985], 299). See also Basser's response to Marcus' article: "Marcus' 'Gates': A Response," *CBQ* 52 (1990), 307–8.

[72]Patte takes this view, *Gospel*, 233. So also Joel Marcus, "The Gates of Hades and the Keys of the Kingdom (Matt 16:18–19)," *CBQ* 50 (1988), 443–55. But Marcus dismisses too quickly R. H. Hiers's proposal that "binding and loosing" denote exorcistic action. Thus, Marcus argues for a halakic meaning, the "promulgation of the true, divinely revealed torah" (450). But Marcus's own concluding paragraph betrays him, when he says that the "church will . . . be the *site of the battle* between the powers of Hades and the power of heaven" and that in the endtime "the kingly power of God . . . will break forth from heaven to enter the [battle] arena against the demons" unleashed from the gates of the underworld (455). This is hardly halakic language! Granted, as Marcus says, it is by teaching the true torah in all the world to the end of the age that believers

catechetical emphasis, as in Jesus' words in the Sermon on the Mount, the former accords more with the context of the repetition of this conferred authority in 18:18. Because of this connection to 18:18 and the general orientation to guarding against sin in this Matthean section, the first dimension of meaning appears to be more strongly in view. But to bind and loose people from the bondage of sin presupposes knowledge of what is right and wrong.[73] Hence, both levels of meaning are in view.[74]

The authority and power here given to the disciples do not exempt from suffering, as the subsequent passion predictions and teaching on discipleship indicate. But it is, nonetheless, an authority that promises the church ultimate victory over Satan and his hosts and also over political powers arraigned against God's work, as Jesus' passion story archetypally signifies.

c. Free from, but subordinate to the powers. Matthew's transitional pericope between the first and second major segments (17:24–27) appears to be unconnected to its context. Why place a fish story about temple tax immediately after the second passion prediction? Is this narrative comic relief from the intensity of the mounting drama and emotion since verse 23 ends by describing the disciples as "greatly distressed"? Or must we forgo narrative intent and say that it simply happened in Jesus' ministry and that Matthew thought it important to record? But why? Especially now when the temple no longer stands and there is no Jewish temple tax for Matthew's readers?[75] The question of narrative meaning cannot be bypassed.

---

are empowered to withstand the erupting powers of the netherworld. But this, in my judgment, puts halakic vigilance into the service of exorcistic victory. Hence both levels of meaning, the exorcistic and halakic, belong to the "binding and loosing" commission.

[73]R. Schnackenburg cites Lev 19:17ff.; 1QS 5:24–26; CD 7:2; 9:8 for Jewish precedence for such mutual disciplinary responsibility within the community: *Matthäusevangelium 16,21–28,20* (Würzburg: Echter, 1987), 172.

[74]D. C. Duling has shown the wide range of possible meanings of "to bind" and "to loose" in his article, "Binding and Loosing: Matthew 16:19; Matthew 18:18; John 20:23," *Forum* 3 (4, 1987), 3–31. One suggestion (by Emerton) is that it is to be connected with the Targum on Isa 22:22: "to open" (*pth*) and "to shut" (*'hd*); another suggestion connects it with the Targum on Gen 4:7 and Num 30, "to loose and forgive" (*šry wšbq*). Duling holds that it is Matthean in origin, but this decision does not solve the question of meaning.

[75]Nor is it likely that tax for the Roman temple Jupiter Capitolinus is in view, for that would put Jesus in sonship relation to that temple's god. To locate meaning for this in relation to some obligation of Jewish Christians in

The answer, in light of Matthew's emphases, appears to be twofold. It underscores Jesus' sonship in relation to the Lord of the temple, and it also declares freedom from the powers of the "kings of the earth" for Jesus' disciples and those who receive the Gospel (the ideal readers). The prior passion prediction put Jesus in relation to the powers: "he will be delivered into the hands of men" who will kill him. But the story, by underscoring Jesus' sonship and his disciples' derived sonship, frees Jesus and his followers from the power of the powers.[76]

The story's influence upon way-conquest theology lies in its depiction of Jesus' and the Christian community's freedom from the powers. The temple tax was instituted as part of the Sinai–tabernacle tradition (Exod 30:11–16) and later supported the centralized cult in Jerusalem.[77] The entire temple complex represents Jewish political and religious power (see ch. 5). Essential to Jewish freedom and independence, the temple complex witnessed to the subjugation of the enemy Canaanite peoples (recall 15:26, discussed in ch. 3). For Jesus to declare freedom for his followers, against Peter's presumption of loyalty, is possible only when the old conquest theology is refused and another basis for freedom has been chosen. Jesus' response shows his choice of this freedom, a freedom not dependent upon or guaranteed by any political power. Further, this freedom is so assured that one can pay the tax even though one is not in theological principle obligated to do so. Hence, to avoid offense Jesus counsels a voluntary subordination that by its freedom is socio-politically revolutionary, for it owes nothing to the political structures for its life and power.

A close reading of this story shows that it is thematically connected to what precedes and what follows. On the topic of the community's relation to the powers, which could produce great distress (ἐλυπήθησαν σφόδρα), the story shows—with some humor—that not all issues with the authorities are life threatening.[78] Believers

---

Matthew's time is difficult. Gundry does so by dating the Gospel prior to the fall of Jerusalem (*Matthew: A Commentary*, 357).

[76]The story may also speak to certain questions facing the Matthean community, such as loyalty to government and/or loyalty to certain ongoing Jewish prescriptions.

[77]See Gundry's citations, dependent on H. Montefiore (*Matthew: A Commentary*, 357).

[78]We should not deduce from this pericope a blanket response to all questions about the Christian duty to pay all taxes. The temple tax, e.g., is quite different from the drachma emperor tax in Mark 12:13–17 and par. See W. M. Swartley, "The Christian and the Payment of Taxes Used for War" (Elkhart: Ind.: New Call to Peacemaking, rev. 1985), 3–7.

should not needlessly offend the powers; hence the miraculous catch of tax! Matthew's Jesus thus advises believers to "avoid offense" (μὴ σκανδαλίσωμεν), a *Stichwort* that connects this story to chapter 18, where the topic of offense shifts to an internal community context. In this way the temple tax episode has narrative unity with that which precedes and follows it.

d. Keeping all members in and all sin out. Chapter 18 may be viewed as a ring composition with verse 14 as the center and the governing accent: "So it is not the will of my Father who is in heaven that one of these little ones should perish." Verses 10–13 and 15–20 expand on both sides the pressing concern to keep each one in and every sin out. Further, these same two concerns are then expanded at both ends by teaching against causing a "little one" or allowing oneself to sin through offenses (vv. 5–9) and the imperative of forgiveness to keep sin from gaining power in a community (vv. 21–35). The key question in verses 1–4, "Who is the greatest in the kingdom of heaven?" then may be regarded as a title introducing the discourse.

The opening paragraph thus introduces all of chapter 18 as extended teaching that stands in some sort of sequential relationship to the second passion-resurrection prediction. But the linkage is not at all clear; we see only that maintaining victory in the community is the focus of the teaching following the second prediction, and that the entire admonition is joined together by key words such as *offense, children/little ones, sin,* and *forgiveness.* Further, the teaching on *binding and loosing* as the responsibility of the whole community connects the entire discourse to 16:19.

It is beyond the scope of this study to expound the various elements of teaching in the chapter. The essential emphasis for this study is that here Jesus prescribes the way the victory of the Son of the Father is maintained in the community (vv. 15–18). The solemn procedure outlined in verses 15–18 shows that sin may not be played with in the community; "binding and loosing" and pronouncements of forgiveness in the name of Jesus are the prescriptions of Matthew's Jesus for maintaining the triumph of Jesus gained by his life, death, and resurrection.

e. Costly discipleship and the call to be a servant. The latter part of Matthew's journey narrative (19:1—20:34) utilizes the synoptic tradition to underscore the cost of discipleship and to focus on Jesus' call to live as a servant. These are essential for sharing with Jesus in his Father's kingdom. The points to be made are the same as for

Mark, except that both the cost and reward are intensified. The cost is intensified by showing that Jesus' hard words about marriage may lead some to become eunuchs for the sake of faithfulness to God's will (19:11–12). The reward for faithful discipleship is intensified by promising the Twelve, who left all, future seats upon twelve thrones, judging the twelve tribes (19:28). Similar to Mark's presentation of Jesus' teachings in this segment, the demands of the kingdom are appropriated into three arenas of life: family, possessions, and exercise of power. The respective accents in Jesus' teaching on these three topics are be faithful, divest and follow, and be a servant. These features of obedient living mark those who, like the two blind men, call Jesus *Lord*, receive sight, and continue to follow Jesus (20:29–34). Thus, Jesus' victory is appropriated into faithful and triumphant living for the believers in Matthew's time and setting.

But a principle of surprise permeates final triumph and reward: "the last will be first, and the first last" (20:16; cf. 19:30). Those who have "left houses or brothers or sisters or father or mother or children or lands for my name's sake, will receive a hundredfold, and inherit eternal life." These are those who, like the disciples, appear to be the losers. *But* remember, "the last (will be) first, and the first last." Further, those who think they enjoy special standing with God are in for a surprise. Those who started late will also get full reward: these last will be first, and the first ones will be last. Though elements of Jewish-Gentile reversal are here readily perceived, the text gives no specific clues for such. The context on either side makes the parable apply to basic ways of thinking about discipleship: specifically Jesus promises that those who give up valued relations and things for the gospel will gain in the end. Faithful work in Christ's vineyard, whether long or short, will be rewarded. Both last and first, if faithful, will realize reward.

Analogically, this pattern of thought matches that of Israel's view that the land was a gift (Josh 24:12; Deut 1:30). Just as active trust in Yahweh as leader in the conquest mattered most, so here trusting and faithful obedience is all that matters in realizing God's reward in the end. Any notion of humanly grasping the promise, or worse, earning it, is completely ruled out.

Apart from the transfiguration narrative, Matthew's journey section has no overt reference to explicit way-conquest motifs from the older story, except the entrance formulas, which in Matthew especially are not adequate to establish explicit connection. But in conceptual form the emphases of the section are analogical to those in the conquest. Gaining and maintaining the promised final reward function is the section's warp; the woof is the synoptic core of Jesus' necessary suffering and death as the way to resurrection victory that opens the "new world" for Jesus' followers.

LUKE

Though Matthew's central section lacks explicit journey motifs or structural features that connect his victory and reward emphases to Israel's conquest traditions, Luke's central section out-Marks Mark in this regard. Few sections of Scripture can boast of such numerous and noble attempts to comprehend its purpose, structure, and essential nature. James L. Resseguie has done scholars a yeoman's service in describing the many divergent and complementing scholarly efforts—from 1856 to 1975—to unlock Luke's enigmatic achievement.[79] Since 1975 Kenneth E. Bailey, M. D. Goulder, and Sharon H. Ringe have provided some new notions, or modifications of old notions, of what Luke intended.[80] As both Resseguie and David Gill discern, the limits of the section are 9:51 and 19:44.[81] The last few verses are distinctively Lukan, and 19:45 locates Jesus in the temple, which marks the beginning of the next section. Verse 41 still has Jesus drawing near the city (ἤγγισεν . . . τὴν πόλιν).

1. Structure, Purpose and Nature of Luke's Journey Narrative

Most, but not all, Lukan scholars agree that the journey motif is central in the structure and purpose of Luke's special section. The numerous proposals regarding Luke's purpose may be outlined and summarized as follows:

a. *The journey (motif) is of central importance.* Luke's use of various forms of πορεύεσθαι (to go on), the key place of ἀναλήμψις (to be received up) in 9:51, and four motion-destiny texts (9:51; 13:13–35; 18:31–34; 19:26–46) unify this section. The journey to Jerusalem

---

[79]J. L. Resseguie, "Interpretation of Luke's Central Section (Luke 9:51–19:44) Since 1856," *Studia Biblica et Theologica* 5/12 (1975), 3–36.

[80]K. E. Bailey, *Poet and Peasant: A Literary Cultural Approach to the Parables in Luke* (Grand Rapids: Eerdmans, 1976), ch. 4: "The Literary Outline of the Travel Narrative (Jerusalem Document): Luke 9:51–19:48"; Goulder, *Calendar*; Ringe, "Luke 9:28–36," 94–96.

[81]Resseguie, "Interpretation," 3, n. 2; D. Gill, "Observations on the Lukan Travel Narrative and Some Related Passages," *HTR* 63 (1970), 213.

"prefigures the real end—the journey via death into his heavenly kingdom" (Davies).[82]

Luke stamped the journey motif on this section to make it conform to his larger view that Jesus' ministry, continued also in the early church, was seen as a continuation of God's salvation history via the motif "way" (ὁδός) or "course" (δρόμος). In Acts, the Jesus movement was designated "The Way" (Robinson).[83]

Luke develops the journey motif (found in Mark) to address a specific christological issue: the necessity of Jesus' suffering and death and the disciples' misunderstanding of it (Conzelmann).[84] Or, better, the christological content is double-sided, even antithetical, with accent on both Jesus' suffering and his glorification (Flender).[85]

Luke concentrates his use of πορεύομαι in his opening verses (9:51–53) and then, occurring throughout the section, his journey references function as settings for teaching on discipleship and mission. By this connection Luke makes Jesus' journey "a type of the Christian life" which embraces both "true discipleship and the mission" that Jesus himself began (Gill).[86]

The journey provides the context for developing both christological and ecclesiastical-ethical emphases (von der Osten-Sacken).[87]

Jesus' journey to Jerusalem and its events also fulfill the announcement of 9:31, Jesus' *exodus*, and represent the Old Testament motif of pilgrimage to the Feast of Tabernacles, the event in the

---

[82]J. H. Davies, "The Purpose of the Central Section of St. Luke's Gospel," in *Studia et Evangelica*, II (TU 87), ed. F. L. Cross (Berlin: Akademie-Verlag, 1964), 164–69. The view of C. C. McCown is similar, except that he holds that the journey is fictitious, a literary device: "The Geography of Luke's Central Section," *JBL* 57 (1938), 53–66.

[83]W. C. Robinson, Jr., "The Theological Context for Interpreting Luke's Travel Narrative (9:51ff.)," *JBL* 79 (1960), 20–31, and idem, *Der Weg des Herrn, Studien zur Geschichte und Eschatologie im Lukas-Evangelium* (Hamburg: Herbert Reich, 1964).

[84]H. Conzelmann, *The Theology of St. Luke*, trans. G. Buswell (New York: Harper & Row, 1961), 60–73. This position is certainly as true of Mark as of Luke. Conzelmann's work was done before the redactional work on Mark's central section appeared. Indeed, Luke does more than Mark and more than Conzelmann perceived.

[85]H. Flender, *St. Luke, Theologian of Redemptive History*, trans. R. H. and I. Fuller (London: SPCK, 1967), 27–33, 73–80.

[86]Gill, "Observations," 199–216, quotation on 214.

[87]P. von der Osten-Sacken, "Zur Christologie des lukanischen Reiseberichts," *EvT* 33 (1973), 476–96.

background of the Transfiguration. The purpose of the journey is to
consummate Jesus' work of liberation (Ringe).[88]
The content of Jesus' journey is modeled after the content of
instruction given during Israel's journey narrated in the book of
Deuteronomy. Luke's central section is a Christian Deuteronomy
(Evans, Drury, Goulder, Moessner).[89]
Other interpretations which argue for multiple journeys in
the section or a Samarian or Perean location[90] add nothing further to
our attempt to assess the degree to which the exodus-conquest traditions influenced the formation of the section.

   *b. The journey is secondary to ecclesial interests, whether didac-
tic or liturgical.* The primary purpose of the section is to fill in the gap
between Galilee and Jerusalem and bring together those teachings of
Jesus that provide ecclesial-didactic direction for Luke's community.
The teachings focus on two dimensions of church life: internal behavior and relations to those outside (Reicke, in part Schneider).[91]
   The structure consists of a ten-step chiasm (nineteen units)
with 13:22–35 as the center. There "is no traveling done at all"; "we
prefer to call it a Jerusalem Document" since Jerusalem is mentioned
at the beginning, center, and end. Its teaching focuses on discipleship,
Jesus' death, and "the eschatological day" (Bailey).[92]

---

[88]Ringe, "Luke 9:28–36," 90–96.
[89]C. F. Evans, "Central Section," 37–53; also in *Saint Luke* (TPINTC;
London: SCM and Philadelphia: Trinity, 1990), 34–36; Drury, *Tradition,* 138–
64; Goulder, *Calendar,* 103 and 306 supp.; Moessner, *Banquet.* Goulder's schedule of Lukan readings, as set beside the Torah cycle, does not always match the
text-correspondences set by Evans, but the overall picture is the same. Moessner's approach is quite different. Building upon Luke's identification of Jesus as
a prophet like unto Moses (Acts 3:22), Moessner argues for four major thematic
correspondences between Luke's journey narrative and Deuteronomy. He
stresses especially Jesus and Moses as "rejected prophets" and the people's
obstinacy which brings judgment. His emphasis on Jesus as "Journeying
Guest"—a major theme of his book—lacks clear analogy in Deuteronomy.
[90]Resseguie, "Interpretation," 7–11, 14–16.
[91]B. Reicke, "Instruction and Discussion in the Travel Narrative," in
Studia Evangelica, I (TU 73), ed. K. Aland (Berlin: Akadamie-Verlag, 1959),
206–16; J. Schneider, "Zur Analyse des lukanischen Reisenberichtes, in *Synoptischen Studien,* ed. J. Schmid and A. Vögtle (Munich: Karl Zink, n.d. [1953]),
207–29. Schneider notes the lack of definite place names and time markers in
the section; thus the didactic-paraenetic purpose is primary.
[92]Bailey, *Poet and Peasant,* 80–83. Bailey's chiastic analysis extends the
earlier work of M. D. Goulder, "The Chiastic Structure of the Lucan Journey,"
in *Studia Evangelica II,* 195–202.

The purpose of its composition, like the rest of Luke's Gospel, was to provide lectionary readings for the church. This section follows the Deuteronomic Torah cycle (Goulder).[93]

How will this diversity in the scholarly assessments of Lukan purpose be evaluated? First, the presence and even prominence of the journey motif cannot be denied. But clarity is needed regarding what is meant by "the journey." By "journey" do we mean Jesus' and his disciples traveling from one destination to another? If so, Schneider's and Bailey's protests are well-placed. Or, does "journey" denote the means of transition from Galilee to the environs of Jerusalem? Granted, this happens in the narrative, but more than once (9:51–10:42 and 17:11–19:41) and in only selected portions.[94] Rather, our perception of the journey imagery should be that of a literary motif that functions with specific narrative roles.[95] Once this is seen, the narrative role(s) may yield theological functions and meanings as well, indeed, as most of those identified above. Gill's work is most helpful in this regard, but he does not indicate the literary nature of the *Reisenotizen*. However, he does specify the narrative role of such "notices": they function to connect Jesus' journey with teachings on discipleship and mission.

Based upon the analysis of Table II below, a threefold function of the travel references is clearly evident: (1) to designate direction to Jerusalem (stated only thrice *between* the beginning and end, but in 9:51–53 and 9:28–44 eleven destiny-to-Jerusalem terms occur); (2) to serve as a setting for teaching on discipleship (six times: 9:57; 10:38; 13:22; 14:25–26; 18:35–45; 19:11–27); and (3) to provide a setting for discourse or action with mission significance (three times: 10:1; 13:22; 17:11–19).

The evidence indicates that the narrative does envision a journey toward Jerusalem. This is supported further by the fact that ἀνάλημψις (9:51) includes a journey with teachings before "assumption," [96] and that several other key words used in this section denote

---

[93]Goulder, *Calendar*, 73–104.

[94]Both accounts of transition accent interaction with Samaritans; each places such a story at the beginning. But the last act of the first journey is the welcome of a woman into learning at the feet of Jesus; the last act of the second is a lament over Jerusalem.

[95]Here Resseguie is not helpful, for he classifies only McCown's essay under the interpretive rubric, "A Literary Device" ("Interpretation," 16–17); McCown regards the journey as fictitious.

[96]Gill, "Observations," 38–40.

"fulfillment of a course" (συμπληροῦσθαι in 9:51; τελειοῦμαι in 13:32; τελεσθήσεται in 18:31). It also shows that the journey motif is a frame for both teaching on discipleship and missional interests, but the evidence does not connect it directly with christological emphases (contra Conzelmann, et al.). In the only passion-resurrection prediction that occurs in this section (18:31), Luke has ἀναβαίνω but lacks any use of ὁδός as found in Mark. The notion that pilgrimage to the Feast of Tabernacles lies behind the journey motif also does not hold, for the events connected to the journey notices show no motifs or themes of the Feast of Tabernacles or Ascent Psalm (except perhaps the Entry itself).

2. Analysis of the Deuteronomy Prototype Theory

Evans's view that the content of the section is modeled on Deuteronomy merits careful analysis. Since Deuteronomy anticipates and gives directions for the conquest ("when you enter the land"), the proposal is crucial to the thesis of this study. Evans's study shows remarkable textual connections, but fails to analyze the possible theological and moral dimensions of this literary phenomenon. Nowhere does he take up the question whether Luke's central section contains a theology of conquest that is in some way analogical to, or different from, that of Deuteronomy. Evans, however, does say that Luke's journey follows that of Deuteronomy's to the promised land "by way of correspondence and contrast."[97] Designated as an ἀναλήμψις, this section echoes in both form and content the Assumption of Moses, clearly modeled on Deuteronomy.[98]

As Resseguie notes, relatively few criticisms of Evans's ingenious contribution have been made, and those put forward are minor in comparison to the weight of evidence.[99] Further, as Evans says, not only the vast number of correspondences, but the fact that the parallels are in sequential order, testifies to design and intention; it is hardly a matter of happenstance.[100] Twenty-one text parallels are substantial,

---

[97]C. F. Evans, "Central Section," 51.

[98]Whether Luke knew of the Assumption (Testament) of Moses cannot be determined; its date of origin is uncertain.

[99]Resseguie, "Interpretation," 13. James Sanders regards Evans's contribution positively (*Canon and Community*, 63–67).

[100] My first impression of this was to dismiss it. But after a third careful reading of the evidence, I concluded that 60–70 percent of the correspondences are substantial. But there are weaknesses: five Deuteronomy sections (14:1–21; 19; 21:1–14; 22:5–23:14; 25:4–19) have no Lukan parallels;

in either word or conceptual connection. In order to assess the data and its significance, Table III (see end of chapter) summarizes the more persuasive correspondences and provides my evaluation as to whether the correspondence is essentially parallel in thought or whether it shows transformation or contrast. Though the relationship might be evaluated differently by some—and I omitted some of Evans's sections—the evidence is much too weighty for the thesis to be discounted. Those correspondences which show either transformation (9) or contrast (7) total together 60%, significantly more than those assessed as only conceptually parallel (11).

This phenomenon in which Luke uses Deuteronomy as a literary model calls for analysis at the level of theological significance.[101] For here we have a New Testament use of the Old that shows both continuity and change between the orders of Moses and those of Jesus. In every case where Deuteronomy prescribed death for what might contaminate the community,[102] Luke's Jesus calls for a reversal of values: the enemy Samaritan is the neighbor who models the Shema; repentance of sinners is the new way to prohibit evil from

---

surprisingly, Deut 18:15–18, containing a key Lukan theme—Jesus is a prophet like unto Moses, has no parallel (Evans ["Central Section"] explains this omission by the connection already made in Luke 9:35, the voice at the Transfiguration [47]). Also I note that the chiastic center of Luke's central section, 13:31–35, has no particular thought correspondence in Deuteronomy. Nonetheless, the evidence for Luke's use of Deuteronomy for his composition is much too strong for the thesis to be dismissed.

[101] This point needs more attention in David Moessner's stimulating study of Luke's use of Deuteronomy. In my judgment, the theme of "rejected Prophet" characterizes Luke's accent more broadly and is not restricted to the journey narrative. Similarly, the Lukan emphasis on Jesus as "Journeying Guest" and Lord of the Banquet is also not restricted to the journey narrative, for Luke 24 contains a finale to this emphasis, as Moessner observes in showing the continuation of the theme in the Passion narrative (22:7–38) and climactically in the Emmaus account (24:13–53). In this respect it is important to maintain, to some extent, the literary dependence of the travel narrative upon the content of Deuteronomy, as C. F. Evans has shown. By slighting this feature, Moessner has not shown the dependence of the travel narrative upon Deuteronomy in a way distinctive from the rest of Luke–Acts. Moessner's summary of correspondences between the travel narrative and Deuteronomy (*Banquet*, 280–85) offers more persuasive evidence, but this appears not to play a crucial role in his contribution as a whole.

[102] M. J. Borg regards *holiness* as a key to Jesus' self-identity and mission. See his stimulating work, *Jesus: A New Vision*, 86–93, 183–84, and his earlier even more extensive treatment of holiness in *Conflict, Holiness and Politics in the Teachings of Jesus* (New York: Edwin Mellen, 1983).

consuming the community; and laws on clean and unclean are stood on their head. When the peace offer/greeting is refused, wiping out the village is replaced by wiping off the dust from your feet as you leave. Also, in the primary conceptualization of the "enemy" we see a major transformation. For us, people are not the enemy, but Satan is the one dethroned in Jesus' vision of victory. At the same time we see basic parallel thought structures on oppression of the poor, obedience to God's word, the primacy of the love command, and the call to put loyalty to the Lord over all other loyalties.

Another significant link to Deuteronomy's way-conquest tradition is Luke's twofold use of the question, "what must I do to inherit eternal life?" (10:25; 18:18). By placing the story of the lawyer close to the beginning and the story of the ruler close to the ending of his special section, thus functioning as penultimate inclusios, Luke is underlining the entire section's thematic linkage with Deuteronomy's emphasis on inheriting the land. We noted above (in Mark) the connection between the Deuteronomic formula "entering into the land" and "entering the kingdom of God." Here Luke connects "inheriting the land" and "inheriting eternal life." The way to inherit eternal life is marked specifically by love for the neighbor, even the enemy, and using wealth for the benefit of the poor. This moral directive reflects the same accent on discipleship found in Mark's story of Jesus' teaching "on the way," leading to the kingdom of God.

Further, while Luke places the transfiguration outside his central section, he links it to the conquest theology of this section by introducing the anticipation of Jesus' *exodus* into the story, an exodus Jesus was about to complete. Ringe is correct in suggesting that the term must be taken to include and extend over the entire journey section. The exodus pushes forward to the ἀναλήμψις, the days for him to be received up (9:51; Acts 1:11), which in turns finds its fulfillment in Jesus' death, resurrection, and *ascension*. For Luke the transfiguration marks the beginning of Jesus' journey from earthly humiliation to heavenly glory and exaltation. The journey begins in the exodus section with Jesus' liberation of others; it ends with Jesus' own liberation and exaltation to the right hand of God.

3. Distinctive Lukan Emphases

With scholarship's many endeavors to discern what Luke sought to do in this section, it is surprising that several features of the narrative have not been adequately considered. Six themes permeate the narrative, here developed as three couplets. Echoing the emphases of the older story, Luke discloses Jesus as: the journeying guest/Lord of the Banquet and rejected prophet, the bringer of peace and justice, and the disarmer of evil and agent of divine judgment. These themes are prominent in the structural design of Luke's travel narrative and disclose the influence of the Deuteronomic "entrance" and conquest traditions.

a. Jesus as journeying banquet guest and rejected prophet. As David Moessner demonstrates, the Lukan journey narrative strongly echoes several Deuteronomic themes by portraying Jesus as a journeying guest and a rejected prophet like Moses. As journeying guest Jesus participates in and speaks of banquets (10:38–42; 11:37–54; 14:15–34; 19:1–10) and calls for proper response to the banquet that he himself will host (22:7–27; 24:13–35). Further, the narrative recalls the Deuteronomic themes of resisting God, stubborn unbelief, and failure to enter the land. As the people rejected Moses, so they reject Jesus, and thus they will miss out on the banquet and rejoicing before the Lord in the land, i.e., in Luke the banquet of messianic celebration. In Luke 9:51ff. "Jesus, like Moses, sends out messengers to secure food and hospitality for them," but, as "if on cue, they are flatly rejected." [103] Moessner identifies many texts which depict Jesus as either a journeying guest or rejected prophet, and these he links to one another and to the theme that Jesus is/will be Lord of the banquet.[104] While this correlation is not as strong as he suggests,[105] it can hardly be doubted that these emphases permeate the narrative. They are also not confined to this section, but tone Luke–Acts more broadly. The distinctive feature of this section consists of the relationship between these themes and their occurrence in Deuteronomy, which functions as a literary archetype for Luke. Hence, Luke's travel narrative witnesses in a special way to Jesus as a prophet like Moses.

---

[103] Moessner, *Banquet*, 273.

[104] Ibid., 3–4, 174–76, 211.

[105] Luke 11:37–54 is the only text which explicitly joins the rejected prophet with the banquet theme, and there the positions are reversed: the Pharisee throws the banquet and Jesus rejects the Pharisees and lawyers. Only in 10:38–42 and 19:1–10 are the journey and banqueting themes linked. Moessner's diagram (ibid., 176) shows how he must choose different texts and hook them together to make his point. True, the texts are all in this section, but the joining of the journeying guest *or* rejected prophet themes with the banquet theme is not as clear in Luke as it is in Moessner. Accordingly, my summary of the Journey (Table II) does not indicate textual correlation between the journey motif and the banqueting motif, even though the two flow together in broad narrative strokes.

Not only is *rejection* of the prophet integral to both units of
literature, literarily and theologically, but the analogical emphasis
upon Israel's journeying to the promised land of milk and honey and
Jesus' journeying to the banquet which he will host is vital. Further,
as Moessner notes, the correspondence also contains a contrast: in
Deuteronomy the people will be divided into households as they come
to the land of banqueting; in Luke those who heed the invitation of and
celebrate with the journeying guest will be gathered together as a new
household at the Banquet.[106] Another correspondence, a parallel, may
also be noted: the journeying Israelites in Deuteronomy are expected
to attend three major feasts annually and to celebrate with thanks-
giving and joy (Deut 16). Luke portrays Jesus frequently feasting and
speaking about feasting (esp. in chs. 14–15). The fault with the Pharisees—and the elder brother of the Prodigal—is that they refuse to
celebrate, feast, and rejoice upon the finding of the lost, the homecom-
ing of the sinner. Further, strong injunctions to do justice that prevents
oppression of the poor and the easily socially marginalized appear following the feast sections in both Deuteronomy and Luke. Precisely
these people, whom the older story barred from the holy space (Lev
21:17–21) and whom the Qumran covenanters proscribed from the
war preceding the messianic banquet (see below), are those welcomed
to the banquet which Jesus as journeying guest will host (14:21–24).

The Lukan journey narrative then, in its echo of the Deuteronomic "land entrance" and conquest traditions, develops a twin theme
of journeying guest/banquet Lord and rejected prophet. This twin
theme is closely intertwined with the next, that of peace and justice,
for the journeying guest offers to people the gospel of peace. Responses to this offer set up a lock-step sequence: if the people respond
by accepting the peace, they prepare for the banquet which Jesus as
Lord will host. If they reject the offer, they reject the journeying
prophet. Further, this twin theme of the journeying banqueting guest-
Lord and rejected prophet can be rightly and fully assessed only when
set within the context of both Luke's *peace and justice* emphases *and*
his thematic focus on the conquest of evil and divine judgment, his
second and third couplets.

b. The journey to peace and justice. The second of Luke's dual
themes lies in his accent on "peace" (εἰρήνη) and "justice" (δίκαιος).

---

[106] Moessner (ibid., 273) speaks of Jesus gathering households for the
Banquet. But Luke 14:26 requires a different conception.

If one regards 9:51–62 as introductory, then the first (10:1ff.) and last (19:28ff.) narratives in the section are laced with Luke's peace accent. The word occurs three times in 10:5–6, including the phrase, "child of peace," and three other times in 19:28–42. Each occurrence is strategic in Luke's literary design and theological intention. In the mission of the Seventy,[107] which prefigures the church's later mission to the Gentiles, the first word of address is "Peace be with you." If a "child of peace" is there, the door will be open; you shall enter, heal the sick and say, "the kingdom of God has come near you" (v. 9). If the peace is refused, it "shall return to you" and you shall wipe off the dust of your feet against them and say, "Nevertheless, know this, that the kingdom of God has come near" (v. 11). Further, the Seventy are "sent" (ἀπέστειλεν), the same word used for Jesus' mission in 4:18 and 43; Jesus sends the Seventy out before his face (πρὸ προσώπου αὐτοῦ, 10:1). While the favorite Lukan verb εὐαγγελίζω does not occur here, the same activity is carried forward by the Seventy under the gospel salutation, "Peace be to this house." A peace response becomes the criterion by which the people receive the kingdom of God or condemnation. Certainly this emphasis, heading up Luke's special section, carries forward his narrative intentions in 2:14 where the angelic choir heralds the meaning of Jesus' birth as "glory in heaven" and "peace on earth."

Paul Minear has suggested a direct correlation between "glory in heaven" and "peace on earth," in Luke's thematic intentions: "the more glory the more peace, and the more peace the more glory."[108] Similarly, Minear correlates the Seventy's rejoicing that their names are written in heaven (10:20) with their šālôm-εἰρήνη shout to the homes they visited; joy in heaven matches the peace, joy and wholeness experienced on earth (15:7, 10, 20–24).[109]

By reintroducing the peace motif at the close of his special section, Luke wants his readers to see that Jesus' entire mission was one of bringing peace.[110] The multitude of disciples that followed Jesus as he descended the Mount of Olives to enter Jerusalem "began

---

[107] Here I follow RSV and NRSV in choosing the textual reading *seventy*.
[108] Minear, *To Heal*, 50. Indeed, glory also is a major thematic accent of Luke's Gospel; see ch. 6 below, pp. 244–45 or n. 120.
[109] Minear, *To Heal*, 50–55; Minear uses the Hebrew word *šālôm*. For evidence that it is appropriate to link εἰρήνη with *šālôm* in Luke, see Swartley, "Politics and Peace," 35–37.
[110] J. Donahue has suggested we read the Lukan journey narrative as "a path to peace" ("The Good News of Peace," *The Way* 22 [1982], 88–89).

to praise God joyfully with a loud voice for all the deeds of power that they had seen, saying, 'Blessed is the King who comes in the name of the Lord! Peace in heaven and glory in the highest heaven' " (19:37–38). This shout becomes an antiphonal response to 2:14. The proclamation of the heavenly host is now complemented by the shout of the multitude of disciples. Earth answers heaven. It is urgent that the praise be given, for when the Pharisees try to silence it, Jesus says, "If they don't shout it, the very stones will cry it out" (my rendering). Luke's narrative exclaims: Jesus comes as king, ringing heaven's bells of peace; a sea of followers has confessed it. But the outcry may also indicate an abortive dimension: the peace has not been welcomed by all on earth. Hence, in sharp contrast to the mood of the praising multitude, Jesus laments over Jerusalem and pronounces judgment: "If you, even you, had only recognized on this day the things that make for peace! But now they are hidden from your eyes" (v. 42). The harsh words of judgment upon the city end with the sad explanatory comment: "because you did not recognize the time of your visitation from God" (v. 44). Thus the section ends. God sent divine peace through Jesus, but the response was full of surprises. Those with standing invitations to the banquet refused; those previously barred from the banquet accepted.

In *The Gospel in Parable* John Donahue notes an arresting parallel between Israel's Holy War regulations in Deuteronomy 20 and Luke's Great Banquet parable in 14:16–24.[111] This correspondence is also cited by C. F. Evans. The excuses of the guests invited first to the banquet echo the same reasons that male Israelites were exempted from responding to the call to Holy War in Deuteronomy 20:

Deuteronomy War Exemptions	*Luke's Banquet Excuses*
1. Built a new house	1. Bought a piece of land
2. Planted a vineyard	2. Bought five yoke of oxen
3. Engaged to a woman	3. Just married a wife

The parallelism is indeed striking. The first are property excuses; the second, work excuses—the oxen tilled the vineyard; and the third, marital obligation. Donahue observes that in OT and later Jewish literature the feast of the messianic age is inaugurated by great violence and war to crush the enemies.[112] Indeed, in Luke Jesus tells this

---

[111] J. Donahue, *Parable*, 140–46.
[112] Ibid., 142. Donahue cites in n. 27, Isa 25:6–8; 55:1–2; 65:13–14; 1 Enoch 62:14; 2 Apoc. Bar. 29:4; Rev 20–21.

parable in response to earlier banqueting instructions (14:7–14) and in response to the exclamation in verse 15, "Blessed is anyone who will eat bread in the kingdom of God." Jesus' Great Banquet parable comes next and ends with the words, "For I tell you, none of those who were invited will eat of my banquet" (v. 24)!

Luke's portrayal of Jesus, says Donahue, departs from the standard Jewish eschatological anticipations in that "he omits those violent elements . . . normally associated with the eschatological banquet." [113] Stressing nonviolence and peace, Luke's Jesus takes the parable into a second dimension in which substitute guests are invited: the poor, the crippled, and the lame—precisely those who in the Qumran literature (1QM 7:4–6; 1QSa 2:5–10) were excluded from the expected messianic banquet.[114] Even after these ritually unclean people are gathered into the feast, a third invitation compels more to come from the highways and hedges. In this new echo of the earlier war tradition, the human enemy has disappeared.

This textual transformation of the Holy War traditions shows thus another link between Luke's Travel Narrative and Israel's conquest warfare traditions. At the same time it contributes to Luke's depiction of Jesus' journey as God's gracious offer of peace, an offer rejected by those earlier called but now accepted by those formerly barred from the banquet.

Complementing Luke's portrait of Jesus' gospel as God's offer of peace is his emphasis on true justice. In this section Luke uses either the verb or noun forms of justice (δίκαιος, δικαιόω, ἐκδικέω, ἐκδίκησις) twelve times, and none have parallels in either Matthew or Mark. Four texts either call for justice (12:57) or designate someone or some group as just: the resurrection of the just in 14:14; the ninety-nine righteous in 15:7—which has an ironic edge to it; and the tax collector for his prayer of contrition who was "justified rather than the other [Pharisee]" in 18:14. A second group of four occurs in the parable of the Unjust Judge. Twice the woman pleads for justice (18:3, 5), and twice Jesus assures the listener that God will grant justice (18:7, 8). Here God's own character is the standard that defines justice. Another four uses describe specific persons or groups who pretend justice or seek to justify themselves: the lawyer in 10:29; the Pharisees in 16:15; likely the Pharisees in 18:9 who "trusted in themselves that they were righteous"; and the scribes and chief priests in

[113] Ibid., 142.
[114] Ibid., 144.

20:20 in setting the tax trap. These counterfeit portraits of justice become a narrative foil for the Gospel's climactic christological confession, "Truly this was a righteous man," in 23:47, a bold alternative to Mark and Matthew. Thus in Luke's theology, Jesus, like God, emerges as the standard of true justice (see ch. 6 for further discussion).

Luke's special section again echoes Deuteronomy's widely recognized emphasis on justice, especially 16:18–20, where God tells Israel to appoint judges to render just decisions and then calls for justice: "Justice, and only justice, you shall pursue, so that you may occupy the land that the Lord your God is giving you." In C. F. Evans's work this particular text corresponds to Luke 14:1–14, a text that promises a reward "at the resurrection of the just" to those who host banquets the Jesus way—inviting in the poor, the maimed, the lame, and the blind.[115] Luke's justice text in 18:1–8 corresponds to Deuteronomy 24:6–25:3, a passage containing numerous injunctions against oppressive treatment of the poor, the resident alien, the orphan, and the widow. This section uses the word "justice" (*mišpāṭ*) only once (in Deut 24:17): "You shall not deprive a resident alien or an orphan of justice; you shall not take the widow's garment in pledge." The widow's persisting pleas for justice in Luke 18 clearly hark back to the Deuteronomic parallel, and thus again Evans's thesis has remarkable support.

Beyond these specific connections, Luke's pervasive emphasis on social justice matches that of Deuteronomy's (see, e.g., Deut 8:11–18 where Moses warns Israel against allowing prosperity in the land to seduce them into forgetting God). In two parables, the Rich Fool in 12:16–20 and the Rich Man and Lazarus in 16:19–31, Luke warns against wealth's blinding of people to the kingdom's call and its justice. These parables are distinctive to Luke and warn against the dangers arising from the apparent gap between rich and poor in the churches of his time and locality. Indeed, Luke's travel narrative includes not only these two parables, but Zacchaeus' giving of half his goods to the poor (19:8), other teaching on almsgiving (11:41; 12:33), and a strong Deuteronomic echo against wealth in chapters 12 and 16 as a whole. Donahue summarizes Luke's special contribution: "Luke presents Jesus in the form of an OT prophet who takes the side of the

---

[115] Evans lifts Deut 16:18ff. out of 16:1–17:7 and puts it with 17:8–18:22 so that this judicial law section is parallel to Luke's parable of the Great Banquet in Luke 14:1–14. By connecting the banqueting and justice themes in this way Luke fuses together the first and second thematic couplets explicated here in my discussion of Luke's travel narrative.

widow (7:11–17; 18:1–8), the stranger in the land (10:29–37; 17:16), and those on the margin of society (14:12–13, 21)."[116] Indeed, this aspect of social justice as one portion of Israel's way to land-conquest traditions resonates loudly in Luke's journey narrative, so loudly that we may assuredly propose that Luke used Deuteronomy imitatively as a literary model.[117]

In light of the contemporary urgent need to correlate peace with justice, Luke creatively and profoundly speaks to our needs as well as those of his time. The meaning of justice in both Deuteronomy and Luke is not to be confused with the Greek notion of rendering to every one their due, but must be understood in parallel to mercy as shown in God's covenant relationship to Israel. Seeing the needs of the poor and marginalized, God responds with compassion. As Lind puts it, "Both justice and mercy arise out of the covenant relationship of God and people." Further, Israel's "law is an expression of that [mercy and justice] norm."[118] Just as law and justice show the design of life within the people's covenant relationship with God, so the Gospel's portrayal of Jesus proclaiming peace and justice reflects also the good news of the kingdom and its pattern for life. It is the way of the Jesus community. It calls people to stop feigning justice, i.e., pretending to be righteous, but to actually live the way of God's kingdom, brought near in Jesus. Failing this, God's justice means judgment, for God's peace and justice confront and overcome evil.

c. The journey leads to conquest and judgment of evil. The third crucial feature in Luke's journey narrative is the gospel's conquest of evil[119] and God's judgment of it, including especially those

---

[116] Donahue, *Parable*, 175.

[117] Of the four intertextual relationships that a literary work might bear to a predecessor—imitative, eclectic, heuristic, or dialectical, according to Thomas Greene—Luke's central section is related to Deuteronomy imitatively on this point of justice. However, where he transforms the Deuteronomic thought, not slaying the Canaanites but forming friendship between Jew and Samaritan, the relationship is dialectical, in conversation with but transforming the emphases also. See Greene, *Light in Troy*, 38–46.

[118] M. C. Lind, "Transformation of Justice: From Moses to Jesus," in *Monotheism, Power, and Justice: Collected Old Testament Essays* (TR 3; Elkhart, Ind.: Institute of Mennonite Studies, 1990), 82–83.

[119] On this, see Garrett, *Demise of the Devil*; especially her treatment of Luke 10:17–20 (46–56). While Garrett argues that this text is proleptic of the victory of Jesus' resurrection and exaltation in Luke's narrative, the effort to understand this text in its present narrative location merits attention. If one makes vv. 17–20 proleptic, then one must do the same for 10:1–12, anticipating

who failed to respond to God's offer of peace and justice. In Luke, Jesus' remark on the mission of the Seventy is most illuminating. From the sequence of the narrative, Luke intends to show that the gospel of peace goes out as victorious power over evil. In the oracle put between the sending out and the return of the Seventy, Jesus speaks woes upon Chorazin and Bethsaida for failing to receive God's peace mission—the *missio Dei* (10:13–16). Jesus' words of judgment recall the downfall of earlier self-exalted and oppressive kings (Isa 14; Ezek 28): "And you, Capernaum, will you be exalted to heaven? No, you will be brought down to Hades" (10:15). Despite the extensive scope of rejection and judgment, Jesus *sees* another result of the kingdom's peace mission: "I saw Satan fall like lightning from heaven" (v. 18, RSV). The reception of the gospel marked the end of Satan's rule; Jesus' rule began! The victory has even more enduring consequence in that " 'your names are written in heaven' " (v. 20).[120]

The next paragraph's scene of Jesus' rejoicing in the Holy Spirit and crying out to God as Father appears to be Jesus' celebration of this cosmic victory: the hidden things have been revealed not to the wise and understanding, but to babes. This voices the simple truth and sheer joy experienced when the gospel word of peace liberates from Satan's bonds. The outburst continues by underscoring the basis of authority for all this to have happened: "All things have been handed over (παρεδόθη) to me by my Father; and no one knows who the Son is except the Father, or who the Father is except the Son and anyone to whom the Son chooses to reveal him" (v. 22). Then comes instruction to the disciples on seeing and hearing and their privileged position: "Blessed are the eyes that see what you see!"

Next Luke narrates a testing (ἐκπειράζων) from a lawyer on the question of inheriting eternal life (v. 25). Will the lawyer see what the disciples have seen? No, for in the face of God's love commands he seeks self-justification. In contrast, the gospel word shows love compassionately aiding not only an unknown neighbor, but a known

---

the later mission of the church. The essential connection between the proclamation of the gospel of peace and the dethronement or disempowerment of Satan cannot be slighted, in faithfulness to the narrative purpose.

[120] By treating the judgment oracle of vv. 13–16 and the visionary episode of vv. 17–20 separately from 10:1–12, U. Mauser slights the crucial interconnection between the two emphases. Otherwise, his fine treatment of Luke's peace theme correlates well with my emphases here. His parallelism in 10:5–6 and vv. 8–11 is especially instructive. See U. Mauser, *The Gospel of Peace* (SPS 1; Louisville: Westminster/John Knox, 1992), 55.

enemy—and the hands of love are those of a Samaritan![121] The narrative shifts from the question, "who is the neighbor whom I am commanded to love?" to "am I a loving neighbor even to the enemy?" To be such a neighbor ensures one of eternal life, and it does not test with evil intent the Teacher of truth and life. The Good Samaritan story climaxes Luke's first segment which is thus framed by the Samaritan theme, for in 9:54 the disciples wanted to rain fire down upon a Samaritan village because of its rejection of the journeying prophet Jesus (cf. 2 Kgs 1:10, 12). But Jesus rebuked (ἐπετίμησεν) them, thus expelling their evil desire.

This first segment (9:51–10:37) of Luke's central section thus develops the theme of the gospel's overcoming of evil through its proclamation of peace and its deeds of love, even to the enemy. As people receive the kingdom's gospel of peace, Satan falls from his throne of power. Enemies are saved from death through love that risks life for life. The gospel of peace and love has conquered.

Since the mission of the Seventy appears to be a narrative follow-up to Jesus' sending messengers ahead to Samaritan towns (9:51–53, 56), another point, blending the two above, comes also into view. The two themes, the peace of the kingdom and the conquest of evil, are developed in the narrative by actions that are located squarely in the territory of the religious and sociopolitical enemy, the despised Samaritans.[122] In light of the older story, this has double significance, for Samaria matches geographically the place where Joshua's or Yahweh's first battles against the Canaanites occurred. But now, rather than eradicating the enemy, the new strategy eradicates the enmity; the Samaritans receive the peace of the kingdom of God. Instead of killing people to get rid of idolatry, the gospel defeats Satan directly. Instead of razing high places, Satan is blown off his throne! Hence the root of idolatry is plucked from its source (see Deut 18:9–14 for the rationale, i.e., idolatry, for destroying the people in the promised land).

Other pericopes also highlight Jesus' conquest and judgment of evil. These are the Beelzebul controversy, which Luke alone places

---

[121] For an excellent description of the identity of the Samaritans, as well as the enmity between Jews and Samaritans, see J. R. Donahue, "Who Is My Enemy? The Parable of the Good Samaritan and the Love of Enemies," in *The Love of Enemy and Nonretaliation in the New Testament*, ed. W. M. Swartley (Louisville: Westminster/John Knox, 1992), pp. 137–56.

[122] The entire segment of 9:51–10:37 thus has Samaria as its locational context.

in this section of the synoptic structure; recurring pronouncements of judgment upon "this evil generation" (ch. 12); and the release of a woman bound by Satan for eighteen years (13:10–17). The Beelzebul controversy contains Jesus' claim of authority and word of victory: "But if it is by the finger of God that I cast out the demons, then the kingdom of God has come to you" (11:20). Again, the theme of the kingdom is correlated directly with victory over the evil hosts. The next verses portray Jesus as the one stronger than the strong man, one who has successfully assailed Satan and rescued those under his dominion. In this context of Jesus' assault and victory over Satan's goods, an earlier saying (9:50) is reversed, "He who is not with me is against me, and he who does not gather with me scatters" (11:23). Even though the statement appears reversed from its other synoptic uses, the shift in context makes its meaning the same in both instances: it is important to be on the side of Jesus in the battle against evil, for Jesus will triumph.

Some themes in this section fit well as sub-themes of peace and victory over evil. Much of the teaching guards against sin or evil threatening to creep into the Christian life, or accents rescue of people from sin and evil (esp. ch. 15). The climax of the Lord's Prayer, "lead us not into temptation," calls on God's power to protect against evil's seductive power;[123] the contrast between evil and good in the subsequent exposition (11:13) shows the pervasiveness of the theme. The extensive warnings against wealth, noted above, exemplify further the point. To be a lover of money is to resist Jesus and his way (16:13–15). By placing close to the end of the section the contrasting stories of the rich ruler (18:18–30) and Zacchaeus (19:1–10), Luke puts attachment to wealth in opposition to the gospel's overcoming of evil (cf. 16:13).[124]

The central section also contains two crucially placed pericopes that accent Jesus' judgment of those who fail to respond to the gospel's peace. According to Bailey's and Goulder's chiastic analyses, the strategic center of the section is 13:31–35. In this saying Jesus describes his ministry—to the Pharisees and Herod who seek to kill him—as one of casting out demons and performing cures. This he must do today, tomorrow, and the next day; then he will accept the prophet's destiny in Jerusalem. An evil/good opposition emerges:

---

[123] Though the later copyists' addition, "deliver us from evil," was influenced by Matthew's text, the petition certainly fits also the larger Lukan emphasis.

[124] On this topic see W. E. Pilgrim, *Good News to the Poor: Wealth and Poverty in Luke–Acts* (Minneapolis: Augsburg, 1981), esp. 109–33.

Jerusalem will kill and stone Jesus as it did the other prophets; Jesus then voices the two-sided reality of his mission, yearning love and judgment upon spurned opportunity:

> How often would I have gathered your children together as a hen gathers her brood under her wings, and you were not willing! See, your house is left to you. And I tell you, you will not see me until the time comes when you say, "Blessed is the one who comes in the name of the Lord" (13:34b–35).

The final segment of Luke's special section sounds a similar note. Luke's parable of the Pounds (19:11–27) contains two levels of story: the nobleman's response to the servants who used the pounds or talents in different ways and the nobleman's response to "the citizens of his country [who] hated him" (v. 14). The final punch of the parable falls upon them:

> But as for these enemies of mine who did not want me to be king over them—bring them here and slaughter them in my presence (19:27).

Even though Luke shows unambiguously that his followers are called to befriend and love the enemy, thus destroying the enmity, the category of "enemy" is not altogether eliminated. While the ethics for humans eschews it, the divine judgment includes it. The parable indicates that the citizens set up the "enemy" reality by their hatred of the nobleman; Jesus' word thus recognizes the reality. In keeping with the older story, judgment falls upon those who hate the God of peace and love. Verse 27 is stark and chilling. The segment's final words reinforce the same reality on a socio-national, corporate level, because the city refused the peace proffered by the humble one seeking royal coronation in God's holy city (19:29–40). Because they did not recognize the things that make for peace, things hidden from their eyes, they now hear:

> Indeed the days will come upon you, when your enemies will set up ramparts around you and surround you, and hem you in on every side. They will crush you to the ground, you and your children within you, and they will not leave within you one stone upon another; because you did not recognize the time of your visitation from God (19:43–44).

Though the end of the narrative carries this somber pronouncement, one detail in the segment especially intrigues the reader: "the whole multitude of the disciples began to praise God joyfully with a loud voice for all the deeds of power they had seen, saying, 'Peace in heaven and glory in the highest heaven (19:37b–38)!' " Who

were all those people in the multitude—hardly many from Jerusalem
(vv. 41–44)—who sang the praises of peace? In light of the narrative's
progression from Galilee through Samaria and the judgment upon
Jerusalem, the composition of this multitude depends upon the swelling crowd that follows the journeying guest to the promised banquet.
It is for these that the walls of Jericho have fallen anew, through the
gospel of peace, love, and justice.

David Tiede rightly says that Luke writes a narrative that
enters "into a complex contemporary discussion of divine justice and
grace, faithfulness and abandonment, vengeance and providence in
Israel's recent history."[125] He concurs with Petersen: "*the rejection of
God's agents by God's people in connection with God's sanctuaries
(synagogues and temples) is the plot device by which the narrative as a
whole is motivated.*"[126] While this is poignantly true in Luke's narrative, another side must be equally emphasized: The Luke 10 narrative
indicates that the announced peace on earth has found some takers
and God's gospel of salvation will triumph in its peace gift, despite the
massive rejection.[127] Both the acceptance and rejection of the gospel
of peace are present in these inclusio narratives of Luke's central
section. Thus the journey from the transfiguration to Jerusalem, the
place of humiliation, was a journey of conquest, disarming the power
of Satan and evil by bringing peace to those who received the peace
of God's kingdom but "a desolate house" to those who refused it
(13:35).[128]

Summary. In form and content Luke's journey narrative thus
shows the older story's way-conquest influences. In form it is a journey, like the older story, and Deuteronomy does appear to be its
literary model. In content, six themes permeate the narrative, here
developed as three couplets. Echoing the older narrative, Luke's journey story discloses Jesus as: the Journeying Guest/Banquet Lord and

[125] Tiede, *Prophecy and History*, 15.
[126] N. Petersen, *Literary Criticism for New Testament Critics* (Philadelphia: Fortress, 1978), 83. Cited by Tiede, *Prophecy and History*, 14.
[127] Note Jesus' post-resurrection greeting to his disciples, "Peace be to
you" (24:36). Peace vocabulary, but more significantly—peace-making events
continue through Acts. See Swartley, "Politics and Peace," 18–37; J. Comblin,
"La Paix dans la Théologie de saint Luc," *ETL* 32 (1956), 439–60; and Mauser,
Gospel of Peace, 89–102.
[128] As D. P. Reid puts it, "If there is a journey to discipleship, there is
also a journey to refusal" ("Peace and Praise in Luke," in *Blessed Are the
Peacemakers*, ed. A. J. Tambasco [New York/Mahwah: Paulist, 1989], 106).

rejected prophet, the bringer of peace and justice, and the disarmer of evil and agent of divine judgment. It is important to note that the first theme in each couplet is inherently linked to the next, as are the second themes in each couplet also. The Journeying Guest/Banquet Lord brings the gospel of peace which is the power that depowers Satan and his arsenal of evil. The rejected prophet is the prophet of justice whose word is judgment for those who refuse the banqueting guest, spurn the gospel of peace, and court evil. All these features, two of form and six of content, provide strong evidence that this section of Luke has been influenced by Israel's way to land-conquest traditions. In light of the above exposition, the journey motif functions primarily, I propose, to signal the reader to hear the Jesus story against the memory of the older story—and, among other things, to see what happens to the Samaritans in the center of the land and story.

CONTINUITY AND TRANSFORMATION IN THE TRADITION: ASSESSMENT AND SUMMARY

The use of Old Testament way-conquest traditions by the Synoptics in their central sections is most explicit in Luke and least explicit in Matthew. Besides his transfiguration story Matthew simply has no overt imagery that reflects OT way-conquest (or exodus) imagery. However, each Gospel presents a strong theology of conquest. Both Luke and Matthew portray the Jesus movement as a triumph over evil. While Mark puts less accent on the theme of evil per se, his entire section is set within imagery derived from the old exodus-conquest story.

For all three Gospels, the means of conquest is similar, if not identical. Jesus' suffering, death, and resurrection mark the road to triumph; for the disciples this means self-denial, cross-bearing, and choosing the role of humble servant. Luke's Gospel further emphasizes that the proclamation and reception of the kingdom gospel dethrones Satan. This accords with his later emphasis in Acts where the spread of the gospel into the Gentile world is framed by stories showing the doom of Satanic power.[129]

If indeed the conquest model lies behind the shaping of this synoptic section in its canonical form, we must give some account of the presence or absence of the divine Warrior and Holy War motifs,

---

[129] Each geographical breakthrough is accompanied by exorcistic encounters: chs. 8, 13, 16, 19.

so central to Israel's theology of the conquest.[130] While the Synoptics' emphases on liberation included dimensions of conquest (ch. 3), in both Matthew and Mark (Luke differs here) stories portraying divine power over chaos are lacking in this section, except the exorcism after the transfiguration. While Jesus doesn't appear so sharply as a warrior figure in these two Gospels in the journey section, he does emerge as Victor nonetheless. How is this possible?

The emergence of Jesus as Victor appears in at least three ways: (1) Jesus continues to battle evil; (2) Jesus himself is the divine Warrior who gives his life instead of taking the lives of others; and (3) the victory of Jesus is to be appropriated by Jesus' followers, in their authority over evil and in the shape of their life together.

1. *Jesus continues to battle against evil.* In Mark the battle is joined over Jesus' messiahship when Peter serves as mouthpiece for Satan. On this front Jesus fought Satan's effort to subvert his messianic rule into the structures of the world, the imperious and oppressive rule of the kings of the earth (10:42–43). Faced with this assault, Jesus *rebuked* the power of Satan, and then instantly announced the suffering of the Son of humanity. From that point onward in the narrative the path of conquest is clear; it is the ὁδός way of faithful obedience to God, a way to suffering and death, and then resurrection. But at this point in the narrative the victory is really through the eyes of Jesus' faith—that God will sustain and vindicate him. What is clear is that the Warrior will become the Holy Martyr.

Matthew declares Jesus' ultimate victory through Peter's confession and appropriates its power into the life of his community. The passion-resurrection *predictions* are there as in Mark, but the outcome is clear: "I will build my church, and the gates of Hades shall not prevail against it." The powers of evil are overcome, for Jesus is the Messiah, the Son of the living God. Victory for the faithful is projected even into the endtime when the disciples shall sit on twelve thrones. The struggle comes in maintaining the victory in the life of the church (see 3 below).

For Luke, the decisive victory of the battle is depicted in this section. The sent-out gospel spells the doom of Satan. From now on the world is divided into those who reject Jesus, thereby incurring judgment, and those who accept Jesus, thereby gaining life now, and

[130] I use both phrases in order not to reduce all divine warfare imagery to the more specific holy war model that has been associated with the Deuteronomist's theology and the work of Gerhard von Rad.

through costly discipleship, in the world to come. Salvation comes to the lost (chs. 15 and 19:1–9), for the goods of the strong man have been plundered. Peace wins, both positively in praise to God and in doom for those who know not "the things that make for peace."

2. *Jesus as dying divine warrior.* Mark's and Matthew's testimony to Jesus as one "who gives his life as a ransom for many" (Mark 10:45; Matt 20:28) is matched by Luke's chiastic center and climactic didactic statement: "I must be on my way, for it is impossible for a prophet to be killed outside of Jerusalem" (13:33) and "For the Son of Man came to seek out and to save the lost" (19:10). As noted in the reversals of Deuteronomy's commands to kill enemies or notorious sinners, Luke's Jesus brings life to those doomed to death under the earlier rules. Sinners are the most welcomed, and the hated Samaritans in the middle of the land (!), emerge as models of the new way.

Precisely on this point, the Gospel tradition shows its most radical transformation. The divine Warrior comes no longer to kill the enemy, but to give his life for others, thus ending the enmity through the gospel of peace and love. The enemy category continues only from the side of those who refuse the gospel's peace and justice. And for those who persist in enmity toward the gospel, divine judgment is portrayed in severe tone.

William Brownlee has helpfully addressed the issue of continuity and discontinuity between the testaments, specifically via the trajectory of holy war to holy martyr, or perhaps better, divine warrior to divine martyr—though it must be emphasized that not all strands of emphasis in the OT support this polarity. Brownlee speaks first of sharp discontinuity: Jesus' victory contrasts sharply to that of the Maccabean warriors (167–130 B.C.) whose blood pleaded "for vengeance like the blood of Abel"; the warrior Jesus' "blood pleads only for forgiveness and redemption." Brownlee sees continuity, however, in that Jesus carries forward Yahweh's warfare. As a human warrior-martyr he is also the divine warrior defeating demonic forces. His exorcisms inaugurate a holy war which climaxes in the victory of his death and resurrection. Brownlee rightly regards this as a crucial trajectory in the relation between the Testaments :

> In the area of biblical theology, we often see modifications and enrichments as we move from the earliest to the latest Scriptures; but in the present case we have the most dramatic development and transformation of all, as we move from the institution of Holy War, with its *ḥērem* of total destruction of the enemy, to the divine-human Warrior, Who gives His life for the salvation of the whole world, including His own enemies. Yet, between the *ḥērem* and the Cross there is not simply

contrast, a radical break with the substitution of one for the other, but
a theological continuity whereby in the history of Holy War the one led
to the other.[131]

This continuity and radical transformation is clearly present
in this central section of the canonical forms of the Synoptic Gospel
tradition. God's battle against evil climaxes and turns to ultimate
victory as Jesus' gospel of peace dethrones Satan and as Jesus the
divine warrior voluntarily enters Jerusalem to suffer and die, to give
his life as a ransom for many. In addition to Brownlee's point is
another: the continuity lies not only in the warfare theme as such:
both the central section's inclusion of the outsider and enemy into the
covenant of love and the themes of peace and justice have deep and
strong roots in the OT. The discontinuity and transformation of which
Brownlee speaks is only a part of trajectory in which story shapes
story. The number of parallels in Evan's correspondences testifies to a
significant unity, and the chords of harmony would be even stronger
if Isaiah or another of the prophets were the literary prototype. But
precisely because this section dialogues with the echoes of Deuteronomy, Brownlee's focus on the theme of warfare, and its changing
expressions, is quite to the point.

3. *Appropriating the victory as believers.* Mark's firm linkage
of Christology to discipleship, Matthew's direct address to the church,
and Luke's mission of the Seventy depict in complementary ways the
appropriation of Jesus' victory for the communities of believers receiving these Gospels. Together these portraits provide three essential
ingredients for the church's continued victory over evil.

Mark's accent means the disciple must keep in focus a twofold truth: that Jesus in his suffering Christology leads the way—
always, faithfully, and perfectly—and that the disciples' role is to trust
in Jesus' victory, not to seek power to win or rule. From human
resources alone, "it is impossible to enter the kingdom," but with God
working through Jesus all things are possible. The hard demands of
discipleship are not an oppressive rule of Jesus over his followers, but

---

[131] W. Brownlee, "From Holy War to Holy Martyrdom," in *The Quest
for the Kingdom of God*, ed. H. B. Huffman, F. A. Spina, A. R. W. Green (Winona
Lake, Ind.: Eisenbrauns, 1983), 286, 291. W. Klassen has noted also a trans-
formation on this topic in the LXX translation of the OT term, "man of war"
(Exod 15:3), which is "The Lord destroys war" (κύριος συντρίβων πολέμους):
W. Klassen, "The God of Peace: New Testament Perspectives on God," in
Towards a Theology of Peace, ed. S. Tunnicliffe (London: European Nuclear
Disarmament, 1989), 127.

an invitation to participate in his victory, for which he gave his all. The call to enter the kingdom like a child, to give up one's wealth, and not to use divorce to bypass a marriage commitment, show in nonnegotiable terms that the kingdom *comes* in power for those who choose to follow Jesus. Disciples do not *inherit* eternal life, but rather *receive* life by humbly and unassumingly giving themselves for the kingdom and for others as servants, in the name of Jesus. Only through prayer and in the name of Jesus will the demons be cast out; only through bearing the cross and forsaking all that hinders following Jesus will God vindicate the disciple. But indeed this is possible only when given *sight,* Jesus' gift, to enable following *in the way.*

Matthew anchors the believers' victory in authority given by the Christ as Son of the living God. The authority has power over Hades, which means triumph over the powers of death and Satan. The authority to *bind* and *loose* means not only moral guidance for believers, but also deliverance from Satan's power and absolution from sin's shame and guilt. Practically, this has the effect of loosing from Satan or allowing the bondage to remain. This is the constitutional prerogative of the church, but its daily life is beset with more subtle troubles and blessings: which taxes to pay, how to avoid offense of "little ones," how to curb internal impulses that lead to ruin, how to reprove a sister who sins and how to put up with a brother who always needs forgiveness. At the heart of the instruction on how to handle these daily inroads into the community's victory over evil is the appeal to seek unendingly the lost one, to forgive untiringly, and thus experience the relational empowerment of "my Father who is in heaven."

Luke's appropriation of the victory of Jesus into the life of the community includes an offense and a defense. The offense is that symbolized by the mission of the Seventy; extending the gospel of peace is the surest way to defeat the enemy. When the kingdom is proclaimed, cosmic power relationships are reordered. The strong man's goods are plundered and jubilation praise rises to heaven, to God as rejoicing Father (10:21–22; 15). The *defense* is to free oneself from anxious cares about money and possessions (chs. 12 and 16; in 18 and 19), and to place simple trust in the Father as exemplified in the Lord's, or Disciples', Prayer, that "the heavenly Father (will) give the Holy Spirit to those who ask him" (11:13). In this way the believers, as babes, will have *authority* given by Jesus "to tread . . . over all the power of the enemy" and even more, to rejoice that their "names are written in heaven," thus taking up the praise of the angelic host, "Glory to God in the highest heaven and on earth peace . . . !"

As Paul's biographer, Luke saw the point as Paul put it: "the God of peace will shortly crush Satan under your feet" (Rom 16:20).[132]

Table II: The Use and Function of Luke's Journey References

9:51–53 Three uses each of πορεύομαι and πρόσωπον; all are linked to Jerusalem as the destiny (one, to Samaria as route)

9:56 Form of πορεύομαι: Jesus and disciples go on. This use, with the six in vv. 51–53, clearly shows that the motif arises from Jesus' actual journey to Jerusalem, even though it carries also other functions in the narrative.

9:57 πορεύομαι is used with ἐν τῇ ὁδῷ and teaching on discipleship follows. The journey is connected with discipleship.

10:1 The Seventy are sent out before his face (πρόσωπον) into every city and town where he was about to come (ἔρχεσθαι). Here the journey is connected with mission.[133]

10:38 A πορεύομαι form is used in connection with the arrival at Mary and Martha's home (no location is given); Jesus commends Mary's learning. Again, a journey notice is used in connection with teaching on discipleship.

13:22 Two forms of πορεύομαι are used (διεπορεύετο and πορείαν ποιούμενος). The one functions to state that Jerusalem is the destiny of the journey. Then teaching both on discipleship and on the inclusion of outsiders (v. 29) follows, i.e., mission.

13:31–33 Three uses of the πορεύομαι form occur, but only two connote motion of Jesus. One use consists of the Pharisees' command for him to *go from* the area, since Herod wants to kill him. The second use connects his *going on* for three days with the Jerusalem destiny for his death.

14:25–35 Jesus' going is accompanied (συνεπορεύοντο) by great multitudes. The term introduces teaching on discipleship.[134]

---

[132] The term ἐν τάχει might also be translated "swiftly," rather than "shortly".

[133] In 10:37, πορεύομαι occurs in the imperative with ποίει, addressed to the lawyer at the end of the Good Samaritan story. It is used in relation to discipleship, but not in relation to Jesus himself, as are the other uses.

[134] Within this pericope is a parabolic saying which speaks of a king going (πορευόμενος) to encounter another king in war. In light of the discussion below on Jesus' portrait in this section, this use may be considered an image of his mission.

17:11–19 Forms of πορεύομαι appear three times (vv. 11, 14, 19).
Only the first use is a *Reisenotiz* to designate Jesus' destiny in Jerusalem. The other two are used in connection with an outsider, the Samaritan leper, who gives thanks for his healing. This is indirectly related to mission.[135]

18:35–45 Jesus is drawing near (ἐγγίζω) to Jericho and a blind man hears of a multitude going through (διαπορευομένου). The journeying motif is correlated with a healing and the man's following, i.e., discipleship.

19:11–27 Jesus speaks a parable in which a nobleman went (ἐπορεύθη) into a far country to receive a kingdom. The parable mirrors Jesus' going away (ἀναλήμψις) and calls disciples to faithful service.

19:28–38 Jesus' entry to Jerusalem uses πορεύομαι twice (vv. 30, 36) and also ἐγγίζω twice (vv. 29, 37; cf. ἐγγύς in v. 11). These uses denote Jesus' arrival at Jerusalem as the destiny of the journey.

19:39–44 In one last indication, Jesus draws near (ἐγγίζω) to the city, which is Jesus' own destiny.

Table III: Correspondences Between
Luke 9:51—19:44 and Deuteronomy

A correspondence of parallel thought is designated (P); one of transformation in thought, (T); reversal of the thought structure, i.e., contrast, (C). Brackets indicate my additions to Evans's content.

Texts	No. Correspondence	Relationship
Deut 1/ Luke 10:1–3,17–20 [really 9:51–53]	1. Israel *journeys* under Moses to Promised Land/Jesus and his disciples journey to Jerusalem:	C
	If Jesus' destiny is viewed as glory, then:	P
	2. The land set "before your face" and Twelve sent out/ Jesus sends out Seventy. Nature of mission:	T

---

[135] In 18:18 εἰσπορεύομαι is used for "entering" the kingdom of God. But again, this use, while connected with discipleship, does not have Jesus as subjective participant in the action, as do the other occurrences. Hence, it is not a *Reisenotiz*.

	[3. People in land are too great and tall; can't conquer and then Lord prevents going/ Mission is successful; Jesus sees Satan falling from heaven]:	C
Deut 2–3:22/ Luke 10:4–16	4. Messengers sent to Sihon and Og with word of peace/ Seventy sent out with word of peace:	P
	5. If rejected, destroy/ If rejected wipe the dust off your feet and leave:	T
	6. What Lord did to two kings/ Jesus prophesies judgment upon Chorazin, Bethsaida, and Capernaum:	P
Deut 3:23–4:40/ Luke 10:21–24	7. Moses is servant mediator/Jesus is revealer-mediator. Both texts contain similar terms: "in that hour," "wisdom and understanding," "seeing and hearing" God's disclosure:	P
Deut 5–6/ Luke 10:25–27	8. Shema and "inherit the land . . . in order to live"/ lawyer asks about inheriting eternal life and answers with Shema:	P/T
Deut 7/ Luke 10:29–37	9. Destroy the foreigner; show no mercy/ Parable of Good Samaritan; show mercy:	C
Deut 8:1–3/ Luke 10:38–42	10. Living by word of God in both:	P
Deut 8:4–20/ Luke 11:1–13	11. Father to son instruction/ Son to Father prayer; "eating" occurs in both:	T
Deut 9:1–10:11/ Luke 11:14–26	12. Lord drives out strong fierce nations/Jesus drives out strong demons; term, "finger of God"/ἐν (τῷ) δακτύλῳ (τοῦ) θεοῦ, in both:	T
Deut 10:12–11/ Luke 11:27–36	13. Lord requires only keeping Torah/ Jesus, "hear word of God and do it." Also a "stiff-necked people" who saw great wonders in Egypt/an "evil generation" who seeks a sign:	P
Deut 12:1–16/ Luke 11:37–12:12	14. Clean and unclean in both: reject/accept:	C
Deut 12:17–32/ Luke 12:13–13:34	15. When Lord prospers you; keep commands to gain inheritance; rejoice in wealth/ Life is more than possessions; seek kingdom, sell, give alms and gain eternal life:	C
Deut 13:1–11/ Luke 12:35–53	16. Death to those who go after other gods; don't let family members entice you/ Reward and punishment as the Lord's stewards; give up family members for Jesus, thus division:	P/T

Deut 13:12–32/ Luke 12:54–13:5	17. Destruction of city for apostasy/Jesus' teachings on discernment and judgment/group calamity, were they worse sinners? No, all must repent:	T
Deut 15:1–18/ Luke 13:10–21	18. Release from debts and slavery/ Jesus releases a woman from bondage:	T
Deut 20/ Luke 14:15–35	19. Excused from Lord's battle for new wife, house, vineyard/ Similar excuses of invited guests to Great Banquet who miss the Feast:	P/T
Deut 21:15–22:4/ Luke 15	20. How father handles rebellious son—stone/ Father seeks prodigal son—celebrates return:	C
Deut 23:15–24:4/ Luke 16:1–18	21. Treatment of fugitive slave; law against usury; granting bill of divorce/Unjust steward forgives oppressed debtors; Pharisees—lovers of money; against divorce—adultery:	P/C
Deut 24:6–25:3/ Luke 16:19–18:8	22. Injunctions against oppressing poor and needy/Lord judges those who oppress poor:	P

5

##

THE FORMATIVE INFLUENCE OF OLD TESTAMENT TEMPLE TRADITIONS ON THE SYNOPTIC PREPASSION (AND PASSION) NARRATIVE

THE TEMPLE TRADITIONS

As Niek Poulssen demonstrates, kingship and temple traditions converge in Old Testament theological understanding.[1] King David brings the Ark to Jerusalem from Shiloh to weld together the kingly rule and the priestly functions of the earlier tabernacle traditions. Poulssen identifies three functions of the king in relation to the temple: "(1) the king is a temple builder; (2) the temple and palace belong to a unified architectural complex; (3) the king has jurisdiction over the temple cult and at times performs priestly functions."[2] Even in the divided kingdom, the connection between king and temple continues in the north. Amaziah, priest of Bethel, silences Amos' prophetic critique against the sanctuary of Israel by threatening Amos with Jeroboam's jurisdiction over the Bethel sanctuary: the temple "is the king's sanctuary, and it is the temple of the kingdom" (Amos 7:13).[3]

As noted in chapter 2, Poulssen assesses negatively the impact that the "southern" traditions of temple and kingship had upon the earlier "northern" Mosaic traditions. Nonetheless, Israel dearly loves

---

[1] Poulssen, *König und Temple.*

[2] Summarized by Bernhard W. Anderson in his review of Poulssen's book: *CBQ* 31 (1969), 450.

[3] Levenson uses this incident to show how the northern and southern theological types are reversed: Amos, a prophet from the south, rails against the king-priest alliance with its degenerate Yahwism; Amaziah, a northern priest, defends the royal temple and palace (*Sinai and Zion*, 202).

its temple; it symbolizes its religious identity. Psalms 48 and 84 (JB) reflect these sentiments:.

> How I love your palace,
>   Yahweh Sabaoth!
> How my soul yearns and pines
>   for Yahweh's courts!
> My heart and my flesh sing for joy
>   to the living God. . . .
>
> A single day in your courts
>   is worth more than a thousand elsewhere;
> merely to stand on the steps of God's house
>   is better than living with the wicked (84:1–2, 10).
>
> God, in your temple
>   we reflect on your love:
> God, your praise, like your name,
>   reaches to the ends of the world. . . .
>
> Go through Zion, walk round her
>   counting her towers,
> admiring her walls,
>   reviewing her palaces;
>
> then tell the next generation
>   that God is here,
> our God and leader,
>   forever and ever (48:9, 12–14).

The canonical accounts of David's desire to build a "house" for the Lord disclose how central Zion's temple and throne were to Israel's faith: "David, your offspring shall build a house for my name, and I will establish the throne of his kingdom forever. I will be his father, and he shall be my son" (2 Sam 7:13–14; cf. 2 Chr 17:12–14). These stand despite the Lord's veto of David's desire through the prophet Nathan; further, the Lord's counter plan promises his building of a house "for my name" through David's offspring. In the later Chronicler's account, the temple dominates the narrative. The people celebrate when the Ark finds its resting place in the sacred tent in Jerusalem (1 Chr 16:7–36; Ps 132). David's farewell speeches focus on the passing of God's promise to Solomon, with the charge to build the temple and a review of the organization of the sons of Levi to care adequately for the temple and its functions (chs. 22–23). David's farewell prayer reaches its zenith on the temple theme (29:16); then the Chronicler devotes nine chapters to the building of the temple (2 Chr 1—9). In 2 Chronicles Solomon's prayer of dedication reiterates God's promise to David (6:4–11) and calls all the people to covenant renewal (vv. 12ff.). Solomon implores the Lord to forgive the people when they sin and depart from his ways (vv. 22–39). A final rehearsal of God's promise and Solomon's charge to the people reflects the unconditional Davidic covenant form *and* the conditional Sinai type (7:11–22).

In the prophetic literature the Zion temple is the object of critique, even judgment, and blessing, for the nations stream to Zion for salvation and *šālôm*. Amos, addressing the north, declares woe to those at ease in Zion and secure in Samaria, for God abhors the songs, feasts, and sacrifices of Israel's worship as long as social injustices abound (5:21–6:7). Isaiah thunders a similar message against Judah (chs. 1 and 3), but he also foresees Zion as the world capital of Yahweh's justice, established by Torah (2:1–5). Because Israel does not trust in Yahweh for defense (chs. 7–8, 10), its doom is imminent, but God's promise to David will not fail (9:1–7; 11:1–9; cf. chs. 30–32). Exilic Isaiah proclaims Zion's endurance and resurrection (esp. ch. 52) and restorationist Isaiah sees foreigners streaming into "my holy mountain," whose burnt offerings and sacrifices will be accepted "on my altar; for my house shall be called a house of prayer for all nations" (56:7). Jeremiah's famous temple court sermon declares doom upon Judah for its deceptive trust in the temple's security (ch. 7), and Micah's castigation of Israel's sham worship (6:1–8) brings doom (ch. 1; cf. Ps 74) and restoration to Jerusalem (7:11ff.), declared by "the Lord from his holy temple" (1:2d). Post-exilic Malachi links the coming of the eschatological "messenger who shall prepare the way before me" with the Lord suddenly coming to his temple (3:1). Throughout all these shifting and yet stable scenarios of God's presence, Israel regularly chants the songs of ascent (Pss 121–35), with either the literal temple the goal of their pilgrimage or God's temple erected in the midst of their worship through eyes of faith.

McKelvey describes the unifying role of the temple in Israel; the various expectations for a new temple in Jewish literature, including the Old Testament prophets, the Apocrypha and Pseudepigrapha, early rabbinic sources; and the notions of a heavenly temple that emerged in Jewish and Greek literature.[4] McKelvey shows how widespread the expectations for a new temple were in the centuries preceding and concurrent to Jesus' coming and the writing of the Gospels.

---

[4]R. J. McKelvey, *The New Temple: The Church in the New Testament* (London: Oxford University, 1969).

Poulssen and others[5] have described the Old Testament historical and theological matrix in which the temple and kingship traditions are linked in Israel. These themes join also in the prepassion and passion narratives of the Synoptic Gospels. Hence, this chapter and the next consider both the prepasssion and the passion narratives. In Mark especially the temple theme not only dominates the prepassion narrative (chs. 11–13) but continues and culminates in the passion narrative proper (chs. 14–15). The kingship theme, as a complementary component, begins in the prepassion narrative[6] and moves into central compositional significance in the passion narrative. For these reasons both chapters 5 and 6 examine the entire Jerusalem component of the Synoptic Gospels' content. That these two themes are so closely intertwined both in the Old Testament theological traditions and in the Synoptic Gospels' structure witnesses to the thesis of this study.

MARK

If the influence of the ὁδός-discipleship emphasis on Mark 8:27–10:52 is the most widely recognized compositional contribution in Mark's structure, the prominence of the temple motif in Mark 11–13 (with consequences in 14–15) ranks second.[7] Four studies are of special importance: Ernst Lohmeyer's *Lord of the Temple* and Lloyd Gaston's *No Stone Upon Another* for both wider background and the role of temple and cult in Mark's Gospel; and John Donahue's *Are You the Christ?* and Donald Juel's *Messiah and Temple* for analyses of how temple and kingship themes converge in the trial narrative against the background of how Mark uses the temple motif in his composition. These contributions together with Werner Kelber's contributions and

---

[5]R. E. Clements, *God and Temple* (Oxford: Blackwell, 1965). F. R. McCurley's study of the "Sacred Mountain" trajectory is also pertinent (*Ancient Myths*, esp. 151–60).

[6]The kingship theme begins even earlier, e.g., Peter's messianic confession (8:29) and Bartimaeus' outcry, "Son of David" (10:47–48). In a still broader sense it begins with Jesus' proclamation in 1:14–15 that the kingdom of God has come near.

[7]One might argue that neither of these is as prominent as is Mark's unfolding Christology linked to his messianic secret. Certainly this is a prominent feature, but it does not provide the distinctive structure of a given section; it provides rather the main theme of the overall plot (Tannehill, "Gospel of Mark," 57–96).

Sharyn Echols Dowd's recent study of Mark 11:22–25 inform the following analysis.[8]

1. Content and Structure

The term "prepassion narrative" here designates the Synoptics' content that is located in Jerusalem but precedes the announcement of the plot of the chief priests and scribes to kill Jesus; this announcement is also identified by the time-marker, "two days before the Passover." In each of the three Gospels the section then narrates the triumphal entry and ends with the Olivet discourse. In Mark this consists of chapters 11–13, which may be divided into three sub-units or segments,[9] as follows:

Ch. 11 Jesus Comes To, Cleanses, and Claims the Temple.

Ch. 12 Jesus Judges and Condemns the Temple Tenants.

Ch. 13 Jesus Foretells the End of the Temple.

Recognized widely by scholarship, the entire section is framed by the temple motif. The word "temple" (ἱερόν), occurs eight times in this section (11:11, 15, 16, 27; 12:35; 13:1, 2). Allusions to Isaiah 5 and a quotation from Psalm 118 in the Parable of the Vineyard's Tenants

---

[8] Kelber, "Kingdom and Parousia" and *The Kingdom in Mark*, cited in ch. 4; S. E. Dowd, *Prayer, Power, and the Problem of Suffering* (SBLDS 105; Atlanta: Scholars, 1988).

[9] J. Donahue (*Are You the Christ? The Trial Narrative in the Gospel of Mark* [SBLDS 10; Society of Biblical Literature, 1973], 116–17), citing Pesch's stichometric analysis, regards chs. 11—12 as three units: 11:1–26, an introductory section with the cleansing of the temple as the central focus; 11:27—12:12, a controversy and parable which by virtue of their content require the temple setting of the preceding material (see 11:27); and 12:13–44, a loose sequence of controversies also located in the temple setting (12:35). D. Juel (*Messiah and Temple: The Trial of Jesus in the Gospel of Mark* [Missoula, Mont.: Scholars, 1977], 128) suggests the joining of 11:27–33 to chapter 12 because this segment is presented as *teaching* in the temple (11:27; 12:35; cf. 14:49, a reference back to these events). The 11:27—12:44 segment thus differs from 11:1–26 consisting of *action* in the temple. Chapter 13 also differs from 11:27–44 in that Jesus leaves the temple, overlooks it from opposite Mount Olivet, and speaks of its doom. E. S. Malbon rightly sees the temple and Mount Olivet functioning in narrative opposition: "Opposite the institution of the temple and its leaders—chief priests, scribes, and elders—is . . . [Jesus'] community of the disciples and its leaders—'Peter and James and John and Andrew' (13:3). Opposite the physical structure of the temple is its future destruction . . . [i.e., Jesus' pronouncement (13:2, 14)]. Opposite the ritual demands of the temple is the command to 'Watch' " (13:37). Malbon, *Narrative Space*, 123–24.

(12:1–12) are also temple-oriented. Further, chapters 14–15 continue the use of temple vocabulary in three crucial texts: 14:58, 15:29, and 15:38. But here a different word, ναός, is used. As numerous scholars note, the meaning here is to the sanctuary itself, whereas ἱερόν designates the complex of temple buildings.[10] Indeed, the temple motif controls the narrative plot of this section. With justification, Eduard Schweizer titles chapters 11–16, "Jesus and the Temple," regarding 11–13 as section A and 14–16 as section B.[11] Leander E. Keck observes that the passion story in Mark, chapters 11–16, "is inaugurated by the entry to the temple . . . [which] alerts the reader to a major motif of the subsequent narrative: Jesus and the temple."[12]

2. Jesus against the Temple

a. Temple (ἱερόν) in chapters 11–13. In Mark Jesus goes directly to the temple, the goal of the triumphal entry (11:11). Verse 11 concludes the triumphal entry and introduces the next events, for which Mark uses his famous literary technique of intercalation, or sandwiching: the cleansing of the temple is sandwiched between the beginning and the end of the cursing of the fig tree episode. Mark thereby casts the shadow of the withered fig tree over the destiny of the temple: the cleansing of the temple is really its judgment.[13] Because the temple has failed to be "a house of prayer for all nations,"

---

[10]In his discussion of ναός, O. Michel says that although there appears to be no absolute distinction between ναός and ἱερόν, ναός does take precedence as a designation for the sanctuary part of the temple (ναός, TDNT, 4.882). Juel makes a similar point but notes also that Mark's use itself calls for a distinction (Messiah and Temple, 127–28). D. E. Garland makes the same point regarding Matthew's use, and considers the two uses that might argue otherwise (12:5; 27:5): D. Garland, The Intention of Matthew 23 (NovTSup 52; Leiden: E. J. Brill, 1979), n. 17 on p. 199.

[11]Schweizer, Good News, 7–10.

[12]L. E. Keck, "Christological Motifs in Mark 14:1–42: A Preliminary, Tentative, Series of Observations," SBL unpub. paper, 1971, 2.

[13]W. R. Telford has brought this view into sharp focus, holding that, for Mark and his readers, the fig tree symbolizes Israel. Thus, Mark intends the cursing of the fig tree to be an eschatological sign that prefigures the destruction of Jerusalem and its Temple: "Mark . . . wishes the fate of the unfruitful tree to be seen as a proleptic sign prefiguring the destruction of the temple cultus." Further, "he invites . . . his readers to understand the Entry and Cleansing traditions as a visit of judgment upon the Jewish people and their Temple, rather than the restoration expected with the coming of the Son of David." See W. Telford, The Barren Temple and the Withered Tree (JSNTSS 1; Sheffield: JSOT, 1980), 39–59, 238–39, quotations on 238 and 262.

its end is inevitable.[14] Jesus casts out (ἐκβάλλω, used elsewhere in Mark for exorcisms) the money-changers; he stops all the commercial traffic and "would not allow anyone to carry anything through the temple" (11:16). The word *anything* translates σκεῦος, likely referring to the goods sold to the pilgrims in the temple.[15] Jesus' actions declare a halt to the separatistic holiness scheme that protects and insulates the sacred from the profane; they mark the end of the system that puts pilgrim Jews and God-fearers at the mercy of the temple merchants and aristocracy. With Jesus' coming as Lord of the temple, the opposition between the sacred and the profane ends; the significance of its regulated access to God ends also—and thus its future destruction is only a matter of course. To Jesus' followers who read Mark's Gospel, the imminent destruction of the physical temple is to be seen as merely the outworking of its essential destruction in Jesus' actions decades earlier.[16]

Jesus then calls the disciples to a faith which dares to say to *this* mountain (τῷ ὄρει τούτῳ) on which the temple stood, "Be cast into the sea." Mark thus reverses the eschatological expectation that in the last days the mountain of the house of the Lord shall be exalted above the hills (Isa 2:2; Mic 4:1). Instead, this mountain is to be uprooted and cast into the sea.[17] True worship will be independent of the temple, and it will be marked by the believer's prayer of faith and forgiveness of sins: "the evangelist has arranged his materials in chapter 11 so as to follow the proleptic destruction of the temple with the necessary assurances about the efficacy of prayer, and he has used the fig tree pericope as a metaphorical clamp to hold the ideas together."[18]

---

[14]Schweizer, *Good News*, 14; Gaston, *No Stone Upon Another*, 474–75. Donahue speaks of the "anti–temple" theme that runs through this section and says that the cleansing, framed by the fig tree cursing, suggests "an eschatological visitation"—presumably judgment—upon the temple (Donahue, *Are You the Christ?*, 113–14). Juel says the temple cleansing in Mark has a didactic function in Mark and implies "the rejection of the official representatives of Israel, the leaders of the temple establishment" (130–31).

[15]Malbon, *Narrative Space*, 121–22.

[16]For the collapsing of the sacred/profane distinction and related emphases I am indebted to Malbon, ibid., 121–24: "Jesus . . . abandons the temple not because its sacrality has been profaned but because he experiences a breakdown of the sacred/profane distinction" (124).

[17]Telford, *Barren Temple*, 163; E. L. Schnellbächer, "The Temple as Focus of Mark's Theology," *HBT* 5/2 (1983), 102–3.

[18]Dowd, *Prayer*, 53.

The cleansing of the temple thus carries a powerful narrative role in Mark's Jerusalem section of the Gospel. Juel identifies four features which highlight its didactic function: the framing of the scene by the fig tree episode; the allusion to Isaiah 56:7 focusing on Mark's distinctive phrase, "for all nations" (πᾶσιν τοῖς ἔθνεσιν); the allusion to Jeremiah 7:11 focusing on "den of robbers" (σπήλαιον λῃστῶν); and the use of the phrase, "house of prayer" in verse 17.[19] Mark's "for all nations" (11:17) carries forward his larger narrative emphasis on Gentiles in this section (13:10; 14:9; 15:39; likely also 14:28; 16:7), turning the temple event into an indictment upon the self-serving practices of the Jerusalem aristocracy. The context of Isaiah 56:7 portrays a fulfillment of God's eschatological promises in which foreigners stream into Jerusalem, are welcomed to worship on God's holy mountain, and present their sacrifices at the temple. But Jesus' act of judgment on the temple disqualifies it from fulfilling the eschatological vision. Hence another place will be chosen as the center for God's eschatological purposes, i.e., Galilee (16:7), and that not centripetally but centrifugally.[20]

Mark's second quotation comes from Jeremiah's temple court sermon (Jer 7:11) which judges Israel's religious leaders for their presumption that they can continue sinning and yet count on God to defend their temple. The fall of Shiloh warns them that God can and will destroy the temple also if they do not repent and change their ways. Mark's use of the phrase "house of prayer" in 11:17, connected to the prayer theme of verses 22–25, may suggest, as Juel notes, that this function can and will continue without the temple. The gathered praying believers will replace the ἱερόν that is now under judgment.[21]

The debate about authority (ἐξουσία) in verses 27–33 follows as a logical consequence of the temple episode. Verse 18 had already indicated that the chief priests and the scribes were seeking a way to destroy Jesus; hence they now zero in on the issue of his authority.

---

[19]Juel, *Messiah and Temple*, 130.

[20]Schnellbächer identifies the Mount of Transfiguration, in Galilee or further north, as the eschatological replacement ("Temple as Focus," 104–5, 107). The text points to Galilee for this function, but hardly the Mount of Transfiguration. Only in Matthew is the return to Galilee connected to a mountain.

[21]Juel relates this phrase, "house of prayer," to that which will be rebuilt (14:58); the author may regard "the Christian [praying] community as a replacement of the rejected temple establishment" (*Messiah and Temple*, 136).

Jesus' counter question about John's baptism silences them; thus he refuses to answer their question. But his following Parable of the Vineyard's Tenants sharpens the conflict. In one of Mark's most allegorical parables, the vineyard represents Israel; the tower, the temple; and the wicked tenants, the temple authorities.[22] With Isaiah's Song of the Vineyard (ch. 5) as background and the quotation from Psalm 118:22–23 in Mark 12:10–11, temple imagery pervades the parable.[23] As Dan O. Via, Jr., has noted, the dominant figures in the parable are not the owner or the son, but the tenants.[24] Mark 12:12 confirms this: "When they realized that he had told this parable against them, they wanted to arrest him, but they feared the crowd. So they left him and went away." The "they" of this verse refers back to the servants in the parable, the "chief priests, scribes and elders" of 11:27 and the "chief priests and scribes" of 11:18 who sought to kill Jesus. Thus, the entire narrative is tightly unified; Jesus, the temple, and the temple tenants all carry major roles in the developing plot.

Next follows a section in which representatives of Jerusalem's religious leadership pose trap questions for Jesus to answer. Mark 12:13 begins: "Then they sent to him some Pharisees and some Herodians to trap him." The Sadducees in verse 18 and "one of the scribes" in verse 28 continue the same effort to best Jesus in public argument. Although each of the three efforts has potentially negative consequences upon Jesus' popularity with the crowds, the first "round" also carries liability for Jesus' personal security. Publicly espousing tax resistance to Rome's oppressive tax policies could be perceived as treason, as Luke 23:1–2 suggests. In each of the three lines of questioning—whether it is lawful to pay taxes to Caesar, the Sadducees' effort to belittle the Pharisees' belief in the resurrection, and the scribes' haggling over the greatest of the commandments—Jesus confounds his opponents. Having deflected their three "fiery darts," Jesus then puts to them a riddle. Rehearsing the scribal view that the Christ is to be the son of David, and then quoting Psalm 110, "The Lord said

---

[22]Gaston, *No Stone Upon Another,* 476; Schweizer, *Good News,* 239–41; Ernst Lohmeyer, "Das Gleichnis von den bösen Weingärtern (Mark 12:1–12," in *Urchristliche Mystik: Neutestamentliche Studien,* 2d ed. (Darmstadt: H. Gertner, 1958), 161–81, and *Lord of the Temple: A Study of the Relation Between Cult and Gospel,* trans. S. Todd (Edinburgh/London: Oliver and Boyd, 1962), 44–45.

[23]Psalm 118:22 speaks of the "festal procession . . . to the horns of the altar." The Psalm was used especially in connection with ascent to Jerusalem for the Feast of Tabernacles.

[24]D. O. Via, Jr., *The Parables: Their Literary and Existential Dimensions* (Philadelphia: Fortress, 1967), 130–37.

to my Lord," Jesus asks how the Messiah-Christ is both David's son and Lord. The exchange occurs "in the temple," which Jesus continues to claim as his platform for teaching and authority, undoubtedly an intolerable nuisance to the temple authorities. The great crowd that listened with delight (12:37) likely remembered the political and religious struggles of their history which had frequently focused on the temple's ownership: Lord *and* king or Lord *versus* king! To whom really did the temple belong? The chapter closes with two contrasting episodes on religious piety: a condemnation of the parading piety of the scribes who "devour widows' houses and for a pretense make long prayers" and a commendation of the humble piety of the poor widow whose alms of two copper coins were "everything she had, all she had to live on" (vv. 38–44).

Then, in chapter 13 Jesus leaves the temple. His disciples extol the temple's architecture, and Jesus declares: "Do you see these great buildings? Not one stone will be left here upon another; all will be thrown down" (v. 2). The apocalyptic discourse answers the disciples' question in verse 4: "Tell us, when will this be, and what will be the sign that all these things are about to be accomplished?"[25] The reference to the "desolating sacrilege" (13:14) recalls the Seleucid control and desecration of the temple in 168–65 B.C., and thus orients the apocalyptic events of the chapter to the temple's doom. But, as Donahue notes, the end of the temple is not the *end* after all: "in ch. 13 Mark looks beyond the destruction of the temple to the formation of the new community."[26] Donahue points out that the Old Testament

---

[25]It is true, as T. J. Weeden, Sr., notes, that the apocalyptic discourse focuses first on Christology—not being duped by false messiahs—and that the temple theme is quite often eclipsed by christological emphases ("The Cross as Power in Weakness" in *The Passion in Mark,* ed. W. H. Kelber [Philadelphia: Fortress, 1976], 122–23). While these features could be used to support a θεῖος ἀνήρ opponent theory linked to an eschatology that connected the temple's doom to the parousia, as Weeden does in his *Mark—Traditions in Conflict* (Philadelphia: Fortress, 1971), 70–100, other textual clues and emphases are more prominent, as the following discussion will show in the correlation between Jesus and new temple conceptions.

[26]Donahue, *Are You the Christ?*, 132. Donahue seems to accept the view advanced by Conzelmann, Pesch, and Kelber that Mark is countering a false eschatology that linked the fall of the temple to the *end.* He then expands this point by suggesting that Mark's community had already been and is hereby further encouraged to distance itself from Jerusalem, and not hook its eschatology to the imminent fate of the temple (assuming Mark is writing in the A.D. 65–70 period when turmoil had besieged the temple). Thus, for Mark's readers the temple stands under judgment not only because it "has become the seat of

texts behind the imagery of verses 24–27 announce judgment. But in Mark the climax is the gathering of the elect: "Salvation awaits the community when the Son of Man comes to gather them into the nucleus of the new community (v. 27)."[27] Thus the events of the passion narrative (14:1ff.) are, on one level, the consequence of the anti–temple stance of Jesus in chapters 11–13: his opponents have their way. But, on another level, the passion narrative carries forward the predictive element of the "cornerstone" text of 12:10–11 via the gathering of the elect in 13:27.[28] A future community there will be! The passion narrative consummates the anti–temple theme, and as such is *its end*, but it also is thus set within a temporal tension in that it comes between the *end* emphases, culminating in chapter 13, and the hints of new beginnings in time as well as the endtime consummation, foretold also in chapter 13.

The intertwining of ends and beginnings is achieved through at least two narrative interplays. As R. H. Lightfoot has persuasively argued, the apocalyptic language of " 'the Son of Man coming in clouds' with great power and glory" (13:26) and the threefold call to watch at the end of chapter 13 have immediate connections to events in the passion story, i.e., Jesus' threefold call in Gethsemane to his sleeping disciples *to watch* (14:32–42) and Jesus' reply to the high priest, *viz*, "you will see the Son of Man seated at the right hand of Power, and coming with the clouds of heaven" (14:62).[29] The question thus emerges: how is it possible for Mark to interrelate so closely the destruction of the temple, the apocalyptic consummation, and the passion story itself? The following analysis of chapters 14–16 provides an answer.

b. Temple (ναός) *in chapters 14–16.* In chapters 14–16 the temple theme continues but with significant alteration. Whereas ἱερόν occurred regularly in chapters 11–13,[30] ναός now appears, in 14:58; 15:29; and 15:38. Mark first uses ναός in the accusation of the false witnesses as grounds for condemnation by the high priest. They

---

evil powers" (132), but because it has fostered a false eschatology that linked its doom to the *end*. But Mark's readers know now that its end was determined by Jesus' actions and words decades earlier, and their future lies elsewhere—with the Son of humanity who shall come to gather the elect (130–32).

[27]Donahue, *Are You the Christ?*, 133.

[28]Ibid., 135.

[29]R. H. Lightfoot, *Gospel Message*, 48–59.

[30]ἱερόν appears only once in chapters 14–16 in a text (14:49) that refers back to Jesus' teaching in the temple (chs. 11–13).

assert: "We heard him say, 'I will destroy this temple that is made with hands, and in three days I will build another, not made with hands' " (14:58). In 15:29–30 those passing by under the cross blasphemed (ἐβλασφήμουν) Jesus, echoing the words of the earlier accusation, "Aha! You who would destroy the temple and build it in three days, save yourself, and come down from the cross!" Then after Jesus expired, Mark's *first* comment is: "The curtain of the temple was torn in two, from top to bottom" (15:38). In all three uses the term ναός occurs.

Two features require comment: the "false accusation" and the "rent veil." First, is the charge really a *false* charge? Juel argues that although it is false at the surface level—i.e., Jesus did not say *he* will destroy the temple—it is ironically and profoundly true at a deeper level, for Jesus' actions and words render its functions meaningless.[31] The narrative repetition of the theme in 15:29 confirms that the charge did not go away, and that Jesus' death is intertwined with that charge. Hence, as Juel puts it: "Jesus is the destroyer of the temple in a figurative and in an ironic sense: its destruction is a result of his death, brought about by those in charge of the temple worship."[32] Elizabeth Struthers Malbon says that we must also recognize that Mark distinguishes between Jesus as "an opponent of the temple and the predictor of its destruction," on the one hand, which 11:12–20 and 13:2 affirm, and "as the destroyer of the temple," on the other hand, which 14:58 denies.[33] Further, several levels of irony are present. The temple charge leads the high priest to accuse Jesus of blasphemy, and then in 15:29 the passers-by are *blaspheming* Jesus—presumably an acknowledgment of the divine (God) in Jesus! Also, those who sought

[31]Juel, *Messiah and Temple*, 74–76, 206. Juel, concurring in part with Donahue's and Weeden's views that the charge is essentially true—as a piece of pre-Markan tradition, but false in that it is placed on Jesus' lips prior to his exaltation via suffering and death—and plays into the false θεῖος ἀνήρ Christology and imminentist eschatology (J. R. Donahue, "Temple, Trial, and Royal Christology," in *The Passion in Mark*, ed. W. H. Kelber [Philadelphia: Fortress, 1976], 67, n. 18), acknowledges that it must have come from pre-Markan tradition (cf. its slightly different forms in Matt and Luke), that it was a sensitive issue for early Christianity and would hardly have been created by the tradition, and that we cannot reconstruct its original form (Juel, ibid., 206–8). But Donahue thinks the pre-Christian Jewish traditions conjoined "the destruction and rebuilding of the Temple" not with the Messiah, but only with Yahweh. Thus, "We affirm that in 14:58 Mk creates a Christian exegesis of Temple expectations which function within his overall theological purpose" ("Temple, Trial," 68).
[32]Juel, *Messiah and Temple*, 206.
[33]Malbon, *Narrative Space*, 125.

to protect the temple by killing Jesus merely hastened its end in that
Jesus' death proleptically signaled its destruction.[34] In sum then, the
false accusation ironically empowers the alleged claim to become
truth, at a level of reality that transcends the power of battering rams
to smash down the temple's walls.

Whether the rent veil refers to the curtain between the Holy
of Holies and the Holy Place or the veil hung at the front of the entire
sanctuary is not clear. According to one view, this alternative is insig-
nificant, for as McKelvey,[35] Lohmeyer,[36] Bartsch,[37] and Gaston, quoting Clement, indicate: "the rending of the temple veil refers to the
destruction of the whole temple."[38] While this view is ultimately
correct (see below), one should, nonetheless, respect two points in
Mark's narrative. First, Mark does not use ἱερόν in 15:38; thus, the
destruction of the temple buildings (ἱερόν) is not directly implied.
The rent veil is the veil of the ναός, and this refers specifically to access
into the holy. Distinguishing between what is most holy, less holy, and
profane is primarily in view. Such distinctions are now abolished
essentially, thus fulfilling the 11:13–17 action and word. Second, the
sequence of 15:38 and 39 confirms that Mark's primary emphasis is
upon the rent veil as that which ends a profane-to-holy regulated
access to the divine presence. Hence, the distinction between the least
holy (the Gentile court) and the most holy (the Holy of Holies) is
abolished by Jesus' death—thus collapsing both curtains,[39] a lock-step
truth which opens the way for the Gentile centurion's confession:
"Truly this man was God's Son." As indicated in 14:58, it is also the
ναός, not the ἱερόν, that Jesus will rebuild in three days.

This distinction also accords with Juel's conclusion regarding
the meaning of "another not made with hands" (ἄλλον ἀχειρο-
ποίητον). That which is to be rebuilt in three days—a temporal narrative marker that joins this text to the three passion-resurrection

[34]Ibid., 125–26. Here Malbon quotes W. H. Kelber, "Conclusion:
From Passion Narrative to Gospel," in *The Passion in Mark: Studies on Mark
14–16*, ed. Kelber, (Philadelphia: Fortress, 1976), 171.

[35]McKelvey, *New Temple*, 58–74.

[36]Lohmeyer, *Lord of the Temple*, 36–52.

[37]H. W. Bartsch, "Die Bedeutung des Sterbens Jesu nach den Synoptikern," *TZ* 20 (1964), 87–102.

[38]Gaston, *No Stone Upon Another*, 480; M. Dibelius, *From Tradition to
Gospel*, trans. B. L. Woolf (New York: Scribner's, n.d.), 195–96.

[39]The sacred/profane collapses, even cosmically, with the reading
(σχίζω) responding antiphonally to 1:10. D Ulansey, "The Heavenly Veil Torn:
Mark's Cosmic Inclusio," *JBL* 110 (1991), 123–25.

predictions—is "the house of prayer for all nations," which the ἱερόν failed to provide. As Juel puts it, "building imagery is being used for some reality that is not really a building." By his use of "another not made with hands," Mark uses "language appropriate to describe the Christian community by using temple imagery. The term would suggest that the new temple is really not a temple; it is a reality of a different order—corresponding to the new character of reality subsequent to Jesus' resurrection."[40]

What is this reality of a different order? The strength of Juel's phrasing is that it avoids a definitive description of what this reality is. But the text does imply another ναός, or something that takes its place. Juel suggests "the Christian community." It is possible to be more precise by considering evidence from a corollary theme of the ἱερόν/ναός in these chapters.

3. Temple and Nations in Chapters 11–16

The term ἔθνη, translated either "nations" or "Gentiles," occurs several times (11:17; 13:10) together with other ways of portraying worldwide (14:9) or Gentile (15:39; 14:28; 16:7) response. Three of these uses occur with statements about the temple (11:17; 13:10; 15:39). If the "going before" to Galilee is linked with the resurrection "in three days," then 14:27 and 16:7 are also to be linked with the rebuilt "not made with hands" ναός of 14:58.

The most crucial association of temple and nations is found only in Mark's account of the cleansing of the temple. While each Synoptic writer contains Jesus' quotation of Isaiah 56:7c, "My house shall be called a house of prayer," Mark alone includes the final phrase, "for all nations," and in the form of a rhetorical question. It appears that Mark regarded Jesus' act to be both a denunciation of the Jewish profanation of the temple and a "demonstration" for the rights of the

---

[40]Juel, *Messiah and Temple*, 155. Juel has an excellent discussion of midrashic, rabbinic traditions associated with Exod 15:17 which speaks of the Lord's hands establishing (building) the Zion sanctuary. A text from the Mekilta of R. Ishmael speaks of God's hands (pl.) building the eschatological sanctuary, which Juel takes as a contrast to human hands. But in Mark, the builder is Jesus, not God. The contrast is not between God and humans, but between "with and without hands." Juel then considers the circumcision texts of Col 2:11 and Eph 2:11 in order to bring into focus the actual contrast of Mark 14:58, one between "made with hands" and "not made with hands." The "not made with hands circumcision" is one of a different order, which Juel calls "spiritual." Against this background of research, Juel proposes the view quoted (150–55).

Gentiles[41] to unhindered worship of God. This is also the rationale for Mark's distinctive phrase, "he would not allow anyone to carry anything through the temple" (v. 16). As Lohmeyer puts it: "Jesus by his action has removed the hindrance to the fulfillment of the reality of the Temple as a house of prayer for all nations."[42]

The second text linking temple and nations is 13:10: "and the gospel must first be preached to all nations (εἰς πάντα τὰ ἔθνη)." Marxsen, following Lohmeyer, holds that verse 10 is a Markan insertion into verses 9–12 both to explain the end of verse 9 (i.e., bearing testimony to kings) and to give an eschatological meaning to the time before the end, in that this is the time for the Gentile mission.[43] Since chapter 13 answers the question of when these things—i.e., not one stone of the temple shall be left upon another—are to be, the word "first" in verse 10 indicates that the mission to the Gentiles must be a precondition of the temple's (ἱερόν) destruction and the end (v. 7, "but the end is still to come").[44]

Mark 15:38–39 is the third text that connects the temple to the inclusion of the Gentiles. By placing these verses in this crucial position in the passion narrative, Mark discloses his theological interpretation of Jesus' death, "Truly this man was God's Son" (v. 39). The temple's function ends; the Gentiles enter through the centurion's confession. Thus 15:38–39 fulfills the plot anticipation of 11:17 and 13:10. By associating these two themes, Mark clearly anchors both the end of the temple (the ναός as stratified access to God) and Gentile belief in Jesus as Son of God, even and precisely in his suffering and death.

The three remaining texts in which "nations" or "Gentiles" occurs are 14:9; 14:28; and 16:7. In these the temple, however, is not directly associated with the nations. The story of Mary's anointing of

---

[41]Quite likely Jesus' prophetic act against the temple took place in the Court of the Gentiles, though some scholars dispute this point. At least Mark's account, by its emphasis, suggests this location.

[42]Lohmeyer, *Lord of the Temple*, 40. See also Schweizer, *Good News*, 233 and W. L. Lane, *Commentary on the Gospel of Mark* (NICNT; Grand Rapids: Eerdmans, 1974), 406.

[43]Marxsen, *Mark the Evangelist*, 175–76.

[44]Whether Mark intends to say that the ἱερόν continues until the mission is completed or that the mission itself is the focus of attention, rather than false prophecies based on this or that sign (vv. 5–8), is difficult to say. If Mark is writing close to the time of the temple's fall in A.D. 70, the former would make little sense to him and his community, unless they believed the parousia also to be imminent.

Jesus beforehand for his burial (14:9) is specified as part of the gospel which will be "proclaimed in the whole world."[45] By connecting verse 9 to verse 8, which speaks of Jesus' burial, Mark again associates the Gentile mission with Jesus' death.

In the remaining two texts, 14:28 and 16:7, "nations" or "Gentiles" does not occur, but, as shown in chapter 2 above, numerous scholars understand the phrase, "I will go before you to Galilee" as Mark's call of the disciples into the Gentile mission. While scholars dispute this point, the consensus is broad enough to proceed on that view.[46] Marxsen's and Brandon's objections are answered by Ralph P. Martin[47] and the proposals of both Norman Perrin[48] and Lloyd Gaston.[49] Perrin and Gaston agree that the Gentile mission is not to be substituted for the parousia in Mark's Gospel; it is rather the locale and context for the parousia. Further, it should be noted that Mark connects Jesus' appearance in Galilee to his resurrection: "after I am raised up, I will go before you to Galilee" (14:28).

Mark also uses the term "within three days" in connection with Jesus' predicted resurrection (8:31; 9:31; 10:33). The two events predicted to occur "within three days" are Jesus' resurrection and the rebuilding of the ναός "not made with hands."[50] In this way Mark connects the themes of temple and nations to Jesus' death and resurrection, on the one hand, and to the Gentile mission as context for the parousia, on the other. Mark thus links the rebuilt ναός to the resur-

---

[45]Like 13:10, this text also is a Markan insertion, according to Marxsen (125). This verse is especially significant for Marxsen since this is the seventh time that Mark introduces the term "gospel" into the tradition.

[46]In my opinion the evidence is convincing. For study of the issue see Boobyer, "Galilee and Galileans," 334–38. C. F. Evans concurs with this interpretation ("I Will Go," 3ff.). Burkill's essay on "Galilee and Jerusalem" (*Mysterious Revelation*, 252–57) contains a helpful resume of the various positions and notes that R. H. Lightfoot, influenced by T. W. Manson (*The Servant-Messiah*, [Cambridge: Cambridge University, 1953], 93ff.) changed his position from a parousia-interpretation, in *Locality and Doctrine*, 124ff.) to a Gentile mission-interpretation in *Gospel Message* (106ff.) See also F. Hahn, *Mission in the New Testament* (SBT 47; London: SCM, 1965), 112–16.

[47]R. P. Martin, "A Gospel in Search of a Life-Setting," *ExpTim* 80 (1969), 361–64.

[48]H. Betz, *Christology*, 43.

[49]Gaston, *No Stone Upon Another*, 483.

[50]The only other use of the phrase "in three days" is in 8:3 where the second feeding functions for Mark as a feeding of the Gentiles, a point that correlates with the resurrected Jesus-ναός calling disciples into the Gentile mission, since that feeding is for the Gentiles (see ch. 3).

rected Jesus calling his church into the Gentile mission. The new ναός is built in the midst of the nations (ἔθνη) where people, like the Gentile centurion, affirm: "Truly, Jesus is Son of God."

In summary then, Mark draws on OT temple traditions of divine blessing and judgment to develop a distinctive theological interpretation of Jesus' prepassion (and passion) ministry. Because the temple tenants misused the temple, the ἱερόν stands under imminent judgment. But Jesus' death and resurrection build a new ναός through mission and blessing to all people. This rebuilt ναός is precursor and precondition of the end of the ἱερόν.

MATTHEW

1. Content and Structure

Matthew's prepassion Jerusalem section consists of chapters 21–25. Containing almost all the content appearing in Mark, it includes more as well:

a. In Matthew, Jesus' entrance into the temple and its cleansing form the climax to the triumphal entry (21:12ff.) and highlight Matthew's christological concerns.

b. Matthew does not sandwich the temple cleansing between two parts of the fig tree episode as Mark. Nor does he give the temple cleansing the Markan purpose "for all nations." Hence, Matthew does not reflect the Markan interconnection of the temple and nations themes.

c. Before and after the parable of the wicked tenants Matthew adds a parable to amplify its import (21:28–22:14), though the first parable of the two sons may also be commentary on the question of Jesus' and John's authority. This has the effect of putting a caesura between the debate over John's and Jesus' authority (21:23–27) and the Parable of the Vineyard's Tenants. It also puts a caesura between the Parable of the Tenants and the controversy dialogues culminating in Jesus' question about the Messiah as Son and Lord of David (22:15–45). Further, Matthew does not locate this controversy cycle "in the temple," as Mark did, though the quoted "stone" text (21:42) and the allegorized temple references in the Parable of the Vineyard's Tenants do afford some temple connections.

d. Most significant for this study, Matthew lacks Jesus' condemnation of the piety of the chief priests and scribes and commendation of the widow for her giving her only mite (Mark 12:38–44).

Matthew's long chapter of woes upon the Pharisees stands in its place (ch. 23); these end with the harsh judgment, "Behold, your house is forsaken and desolate" (v. 38, RSV). This judgment is followed by the words, "For I tell you, you will not see me again until you say, 'Blessed is the one who comes in the name of the Lord.' " Literarily, these words provide the transition to the Mount Olivet discourse, which ironically begins with Jesus exiting the temple, never to return (24:1). The way *into* the discourse necessitates a final *out*, from the temple.

e. The beginning (24:3) and the ending of the eschatological discourse (24:36ff.) have been shaped to make it focus primarily on the parousia. Some commentators thus regard chapter 25 as a continuation of the discourse in that both reflect parousia emphases. In any case, the end of chapter 24 and all of 25 consist of content found only minimally in Mark (Matt 25:13 par. Mark 13:35). Only 24:15, "the desolating sacrilege," refers to the temple as such.

On first blush then, except for the temple cleansing and the transition between chapters 23 and 24, temple imagery and emphases seem to be minimal in this section of Matthew. It is not clear that Matthew's use of the ναός theme carries any particular emphasis (Matt 26:61 is a shortened form of Mark 14:58; Matt 27:40, 51 is an expanded form of Mark 15:29, 38). One section though, the "Woes on the scribes and Pharisees" (23:16–22), uses temple imagery, but hardly with the purpose of showing distinctive temple theology, unless it supports temple themes evident more broadly in the narrative.

If it were not for the transition between chapters 23–24, and its implications, a judgment of "minimal temple interest" might stand. But when the 23–24 transition is examined closely in the context of 23:34–38, temple emphases peak to steeple height. Further, some earlier Matthean distinctives, mentioning temple (12:6) and house (10:5; 15:24), fuel Matthew's fire over the temple. Even the episode about the temple tax (17:24–27) shows interest in the temple, but makes it subservient to Christology and ecclesiology: "the sons are free," a point paradigmatic of Matthew's interests in the temple.

The structure of Matthew 21–25 is difficult to discern. With its content almost twice that of Mark, where does one segment end and another begin? Schweizer avoids the problem by simply listing seventeen thematic units of varying length.[51] Gundry puts chapters 21–22 and 23–25 together.[52] Patte keeps 24–25 together but treats 23

---

[51]Schweizer, *Good News*, 8–9, 401–82.
[52]Gundry, *Matthew: A Commentary*, vii–ix, 415–515.

separately and divides 21–22 (with 20:17ff.) into three segments.[53] The lack of agreement shows the difficulty, which is best resolved by regarding 23 as a hinge chapter between 21–22 and 24–25.

This section also has much to contribute to Matthew's view of kingship—not least of which is the triumphal entry with its Zechariah 9:9 quotation—to be considered in the next chapter. Even though temple and kingship emphases are woven together, e.g., in 21:15, this chapter focuses on the temple theme.

The oppositional markers of Jesus' *entering the temple* (21:12) and *leaving the temple* (24:1) may be taken as the subsectional titles, thus dividing the section into two basic subsections, with chapter 23 hinging the two sections together. This decision has the advantage of highlighting all that follows 21:12 as that which results from Jesus' entering the temple: the rounds of judgment express the temple Lord's indictment upon the leaders and people who failed to manage the "house"—hence its desolation. Antiphonally, all that follows 24:1–2 lies beyond the temple era and thus prepares one for the eschatological consummation. Even so, the key motifs associated with the temple theology extend themselves into that era as well.

Discussion of this section proceeds then, first, by examining the temple cleansing in relation to the triumphal entry—and the emphases that follow from these provocations; second, by focusing on judgment in chapters 23–24; and, third and fourth, by understanding narrative emphases related to the temple, namely, Jesus as Wisdom and the temple's *šᵉkînâ*.

2. Temple Cleansing: Context and Consequence

As Daniel Patte notes, the triumphal entry has its interpretive climax in Jesus' cleansing of the temple, his healing of the blind and the lame in the temple, and the outcry of the children's praise, ratified by Jesus' quotation of Psalm 8:2 in 21:16: "Yes; have you never read, 'Out of the mouth of infants and nursing babies you have prepared praise for yourself'?"[54] Matthew's fulfillment quotation of Zechariah 9:9, however, already interprets the entry as that of a peaceable,

---

[53]Patte, *Matthew*, viii–ix, 281–352. The three segments are: 20:17–21:17, Going Up to Jerusalem and the Temple; 21:18–22:14, By What Authority Are You Doing These Things?; 22:15–46, Whose Son Is Christ?

[54]Ibid., 286–88. Patte says Matthew portrays the response of the crowd in 21:9–11 as ambiguous. Yes, Matthew wants Jesus acclaimed "Son of David"; but he does not trust the crowds' acclaim, only the children's.

humble king. But since Matthew knows that the stories to follow do not show rejoicing, he substitutes the first line of Zechariah 9:9, "Rejoice, greatly" with that of Isaiah 62:11, "Say to the daughter of Zion." The change makes the entire quotation "an evangelistic challenge to unconverted Israel,"[55] standing in tension with the crowds' acclaim in verses 9–11; it sets forth the moral and even ontological character of "Hosanna to the Son of David." The modified Zechariah 9:9 and the Psalm 8:2 quotations in verses 5 and 16 respectively may be regarded as the interpretive inclusios to the combined entry and cleansing. They interpret these kingly acts in accord with the Son of humanity's humble servanthood in 20:20–28.[56]

The festive branches on the road, the "Hosannas," and the acclaim, "Blessed is the one who comes in the name of the Lord" (vv. 8–9) all echo Psalm 118:25–26. Clearly, Jesus' entry is portrayed in line with and as consummation of this festal entry into Jerusalem and to the temple with the eager hope that God will save his covenant people—Save us (Hosanna). The crowd's answer to the "shaken" city's (ἐσείσθη πᾶσα ἡ πόλις) question, "Who is this?" (v. 10), identifies Jesus with earlier salvific themes linked to Nazareth and Galilee: "This is the prophet Jesus from Nazareth of Galilee" (recall 1:21–23). By now the story has set forth the announcement of and invitation to salvation.

Then Jesus entered "the temple [of God][57] and drove out all who were selling and buying in the temple. He said to them, 'It is written, "My house shall be called a house of prayer," but you are making it a den of robbers.' " Unlike Mark's rendering of Isaiah 56:7 as a rhetorical question, Matthew makes it a pronouncement on the will of God for the temple, a sharp contrast to its present functioning as "a den of robbers." When Jesus then begins to heal the blind and lame in the temple, he violates David's prohibition in 2 Samuel 5:8, which forbids the blind and the lame to enter the temple. In keeping with Matthew's earlier portrait of Jesus (twice quoting Hosea 6:6 on God desiring mercy, in 9:13 and 12:7), Jesus is a minister of mercy. By ending the commerce of robbery, and offering healing instead, Jesus defines the proper cultic activity of the temple, even if it means revising the law of David—thus anticipating the "Son/Lord of David"

---

[55]Gundry, *Matthew: A Commentary*, 408.

[56]Patte's division of 20:20–21:17 as one segment shows this unity of thought.

[57]Though the phrase "of God" does not have the best MS support, internal evidence argues for it. Nestle-Aland and NRSV omit it; RSV includes it.

query at the end of this subsection. For the blind and the lame, even Israel's Jebusite enemies,[58] salvation has now come to the temple! And the children acclaim it: "Hosanna to the Son of David." Now the salvation announced and proffered had taken concrete expression.

But the chief priests and the scribes are indignant (21:15d). This indignation—in opposition to God's offer of salvation in Jesus—sets the atmosphere for all that follows until Jesus leaves the temple, never to return (24:1). The cursing of the fig tree dramatizes for the disciples the severity of God's judgment and the power of faith—a kind of "get ready to play some hard-ball." The debate over authority (ἐξουσία) in verses 23–27 focuses the issue: the authority of the chief priests and elders of the people is in fatal contest with the authority of Jesus, and the authority of John. Since they can not answer Jesus' counter question, Jesus refuses to specify his source of authority—which indeed they know full well. Only their effort to publicly taunt him fails.

Withholding his answer, Jesus then takes the opportunity to tell several stories: about two sons—a "yes-but-didn't-do" son and a "no-but-did-do" son; about a householder who leases a special vineyard out to tenants who kill the owner's servants and son; and about a king who throws a marriage feast to which the invited guests refuse to come, though one person shows up without a wedding garment, presumably thinking it isn't really wedding time! Each story ends, not with cheers and applause, but with a harsh word of judgment against those refusing God's offer of salvation:

> Ending 1: "Truly, I tell you, the tax collectors and the prostitutes are going into the kingdom of God ahead of you. For John came to you in the way of righteousness, and you did not believe him, but the tax collectors and the prostitutes believed him; and even when you saw it, you did not change you minds and believe him" (21:31b–32)

---

[58]Gundry says that the context of 2 Sam 5:8 indicates that David by the phrase, "lame and the blind," was referring to the Jebusites. Jesus' action "denies the Jews' false deduction from David's statement (cf. 1QSa 2:19–25; 1QM 7:4–5; 4QD^b/CD 15:15–17; *m. Ḥag.* 1:1)" (*Matthew: A Commentary*, 413). Rather than concluding, as Gundry does, that Matthew thus combines the traditions of Jesus as royal messiah with that of miracle worker, I suggest that Matthew has his own version of Mark's "for all nations." If Matthew's Jesus corrects the Jews' misunderstanding of "blind and lame," then he also reverses David's policy against the enemy: rather than exclude, Jesus welcomes and heals, i.e., transforms the symbol of enmity into a condition of *šālôm*—they are welcomed to the holy place.

Ending 2: "Have you never read in the scriptures:
'The stone which the builders rejected
has become the cornerstone;
this was the Lord's doing,
and it is amazing in our eyes?'

Therefore I tell you, the kingdom of God will be taken away from you and given to a people that produces the fruits of the kingdom" (21:42–43).

Ending 3: "Go therefore into the main streets, and invite everyone you find to the wedding banquet" (22:9) and to the one without a wedding garment, " 'Bind him hand and foot, and cast him into the outer darkness; where there will be weeping and gnashing of teeth.' For many are called, but few are chosen" (22:13b–14).

The "stone" quotation, like the "Hosanna" and the festal procession with tree branches strewn on the road, derives from Psalm 118. Hence, the stone of the building suggests, on one level, the temple and, in its present Matthean context, Jesus as the cornerstone of that temple. Thus, in 21:42–43 the rejection of the stone is in metonymic relation to "the kingdom of God will be taken away from you."[59] The Jewish leaders' conduct, mirrored by the "yes-but-didn't-do son" of the first parable, as well as by the tenants who killed the servants and the son, warrants the loss of their stewardship (οἰκονομία) of the kingdom of God.[60] The "householder" (οἰκοδεσπότης) now gives it to another. The last parable reiterates the key points on two complementing levels: *others* are now invited to the marriage feast, and if one who still thinks he is entitled to manage the vineyard and the kingdom shows up at the feast with no wedding garment because he says in his heart that this is not the time of God's *wedding* feast, he will be shut out into outer darkness.[61]

---

[59]For Matthew, rejection of the stone entails rejection of Zion, God's covenant presence in the temple on the holy mountain. For this Zion theology, see Pss 20, 33, 48, 65, 84, 118 and numerous sections of Isaiah. A thorough and incisive study of Zion theology, which functions critically upon royal theology, is Ollenburger's *Zion*; see T. N. D. Mettinger, *The Dethronement of the Sabaoth: Studies in the Shem and Kabod Theologies* (Lund: C. W. K. Gleerup, 1982).

[60]The language of stewarding God's house is a primary metaphor for this discussion, and the basis for judgment and reward in Matthew. See n. 69 for discussion of this in M. Crosby's work.

[61]In the communities receiving and using Matthew's Gospel, these parables—as well as the narrative more broadly—functioned on two levels: to explain Jesus' rejection by the Jewish leaders together with Israel's standing outside the Messianic community, and to warn Christians against presumption

The next segment of controversy stories, 22:15–46, shows Jesus sparring and winning in verbal debate with the Pharisees and Sadducees, who are also competing against each other, using Jesus to score points against the other party's position. All three Synoptics include this section in much the same form. While Mark locates it in the temple (12:35), Matthew prepares for his distinctive chapter 23 by identifying the opponents as Pharisees in both verses 34 and 41.[62] This segment of synoptic tradition in Matthew thus amplifies the tension and distance between Jesus and the religious leaders and, by identifying the opponents as primarily Pharisees, prepares for chapter 23.

3. Judgment on the Pharisees

Though 23:13–26 (and possibly 37–39) is styled as direct address to the "scribes and Pharisees," the discourse is spoken to "the crowds and to his disciples" (v. 1). Hence, like the parables above (see pp. 174–75, n. 61), the discourse functions on two levels.

An engulfing torrent of fiery judgment upon the Pharisees, the chapter leaves no question about Matthew's view of Israel's status as a people in their relation to Jesus as Messiah. Judgment falls "upon this generation" (ἐπὶ τὴν γενεὰν ταύτην), i.e., the generation that rejected Jesus. The use of γενεά here brings to a head the earlier warnings and condemnations of "this evil generation" (γενεά, 11:16; 12:39, 41, 45; 17:17). If for Mark the temple-ἱερόν with its ναός is eclipsed by a nations-sanctuary (ἔθνη-ναός), in Matthew the judged γενεά is eclipsed by the ἔθνη who will hear and respond (12:15–18; 21:43; 28:19). In both cases the temple goes under in the shuffle, signified by Matthew's Jesus declaring, "Your house is forsaken and desolate," and then decreeing in the Olivet discourse, "Not one stone shall be left here upon another."

---

upon their own standing. As Donahue puts it: "they summon Christians who are the heirs of Matthew, not merely to respond with promises of labor in the vineyard, but to bear fruit and to 'put on Christ' by deeds of justice and charity" (*Parable*, 96).

[62]This diverges significantly from Mark. As M. Cook observes, in Mark Jesus' opponents in Galilee are Pharisees; in Jerusalem they are the chief priests, elders, and Sadducees. When the opposite group appears in either section of Mark's narrative, there is linkage of that group with the home area (i.e., "scribes from Jerusalem" in 3:22). Mark 12:13 may be an exception, but narrative unity hooks it back to 3:6. See M. Cook, *Mark's Treatment of the Jewish Leaders* (Leiden: E. J. Brill, 1978).

This vendetta against the Pharisees is toned by Matthew's church's struggle against the synagogue. The chapter is not the source for a fair assessment of the Pharisees in Jesus' time.[63] But neither can the chapter be ignored, since some points of continuity between Jesus' view of the Pharisees, dependent upon their practices of piety, and Matthean polemic certainly exist. Gaston may be right in saying that Matthew here begins a practice now of long-standing, using "the Pharisees . . . [as] a Jewish stick with which to beat Christian dogs, for legalism and enthusiasm and hypocrisy are essentially Gentile-Christian problems."[64] Matthew is indeed warning against "Pharisaic" conduct in his own church community, but he is also doing more. He is setting forth the narrative basis for the harsh word of judgment upon "this generation," lined out in 23:34–24:2. This theological reflection provides the underpinning for the historical enigma: how the Messiah of Israel has become the Lord of the Jewish and Gentile Christians, to use Gaston's captions.

While chapter 23 generally shows Jesus' indictment of the Pharisees' for their misuse of the householder's (the image of 21:33) law and temple, one paragraph, verses 16–22, focuses specifically on the Pharisees' flawed vision of the temple. The Pharisees consider swearing by the "gold of the temple" or "the gift on the altar" to be binding; however, according to this text, they do not regard swearing by the temple or by the altar to be binding. Are the gold and the gift of more value or power than the temple and the altar? Isn't it the altar that makes the gift sacred? Isn't the temple the focal symbol, the "presence" of God's throne and God himself? These questions, turned then by the text into declarations, expose the Pharisees' distortion of holiness and the sacred. Gold and gift, the trappings of the holy, have eclipsed the holy itself. Like Christmas for many Christians, the truest and deepest meanings of the sacred have been forfeited for the tinsel and glitter. This indictment is an important pillar in the rationale for

---

[63]For this see E. Rivkin, "Pharisees" in *IDB Supplementary Volume* (Nashville: Abingdon, 1976), 657–63; Rivkin, *A Hidden Revolution: The Pharisees' Search for the Kingdom Within* (Nashville: Abingdon, 1978); J. Neusner, *From Politics to Piety: The Emergence of Pharisaic Judaism* (Englewood Cliffs, N.J.: Prentice-Hall, 1973); and A. J. Saldarini, "Pharisees," *ABD* (New York: Doubleday, 1992), 5.289–303.

[64]L. Gaston, "The Messiah of Israel as Teacher of the Gentiles: The Setting of Matthew's Gospel," in *Interpreting the Gospels*, ed. J. L. Mays (Philadelphia: Fortress, 1981), 95.

words soon to be spoken, threatening the pillars and foundation of the temple itself.

The imagery of the parable of the householder and wicked tenants is utilized in two ways in Jesus' indictment. The killing of the servants sent by the householder has here a parallel in "your fathers" who shed the blood of the prophets (v. 30). The parallel extends to *now*, for "you are the descendants of those who murdered the prophets. Fill up, then, the measure of your ancestors. You snakes, you brood of vipers! How can you escape being sentenced to hell?" (vv. 31b–33). The indictment continues into Jesus' time, upon the "scribes and Pharisees" (v. 29):

> Therefore I send you prophets, sages, and scribes, some of whom you will kill and crucify, and some you will flog in your synagogues and pursue from town to town, so that upon you may come all the righteous blood shed on earth, from the blood of righteous Abel to the blood of Zechariah son of Barachiah, whom you murdered between the sanctuary and the altar. Truly, I tell you, all this will come upon this generation (vv. 34–36).

Two points are distressingly clear: the convergence of guilt and punishment upon *you* and *this generation*. Apparently, *you* and γενεά are here identified.[65] Second, the catalog of offenses—from A to Z—culminates in a murder that took place between the temple ναός and altar, a picture proleptic of a scene surrounding Jesus' own death. In 27:3–10, Judas, having repented of his deed, seeks to return the thirty pieces of silver to the chief priests and elders. Since they won't accept it, he throws down the silver into the temple (εἰς τὸν ναόν), then goes out and hangs himself. The falling of the silver into the ναός connects Jesus own death with the temple ναός. As blood money, it defiles the temple, pollutes it, and disqualifies it for continued service as a house of prayer.[66] Jesus' death is thus portrayed as consummating a long history of Israel's religious leaders shedding the blood of the prophets, even now into the very temple ναός precincts.

---

[65]γενεά, therefore, could mean both the Jewish people and the generation of those living at that time. In light of 24:34, Matthew's emphasis falls upon the former, since by the time of his writing the temporal generation of Jesus' time had already died. Should we ascribe to Matthew a hermeneutic of existential contemporeity, "this γενεά" could be "every generation" hearing the story. To some extent the gospel functions that way in every telling, but my judgment would be that "this γενεά" carried a fixed reference also, i.e., God's chosen people who rejected Jesus as Messiah.

[66]W. C. van Unnik, "The Death of Judas in Saint Matthew's Gospel," *ATR* Suppl. Series 3 (1974), 44–57.

The next oracle, combining compassion and judgment, addresses Jerusalem directly:

> Jerusalem, Jerusalem, the city that kills the prophets and stones those who are sent to it! How often would I have gathered your children together as a hen gathers her brood under her wings, and you were not willing! See, your house is left to you, desolate. For I tell you, you will not see me again, until you say, "Blessed is the one who comes in the name of the Lord" (vv. 37–39).

The motif of "killing the prophets and stoning those sent" here recurs.[67] But its harshness is temporarily muted by an abrupt shift to imagery of compassionate protection, a mother hen gathering her chicks under her wings. But like an earlier story when Israel spurned God's tender love that eased the yoke upon their jaws (Hos 11:1–4), "you would not!" (RSV). Again, as in an earlier story, the house is forsaken and desolate. The word "house" (οἶκος) plays a crucial narrative role. Three earlier narrative occurrences here reach their denouement: the (lost!) "house" (οἶκος) of Israel in 10:5 and 15:24; the twofold use of "house" (οἶκος) in the temple cleansing pericope: "My house shall be called a house of prayer"; and the allegorical allusion to God as the "householder" (οἰκοδεσπότης) in the parable of the wicked tenants (21:33; also 20:1 and 11). Within this narrative context οἶκος, in 23:38, carries at least a double meaning, including both the temple and the people of Israel.[68] For both, God is the Householder, the One to whom the house belongs.[69] The first

---

[67] See Garland, *Intention*, 179–87, for a good discussion, using O. H. Steck's thesis, on the pervasive impact that the theme of "violent rejection of the prophets" had upon Israel's literature.

[68] This double meaning of *house* (Heb. *bêṯ*) goes back to the planning stage of building Israel's first temple (2 Sam 7). See the foundational discussion of S. Aalen, " 'Reign' and 'House' in the Kingdom of God in the Gospels," *NTS* 8 (1962), 215–40, and Juel's discussion of the use of *house* (*bayiṯ* and *bêṯ*) in Qumran to designate "temple" (*Messiah and Temple*, 159–64). Garland argues rightly that οἶκος in Matthew has three levels of referent: the city of Jerusalem, the Temple, and the entire nation of Israel. Several levels may be present in a single use, or only one may be in view (*Intention*, 197–200).

[69] M. H. Crosby has studied the role of "house" and "household" in Matthew's Gospel to emphasize issues of justice and stewardship. His work stimulated my insights on the significance of Matthew's use of "house" and related terms (*House of Disciples: Church, Economics and Justice in Matthew* [Maryknoll, N.Y.: Orbis, 1989], esp. 72–75). Hebrews 3:1–6 employs at length the term "God's house," which conveys a similar meaning. The "house" refers to God's covenant people. Both Moses and Jesus are builders of "houses"

verses of chapter 24 carry forward Jesus' doom on the temple. God's forsaking Israel as the people of the kingdoms finds its narrative consummation in 28:19, where the mission of Jesus' disciples is directed toward the Gentiles, an opposition that extends the earlier restricted mission to Israel in 10:5.

4. Wisdom and Shekinah Depart

Beneath the surface of this text declaring the house forsaken and desolate are two motifs associated with temple theology in Israel's tradition: wisdom and glory. A comparison of Matthew with Luke indicates that Matthew identifies Jesus with Wisdom in 23:34:

Matt 23:34	Luke 11:49
Therefore	Therefore
	also the Wisdom of God said,
I send you prophets,	'I will send them prophets
sages, and scribes,	and apostles,
some of whom you will kill	some of whom they will kill
and crucify,	
and some you will flog	
in your synagogues	
and pursue [persecute, RSV]	and persecute.'
from town to town.	

What Luke regards as a saying of Wisdom that addresses the people in the third person, Matthew attributes to Jesus who addresses the people directly in the second person.[70] Because Matthew avoids ascribing this saying to Wisdom, it may be argued that any discussion of Wisdom on the basis of this text should be likewise avoided. An alternative view, widely espoused, is that Matthew intentionally identifies Jesus with Wisdom.[71] Since Matthew has already identified Jesus

---

(οἶκοι), though God ultimately is the builder of all things. Moses was faithful as a servant; Christ, as a son.

[70]Most scholars speak of this as Matthew's modification of Q, which gave significant place to Wisdom. Since my methodological intention in this study is not to make insights dependent upon a given theory of source criticism, I have avoided that language and conceptual framework insofar as is possible.

[71]J. M. Robinson says, "It is not enough to say Matthew simply eliminates the reference to Sophia. Rather one must recognize that he identifies Sophia with Jesus, by attributing to Jesus not only a saying previously attributed to Sophia, but by attributing to Jesus the content of the saying, namely Sophia's role as the heavenly personage who throughout history has sent the prophets and other spokesmen. It is to himself as preexistent Sophia that he refers in saying a few verses later (Matt 23:37): 'How often would I have gathered your

with Wisdom in 11:19,[72] it is correct to make this connection in 23:24, for the saying Luke attributes to Wisdom, Matthew attributes to Jesus.[73]

This view is supported by Matthew's reading in 11:19 where "wisdom is justified by her deeds," in contrast to Luke's "wisdom is justified by her children" (7:35). Whereas in Luke the *children* are *God's*, in Matthew the *deeds* are *Jesus'*. This shift arises from harmony with the context in Matthew 11 where the deeds Jesus has done answer John's question about Jesus' identity. As Celia Deutsch puts it, "Matthew has . . . thus altered the Q saying to identify Jesus with Wisdom in order to make clear the proper ranking of John with respect to Jesus. In so doing, he has associated, identified the deeds of Wisdom with the deeds of the Christ."[74] Focusing on Matthew's purpose in this identification, Deutsch rightly proposes that Jesus, by virtue of wisdom's functions in Israel's traditions, is thus linked to both revelational and authoritative teaching (instructional) roles; by identifying Jesus with wisdom Matthew legitimates Jesus' Torah teaching and prophetic proclamation.[75]

---

children together as a hen gathers her brood under her wings.' " See Robinson, "Jesus as Sophos and Sophia: Wisdom Tradition and the Gospels," in *Aspects of Wisdom in Judaism and Early Christianity*, ed. R. L. Wilken (Notre Dame: Notre Dame, 1975), 11.

[72]See also Matt 11:25–30 where Matthew connects vv. 28–30 to vv. 25–27, which bear the marks of wisdom. In Luke the term *children* plays upon a phrase in 7:29, "all the people and the tax collectors justified God." These people contrast to the "Pharisees and the lawyers who rejected the purpose of God," refused John's baptism, and repudiated Jesus' prophetic deeds. The *children* in 7:35 is thus a weapon word, designating those who "justify God." Thus, in Luke the *children* are linked to *God*, just as in Matthew the *deeds* are linked to *Jesus*. In this way Luke correlates wisdom with God, whereas Matthew correlates wisdom with Jesus.

[73]F. Burnett's study is generally convincing on this: *The Testament of Jesus-Sophia: A Redaction-Critical Study of the Eschatological Discourse in Matthew* (Lanham/New York/London: University Press of America, 1981), esp. 51–54. See also Schweizer, *Good News*, 447; J. Robinson, "Jesus as Sophos," 10–14; and the pioneering work on this by M. J. Suggs, *Wisdom, Christology and Law in Matthew's Gospel* (Cambridge, Mass.: Harvard University, 1970), 59–60. In an even earlier essay W. A. Beardslee regarded this Matthean identification as "not improbably right" ("The Wisdom Tradition and the Synoptic Gospels," *JAAR* 35 [1967], 237). H. von Lips's recent extensive study, *Weisheitliche Traditionen im Neuen Testament* (WMANT 64; Neukirchen-Vluyn: Neukirchener Verlag, 1990), also argues persuasively for this connection (280–90).

[74]C. Deutsch, "Wisdom in Matthew: Transformation of a Symbol," *NovT* 32 (1990), 35–36.

[75]Ibid., 47. Hermann von Lips offers an alternative reason, less convincing in my judgment. He theorizes that Matt 11–13 develops a wisdom

The wisdom tradition had originated and flourished in Israel's courtly (temple complex) environment. Proverbs already shows a personification of wisdom, in which wisdom is an hypostasis of God (Prov 1–9; so also Job 28; Bar 3:9–4:4; Sir 1; 4:11–19; 6:18–31; 14:20–15:10; 24; Wis 6–9). By intertestamental times, Wisdom of Solomon shows a sapientializing of Israel's history (chs. 10–11),[76] in which Wisdom is the God-acting subject in Israel's *Heilsgeschichte.* In Sirach 24:10–11, Wisdom dwells as God's presence in the temple:

> In the holy tent I ministered before him,
>   and so I was established in Zion.
> Thus in the beloved city he gave me a resting place,
>   and in Jerusalem was my domain.

In Sirach 24:4, Wisdom's throne is "in a pillar of cloud,"[77] the cloud of God's presence with Israel (Exod 13:21; 40:34–38). So "the glory of the Lord filled the tabernacle" (Exod 40:35). God's glorious presence was thus said to dwell (Heb. *šākan*) among the people, from which arose the image of God's Shekinah, God's glory dwelling among the people. Hence, referring to the door of the tent of meeting, it is said:

> I will meet with the Israelites there,
>   and it shall be sanctified by my glory; . . .
> And I will dwell among the Israelites,
>   and I will be their God (Exod 29:43, 45).

In Psalm 24 the Lord as the King of glory enters the temple, thus reigning there to receive the people's worship (cf. Pss 29, 48, 50; Isa 6:3; Ezek passim, esp. 43:2–5).[78] In Sirach 24, Wisdom, enthroned upon the *kābôd* cloud of God's presence, mediates also the divine presence in Israel's worship.

In view of this joining of Wisdom and Shekinah, Burnett contends that in 23:37 the speaker "is *heavenly* Wisdom depicted as the Shekinah who seeks to gather Jerusalem under its wings."[79] But Jerusalem would not give a home to Wisdom and Shekinah. The

---

Christology which links the Q wisdom tradition with a Spirit tradition (possibly Mark's). Thus, wisdom and Spirit are joined in Matthew's Christology, especially in chs. 11–13 (281, 289–90).

[76] A phrase used by Childs in class discussion. Robinson describes it as "Sophia . . . superimposed on Israel's *Heilsgeschichte*" ("Jesus as Sophos," 2).

[77] Verses 23–29 speak of wisdom dwelling also in Torah.

[78] Mettinger's discussion of Yahweh's *kābôd* in the Priestly writings and Ezekiel is extensive and excellent (*The Dethronement of the Sabaoth*, 80–123).

[79] Burnett, *Testament of Jesus-Sophia*, 66.

connective "For" (γάρ) which begins verse 39 and is linked to "me," i.e., Jesus, "*virtually equates Jesus with the Shekinah of God.*"[80] Thus when Jesus as Wisdom declares the city to be "forsaken and desolate," then says it will not see him again until . . . , and then leaves the temple (24:1), both Wisdom and Shekinah depart. The holy mountain is no longer holy, for the Lord's presence has gone from it.[81]

5. From Temple to Parousia

Chapters 24–25 unwind the spring of doom on the temple and also transfer the tension of that spring of judgment to Christian believers awaiting Christ's parousia. Burnett argues that 24:3 has the Christian church community as its referent. The "desolating sacrilege" now points to Satan's spoiling of the church (24:1–2).

> For Matthew the loss of Jesus' presence *was* the desecration of the Jerusalem temple. . . . 24:3 creates a new scene in which Jesus-Sophia centers upon the question of his return as Son of Man. The theme of the Jerusalem temple is not discussed again in the eschatological discourse—even in 24:15–22.[82]

While Burnett is correct in identifying where Matthew's accent falls, his separation between temple and parousia is too sharp. Granted, verse 3 focuses the disciples' question on "the sign of your coming and of the close of the age," yet it retains the question, "when will this be?" This refers back to verses 1–2; Burnett's caesura between verses 2 and 3 is more his than Matthew's.

Rather, it seems more correct to say that Matthew respects the first referent of the language in verses 3–22, i.e., the era between Jesus and the fall of the temple, and also appropriates it into his own

---

[80]Ibid., 73; also Schweizer, *Good News*, 444, and G. Strecker, *Der Weg der Gerechtigkeit*, 3d ed. (FRLANT 82; Göttingen: Vandenhoeck & Ruprecht, 1971), 113.

[81]The term *forsaken* aptly describes Wisdom's act of withdrawal, as in *1 Enoch* 42:1–2:

> Wisdom went forth to make her dwelling among humans;
> And found no dwelling-place:
> Wisdom returned to her place,
> And took her seat among the angels.

The term *desolate* similarly aptly describes the condition of the city and temple, once God's Shekinah presence has left it.

[82]Burnett, *Testament of Jesus-Sophia*, 310–11. His discussion extends through p. 353.

era, drawing its tones of warning and correction of false eschatological hopes into parenetic service for Christian believers anticipating
Jesus' parousia and the consummation of the age. This is not a "replacement" scheme—the church for Israel—but a typological correlation. Even the seven parousia parables draw on the imagery of Jesus'
earlier indictments of Israel's leaders and his discourses on the temple.
The temple's shadow lengthens into the age of the church expecting
the parousia. The significant connection lies in the matter of destiny:
how will the Christian believers fare when the judgment of Jesus-Sophia on Israel becomes the judgment of the Son of humanity on the
church, the house Jesus built (16:18; cf. 7:24–27)?[83]

Specific terms in Matthew's third and fourth parousia parables,
which disclose his distinctive emphases, link his address to church
believers back to the earlier parables indicting Israel's temple manag-
ers. Verse 43 designates the Son of humanity (vv. 40 and 44) as the
householder and v. 45, in beginning the next parable, speaks of a lord
and his *household* (οἰκετείας). In the parable of the talents (25:14ff.)
the man going on a journey and entrusting his property to his servants echoes the imagery of the parable of the householder and the
tenants (21:33ff.) The image of the Son of humanity as the king in the
last parable (25:31–46) parallels the king image in Jesus' last parable
to Israel's leaders (22:7, 11). Further, those on the left, the goats, will
fare like the one who came without a wedding garment. Overall, the
three parables of chapter 25 parallel the three in 21:28–22:14 in their
respective emphases and images.

Preparedness and faithful stewardship permeate both sets of
parables—those to Israel and those to the church. Michael Crosby's
study of *house* and *household* imagery in these parables articulates the
tone of both parable sections:

> As the final section of the discourse makes clear in the separation of the
> just from the unjust, when the master "comes in his glory" (25:31), the
> possession of the reign of God will depend on how members of the
> household communities shared their resources with the least of their
> brothers and sisters and, indeed, how the resources of "all the nations"
> (25:32; see 28:19) would be shared not only with the disciples, but with
> all those in need (25:33–46). Those to be blessed will be those called
> "just." Because justice refers to rightly-ordered relationships and re-
> sources, at the end of the age those who have lived in fidelity to the

---

[83]Burnett argues that Matthew puts a humble Wisdom and an authoritative apocalyptic Son of Man Christology side by side in a complementary
relationship (ibid., 363–70).

ordering of the house will be called "just." The king will call them "blessed of my father" (25:34) because they did the Father's will.[84]

LUKE

1. Luke's Perspective and Structure

The corresponding section in Luke is relatively brief, extending from 19:28(45)—21:38. Luke's temple emphases, however, stretch over his entire two-volume work; the temple obviously functions within God's salvation purpose, but also functions transitionally in that purpose. Though scholarly interpretations have varied,[85] consensus holds that Luke has a place for the temple in God's salvation purpose, unknown to Matthew and Mark. In Luke the gospel story originates in the temple (chs. 1–2) and culminates in Jesus' disciples continually blessing God in the temple (24:53).[86] According to K. Baltzer, Jesus' coming to the temple means the blessing of the temple with God's glory (kāḇôḏ/δόξα).[87]

---

[84]Crosby, *House of Disciples*, 75. While Crosby applies the term "nations" in 25:32 both to the believers—in their ethical responsibility in the household churches—*and* to the nations of the world, the more precise referent in Matthew appears to be *nations* in the sense of *Gentile* peoples, since a certain opposition between ἔθνη and γενεά appears in Matthew. Similarly, Jewish and Gentile Christian believers, scattered throughout those nations, appear to be the primary referent of "the least of these my brethren" (v. 40). But this sets up an unresolvable irony in the text, since it is directed to Christians. Thus, it is wiser exegesis to take the parable as a cosmic scene (apocalyptic) which sets up categories of ethical accountability applicable to Christians in their self-assessment of their response to the hungry, thirsty, and naked. For a review of the various interpretations, see S. W. Gray, *The Least of My Brothers, Matthew 25:31–46: A History of Interpretation* (Atlanta: Scholars, 1989).

[85]C. van der Waal's essay represents a minority position in holding that Luke agrees with Matthew and Mark in stressing judgment upon the temple, even though he shows also how "the glory of Jahweh has come in Christ to the temple": "The Temple in the Gospel According to Luke," *Neot* 7 (1973), 58. Most writers note Luke's difference from Matthew and Mark and stress his positive view of the temple. See esp. F. D. Weinert, "The Meaning of the Temple in Luke–Acts," *BTB* 11 (1981), 85–89, and J. B. Chance, *Jerusalem, the Temple, and the New Age in Luke–Acts* (Macon, Ga.: Mercer University, 1988)—a most helpful study.

[86]Luke's two-volume work may be viewed geographically as "From Temple to Rome."

[87]K. Baltzer, "The Meaning of the Temple in the Lukan Writings," *HTR* 58 (1965), 263–77. Baltzer's view, appealing to Luke's larger distinctive emphasis on Jesus as mediating God's glory (2:14, 32; 9:31–32; 19:38; Acts 1:9),

A full study of Luke's temple theology must take into account the view of the temple (and Jerusalem)[88] in Luke 1–2 (also 3:9–12), Luke 19:28–21:38; Luke 24:52–Acts 5; Acts 6:1–8:4; 15:15–18; and 21–23. This study focuses on Luke 19:28–21:38 but is informed also by the content of the other sections. Scholars differ on Luke's view of the temple in part because of the general ambiguity of these texts. While most interpreters emphasize the positive place of the temple in Luke,[89] Esler concentrates on the strong negative critique of the temple in Acts 6–7 (and the negative role the temple plays for Paul's destiny in Acts 21) in an attempt to situate such within an ethnic religious conflict that causes Stephen and Paul to lose their lives over temple issues.[90] Luke 19:28–21:38, with both positive and negative strands vis-à-vis the temple, serves as a window through which to glimpse Luke's overall emphasis.

Luke's prepassion section falls into three segments:

19:28–46   Jesus' Temple Processional
19:47–21:4 Jesus Teaches in the Temple
21:5–38   Jesus Teaches in the Temple despite its Doom

The narrative emphasis on Jesus as Teacher in the temple is so strong that it forms an inclusio for the section proper: 19:47–48 and 21:37–38. Jesus' temple processional—recall that his entry acclaimed him the king who laments the city's rejected peace (ch. 4)—leads to and includes the temple cleansing. Thus, Jesus establishes his right to use the temple as his teaching platform. By means of this temple inclusio Luke "gives the temple ministry a definite beginning and ending. Here, and only here, the Messiah of Israel confronts the whole of Israel with the message of eschatological salvation."[91]

---

has serious weaknesses. Luke 1–2, prior to and apart from Jesus, does not present the temple and its cult as devoid of God's glory. Jesus' word on the "house as desolate and forsaken" in 13:35 doesn't fit Baltzer's thesis, and 19:41–44, by intervening the acclaim of glory (19:38) and Jesus' temple entry, gives further trouble to his argument.

[88]Here Chance sides with Bachmann against Weinert and Conzelmann who tend to dissociate the city and the temple in the role they play in Luke's theology (Chance, *Jerusalem*, 2).

[89]Chance; Weinert; Baltzer; M. Bachmann, *Jerusalem und der Tempel: Die geographisch-theologischen Elemente in der lukanischen Sicht des jüdischen Kultzentrums* (BWANT 109; Stuttgart et al.: W. Kohlhammer, 1980).

[90]P. F. Esler, *Community and Gospel in Luke-Acts: The Social and Political Motivations of Lucan Theology* (Cambridge/New York et al.: Cambridge University, 1987), 131–63.

[91]Chance, *Jerusalem*, 62.

2. Luke's Differences

Luke's differences from Matthew and Mark are striking:

a. The account of the cleansing is much shorter; Luke does not portray the abuses to be of such a degree that it cannot be truly cleansed and thus restored for its God-intended functions. Through its cleansing Jesus claims the temple for all his Jerusalem ministry: "The temple is now *his* place where he is free to teach the people."[92] He really never leaves it until he goes out to the Mount of Olives on the eve before his death (22:30). For in the passion events preceding that exit the temple and city appear to be blended together. When he, the resurrected One, departs from his disciples to go into heaven, they return to the temple (24:50–53).

b. Quite astonishingly, Luke has no cursing of the fig tree; hence its withered leaves extend no shadow over the temple. Nor are there any subsequent instructions about prayer and forgiveness, indications that Christian piety will flourish apart from the temple. No, the temple stands and functions for God's purposes, for Jesus' ministry continues in it after its doom is foretold (21:37–38). Even beyond Jesus' death, in Acts, the temple continues both as a center for the Christian community and as a pivot to move the disciples into worldwide mission (via Stephen's critique and martyrdom which scatters the believers for mission, and via James' quotation of Amos 9:11–12 in Acts 15:15–18: " . . . I will rebuild the dwelling of David, which has fallen; . . . so that all other peoples may seek the Lord—even all the Gentiles over whom my name has been called").[93]

c. Luke has no equivalent to either the temple accusation of false witnesses in Mark 14:58 or the mockery of the passers-by—for Jesus to destroy and rebuild the temple in Mark 15:29 (both have Matthean parallels). Hence, the Lukan narrative makes no connection between Jesus' arrest and any anti-temple stance.

d. The tearing of the temple veil (Luke 23:45b) occurs before Jesus' death. This precludes the point that Jesus' death marks the end of the temple veil and what it signifies. For whatever meaning the rent

---

[92]Ibid., 58.

[93]Chance, following Earl Richard (*Acts 6:1–8:4: The Author's Method of Composition* [SBLDS 41; Missoula, Mont.: Scholars, 1978], 326–30), rightly says that this quotation does not indicate that Luke views the church or Gentile mission as replacing the temple, but that the rebuilding of the fallen booth of David is the restoring of Israel, i.e., Jesus' mission, which makes the Gentile mission possible (*Jerusalem*, 41).

temple veil may have for Luke, the view that Jesus himself becomes the
new temple (Mark) or that the temple is to be replaced by the Christian
mission or the church (Matthew), cannot be attributed to Luke.[94]

3. More Distinctive Features

Several narrative features disclose Luke's view of the temple.
Just as the cleansing of the temple enabled it to become a house of
prayer and a platform for Jesus' ministry, so God's people, the λαός,
hang on to Jesus' words (19:48) and protect Jesus against the evil
intent of the "chief priests and scribes and the leaders of the people"
(19:47). The temple and God's people (λαός) play corollary, positive
roles in Luke.

The λαός are mentioned eleven times throughout this sec-
tion, 19:47–22:2 (they, referring to the λαός, also occurs frequently).[95]
Five times the λαός protect Jesus (19:47; 20:6; 19, 26; 22:2). Five times
also the λαός receive his teaching (19:48; 20:1, 9, 45; 21:38). In response to God's judgment, the λαός ("they" refers to λαός in 20:9) say,
" 'God forbid!' " Later, the leaders accuse Jesus that he stirs up and
perverts the λαός (23:5, 14). In the events leading to Jesus' crucifixion,
the people (λαός) are distinct from the prosecuting Jewish rulers
(23:24); in 23:35 the scoffing of the rulers contrasts to the watching of
the people (λαός). Nonetheless, the two groups are linked in the
phrase, the elders of the people (22:66), in Pilate's calling together
"the chief priests, the leaders, and the people" (23:13), and in the
briefly recurring "they" who cry to Pilate for Jesus' death (23:18–23).
When Pilate is the opponent, the people (λαός) blend with the leaders;
otherwise the leaders and the people remain distinct in the narrative.
This distinctive use of λαός is further confirmed by the complete
absence of ὄχλος (crowd) in 19:47–22:2. When it does occur in the

---

[94]See Chance's discussion of this point, Jerusalem, 35–37. This view
disagrees with that of F. X. Reitzel, that Jesus here begins to abandon the temple,
anticipating the tearing of the veil which signals "the beginning of the reign of
Christ" (Rietzel, "St. Luke's Use of the Temple Image," Review for Religious 38
[1979], 4).
[95]R. C. Tannehill mentions Luke's frequent use of λαός and makes
some of the points that follow: Narrative Unity, 158–66. G. Lohfink also observes Luke's extensive use of λαός as part of his narrative strategy to show that
Jesus' ministry in the Gospel is directed to "das gesamte Volk Israel": Die
Sammlung Israels: Eine Untersuchung zur lukanische Ekklesiologie (Munich:
Kösel-Verlag, 1975), 33–37. See also R. J. Cassidy, "Luke's Audience, the Chief
Priests, and the Motive for Jesus' Death," in Political Issues in Luke–Acts, ed. R. J.
Cassidy and P. J. Scharper, 150–52.

preceding (18:36; 19:3, 39) and subsequent (22:6, 47; 23:4, 48) sections, it always refers to a crowd in the sense of a multitude. Thus ὄχλος carries a different meaning from λαός, and it is not used in this temple section, where the role of the λαός is carefully portrayed.

For Luke the dominant role for both the λαός and the ναός is positive, enabling Jesus' ministry to be consummated for Israel's restoration, in keeping with God's covenant promise. However, both—the λαός and the temple—are judged in chapter 21. Concerning the temple Jesus says, "not one stone will be left upon another; all will be thrown down" (v. 6). Concerning the city when it is surrounded by armies, Jesus says, "there will be great distress upon the earth and wrath against this people" (λαός, 21:23). Again, when Rome is the opponent and now aggressor, the people and the leaders are blended together into one as recipients of judgment; both the temple falls and the people lose their pivotal place and role: "they will fall by the edge of the sword, and be taken away as captives among all nations; and Jerusalem will be trampled on by the Gentiles, until the times of the Gentiles are fulfilled" (21:24).

Writing ten to twenty years after Jerusalem's fall, Luke knows that the predicted future judgment is already past. He knows also the ambivalent role that Jerusalem and the temple played in the Christian church's life and growth (so Acts).[96] In the opening infancy narrative and in the post-resurrection Emmaus story Luke views Jesus' coming as being for the redemption of Israel; he brings salvation to God's people (1:68, 77; 2:30, 38; 24:21). Was this vision and hope fulfilled in Israel's role in the Luke–Acts narrative, or is the "redemption" of Israel to be consummated after the "times of the Gentiles?" The announcement of "redemption drawing near" in 21:28 further complicates the question. Since this discourse is addressed to the λαός, this verse suggests a positive answer.[97] Yes, the redemption of Israel is

---

[96]This ambivalence may arise from Luke's distance from the history itself. This, at least, is the view that S. G. Wilson takes on Luke's inconsistent view—both positive and negative—of the law: *Luke and the Law* (SNTSMS 50; Cambridge et al.: Cambridge University, 1983), 57. In my judgment, however, Luke's positive presentation of law and temple cannot be the result of disinterest arising from distance. Other theological and ecclesiological—and perhaps political—motives were at work.

[97]A. J. Mattill, Jr., takes this view to its shocking conclusion so that all Luke's anticipations of "salvation for the people," "redemption of Israel," "Year of Jubilee," "seasons of Refreshing," etc. are postponed until after the "times of the Gentiles" (*Luke and the Last Things* [Dillsboro, N.C.: Western North Carolina, 1979], 136–45, and chart (!) on 156–57).

expected to take place after the times of the Gentiles are fulfilled. This would mean, in keeping with numerous earlier texts (Isa 63:18; 2 Bar 67:2; Dan 8:13; 1 Macc 3:45; 51; Ps Sol 17:23–25), that the "trampling of Zion" would last only for a given period of time.[98] But the redemption of 21:28 is linked to " 'the Son of Man coming in a cloud' with power and great glory" (v. 27). Likewise, the final call to "watchfulness" is linked to standing before the Son of humanity (v. 36). Hence, the temporal and spatial referents after verse 24 appear not to fit the tradition of restoration. And indeed this text is addressed to Gentile Christians who are now called to be alert and watch for the ultimate endtime crisis, the coming of the Son of humanity. Thus, while Chance is inclined to think that Luke did envisage a final restoration of Jerusalem with the Gentiles coming for worship, thus again fulfilling "its eschatological destiny as the city of salvation,"[99] the evidence for this in the subsequent text is slim.

The text does not state explicitly such future expectations. Rather, in Luke the temple functions as the worshipping, instructional, and eschatological center for God's people; it witnesses to and facilitates the dawning of God's eschatological salvation for Israel in Jesus, the Messiah. But because the leaders rejected Jesus the Prophet and Messiah-King, the temple's destruction, together with that of the holy city, was inevitable, because:

> the things that make for peace . . . are hidden from your eyes. Indeed, the days will come upon you when your enemies will set up ramparts around you and surround you, and hem you in on every side. They will crush you to the ground, you and your children within you, and they will not leave within you one stone upon another; because you did not recognize the time of your visitation from God (19:42–44).

This echoes Jesus' earlier word anticipating his Jerusalem ministry:

> Yet today, tomorrow, and the next day I must be on my way, because it is impossible for a prophet to be killed outside of Jerusalem. Jerusalem, Jerusalem, the city that kills the prophets and stones those who are sent

---

[98]Chance cites these and other texts regarding expected restoration (*Jerusalem*, 134–35).

[99]Ibid., 138. See also Tiede, *Prophecy and History*, 92–95. This view would align Luke quite closely with Paul, as in Rom 9–11. Based upon the role of the temple in Acts as a pivot in the mission to the Gentiles—in negative and positive ways—one could propose, in accord with J. Munck's view (*Christ and Israel: An Interpretation of Romans 9–11*, trans. I. Nixon [Philadelphia: Fortress, 1967], 9–11), that the Gentile mission itself would hasten the precondition of the restoration, the turning of Israel to its Messiah.

to it! How often have I desired to gather your children together as a hen gathers her brood under her wings, and you were not willing! See, your house is left to you. And I tell you, you will not see me until the time comes when you say, "Blessed is the one who comes in the name of the Lord" (13:33–35).

To the same degree that Luke accentuates the temple's and the city's role in God's eschatological salvation, so also he shows the certainty of the temple's and the city's doom because it rejected the One preaching the gospel of peace. Thus, its leaders and the people crucify the Messiah.[100] Even so, the temple continues to function in Acts as a focal center for salvation to both Jews and Gentiles (Acts 2–5; 15; 21). Even though the Pauline missionary team is sent out from Antioch, yet Jerusalem and the temple continue to function as a significant center, despite what Esler reconstructs to be a strong critique of the temple and law by Greek-speaking Jewish Christians (chs. 6–7).[101] Even in Acts 21, not Jews from Jerusalem, but Jews from Asia, accuse Paul of defiling the temple by taking the Ephesian Trophimus into the forbidden temple precincts. Hence, Paul is arrested for the very issue that Stephen's death protests.[102]

Thus, despite the pro-temple stance in Luke–Acts, the certain doom of the temple declared by Jesus is matched in Acts by recurring sharp critique.[103] This critique, though never clearly explicated in

---

[100] See the discussion in ch. 4 (133–34) of Jesus as the rejected journeying guest and prophet. Moessner (*Banquet*, 131–86), in his treatment of the theme of rejection, fails to distinguish between "crowds" (ὄχλοι) and "people" (λαός) in the narrative; there is a difference, in that the latter designates the people of Israel as God's covenant people.

[101] Esler, *Community*. This critique arose because "the God-fearers were successful in convincing their Greek-speaking Jewish friends who had become disciples that they, too, should be admitted to discipleship" (158). Because they as God-fearers (i.e., Gentiles) continued to experience restrictions in temple worship but as Christians shared equally with Jewish Christians, the critique of the temple naturally arose. This stirred the animosity of the Jews against the Hellenist Christians—Greek-speaking Jews who earlier supported the Jew/God-fearer distinctions. This, Esler cogently proposes, is the background to the events of Acts 6–7.

[102] According to Esler, the issue was: since the *soreg* (a five foot high wicket fence that separated the temple's Jewish courts from the Gentile court) had already fallen between Jewish Greek-speaking (Hellenist) Christians and Gentile Christians, it should also fall between Jews' and God-fearers' access to worship in the temple—or else the temple itself should fall—and it did! It is striking how parallel this logic is to Mark's theology of the temple.

[103] R. Maddox, in *The Purpose of Luke–Acts* (Edinburgh: T. & T. Clark, 1982), notes that Stephen's speech regards the building of the temple originally

Acts, appears to have centered on Gentile-Jewish relationships, and is thus similar to that of Mark's Gospel. As noted in chapter 4, Luke is careful not to locate Jesus outside Israel to contact Gentiles, since he reserves such "going out" for the early church's history in Acts. So likewise, he is careful not to show in his Gospel a critique of the temple that arises from its inefficacy for God-fearers. That phase of theological emphasis belongs, according to Luke, to the history of the early Christian church's mission, A.D. 30–60.

CONTINUITY AND TRANSFORMATION IN THE TRADITION: ASSESSMENT AND SUMMARY

That temple traditions from the Hebrew Scriptures and post-biblical Judaism influenced the Jesus traditions in this prepassion section of the Synoptic Gospels is quite evident. But the influence appears limited to the temple motif and the temple itself. Except for the implied departure of Shekinah in Matthew, nothing is said about the various aspects of the temple cultus: sacrifice, priesthood and other temple symbolisms. This indicates that the synoptic tradition, in its pre-Gospel form or in its Gospel redactions, did not undertake a theological assessment of priestly theology as did the book of Hebrews. The Gospels present Jesus as seeking to renew Judaism, and as such the stories of this section function within God's covenant made with Israel. Prophetic criticism of the temple must be seen within this context also, in line with the Old Testament prophets' critique of the temple.

The Synoptic Gospels' assessment of the role of the temple shows both unity and diversity. Unity emerges in that all three Gospels envision an end to the temple. More significantly, from a theological perspective all three also connect the end of the temple with God's judgment. But in detailing the precise rationale for that judgment, diversity emerges.

For Mark, the temple is judged because it fails to provide a "house of prayer for all nations." This assumes, on the one hand,

---

as an act of rebellion (Acts 7:44–50). He sees this point as so contradictory to Luke's emphasis elsewhere that it must be assigned to old traditions which Luke is here using. Nowhere else does Luke "hint that the Temple is an evil institution" (53). But Maddox holds also that the speeches finally are Lukan compositions, despite the traditions utilized. Hence, he concludes that "Luke himself may well have thought that Stephen's summing up of past and present Jewish history, even if unusually sharp and pessimistic, was on the whole a fair statement of the case" (54).

Israel's abuse of the temple's functions; on the other hand, it represents Mark's desire to promulgate the church's mission to the Gentiles. The temple's end, in both its ναός function and its standing as ἱερόν, is connected to Jesus' death as opening up for Gentiles full access to God—for salvation and worship. The temple's failure to fulfill Israel's call to be a light to the nations (Isa 49:6) becomes a causative factor in Jesus' death—in the temple accusation (14:58) and logically: Jesus dies in order to achieve what the temple couldn't. Thus, the confession of the Gentile centurion (15:39) manifests the efficacy of Jesus' death. The temple's rent veil (15:38), declaring the end of its efficacy, provides the logical—and theological—warrant for the new reality to emerge, a reality in which Jesus, in place of the temple, is the Gentiles' access to God. Hence, Mark's theology of the temple is christologically and missionally focused.

The emphasis on prayer and forgiveness in 11:22–25 implies that the new reality, in replacing the old, embraces also the life of true worship. The means by which covenant relationship is maintained and renewed are now possible without the temple's functions. Since it is Jesus' disciples who are called to this new freedom in worship, Mark suggests an ecclesiological tension and perhaps shift as well. The Parable of the Vineyard's Tenants' saying, "he will come and destroy the tenants, and give the vineyard to others," suggests an ecclesiological displacement for the management of the vineyard (temple). Others will be invited to care for the vineyard. Further, the false accusation that Jesus said he would build a temple not made with hands ironically predicts the future course of events: in three days Jesus will build a temple-reality of a different order (Juel). Likewise, the Son of humanity's coming is for the gathering of the elect (Donahue).

Mark's theology of the temple thus consists of a replacement with both christological and ecclesiological dimensions. The christological dimension is the stronger and clearer in Mark; the ecclesiological is an implied consequence of the christological.

In Matthew, however, the balance of emphasis is reversed. Emphasis on the ecclesiological dimension takes precedence over the christological. Matthew makes this clear by framing the parable of the vineyard's tenants with parables that show the failure of one people to respond (the "Yes-but-didn't-do-it son") and extends God's invitation to another people, symbolized by the "No-but-did-do-it son" and the people invited from the highways and byways. His distinctive ending to the parable of the vineyard's tenants also makes the point: " 'Therefore I tell you, the kingdom of God will be taken away from you, and be given to a people (ἔθνη) that produces the fruits of the kingdom.' " Matthew's distinctive portrait of Jesus as One who builds his church upon the "rock" emphasizes also a new community's beginning. Matthew's temple theology thus accents ecclesiological dimensions, and it lacks sharpness of depiction on the christological level. Matthew lacks the phrase so crucial to Mark's account of the temple cleansing, "for all nations," a phrase that blended missional ecclesiology and Christology. In keeping with Matthew's larger portrait of Jesus as One to be worshiped as Lord and/or Son of God, the commentary that follows Jesus' death evokes awe and wonder (27:51–54). The centurion's confession serves the point of Gentile access to God—in which Jesus eclipses the temple's function—less than it amplifies the apocalyptic cosmic response to Jesus' death. Matthew's unique word in 12:5–6, "I tell you something greater than the temple is here," however, is clearly christological. But this emphasis is not as dominant as the ecclesiological. Matthew's ecclesiological focus is a typological relationship that functions for purposes of catechetical admonition. While statements can be cited to support the new people's displacement of Israel's leaders and people, such emphasis violates the call of the narrative to both communities. Rather, the motif of spurned opportunity in Israel's response warns the Christian community against unpreparedness and presumptuous careless stewardship.

Luke rejects any notion of temple replacement within the narrative time of the Gospel; neither shall it be so christologically or ecclesiologically. In Acts, however, with the "false witness" (!) against Stephen in 6:13—that "he never stops saying words against this holy place and the law"—and Stephen's sharp critique of the temple in Acts 7, the temple falls under such strong prophetic judgment that its end, known historically in Luke's time, is thus theologically legitimated. But Luke does not allow this to undermine continuity between Israel and the Jesus movement. Even the Christian movement is denoted as the Way sect within Judaism (9:2; 22:4). In this Luke reflects the temple tradition which portrays Israel at the center of God's purpose to bring blessing to all nations (Gen 12:3). It reflects the tradition of all people flowing into Zion's temple to share in God's eschatological salvation.[104] Acts 2 plays a central role in this fulfillment. This theological emphasis means, as Chance argues, that Luke does not "de-eschatologize" in view of a delayed parousia (contra Conzelmann and

---

[104] McKelvey's survey of temple traditions identifies this emphasis in many OT and intertestamental texts (*New Temple*, 9–24). Some of the Sybilline Oracles even view this new temple center as a reversal of Babel (these Oracles, though, may be later than Acts).

company) but highlights the Christ event as the fulfillment of Israel's consolation (2:25) and redemption (24:21).[105] This Christ event inaugurated the fulfillment of Israel's eschatological hopes, which included the salvation of the Gentiles and their reception into the kingdom (Acts 1:8; 15:1–21). The predicted (and remembered) destruction of the temple was not the result of the temple's flawed function, but because its tenants, the Jewish religious leaders, rejected its Lord, Israel's Prophet and Messiah-King. In accord with Luke's view of the temple, the Christians who nourish their faith by his writings continue to think of the temple symbolically, despite its historical demise and literal end, as the channel of God's salvation blessings through Israel to all nations.[106]

How then are these Synoptic theologies to be assessed in relation to continuity and discontinuity with Israel's temple traditions? Both McKelvey and Chance contend that Israel's hope of eschatological salvation includes a restored temple as a significant part in the drama (Isa 27:12–13; 40:11; 41:17ff.; 43:5; Jer 23:3; Ezek 40–48, Zech 8), and that this drama includes the streaming of the Gentiles into Zion (Isa 25:6–8; 60:3ff.; Zech 8:22) to the temple to worship (Isa 56:6–7; 66:23; Hag 2:7)—with Israel's law and šālôm thus going out to the Gentiles (Isa 2:2–5, par. Mic 4:1–3),[107] (although it must be said that other traditions envision the annihilation of the Gentiles!). A more confined tradition sees the Messiah as restoring and rebuilding a purified temple.[108] Four conclusions can be drawn on the question of continuity and discontinuity.

1. Each of the three Gospels shows continuity with the Old Testament on the role of the temple in God's eschatological purposes. That each of the Gospels gives considerable place to the temple in Jesus' Jerusalem ministry shows that the gospel story could not be told without taking this stream of tradition into account. Jesus' inauguration of the kingdom of God will have, must have, some bearing upon the temple, and the temple must have some bearing upon it.[109]

---

[105] Chance, *Jerusalem*, 139.

[106] The issue of Christians offering sacrifices at the temple, and the concomitant theological implications, is surprisingly not addressed in Acts.

[107] McKelvey, *New Temple*, 9–24; Chance, *Jerusalem*, 5–14, but esp. 12–14.

[108] Chance, *Jerusalem*, 14–18; Juel, *Messiah and Temple*, 169–79. Most striking here is the Isaiah Targum on 53:5: "He will build the temple which was profaned for our transgressions and delivered up because of our sins" (Juel, *Messiah and Temple*, 181; Chance, *Jerusalem*, 16).

[109] Zion theology (see Ollenburger's *Zion*) emphasizing Jesus' call to

2. Luke diverges significantly from Matthew and Mark in
portraying a positive role for the temple in Jesus' and the early church's
involvement in God's dawning eschatological salvation, though this
does not exclude Luke's portraying prophetic critique of the temple
as well. Matthew and Mark, however, portray the temple to be a
hindrance to Jesus' mission. For Mark, Jesus' mission brings the
temple under judgment; its exclusivity prevents it from serving God's
messianic purpose of breaking barriers among humans, and between
humans and God. For Matthew, the kingdom which the temple serves
must be reassigned its stewardship since its tenants would neither
"work" nor come to "the party." The kingdom stewardship is trans-
ferred, but the temple falls under the doom of God's judgment upon
the Pharisees. Luke represents continuity with this larger stream of
tradition; Matthew and Mark, representing a break with this particular tradition—of the temple's role in the ingathering of the Gentiles—
reflect another tradition, that of Jeremiah's doom upon the temple
(Jer 7) and the Zion theology's critique of establishment royalty and
priestly power. Although in Isaiah this Zion theology is most clearly
expressed in its critique of "the attempts of Israel and Judah to find
security in international alliances and military armaments," its critique falls also on exclusivistic priestly institutions, for Zion theology
means that human institutions "are appropriate and can 'succeed'
only insofar as they acknowledge that order of creation" which consists of God's establishment of "a good and just world-order," in
which humans in humility, trust, and subordination acknowledge
God's kingship.[110] In Mark and Matthew, Jesus applies God's "exclusive prerogative" of Zion theology's judgment against the exclusivity
of the temple.

3. Mark's and Matthew's implied rebuilding of another
temple continues *and transforms* the few traditions that speak of the
Messiah who will purify and/or rebuild the temple (Mal 3:1–2; Tg.
Zech. 6:12; Tg. Isa. 53:5).[111] Luke does not transform this aspect of

---

humble trust in God as One who provides for and defends the disciples—and
this runs through the whole story in each Gospel—might be seen as another
point of continuity between the Synoptic Gospels and temple traditions. Certainly the universalistic aspects of Zion theology, as emerge in Isa 40–55, are
part of the Scripture tradition which informs the Synoptics' theology—and
indeed Jesus' mission as well.

[110] Ollenburger, *Zion*, 156, 160.

[111] Later texts, in the Sibylline Oracles, also associate the Messiah with
rebuilding the temple (5:420–7). The 4QFlor 1:11–13, in its commentary on
2 Sam 7:11–14, speaks of the Messiah (i.e., Branch of David) ruling in Zion; but

the tradition, but portrays Jesus' coming to the temple with his almost perfunctory cleansing as *fulfilling* the "purification" of the temple.

4. All three Synoptics link the messianic story to the anticipated eschatological inclusion of Gentiles. All three stand in continuity with this stream of Israel's traditions, but stress the centrifugal dimension. The good news of God's reign goes out from Jerusalem to the nations of the world. While Mark and Matthew put the fulfillment of this eschatological hope in tension with the temple itself, Luke views the temple assisting that end. Luke's second volume fleshes out his Gospel's universal *vision* by showing the spread of the gospel from Jerusalem's temple to the empire's capital. As one continuous story, Luke–Acts shows how the temple rendered and "surrendered its redemptive significance to Jesus and his church."[112]

11QTemple 29:10 explicitly designates God as the builder of the temple. Other rabbinic commentary associates the coming of the Messiah with the reestablishing of the temple (Gen. Rab. 2:5, 56:2; Ex. Rab. 31:10), but falls short of designating the Messiah as the One who builds it. Hence the tradition has limited witness.

[112] Telford, *Barren Temple*, 232, quoting from R. E. Dowda's diss., "The Cleansing of the Temple in the Synoptic Gospels" (Duke University, 1972).

6

✾

THE FORMATIVE INFLUENCE OF OLD TESTAMENT KINGSHIP TRADITIONS ON THE SYNOPTIC PASSION NARRATIVE

This chapter examines the influence of Israel's kingship traditions upon the passion narratives of Mark, Matthew, and Luke. In each of these Gospels, however, the study of kingship in the passion narrative necessitates attention also to its function in the earlier parts of the Gospels. For Mark and Matthew, at least, the kingship theme in the passion narrative climaxes earlier compositional emphases.[1] Further, the theme is not limited to explicit kingship statements, but embraces a variety of images and titles: kingdom of God, Messiah-Christ, Son, Son of David, and Son of God—possibly also Son of humanity (υἱὸς τοῦ ἀνθρώπου).[2] It is intertwined also with the temple and Zion traditions. A complete analysis of the uses of all these terms in each Gospel is impossible. Rather, this chapter focuses on the passion narrative, using the earlier narrative at appropriate places in order to assess the full meaning of kingship in the passion story.

---

[1] Perhaps this confirms M. Kähler's dictum that the Gospels are passion stories with extended introductions: *The So-called Historical Jesus and the Historic Biblical Christ*, trans. and ed. C. E. Braaten (1890; rep. Philadelphia: Fortress, 1963], 80, n. 11. But viewed from the standpoint of a literary composition, the passion story is the climax of the plot. The occurrences of the kingship theme throughout the narrative anticipate the denouement—how the issue of Jesus' identity as King is resolved.

[2] For the rationale for this particular English translation, see p. 99 above.

ISRAEL'S KINGSHIP TRADITION

As in Israel's story, so in the Synoptics the kingship theme appears in relationship to the exodus-Sinai, way-conquest, and temple traditions. Both in the Gospels and in the Hebrew Scriptures these traditions and themes closely interact with and shape one another. Bernhard W. Anderson summarizes the vast Old Testament literature on kingship traditions[3] in order to illumine Peter's confession, "You are the Christ."[4] The main points are:

1. The metaphor "son of God" is applied to Israel as God's people in the Mosaic tradition (Exod 4:22–24; Hos 11:1–11; Jer 31:9; Isa 1:2–3b). In the royal Davidic and Zion traditions it is applied to the king (Ps 2:7; Isa 9:2–7; 2 Sam 7:11–17).

2. The Davidic king who is son of God is the anointed one (*māšîaḥ*), from whence the messianic hope and the title Messiah arise. The king functions as the anointed of Yahweh, the cosmic King enthroned in the heavens; Yahweh reigns in Zion, and there as Yahweh's servant the Davidic king is installed to implement Yahweh's rule (Pss 2; 46; 47; 93; 95–99; 132): "Yahweh is hailed as the King, enthroned in the heavens, who has chosen the Davidic king to be the representative of Yahweh's rule on earth and has chosen Zion as the place where Yahweh becomes present in the midst of the chosen people."[5]

3. Though the Davidic-Zion tradition has affinities with ancient Near Eastern kingship conceptions, kingship in Israel "does not have primordial status. . . ; monarchy and temple are historically conditioned. . . ; in Israel kingship had a humble historical origin in the time when Yahweh raised David from the sheepfolds . . . to be shepherd of the chosen people (Ps 78:70–72)."[6]

---

[3] These include T. N. D. Mettinger, *King and Messiah* (Lund: C. W. K. Gleerup, 1976); H. Ringgren, *The Messiah in the Old Testament* (SBT; Chicago: Allenson, 1956); J. H. Eaton, *Kingship and the Psalms* 2d ed.; The Biblical Seminar 3 (Sheffield: JSOT, 1986.); G. Cook, "The Israelite King as Son of God," *ZAW* 73 (1961), 202–25; G. E. Gerbrandt, *Kingship According to the Deuteronomic History* (SBLDS 87; Atlanta: Scholars, 1986); B. Ollenburger, *Zion*; M. Z. Brettler, *God Is King: Understanding an Israelite Metaphor* (JSOTSS 76; Sheffield: JSOT, 1989). D. M. Hay's *Glory at the Right Hand,* a study of Ps 110 and its influence upon the NT, is crucial also.

[4] B. W. Anderson, "The Messiah as Son of God: Peter's Confession in Traditio-historical Perspective," in *Christological Perspectives: Essays in Honor of Harvey K. McArthur,* ed. R. F. Berkey and S. A. Edwards (New York: Pilgrim, 1982), 157–69.

[5] Ibid., 165.

[6] Ibid., 166.

4. Because the Davidic king was accountable to Yahweh as King, the failure of kingship in Israel to follow Yahweh led to eschatological expectations of a coming ideal Son of God, Messiah, King, who will reign in righteousness and shower the earth with the truth and justice of Yahweh. Israel's way into this future will entail suffering (Isa 53) and the necessary recreating of heart and spirit (Jer 31:31–34).

5. Despite the turns and shifts in the David/Zion tradition, through Israel's exile and disappointments upon return to Jerusalem, this tradition "survived intact and provided a major resource, if not a hermeneutical guide, for understanding the messianic identity of Jesus." Anderson then sums up three basic components of the tradition:

> (a) God's cosmic kingship in heaven and on earth; (b) the elected king (the Anointed One) as the Son of God and therefore God's viceroy on earth; and (c) the exaltation of the "messiah" on Zion, the "holy hill," against which the assaulting hosts of chaos and evil cannot prevail.[7]

Indeed, this tradition does provide a major resource for the early church's understanding of Jesus. But this study shows a necessary major transformation in the tradition, so much so that it cannot be considered an unambiguous hermeneutical guide. In some respects it becomes a foil against which truer understandings of Jesus' identity—and of the tradition itself—are forged.

This ambiguity is already present in the Old Testament. A major stream of Old Testament tradition views kingship negatively. Second Samuel 8 understands Israel's desire to have a king, like the nations, as a departure from God's pattern for Israel—a direct threat to Yahweh's kingship. Some of the prophets echo this tradition, "I have given you kings in my anger, and I have taken them away in my wrath" (Hos 13:11). Indeed, as Millard C. Lind has shown, Israel's entire experience of human kingship may be viewed negatively, as usurping Yahweh's role and willfully disobeying God.[8] It is not surprising then that the kingship motif plays an ambiguous role in the Gospels.

James Will introduces another tradition of royal messianism which he contends is a more relevant background for Jesus and the Gospels than is the royal Davidic political messianism.[9] Will desig-

---

[7] Ibid., 169.

[8] M. Lind develops this view in his textual study of the Pentateuchal narrative and the Primary History. See Lind, *Yahweh Is a Warrior*, 50–170.

[9] J. E. Will, *A Christology of Peace* (Louisville, Ky.: Westminster/John Knox, 1989).

nates this tradition as the "Solomonic-Sapiential Royal Messianism." Drawing on the *Psalms of Solomon* and the *Testament of Solomon*, he points out that this tradition, linked to David's royal son, King Solomon, to whom God promised an eternal throne (2 Sam 7:14), depicts the Messiah as excelling in wisdom and exercising lordship over demonic powers. This wise One will enter his kingship only through suffering and death (Wis 2:19), and will also be vindicated by God (Wis 2:16; 5:1; 18:3).[10] Will's proposal is appealing, but his inclusion of Psalm 72 in this tradition, in order to link the kingly role with "wisdom, justice, and peace," is questionable. In fact, data from this sapiential tradition to support the justice and peace role of the Messiah, though strongest in *Psalms of Solomon*,[11] is overall comparatively meager. Granted, the Synoptics' portrait of Jesus as a paraboler and an exorcist seems to fit well with this tradition. But, as this study shows, portrayals of Jesus in this way (primarily the first three sections, though exorcism occurs mostly in the Galilean section) do not focus on Jesus' identity as King, though the kingdom of God motif does abound.

This literary phenomenon calls for caution in aligning the Gospels' portrait of Jesus' royal messiahship with the Solomonic rather than the Davidic tradition. Arguably, however, the first three sections of the Synoptics do create a messianic portrait of a paraboler and exorcist which then climaxes in the issue of Jesus' royal identity, the focus of the conflict in the passion section. But a more serious objection to Will's proposal is that the Synoptic texts, when they discuss kingship, frequently mention the Davidic and/or the Zion traditions in one form or another. The Gospel texts do not explicitly link kingship to the Solomonic tradition.[12]

Two other traditions, moreover, do appear to be intertwined with the royal messianic theme. One of these, the Son of humanity tradition, is explicitly linked with the messianic theme by the juxtaposition of the two titles, Messiah and Son of humanity, in Mark 8:29–31 and parallels. Scholars disagree on how these two titles are related. Countering the mainstream view, Hartmut Gese proposes

---

[10]Ibid., 39–40.

[11]A. Shank, "Peace Themes in the *Psalms of Solomon*," unpub. paper (Elkhart, Ind.: Institute of Mennonite Studies, 1985).

[12]The sources used for this tradition are actually quite late. While both *Wisdom* and *Psalms of Solomon* are dated in the middle to late first century B.C., the *Testament of Solomon*, upon which the exorcistic tradition rests, is likely third century A.D., though a few scholars have proposed a first century A.D. date (D. C. Duling in Charlesworth, *OTP*, 1.940–43). See also n. 38 below.

that Scripture as early as Daniel already associates the two traditions.[13] Gese also notes that *1 Enoch* "consciously draws on Davidic
messianism" by using the "title *māšîaḥ* for the Son of humanity
(48:10; 52:4)."[14] On the other hand, Jack Dean Kingsbury regards Son
of humanity in Mark as functioning in virtually a reverse role to that
proposed by Gese.

Kingsbury argues that Son of humanity functions
distinctly and differently from the Christ/Messiah title and its associates,
Son of David, King of the Jews (Israel), and Son (of God). Holding
that Son of humanity is neither simply a circumlocution for "I, Jesus, a
man" nor a use of the Danielic apocalyptic tradition, he proposes that
it is a title of majesty, used publicly not to disclose Jesus' identity—
thus there would be no messianic secret (so H. Räisänen)—but to
describe Jesus' special vocation as "the Man." It plays no role in dis-
closing who Jesus is. Challenging a broad consensus in Markan scholarship, Kingsbury argues that the title Son of humanity does not *correct*
Peter's messianic confession.[15] Rather, Peter's confession is correct
but not sufficient. Jesus' question to the scribes, How can the Messiah
be both David's Son and Lord?, does not repudiate Davidic lineage but
affirms both the Messiah's Davidic sonship *and* something more.[16]

---

[13]Gese, *Biblical Theology*, 154.

[14]Ibid., 158. B. McNeil, in "The Son of Man and the Messiah: A
Footnote," *NTS* 26 (1980), 419–21, has also noted the Targum on Ps 80:15b,
which reads "King Messiah" (*mlk' mšyḥ'*) for "son" in the phrase, "and upon the
son whom thou hast reared for thyself," usually regarded as a late MS addition
(though the Syriac testifies to its presence as a non-*parablesis*) parallel to 17b.
The Targum thus has "King Messiah" (15b) as a metonymic parallel to Son of
man in 17b. Again, any proposed dating of the origin of this Targum (certainly
prior to final redactional form) before the writing of Mark is controversial.

[15]Kingsbury does not deal with Mark's distinctive rendering in 8:30
which has Jesus rebuking (ἐπιτιμάω) Peter right after his confession. Kingsbury
is asking us to accept the prediction of suffering as a corrective (v. 31), but not
to see *Son of humanity* in tension with *Christ* as a title in Peter's confession. But
this is asking that we separate the titles from the traditions they represent. Nor
is it a case where *Son of humanity* can simply be added as a complement to
Messiah. Rather, *Son of humanity* and the tradition it represents relate trans-
formationally to *Messiah*.

[16]F. J. Matera has noted that scholarly interpretations of this pericope
fall into two camps: "the evangelist did not deny Davidic descent but believed
that the Messiah would be more.... [or] the evangelist did not consider Davidic
descent essential for messiahship and probably denied it" (*The Kingship of Jesus
in Mark* [SBLDS 66; Chico, Calif.: Scholars, 1982], 85). Kingsbury represents
the former view. While this is essentially correct, the Markan care to qualify and
even transform the notions of kingship associated with the Davidic tradition
are indeed more significant than Kingsbury's discussion shows.

In evaluative response, Kingsbury's distinction between Messiah-Son of God as titles of identity and Son of humanity as descriptive of vocation is overdrawn. The prevailing understanding in the Judaism of Jesus' time was such that Son of humanity did not yet connote messianic hope (contra Gese) but had a sufficient independence, as Kingsbury argues, to signify something else (as in Mark 8:38 and 14:62) and even blend apparently with the servant tradition (in 8:31; 9:12, 31; 10:32) in order to function as a qualifying control upon the Messiah-Son of God titles (contra Kingsbury).

The second linkage between traditions is that of kingship and the servant of Isaiah 40–55, also in ch. 61. The Isaianic servant is chosen and endowed with the Spirit (42:1); if the "me " of 61:1 is connected to the servant, then the servant is "anointed" by the Spirit. While the anointing by the Spirit may signify prophetic tradition, royal identity marks the servant here as well (see ch. 7, n. 28). Specifically, against the background of the suffering and death of the servant in Isaiah, culminating in 52:13–53:12, and the royal-servant lament Psalms 22, 31, and 69, the Synoptics' portrait of the suffering and crucified Messiah makes sense. The Second Isaiah corpus conveys understandings that illumine Jesus' post-resurrection return to Galilee, a climactic emphasis for Matthew and Mark (see ch. 7). The mission of the servant Messiah continues beyond death.[17]

MARK

1. Content and Structure

Mark's passion narrative begins at 14:1 and ends at either 15:39 or 16:8. If one focuses on the disclosure of Jesus' christological identity in the passion, then 15:39 is the climax—but even then Jesus' resurrection may be viewed as confirmation of this confessional disclosure that Jesus is Son of God. If one looks at the passion as one piece with Jesus' resurrection (as the passion-resurrection predictions in 8:31; 9:31; 10:32 do), then 16:8 is the end.

The internal structure of the section consists of six segments:

14:1–25. Three levels of preparation: (1) the chief priests' and Judas' plotting (vv. 1–2 and 10–11), intercalated with (2) Mary's

---

[17]The conjoining of these traditions to understand Jesus has been done by Manson, *Servant-Messiah*; J. W. Bowman, *Which Jesus?* (New York: Macmillan, 1970), 136–55; O. Cullmann, *The Christology of the New Testament* (London: SCM, 1959), 51–82; 109–92.

anointing (3–9) and (3) Jesus' own preparation (including Judas' action in the center) climaxing with the phrase "kingdom of God" (12–25).

14:26–65. A Jesus-Peter narrative into which are interwoven three major events: Gethsemane (32–42), Jesus' arrest by Judas and a crowd (43–49), and a "trial" before the chief priests and Sanhedrin followed by a mockery (53–65). The first paragraph of this segment introduces two motifs which recur later: Jesus' word, "strike the shepherd, and the sheep will be scattered" (27) is echoed in vv. 50–52 when all forsake him and a young man runs away naked. Second, Peter's vow never to forsake Jesus followed by Jesus' prediction of Peter's denial (29–31) is consummated in the account of Peter's denial in vv. 66–72. In this segment the kingship topic arises in the trial interchange between the high priest[18] and Jesus.

15:1–20. Jesus', the leaders', and the crowd's trial before Pilate, followed by the soldier's mockery. The big issue is: whether Jesus is King of the Jews—with four casts of the motif, in verses 2, 9, 12, and 18.

15:21–39. Jesus' crucifixion as "King of the Jews," mockery as "the Christ, the King of Israel," and death. To these ring out an antiphonal encore: the rent temple veil and the centurion's confession, "Truly, this man was God's Son."

15:40–47. Surprise players on the stage: women who followed him in Galilee and Joseph of Arimathea. Joseph, "who was also himself waiting expectantly for the kingdom of God, went boldly to Pilate and asked for the body of Jesus." Joseph and his friends bury Jesus.

16:1–8. News of the resurrection and its reception. The women, going to the tomb and worrying about the huge stone, find the stone rolled away. Upon entering the tomb, they encounter a young man who gives them resurrection news and commands them to tell the disciples *and Peter* to go to Galilee to see Jesus. But, shaken and astonished, they run away and tell no one anything.

In addition to identifying explicit references to kingship, I will consider two other factors as well. First, various scholars include aspects of the narrative that develop the royalty theme only implicitly.

---

[18]In Mark the high priest is unnamed; Matthew (26:3, 57) and Luke (3:1–2) specify the name, Caiaphas. For a convincing explanation why Mark withholds the name, see G. Theissen, *The Gospels in Context: Social and Political History in the Synoptics*, trans. L. M. Maloney (Minneapolis: Augsburg/Fortress, 1991), 171–74.

For example, Sherman E. Johnson regards Mary's anointing as an anointing for kingship, even though none of the Gospels identify it as such.[19] Similarly, Frank J. Matera regards Jesus' E'lo-i, E'lo-i cry and the bypassers' response, "he is calling Elijah," as a mockery of Jesus' kingship. I treat these two instances separately from clear, explicit references to kingship.[20]

Second, defining the scope of images that contribute to the kingship motif is necessary. The term "kingdom of God" occurs twice in these chapters and is clearly a kingship motif. As Paul Minear has pointed out, Old Testament images for God, such as Father, King, Shepherd, etc. are really part of a paired image, Father and son, King and people of the kingdom, Shepherd and sheep.[21] These considerations, the distinction between explicit and implicit and the scope of images included in the kingship motif, must be kept in mind also when using earlier parts of the Gospel to see how the narrative anticipates the kingship theme in the passion.

2. Explicit Occurrences of the Kingship Motif in Mark

In the passion narrative two explicit uses of the kingship theme form the heart of the trial interrogations (Jewish and Roman respectively). In the Jewish trial, the high priest asks Jesus, "Are you the Messiah, the Son of the Blessed?" (14:61). In the Roman trial before Pilate and in the subsequent crucifixion narrative, the phrase "King of the Jews/"King of Israel," occurs six times (15:2, 9, 12, 18, 26, 32), indisputably one of the leit-motifs of the narrative.[22] This motif prepares for the centurion's confession of Jesus as Son of God, which thus brings to a climax the royal imagery of the chapter and the Christology of the entire Gospel. By making this confession of Jesus' royal identity as Son of God the interpretive response to Jesus' death, Mark "poses the paradox that the crucified Jesus is God's royal Messiah."[23]

---

[19]S. E. Johnson, "The Davidic-Royal Motif in the Gospels," *JBL* 87 (1968), 139.

[20]F. J. Matera, *The Kingship of Jesus: Composition and Theology in Mark 15* (SBLDS 66; Chico, Calif.: Scholars, 1982), 133.

[21]P. Minear, *The God of the Gospels* (Atlanta: John Knox, 1988), 12.

[22]A second is the recurring use of παραδίδωμι, to hand over, to betray, occurring in 14:10, 11, 18, 21, 41, 42, 44; 15:1, 10, 15. The "handing over/betrayal" is in three stages: Judas to the chief priests, the chief priests to Pilate, and Pilate to the death sentence.

[23]Matera, *Passion Narratives*, 8.

The occurrence of both *Christ/Messiah* and *Son of the Blessed* in the high priests' question intensifies the kingship theme. In keeping with the Psalm 2 and Isaiah 9 traditions, *Son of the Blessed* implies messianic identity as well. In Mark, Jesus' answer to the question is affirmative, "I am" (ἐγώ εἰμι). But this response is more than simple affirmation, since in Mark (cf. 6:50) it conveys christological disclosure; it is a "revelational formula," to use Donahue's phrase.[24] While Donahue holds that this formula leads to the Christophany in verse 62, i.e., seeing the Son of humanity coming on the clouds of heaven, the entire narrative, with its numerous royalty titles and the controversial temple saying (14:58), is christological disclosure. Donahue's arresting picture, summarizing Best, that "the titles *Christos* and Son of God 'chase' each other through the Gospel" and here the chase ends[25] is well put.[26] But other christological disclosures play into this narrative chase as well: the revelational "ἐγώ εἰμι" and the title Son of humanity. As in 8:29–31, the Son of humanity self-designation stands in tension with and qualifies the χριστός confession.[27] Thus, the ἐγώ εἰμι declaration affirms and intensifies the χριστός identity of Jesus while the suffering (8:31; 9:12, 31; 10:32) and the future power and glory of the Son of humanity (8:38; 13:26; 14:62) qualify and redirect it. Kingsbury's effort to show that the title Son of humanity is not a corrective to the title Messiah appears valid, but it does not acknowledge the plain narrative technique of using functions associated with Son of humanity to qualify the messianic role.[28] Thus in 8:31 Jesus resumes his earlier Son of humanity self-designation (2:10, 28)—

---

[24]Donahue, *Are You The Christ?*

[25]Ibid., 91.

[26]Assuming the textual authenticity of the longer reading in 1:1, which Nestle-Aland include in brackets, the readers of the narrative have known all along that these two claims about Jesus belong together.

[27]In his essay, "The Earliest Use of *Christos*, Some Suggestions" (*NTS* 32 [1986], 321–43), M. de Jonge concludes that in view of the varied roles associated with the Messiah in first-century Judaism—"prophet-preacher-teacher-healer-exorcist" (334), there is no reason why Jesus should "have avoided the title 'Messiah,'... if he could give his own creative interpretation of it" (336). But as his early references to N. Dahl's essay indicate, Messiah, who voluntarily suffers and is crucified, offends all expectations. Hence, Jesus could not own the title without transforming it. But early Christianity assigned that title to Jesus, in the very designation, Jesus Christ. Further, as Dahl has argued, Jesus was crucified as Messiah, clearly a political charge. Hence a major task of early Christian theology was to transform the political understanding of Messiahship: Dahl, *Crucified Messiah*, 10–36.

[28]As N. Perrin has shown: "Creative Use, 357–65.

which indeed is not part of the "secret"—to describe aspects of his vocation intrinsic to his work as Messiah.[29]

Furthermore, the placement of this messianic confession in the context of the charge that Jesus said he would destroy and rebuild the temple (14:58) adds another component of messianic disclosure. Regardless of whether God or Jesus would rebuild the temple in the messianic age,[30] the Markan narrative clearly links the two themes together. Later on in the narrative when asked by the high priest for some response to the temple charge, Jesus simply remains silent. His refusal to deny or affirm the charge leads directly to the high priest's question, "Are you the Messiah, the Son of the Blessed?" As Kingsbury notes, in asking this question "the high priest unwittingly calls upon Jesus to acknowledge in public who he is really is," a critical dilemma for Jesus.[31] His reply, ἐγώ εἰμι, affirms then his acceptance of both the messianic and divine sonship identities. He then continues with a Son of humanity saying in which Jesus claims for himself future vindication: " 'you will see the Son of Man seated at the right hand of Power,' and 'coming with the clouds of heaven.' " Exasperated, the high priest declares Jesus guilty of blasphemy.

But on what basis does the high priest pronounce judgment, since the messianic claim, even as God's Son (see the OT background above) is no cause for such an indictment? Drawing the connection in the narrative between the temple charge and Jesus' messianic claim resolves this problem. Scholars agree that earlier sources designate God as the One who would rebuild the temple when the Messiah comes.[32] The narrative flow thus "grounds" the charge of blasphemy in Jesus' acknowledgment of himself as the Messiah *and* that he would do *God's* work of rebuilding the temple—since he did not deny the temple charge. But, the rebuilt temple anticipates an order of reality that the high priest cannot grasp. The same holds true for Jesus'

---

[29]Moreover, 8:30, "And he charged (ἐπετίμησεν) them to tell no one about him," indicates that the secret is linked to Jesus' messianic identity. Peter's and the disciples' view of Jesus' messiahship cannot be proclaimed because it distorts Jesus' own view. Hence, the use of ἐπιτιμάω (rebuke) already in v. 30.

[30]See the discussion in ch. 5; also esp. Chance, *Jerusalem*, 14–18. Tg. Zech. 6:12 and Tg. Isa. 53:5 are clear that the Messiah will rebuild the temple. But the only certain preChristian evidence assigns the work to God when the Messiah comes (4QFlor 1:11 and 11QTemple 29:10).

[31]Kingsbury, *Christology of Mark's Gospel*, 120.

[32]Juel, *Messiah and Temple*, 174–79, in assessing the Qumran literature. The same point appears in later rabbinic literature (ibid., 151). Both texts are midrash on Exod 15:17.

messianic identity. The reader understands Jesus' messiahship and sonship in a way that the high priest cannot. Thus the irony of the temple truth extends to the Messiah truth.

If, on the one side of the χριστός declaration, Jesus as Messiah claims to do God's work of rebuilding the temple, so on the other side "the Son of humanity seated at the right hand of Power (τῆς δυνάμεως)" and "coming with the clouds of heaven" identify Jesus again with what was held to be the prerogative and work of God. As Donahue notes, it climaxes a long narrative debate over Jesus' authority (ἐξουσία)—whence comes Jesus' authority (1:22, 27; 2:7–10; 11:11–12:44)?[33] Jesus' authority, associated with the Son of humanity title, and his identity as Christ and divine Son are now merged within the context of the alleged claim that he will destroy and rebuild the temple. Only joining Jesus' claims of his identity with his claim of doing the work of God clears the way for the high priest's vexed declaration that Jesus blasphemes. Thus, some of the people began to mock him, saying " 'Prophesy!' "—in deriding response to his Son of humanity prophecy in 14:62.[34]

The use of "Son of humanity" in Mark 14:62 clearly designates a transcendent figure with divine authority.[35] Gese's distinction between the royal Davidic messiahship and transcendent Son of humanity traditions—though both acquire universalistic aspects—fits well their theological significance in Mark. But the extreme importance of the Son of humanity theme correlates with imminent suffering and death, as established earlier in the passion-resurrection predictions.[36] This connection tones the Son of humanity saying in 14:62 as well. The two emphases, imminent suffering and future vindication, must be held together. Thus Jesus' "coming with the clouds of heaven" stands in christological tension with the passion narrative itself. Jesus' prophecy of his royal power arises ironically from the setting of his condemnation as a blasphemer, his suffering as

---

[33]Donahue, *Are You the Christ?*, 119–20.

[34]Juel notes here the irony that while Jesus is mocked as a false prophet (v. 65), his prophecy of Peter's denial (14:30) is coming true at this very time (vv. 66ff.): "at the very moment he is being ridiculed as prophet, his prediction about Peter is being fulfilled to the letter" (ibid., 72).

[35]Matera holds that the "Son of Man figure in Daniel (whether an individual or a corporate figure) is represented as a royal figure; see Dan 7:14, 18, 22, 27" (*Passion Narratives*, 231, n. 35).

[36]Gese notes that Enoch's exaltation after his faithful life is not an adequate parallel, in that the suffering and exaltation are more closely linked in the Gospels' Christology than in Enoch (*Biblical Theology*, 164).

one publicly humiliated, and his crucifixion as a criminal—an alleged political threat to Rome.

A second christological feature is the sixfold use in chapter 15 of "King of the Jews (Israel)," which must be considered together with the centurion's confession of Jesus as Son of God. As Matera argues, "the overall theme of chapter 15 is the 'Kingship of Jesus,' " which Mark develops through use of irony and the three mockeries, culminating in the centurion's confession. Thus, "Pilate learns that Jesus has died from the centurion who proclaimed the King of the Jews to be the Son of God."[37] Further, in the larger context of chapters 14–15, Mark clearly uses the title "Son of God" in its royal sense, reflecting the Old Testament messianic tradition.[38]

The first and last uses of "King of the Jews" frame the narrative: Jesus accused as "King of the Jews" (v. 2) and crucified under the placard, "King of the Jews" (v. 26). The intervening uses identify Jesus as rejected as "King of the Jews" (vv. 9, 12) and mocked as "King of the Jews" (v. 18). Each of these uses comes from the Romans and possibly connotes an indictment of Jesus as a political insurrectionist. But through the narrative tone the Roman acclaim ironically affirms what the Jewish leaders will not acknowledge. Jesus remains noncommittal (v. 2, σὺ εἶπας), standing in agonizing silence (v. 5) so that Pilate marvels (θαυμάζω). Pilate then seeks to extricate himself by offering Barabbas as an alternative, asking, "Do you want me to release for you

[37]Matera, Kingship, 63.
[38]Ibid., 62; Juel, Messiah and Temple, 82. Some scholars have urged that "Son of David" should be understood in line with a charismatic exorcist tradition which links the "Son of David" title to Solomon as exorcist. K. Berger makes this connection in Mark 15 in the second mockery where Jesus fails as a charismatic miracle worker to fulfill the prediction of 14:58, and is thus mocked: "Die königlichen Messiastradition des Neuen Testaments," NTS 20 (1973), 1–44, and "Zum Problem der Messianität Jesu," ZTK 71 (1974), 1–30. A similar connection is suggested by C. Burger in Jesus als Davidssohn: Eine traditionsgeschichtliche Untersuchung (FRLANT 98; Göttingen: Vandenhoeck & Ruprecht, 1970). Burger (ibid., 66, 169) sees some parallel in this to the Hellenistic θεῖος ἀνήρ tradition; hence, Jesus is addressed as "Son of David" in contexts of healings in Mark (10:47). See also D. C. Duling, "Solomon, Exorcism, and the Son of David," HTR 68 (1975), 235–52. Duling rightly questions: if this link is valid, why is Jesus not addressed as "Son of David" in an exorcism? By locating this address with a healing, Mark shifts the title and perception of Jesus away from this tradition. In my judgment, this fact should be interpreted to mean that this tradition is not a factor in understanding Mark's portrait of Jesus, either in his miracles or in the royal titles of the narrative. For further sources, see M. de Jonge, "Earliest Use," 335 and 342, n. 93.

the King of the Jews?" (v. 10). But the chief priests and the crowd cry for Jesus to be crucified. Then Pilate sarcastically attributes the appellation to them: "Then what do you wish me to do with the man whom you call the King of the Jews?" (v. 12). When they cry, "Crucify him," Pilate insists on some clearer account of Jesus' culpability, "Why, what evil has he done?" (v. 14). They give no evidence, but because they persist in their cry, Pilate delivers Jesus to be crucified. The Roman soldiers mockingly adorn him with a royal purple robe, place a crown (στέφανος) of thorns on his head, and salute him saying, "Hail, King of the Jews!" (v. 19), even kneeling in homage to him. After noting that they cast lots for his coveted garments, the narrative indicates that the inscribed ἐπιγραφή of his charge (αἰτία) was "The King of the Jews" (v. 26).

This sets the stage for the next two ironic references to Jesus' royalty. Until now, only Romans allege him as king of the Jews. But once Jesus is on the cross where they want him, the chief priests and scribes begin ridiculing him, saying, "He saved others; he cannot save himself. Let the Messiah, the King of Israel, come down from the cross now, so that we may see and believe" (v. 32). Only in jeering at him do the Jewish leaders acknowledge Jesus' identity as the Messiah, the King of Israel. Also, the shift from "King of the Jews" to "King of Israel" reflects the shift from Roman to Jewish voices.[39] This mockery links chapter 15 to the christological disclosures of 14:58–62; the Jewish leaders here deny what Jesus there affirms. In mockery lies the fear of truth denied.

Ironically the narrative denouement comes in a Roman voice, the officiating centurion who, as he sees (ἰδών) the suffering Jesus breathing his last, exclaims, "Truly this man was the Son of God" (RSV). Here, on the lips of a Gentile, is *Israel's* royal coronation acclaim of Psalm 2:7: the faithful dying king is indeed the royal Son of God who executes the Lord God's reign in justice and faithfulness (cf. Pss 72 and 45). Jesus' kingship, thrown into comic relief from the Roman side and tragic relief from the Jewish side by Pilate's placard, is first mocked by the Jewish leaders, and then in sharp contrast, affirmed by a *Gentile* soldier. In this triple contextual convergence of shameful cross, royal Son, and defiled Gentile, truth transcending paradox is spoken!

3. More Royalty Indicators: Scope and Implicit References

When the terms and implicit references connected to the christological royalty theme in the passion narrative are considered,

---

[39]Juel, *Messiah and Temple*, 50.

14:1–25 and 15:40–16:8 add additional depth to the focus on christological titles noted above.

   a. The Eloi cry and mockery. Matera points out that at the implicit level, Jesus' *E'lo-i* cry is followed by a mockery, so that chapter 15 contains three mockeries. The mockery by the bystanders, "Wait, let us see if Elijah will come to take him down," contrasts sharply to the centurion's confession, since both are responses to Jesus' cry, "*E'lo-i, E'lo-i, la'ma sabach-tha'ni?*" Matera argues that Mark intended the apparent misunderstanding of the bystanders, Elijah for *E'lo-i,* really to be mockery. Matera further holds that Jesus' cry quotes Psalm 22 and that the reader should bring that entire Psalm to mind since three explicit connections to the psalm are made elsewhere by Mark: 15:24 (garments) with Psalm 22:19; 15:29 (mockery) with 22:8 and 15:34 (cry) with 22:2f., 12, 20–22.[40] Old Testament scholars note the royal function and emphasis of Psalm 22: Eaton "refers the entire psalm to the sacral king and claims that the enemies possess an archetypal character," and "Gese draws attention to the relationship between the Holy One enthroned in v. 4 and God's kingship in v. 29."[41]

   In this context, Matera proposes that Mark intends his community to understand

> the cry of 15:34 as the cry of the Messiah King, a cry first uttered by David himself. Thus, by juxtaposing the great cry of Psalm 22 and the Elijah mockery, the evangelist shows in still another way that the bystanders mock Jesus as Messiah King.[42]

Whether Mark and/or his community of readers/hearers had the entire Psalm in mind is debatable (Matera believes they did, and he considers and counters the opposing arguments). The citations and allusions between the two passages and the way in which the cry followed by a mockery fits the structure of chapter 15 argue forcefully for Matera's conclusion. The cry and mockery thus extend the royal kingship theme through the last phase of the crucifixion narrative.

   b. Recurrence of "kingdom of God." The occurrence of "kingdom of God" in 14:25 and 15:43 merits notice. In the first use, it

---

[40]Matera also cites the works of C. O. Peddinghaus and J. Oswald, which together identify five additional implicit connections (*Kingship,* 128–29). See also O. L. Cope, *Matthew: A Scribe Trained for the Kingdom of Heaven* (CBQMS 5; Washington, D.C.: CBA of America, 1976), 102–10.

[41]Matera, *Kingship,* 127–28. Matera cites church fathers who understood Ps 22 as a royal psalm fulfilled in Christ (130–31).

[42]Ibid., 132–33, quotation on 133 (emphasis in the original).

functions as the "ending word" of Jesus' last meal with his disciples.
After decreeing the bread and cup to be bearers of his presence, with
the cup to be his covenant blood poured out for many, Jesus tells his
disciples, "Truly I tell you, I will never again drink of the fruit of the
vine until that day when I drink it new in the kingdom of God."
Though Jesus has just announced that his betrayal is imminent (14:21),
this statement clearly marks the future as anticipating and bringing
the kingdom of God. Verses 27–28 continue the same contrast of
imminent crisis and new beginning: " 'I will strike the shepherd, and
the sheep will be scattered.' But after I am raised up, I will go before
you to Galilee." Again, royal imagery appears. The "shepherd" quotation from Zechariah 13:7b comes out of the context of God's desolating Israel by striking the royal leader and scattering the people.[43]

The same themes reappear in the closing frame. Jesus' burial
becomes christologically significant through the way Mark introduces
Joseph of Arimathea: "a respected member of the council, who was
also himself waiting expectantly for the kingdom of God" (15:43).
This links the burial itself with hope for the future. Once again, irony
discloses truth: a Jewish leader—of the group that betrayed Jesus to
the Roman authority on the charge that he was a messianic pretender—musters the courage to ask for the body of Jesus, as one who
also himself (καὶ αὐτός) was looking for the kingdom of God.[44] This
comment on Joseph's hope tones the entire narrative with the underlying hope of others who also were longing, hoping, yearning for the
kingdom of God to come—in fulfillment of the proclaimed promise
of the now crucified King, issued at the narrative's beginning: "Jesus
came to Galilee, preaching the good news of God, and saying, 'The
time is fulfilled, and the kingdom of God has come near; repent, and
believe in the good news' " (1:14b–15).

Where does the Markan narrative leave this hope for the
coming of God's kingdom? The enigmatic ending picks up the theme
of 14:27–28. The young man at the tomb announces that the stricken
Shepherd-King is risen; he is no longer in the tomb. Rather, the young
man says, Jesus goes "before you to Galilee; there you will see him, as
he told you." With three converging emphases the narrative clearly
reaffirms the coming of the kingdom. The risen Jesus returns to
Galilee, the place of earlier manifestations of kingdom deeds and

[43]Gese, *Biblical Theology*, 145, 151.
[44]The καί (also) is perplexing. Apparently its *other* referent is "respected member of the council" (εὐσχήμων βουλευτής).

words. Second, the promise, "there you will see (ὄψεσθε) him," fulfills
the theme introduced in 9:1, "Truly, I tell you, there are some standing
here who will not taste death until they see (ἴδωσιν) that the kingdom
of God has come with power," as well as Jesus' similar "Truly, I tell
you" announcement of the kingdom (14:25). Here the connection
exists through both the *seeing* and *kingdom* themes. Third, the specific
mention of Peter, "go, tell his disciples *and Peter*" (emphasis mine),
climaxes the prominence of Peter's earlier role in the narrative, both
in his confession of Jesus as the Messiah (8:29) and in his denial of
Jesus precisely when his messianic identity was tested by the high
priest (14:61–72). Earlier, when Jesus spoke of his imminent suffering,
Peter rebuked Jesus. Now when Jesus is arrested and mocked, Peter
denies him. Jesus' meeting of Peter in Galilee anticipates a *resurrection*
of what Peter denied, namely, the *crucified* Messiah! The resurrected
Jesus meeting with his disciples in Galilee not only gathers the scattered disciples physically but also gathers them around the truth from
which they fled, i.e., the messianic identity and kingdom reality of the
crucified Jesus, Son of God.

In addition, the announced resurrection and reappearance in
Galilee consummate the three passion-resurrection predictions and
(false?) declaration of the rebuilt temple not made with hands, both
of which are linked to the "three days" motif. The predictions begin
in the context of Peter's confession; the temple charge triggers Jesus'
own "I am" declaration before the Jewish high priest and Council, as
well as the sequence of events that led to Jesus' execution as "King of
the Jews." Thus, wending its way through the Gospel narrative, including transformed and reversed notions of how one gains entrance
into the kingdom (9:35–10:45), the kingdom hope bursts forth anew
on Easter morning. In Galilee, the resurrected, stricken Shepherd
gathers the scattered sheep; 16:7 thus consummates the narrative
themes first mentioned in 14:27–28.[45]

c. The narrative role of the women. The flight of the women,
however, appears to short-circuit the commission and its restoration
of the kingdom hope. Framing the passion narrative is the crucial role
of women at the beginning and end: Mary's anointing of Jesus in
14:1–9 and the women who suddenly appear in the narrative after

_____

[45]Johnson, "Davidic-Royal Motif," 137, suggests that Mark's account
of Jesus' feeding of the five thousand, in its description of them as "sheep
without a shepherd" (6:34), echoes the royal shepherd-kingship imagery of the
OT: Joshua (Num 27:17), Micaiah's vision (1 Kgs 22:17), Ezekiel's vision (Ezek
34:1–6).

Jesus died (15:40–41), remaining also at the center of the narrative until the very end (16:8). As Johnson has suggested, Mary's anointing of Jesus functions at the implicit level as an anointing not only for burial but for Jesus' kingship as well.[46] At the end of the narrative, women from Galilee, Mary Magdalene, Mary the mother of James the less and Joses, and Salome, were beholding the crucifixion and Jesus' death from a distance. They had followed him and ministered to him while he was in Galilee.

These women are the key witnesses to the continuity between the historical Jesus and the resurrected Christ. But their flight from the tomb suspends the ending of the story in order to privilege its call and impact upon the reader. The historical continuity, here in the form of testimony, is actualized when the link between Jesus' past and the reader's present is closed by the reader's "yes" to meet Jesus in "Galilee" to receive the call to take up the kingdom mission. The restoration of the kingdom hope lies in the Gospel's appeal—and hence commission—to its readers. Strikingly, Mary's anointing of Jesus closes with Jesus' prophetic word that what she did will be told "wherever the gospel is proclaimed in the whole world" (14:9). In both cases, at the beginning and at the end of the passion narrative, women provide the impetus for the worldwide proclamation of the gospel.

Does this feature of Mark's Gospel have anything to do with understanding the nature of Jesus' kingship? In the Gospel as a whole women regularly appear in narrative roles that model exemplary responses to Jesus within given sections.[47] What is the significance of women framing the passion narrative in this way? Does this feature illumine Mark's view of Jesus' kingship? Possibly so, in that it effectively disarms kingship from all standard and expected representations. When Jesus' kingship is publicly decreed, the men have fled and women in their uncalculating devotion, lingering commitment, and fearful flight beckon the readers to their own encounter with the

---

[46]Ibid., 139.

[47]See W. M. Swartley, "The Role of Women in Mark's Gospel: A Narrative Analysis," 1987 *SBL Abstracts*, 283–84; E. S. Malbon, "Fallible Followers: Women and Men in the Gospel of Mark," *Semeia* 28, ed. M. A. Tolbert (Chico, Calif.: Scholars, 1983), 29–48; and J. A. Grassi, *The Hidden Heroes of the Gospels: Female Counterparts of Jesus* (Collegeville, Minn.: Liturgical, 1989), 12–44. This phenomenon, especially the role of the women present at the resurrection, may be seen as a structural parallel to the role of women in the OT heralding the news of a battle.

risen, crucified Son of God. The narrative does not deny kingship, but through a series of ironies (Roman taunt, Jewish denial, and a Gentile's confession), it leads us to exclaim, "how strange and disarming this kingship!"

d. *Connections to earlier royalty emphases.* Kingsbury noted three additional ways in which the resurrection narrative is linked to Mark's larger story and/or the passion story with its confession that Jesus is the (royal) Son of God. First, the identification of "Jesus the Nazarene (of Nazareth)" in 16:6 loops the reader back to 1:14, to "Jesus [who] came from Nazareth of Galilee." In the baptism this Jesus was designated by God as "my beloved Son," a royal title, who is now raised from the dead. Second, "the resurrection does not 'undo' the crucifixion" but rather the young man's announcement indissolubly links the crucifixion and resurrection. The One who was crucified is the One who has risen. Though the centurion said Jesus *was* the Son of God, the resurrection makes the *was* become *is*: "the crucified Jesus, who is said upon his death to have been the Son of God, has been raised and so 'is' the Son of God."[48] Third, the passive voice ἠγέρθη in 16:6 points to God as the One who raised Jesus from the dead. This divine action echoes the ending of the parable of the vineyard, in which the stone that the builders rejected will be placed by God as the "head of the corner." Thus, "God has vindicated the 'rejected stone—his beloved Son.'"[49] This analysis shows that the resurrection does not divert from or eclipse the royal Sonship motif of the Gospel, but consummates it. The resurrected One is the baptized, rejected, crucified, and now vindicated royal Son of God.

MATTHEW

1. Content of the Narrative

Matthew's passion and resurrection narrative extends over three chapters, 26–28. The resurrection narrative continues considerably beyond Mark's, but the passion narratives are so similar in content and order that it is unnecessary to repeat the outline. The most significant differences in the passion narratives consist of additional material in 26:2–5, 52–54; 27:3–10, 19 with 24–25, 43, 51b–53b, 62–66. The first two passages highlight the nonpolitical and non-

---

[48]Kingsbury, *Christology of Mark's Gospel,* 134.
[49]Ibid., 135.

military nature of Jesus' kingship. By recounting the Son of humanity passion prediction a fourth time (v. 2b), Matthew stresses the divine ordination of Jesus' death. Similarly, Jesus' specific command to sheath the sword that cut off the ear of the high priest's servant and his statement that he could appeal to his Father for twelve legions of angels to protect him decisively establish that Jesus is a Messiah who will not launch a military revolt.

The next two passages underscore one of Matthew's more prominent emphases, the guilt of Judas (27:3–10) and the Jewish leaders (27:3–10, 19, 24–25). Both the dream of Pilate's wife (v. 19) and Pilate's washing of his hands (v. 24) accentuate Pilate's desire to free Jesus, in contrast to his actual deed when under pressure. Sealing the sepulcher and posting a watch (27:63–66) illustrate this guilt as well as the unspoken fear that their attempt to eliminate Jesus would backfire. The two remaining passages emphasize Matthew's christological focus upon Jesus as Son of God: his impotence as *Son of God* to save himself in 27:42–43 and, intensified by the cosmic convulsions (earthquake and opened tombs in 27:51b–53b), the centurion's awe-filled confession of Jesus as *Son of God* in verse 54.

In two places Matthew has a shorter account than Mark: (1) in the temple charge, 26:61, the Markan contrast of "made with hands" and "not made with hands" is absent. This is followed by a more ambiguous version of Jesus' claim: from "I will destroy" (Mark) to "I am able to destroy." (2) Matthew does not describe Joseph of Arimathea as one who is "looking for the kingdom of God." Some other more minor but significant differences appear in Matthew's view of Jesus' kingship as well.

In presenting a fuller resurrection narrative that goes beyond Mark 16:8, Matthew 28:8–10 portrays the women running with fear and joy to give the angel's message to the disciples.[50] While they are running, Jesus himself meets them, and the women worship him. Jesus then commands them, "Do not be afraid; go and tell my brothers to go to Galilee; there they will see me." Matthew then tells how the earlier fear of the chief priests now leads to their fraud: they pay the soldiers to tell the people that his disciples came by night and stole Jesus' body. The Gospel climaxes with the eleven going to a mountain in Galilee, worshipping the resurrected Jesus who claims "all author-

---

[50]For discussion of how this angel and the young man of Mark are to be understood, see A. K. Jenkins, "Young Man or Angel," *ExpTim* 97 (1983), 237–40; Swartley, *Mark*, 35–36.

ity in heaven and on earth" and commissions his disciples to "make disciples of all nations, baptizing them in the name of the Father and of the Son and of the Holy Spirit." (16–20).

2. *Kingship in Matthew's Passion Narrative*

In keeping with Matthew's explicit Christology earlier in his Gospel, his passion story shows more fully than Mark's the nature of Jesus' kingship.[51]

a. *The Jewish trial and mockery (26:57–68)*. We observe three differences from Mark. Instead of "Son of the Blessed" in the high priest's question, Matthew reads "Son of God." But, with Luke, Matthew gives Jesus' answer as "So you say" (σὺ εἶπας), instead of Mark's ἐγώ εἰμι. Hence, while the high priest's question is more explicit in Matthew than in Mark about Jesus' divine Sonship, Jesus' acknowledgment is decidedly more ambiguous, though comparison with Jesus' own earlier use of σὺ εἶπας (26:25) would indicate a fully affirmative answer—but one which puts the "burden" of the affirmation back on the inquirer!

A third difference appears in the mockery, in that the hecklers who call for Jesus to prophesy address him as "you Christ" (χριστέ). Matthew's Gospel earlier makes clear Jesus' identity as Messiah (1:1, 16, 18; 16:16, 20, 21[52]; the trial scenes shift the title into a derisive taunt, from both the Jewish and the Roman sides, thus intensifying the Jewish rejection of Jesus as *their* rejection of *their* Messiah.

b. *The Roman trial and subsequent mockery (27:11–31)*. In two of the four Roman taunts in Mark and Matthew against Jesus as "King of the Jews," Matthew's Pilate uses the word "Christ" (vv. 17, 22). Two possible explanations are: since some manuscripts designate Barabbas as Jesus Barabbas in v. 16, the phrase "Jesus who is called Christ," could simply be a way to distinguish between the two Jesuses; or Matthew has Pilate use the term *Christ* to drive home to the Jewish leaders their claim against Jesus, i.e., "so he is your alleged Messiah whom you refuse and wish to crucify." This second explanation is

---

[51]G. M. Styler, "Stages in Christology in the Synoptic Gospels" (*NTS* 10 [1963–64], 404–6; followed by D. Hill, *The Gospel of Matthew*, NCB (London: Oliphants, 1972), 64. Some of the following observations have been noted by Matera, *Passion Narratives*, 121.

[52]Here I follow the reading supported by Sinaiticus and Vaticanus, Ἰησοῦς Χριστός, as do also Nolan, *Royal Son of God*, 146, and Kingsbury (who leans toward accepting it), *Matthew*, 96–97.

supported by Pilate's twice stating his desire to exonerate himself of all guilt (vv. 19 and 24), thus shifting the blame onto the Jewish leaders.

In the soldiers' mockery, Matthew dramatizes Jesus' royalty even more than Mark. In addition to the scarlet robe and crown of thorns, Matthew notes that they put a "reed in his right hand" (29b), a parody of the royal scepter (Gen 49:10), thus intensifying their sarcastic regard for his kingship.

c. *The crucifixion, mockery, and centurion's confession.* The inscription over the cross identifies both the crucified one and the charge, "This is Jesus the King of the Jews" (27:37). It also declares the truth denied by those who cried for his crucifixion.

In 27:42 the mockery of the chief priests, scribes, and elders lacks the word "Christ" (ὁ χριστός) present in Mark (15:32), possibly because it was already used by the same group in earlier ridicule (26:28). Whatever the reason, its absence intensifies the extended mockery of Jesus as *Son of God*: "He trusts in God; let God deliver him now, if he wants to; for he said, 'I am God's Son' " (v. 43).

This feature has a fourfold significance. First, it ties the ending of the trial narrative to its beginning, when the high priest asks if "you, Jesus, are the Son of God." Second, it enables the trial narrative as a whole, and especially the taunt sequence (in Mark 15 the sixfold "King of the Jews [Israel]"), to play upon a larger christological repertoire, i.e., King of the Jews, Christ, and Son of God. Earlier in the Gospel these titles were already used to define Jesus' identity (chs. 1–2). To use them now as sarcastic taunts heightens the culpability of those who refuse Jesus as their King, Christ-Messiah, and Son of God. Third, by putting a "Son of God" taunt at the end of the series, Matthew highlights his christological focus. This truth, so central to Matthew's Christology, is thus disdained by the unbelief, rejection, and hatred of Jesus' own people who refuse him as Son of God.

Fourth and as the narrative's climax, the Jewish leaders' taunt of Jesus as Son of God contrasts sharply to the Roman centurion's confession of Jesus as Son of God (27:54). Climaxing Matthew's narrative christologically, the contrast also links his Christology with his ecclesiology and missiology. It loops the reader back to Matthew's distinctive emphases in 4:15–16, 23–25, and 8:5–13. Jesus' earlier words to another centurion apply here also:

> "Truly I tell you, in no one in Israel have I found such faith. I tell you, many will come from east and west and will eat with Abraham and Isaac and Jacob in the kingdom of heaven, while the heirs of the kingdom will be thrown into the outer darkness, where there will be weeping and

gnashing of teeth." And to the centurion Jesus said, "Go, let it be done for you according to your faith" (8:10–13).

d. Burial and resurrection narrative. Matthew's royal Christology, profusely presented throughout the Gospel, significantly culminates in Jesus' final words in 28:17–20. The centurion's confession that Jesus is the Son of God is specifically confirmed and vindicated by: (1) the phrase, "All authority in heaven and on earth has been given to me"; (2) the charge to make disciples of all nations, thus highlighting Gentiles as recipients of the gospel; and (3) the inclusion of "the Son" in the baptismal formula: "in the name of the Father and of the Son and of the Holy Spirit." The long tradition of the King as God's royal Son has reached its apogee—indeed, upon a mountain which in the Sinai–Zion tradition symbolizes the place of God's presence and rule.

3. Matthew's Larger Gospel Perspectives on Royal Christology

The royal Christology that permeates Matthew's passion narrative consummates the christological emphases of his entire Gospel. As Kingsbury contends, among the plethora of Matthew's christological titles, "Son of God" ranks foremost. Our analysis of Matthew's passion narrative confirms Kingsbury's view with double-sided evidence. Contra those who have argued for the primacy of the "Son of David" title, it is virtually absent from the passion narrative, and thus clearly cannot be the point upon which Matthew wants final emphasis to fall. Conversely, the title "Son of God" functions in foremost position, both at the end of the trial narrative, with its mocking taunt, and in the centurion's confession, the only direct speech responding to Jesus' death. Besides, Jesus' mountaintop commissioning of his disciples, in its baptismal formula, clinches the acclaimed royal identity of Jesus as Son of God.[53]

Matthew's many depictions of Jesus as Son of God, according to Kingsbury, portray "the abiding presence of God with his people in the person of the earthly and exalted Son of God (1:23; 14:27, 33; 18:20; 28:20)." This motif occurs within "the time of Jesus" which extends from his birth to his parousia, including this age in which "Jesus is worshiped (cf., e.g., 14:33; 28:9, 17), confessed (14:33; 16:16–17; 27:54), and 'followed' (cf., e.g., 4:18–22; 9:9; 10:38; 16:24; 19:27–

---

[53]Kingsbury had noted this already in his article, "The Composition and Christology of Matt 28:6–20," *JBL* 93 (1974), 573–84. Also, *Matthew*, 77–78.

29) as the Son of God by the church."[54] By designating Jesus "Son of
God" Matthew does not discount either the traditions of Davidic
royalty or those of Jesus' kingship. Rather, other royalty titles play
narrative roles that embellish the portrait of Jesus as Son of God. This
is especially true of Messiah-Christ, Son of David, and King of the
Jews. But it is also true of Lord and Son of humanity, which stress
different christological traditions and emphases. Each of these five
titles may be regarded as major christological titles for Matthew, in
distinction to those which play more minor roles (Jesus, Son of
Abraham, The Coming One, Shepherd, Prophet, Rabbi–Teacher, Ser-
vant/παῖς, Emmanuel).[55]

Since Messiah-Christ and Son of David are the two most
prominent titles which, like Son of God, bear directly upon Matthew's
portrait of Jesus as King, this discussion focuses only on the occurrences and function of these two titles, as they prepare for Matthew's
climactic portrait of Jesus as Son of God in the passion narrative. In
addition, the examination includes more general portraits of Jesus as
king, and most importantly, how portraits of Jesus as Son of God
function in the Gospel as a whole.

a. Messiah-Christ. Brian Nolan, in Royal Son of God, gives
extensive attention to the function of Jesus as Christ and Son of David
in Matthew. He identifies three uses of "Christ" in the Gospel.[56] First,
Christ is used with the name Jesus, defined as one "who saves his
people from their sins" (1:21). In the six references where "Christ" and
"Jesus" appear together (1:1, 16, 18; 16:20f.; 27:17, 22), Christ's role
as one "who saves from sin by his atoning death"[57] is conveyed as one
aspect of Matthew's royal Christology. This too is part of the truth
that Pilate rivets on the Jewish conscience in his appellation of Jesus
as the Christ. Pilate's washing of his hands and the Jewish people's
declaration, "His blood be on us and on our children" (27:24–25),
both appear as responses to guilt. Thus, the Jewish response rejects

---

[54]Kingsbury, Matthew, 123.
[55]Ibid., 84–96. Kingsbury subsumes "King of the Jews" under "Messiah-King" (98–99), but it should be considered separately since it is used
specifically to show how Gentiles designate him, the magi in worship (2:2),
Pilate in interrogation (27:11) and criminal declaration (27:37), and the soldiers in mockery (27:29). The worship and the mockery illustrate contrast
between the birth and passion narratives. For numerous other parallels and
contrasts, see Nolan, Royal Son of God, 104–8. Like Pilate, Herod also refers to
Jesus as "the Christ" (2:4; Nolan, Royal Son of God, 104)
[56]Nolan, Royal Son of God, 146–49.
[57]Ibid., 147.

this salvific efficacy of Jesus' death as the Christ. Though some have proposed that Matthew intends this Jewish outcry to be an acceptance of forgiveness, the placement of this outcry immediately after Pilate's evasion of responsibility does not support this interpretation.[58]

Second, in both 11:2 where John hears about the "deeds of the Christ" and 23:10 where Christ is to be the only Master of the disciples, the term "Christ" is used to designate Jesus as One with prophetic anointing as Teacher. Matthew's distinctive word for "Teacher" in 23:10 (καθηγητής) designates Jesus as head of a scribal school. In this capacity as prophetic teacher he also heals (11:2ff.) and prophesies (26:68).

Third, though "Christ" is implicitly equivalent to Son of David and King, Matthew refuses "to link the Messiah explicitly with the Son of David and King of Israel."[59] Granted, these titles coincide in 1:6, 20–21; 2:2–6; 21:5–9, yet in three instances Matthew backs off from using the term Messiah in places where it might connote political royalty. After Peter's confession, Jesus commands the disciples to tell no one (16:20). In the "Son of David" riddle, Matthew puts distance between "Christ" and "Son of David" (22:42–45), although he does not deny that the Christ is the Son of David. And in 27:42, as noted above, "Christ" is not joined to "King of Israel" in the mockery of Jesus on the cross, as in Mark 15:32 and Luke 23:35, 39. This point gains significance when, on the other hand, "Christ," "Son of David" and "King of the Jews (Israel)" are all explicitly linked with "Son of God" (16:16; 26:63; 22:42–45; 2:2, 4, 15; 27:42–43). This indicates that Matthew's "control" on the royal Davidic Messianic tradition is "Son of God," and *only* "Son of God."

Fourth, Matthew explicitly links "Christ" and "Son of God" at the most crucial places in the unfolding story of the Gospel, a point that, surprisingly, Nolan fails to note. Peter's confession of Jesus as the

---

[58]In two separate papers at the Annual SBL 1988 meeting, F. A. Niedner, Jr. ("Re-reading Matthew on Jerusalem and Judaism" [*1988 Abstracts*, §38], 263) and Timothy B. Cargal (" 'His Blood be upon Us and upon Our Children': A Matthean Double Entendre" [*1988 Abstracts*, §153], 363) proposed this interpretation: the outcry of the Jewish crowd should be understood as their acceptance of Jesus' blood for the forgiveness of their sins, fulfilling the narrative theme of 1:21. While their evidence appeared somewhat convincing (Cargall noted, among other evidence, 26:28 in which Jesus' blood is associated with forgiveness of sins), neither considered how this saying relates in the narrative to Pilate's preceding word.

[59]Nolan, *Royal Son of God*, 149, 148. The closest case for linkage is Pilate's interchange between the titles "King of the Jews" and "the Christ." But even there it is "the one called Christ."

Messiah is joined to "the Son of the living God" (16:16). In his adjuration at the trial, the high priest demands to know if Jesus is "the Christ, the Son of God" (26:63). Further, since "King of Israel" belongs to the Messiah-Christ complex, the mockery which links "King of Israel" and "Son of God" (27:43) should also be included.[60] The infancy narrative's christological titles, "King of the Jews" and "Christ" in 2:2, 4 culminate in Matthew's citation (in 2:15) of Hosea 11:1, "Out of Egypt I have called my son." The narrative sequence of this link between Christ and Son of God is: (1) God's declaration in the Old Testament citation (2:15); (2) Peter's confession (16:16); (3) the high priest's interrogating adjuration (26:63); and (4) the chief priests', scribes', and elders' mockery (27:43). Thus Matthew makes clear that this *revealed* truth (16:17; cf. 2:15 as OT citation) is rejected by the Jewish leaders.

b. Son of David and kingship. As Nolan contends, *a* son of David must be distinguished from *the* Son of David. The former concerns lineage and royal paternity; the latter, messianic authority from a theological point of view.[61] Matthew's narrative clearly establishes both points.

The salient features of *a* son and *the* "Son of David" in Matthew adhere to three main emphases. First, the birth and infancy narratives establish that Jesus is of royal Davidic lineage (1:1, 6, 17, 21). He is born King of the Jews (2:2) as the Christ (2:4) in Bethlehem, the city of David (2:5–6); believing non-Jewish royalty (the Magi) worship him (2:11). Jesus' royal credentials thus contrast to Herod's semi–Jewish but nonDavidic, unbelieving rule in Jerusalem,[62] whose desire for the Christ-Child is death.[63]

---

[60]Kingsbury holds that "Messiah" is qualified, on one side, by "King of the Jews (Israel)" which carries political overtones that are closed out in the narrative by the taunting and mockery in the passion narrative and, on the other side, by "Son of God" which carries Matthew's positive aspects of royal Messiahship (*Matthew*, 97).

[61]Nolan, *Royal Son of God*, 149. Nolan has an extensive treatment of this title through all of Matthew and examines understandings in the Jewish literature as well (149–215). After studying the wider Matthean uses and Jewish backgrounds, he focuses on Son of David and Kingship in Matt 1–2 (210–15).

[62]Ibid., 205.

[63]Nolan treats Davidic Sonship so comprehensively that it subsumes "Son of God." His Son of David section includes the voice at the baptism and transfiguration, the testing in the wilderness, and Jesus' proclamation of the kingdom (ibid., 170–73). While Nolan devotes sixty-five pages to "Son of David," only eighteen are given to "Son of the Lord God" in which the title κύριος is considered also. Even here "Son of David" holds sway alongside "Son

Second, the acclaim of Jesus' Davidic Sonship throughout his Galilean ministry is actually the positive response of the "underside of history" to Jesus' proclamation of the kingdom of God. The blind men's outcry, "Have mercy on us, Son of David" (9:27), climaxes Matthew's section of ten miracles and prepares for the testimonial, "Never was anything like this seen in Israel" (9:33c). These miracles are Jesus' deeds of the kingdom, of the Christ; even John hears of them in prison (11:2). As Kingsbury says, "the 'blind,' a 'dumb' man, the 'children,' and even a Gentile 'woman' are able to 'see' and 'confess' what Israel does not (cf. 9:27; 12:22; 15:22; 21:15; with 13:13; 15:14; 23:16–17, 19, 14, 16)."[64] Indeed, even the blind see that Jesus is the Son of David. In 12:22 "all the people" hopefully query, "Can this be the Son of David?" This question comes immediately after an extended quotation of Isaiah 42:1–4 which envisions Jesus' ministry as including the Gentiles (12:18–21), and Matthew's depiction of Jesus as One "greater than the [Davidic] temple" (12:3–6). This implies that those beyond/outside Israel will recognize Jesus' Davidic Sonship. The Pharisees immediately contravene a positive answer and attribute the deeds of Jesus to Beelzebul (12:24). To climax the healing deeds of Jesus' Galilean ministry, the Canaanite woman calls out for Jesus' mercy, "O Lord, Son of David" (15:22). These three uses of the title in Jesus' Galilean ministry form a choir of recognition, a choir in which the blind and the Gentiles see and sing that the Proclaimer of the kingdom is indeed David's royal Son.

Third, the repeated cry of the two blind men west of Jericho, "Have mercy on us, Son of David" (20:30–31), carries the Galilean choric toward Jerusalem and prepares for the twofold acclaim of the triumphal entry, "Hosanna to the Son of David." The crowds first shout it in 21:9, and then the children chant it in the temple—to the irritation of the chief priests and scribes (21:15). Jesus approves the praise, clinching it with a quotation from Psalm 8:2: "Out of the mouths of infants and nursing babies you have prepared praise for yourself."[65] Jesus' controversies with the religious leaders climax then

---

of God" and "Lord." This reflects his regard of Matthew as a presentation of Jesus' enthronement as Christ-King (reflecting the fall New Year's Tishri festival as a ritual enactment of the king's accession to divine sonship). Thus he concludes: "In short, Jesus the Christ [in Matthew] actualizes the ultimate mystery which Tishri celebrates" (240).

[64]Kingsbury, *Matthew*, 101.

[65]The LXX has *praise* (αἶνος) for the MT *strength* ('*ōz*). In both cases the praise/strength is because of the enemy, a point most appropriate in this

with his question of how the Christ can be both David's son and his Lord (22:42–45). In all of this Jesus' Davidic Sonship is endorsed, but the final appeal is to demonstrate that it is not enough; it requires something more.[66] For this something more, the titles Lord, Son of God, and also Son of humanity are essential.

Most significantly, Matthew's treatment of Jesus' Davidic Sonship shows a specific *Tendenz*. Though of the lineage of David (1:2–16), Jesus' parent was not a human male king (1:18–25); Jesus was conceived of the Holy Spirit, an ultimate development in the trajectory of spiritualizing the Son of David messianism, evident already in Isaiah 9:6–7; 11:1–5 (7:14).[67] Born in Bethlehem—thus its lowliness is exalted—according to prophetic decree, Jesus comes as a ruler to shepherd (ποιμαίνω) Israel (2:5–6). In Jesus' infancy, when Jesus is already designated as "King of the Jews," Herod the king in Jerusalem seeks to kill Jesus; in the passion narrative the Jerusalem powers do kill him. In his Galilean ministry as Son of David, Jesus appears as a compassionate healer, and One who, like Wisdom in the royal court, calls people to his humble and easy yoke (11:25–30).[68] He enters Jerusalem in humility, riding upon the royal, but lowly, donkey (1 Kgs 1:38), thereby fulfilling the peaceable vision of Zechariah 9:9–10.

> Rejoice greatly, O daughter of Zion!
> Shout aloud, O daughter of Jerusalem!
> Lo, your king comes to you;
>   triumphant and victorious is he,
> humble and riding on a donkey,
>   on a colt, the foal of a donkey.
> He will cut off the chariot from Ephraim
>   and the war horse from Jerusalem;
> and the battle bow shall be cut off,
>   and he shall command peace to the nations;

Matthean context. While the NRSV, following the MT, continues with "to silence the enemy and the avenger," the LXX has καταλύσαι for its verb, the same verb used in the temple charge. Quite likely Matthew intends that this quotation be heard by the opponents as praise that activates God's defense against the enemy, a recurring motif in the Psalms.

[66] Kingsbury (*Matthew*, 97ff.) rightly seeks to show that "Son of David" is not "the foremost title in the first Gospel" (contra G. Strecker, R. Hummel, and A. Suhl).

[67] On this, see Gese, *Biblical Theology*, 147.

[68] Here D. Verseput's study of Matthew's kingship theme is helpful: *The Rejection of the Humble Messianic King: A Study of the Composition of Matthew 11–12* (New York et al.: Peter Lang, 1986).

his dominion shall be from sea to sea,
and from the River to the ends of the earth.

Here the view of the Davidic Messiah as a military conqueror forcefully freeing Israel from political oppression, crushing the Gentiles, is
already repudiated. Still another degree of transformation in the
Messiah/Son of David expectations may be seen in the Zechariah 13:7
portrait of the stricken shepherd, with its NT portrayal in Matthew
26:31; 28:7 (and par.). Gese points to the development in the Ptole-
maic period in which "the Messiah appears as the one who fights . . .
as a martyr."[69] Indeed, Jesus' question on the Messiah's Davidic Sonship and Lordship calls for radical reflection. How much of these
earlier understandings is intended in Matthew's use of the title? His
use of other titles and overall narrative emphases provide the clue.

c. Son of God. Matthew uses "Son of God" for Jesus in order
to qualify and "shepherd" Jesus' identity as Davidic son. Granted, the
Old Testament "Son of God" identity of the king is very much part of
the Davidic kingship tradition. But, as Gese points out, this identity
of political royalty and divinity, so commonplace in the Ancient Near
East ideologies, is broken in Israel. Precisely when the political structure of Israel crumbles, kingship intensifies and deepens into the
messianic hope. God "rejects the reigning house of David" and in-
spires the hope for a new son, Emmanuel, to be born. "The concept
of son of God does not disappear but is transformed. No specific
family can come forward as bearer of the promise given to the Davidic
dynasty, but somewhere in the great Davidic clan, not perceptible in
specific detail, God will choose the one to fulfill the dynastic promise
of eternal lordship in Zion."[70] In a similar way of both affirming and
refining the tradition, the Zion tradition functions as a critical force
upon the Davidic royalty traditions in Psalms and Isaiah. In keeping
with and extending this tradition, Matthew designates Jesus as Son of
God to critically qualify and define the Davidic royalty tradition.

This is evident in the birth and infancy narratives in that
Jesus' conception by the Holy Spirit overshadows Jesus' Davidic lineage. As Kingsbury puts it, "Suffice it to say that the adoption of Jesus
by Joseph, which makes him Son of David, cannot compare to his
conception by the Holy Spirit, which makes him Son of God."[71]

---

[69]Gese, Biblical Theology, 150. See p. 114, n. 55, for primary source
documentation.
[70]Ibid., 146–47.
[71]Kingsbury, Matthew, 101.

Linked to this superior emphasis is the interpretation of Jesus' miraculous birth by the word Emmanuel: in Jesus *God* is with humanity. Similarly, the sequence of identity-titles for Jesus in chapter 2 moves through "King of the Jews" and "Christ" to "God's Son called out of Egypt." The repeated phrase, "the child and his mother" (2:11, 13, 14, 20, 21) also calls attention to his divine paternity.[72]

The preparation narrative, climaxing in Jesus' baptism and temptations, affirms and confirms Jesus as God's Son,[73] in fulfilling all righteousness and sustaining perfect obedience under test (3:15–4:11). God's pronouncement at Jesus' baptism, "This is my Son, the Beloved, with whom I am well pleased," marks Jesus' royal identity since it quotes from the coronation Psalm 2 (v. 7), echoes also the beloved son of sacrifice in Genesis 22, and links the Son designation to that of the obedient servant in Isaiah 42:1–4. The last temptation—all three prefaced by "Since you are the Son of God"—rightly images the "kingdoms of the world" as Jesus' prerogative, but on Satan's terms. Loyal as Son in his worship and obedience to God, Jesus triumphs over Satan's testing and then begins his ministry of announcing that the "kingdom of heaven has come near" (4:17).

In the Galilean ministry Jesus' identity as Son of God gives way to more public identifications such as Lord (reflecting the address of Matthew's post-Easter Christian community), Son of David (see above), and Son of humanity (Jesus' self-identification in the Synoptic tradition). In contrast to Mark's three uses (1:25; 3:11; 5:7), Matthew has demons decrying Jesus as Son of God only once (8:29), and this plays no role in Matthew's overall narrative strategies.[74] In calling his disciples to become "sons of God" by becoming peacemakers (5:9) and loving the enemy (5:45), Jesus alludes to his own divine Son-

---

[72]Ibid., 45; Matera, *Passion Narratives*, 123; Nolan, *Royal Son of God*, 41–42.

[73]In his essay, "Stages in Christology," 404, G. M. Styler suggests that Matthew begins an "interest in ontology, the divine nature of Christ." Steeped as Matthew is in the OT royal traditions, I find this suggestion unlikely.

[74]One might argue that it climaxes the christological sequence of "Son of man" (8:20), "Lord" (8:25), and then "Son of God" here in 8:29. But why would Matthew have a christological confession by demons climax Jesus' own self-identification and the disciples' address of Jesus as Lord—voicing the title of full faith in the Matthean community? Further, the title "Lord" is not to be put in any comparative role with "Son of God." It reflects the address of disciples in Matthew's community whose speech of Jesus is most commonly "Lord"; it recognizes Jesus' exalted status as Lord (cf. Phil 2:9–11). Indeed, this assumes Jesus' divine Sonship, which the narrative carefully establishes.

ship.[75] In addition, his frequent use of "Father" (11:25, 26), "the Father" (11:27b, 27c),[76] "my (heavenly) Father (in heaven)" (7:21; 10:32–33; 11:27a; 12:50; 15:13; 16:17),[77] "your (pl.) Father (in heaven)" (5:16, 45, 48; 6:1, 8, 14, 15, 26, 32; 7:11—ten times in the Sermon; 10:20, 29),[78] and "our Father" (6:9) continue to disclose Jesus' personal identity as Son of God. All these uses speak of God only in contexts where Jesus addresses his disciples and the crowds, which in Matthew are regarded as potential disciples.[79] God is never referred to as Father in discourse with the religious leaders. In Matthew the address of God as Father attests often, but not always, to intimacy in relationship and regularly appears to assume identity in character, based ultimately on Jesus' own identity with God as his true Son.

As the Galilean ministry draws to a close, Jesus is twice called Son of God, first by the disciples as a spontaneous worshipful response to Jesus' sea miracles (14:33) and, second, in Peter's confession (16:16). God's voice at the Transfiguration (17:5) confirms Peter's declaration. For the disciples, Jesus' royalty as Son of God is now certified truth, reflected in Jesus' Olivet discourse to his disciples (24:36). In two parables, the Vineyard Tenants and the Marriage Feast (21:33–22:14), Jesus intimates to Jerusalem's religious leaders that he is God's son/Son. In the flow of the narrative this prepares the way for the high priest's interrogation, "I put you under oath before the living God, tell us if you are the Messiah, the Son of God" (26:63). Then the narrative sequence of the religious leaders' mockery of Jesus as Son of God (27:43), the contrasting centurion's confession (27:54), and Jesus' commissioning of his disciples to baptize in the name of the Father, Son, and Holy Spirit, consummates this important Matthean christological emphasis.

---

[75]I find Kingsbury (despite his appeal to H. Frankemölle) unconvincing in connecting this with any Matthean emphasis on the disciples being "with" (μετά) Jesus (*Matthew*, 56). Matthew's parallel (10:1–4) to Mark's 3:13–19 lacks the point that Jesus made the Twelve to be "with" (μετά) him. Rather, Matthew emphasizes God-in-Jesus with us (1:23; 28:20).

[76]Also later in 24:36 and 28:19.

[77]These references continue to the end of the Gospel (18:10, 19, 35; 20:23; 25:34; 26:29, 39, 42, 53).

[78]Two references occur later: 18:14; 23:9.

[79]For this data I am indebted to R. L. Mowery for his speech and handout at the Boston SBL meeting, 1987, "God the Father in the Gospel of Matthew." See now a companion essay: "God, Lord and Father: The Theology of the Gospel of Matthew," *BR* 33 (April 1988), 24–33, in which he compares the uses of God, Lord and Father. Matthew is the only Synoptic to use πατέρ almost as often (44x) as "God" (51x); "Lord" occurs 18 times to address God.

4. *Gather on the Mountain*

To understand how Matthew employs the divine Sonship theme as well as, by interrelationship, the Davidic Sonship and Christ-Messiah themes, we return to the mountain of 28:16–20. While scholars commonly recognize this pericope as the climax of Matthew's Christology, ecclesiology, and missiology, their form analyses of the unit suggest numerous prototypes:

(1) an 'enthronement hymn' such as is found in Phil 2.9–11, 1 Tim 3.16 and Heb 1:5–14 [Michel, Jeremias, Bornkamm]; (2) a 'divine utterance' . . . [Trilling]; (3) an 'official decree modeled on 2 Chron 36.23 [Malina, Nolan, Senior, Schweizer]; (4) a 'covenant renewal formulation' [Frankemölle]; (5) part of a 'theophanic form' modeled on the Sinai theophany [Smyth]; (6) a 'commissioning *Gattung*' [Hubbard, O'Brien, Ellis].[80]

But none of these discuss the significance of the mountain setting per se in relationship to eschatological hopes surrounding Israel's Zion traditions, as does Terence Donaldson, whose work influences this section. Matthew's attention to mountain settings reflects both Sinai and Zion themes (see ch. 3 above), with the latter often absorbing the former. In this text we see Zion theology in each of the three parts of the commissioning scene.

a. All authority given to Jesus. Jesus receives (ἐδόθη μοι) "all authority in heaven and on earth" (πᾶσα ἐξουσία). Anchored in Yahweh's Father-Son oath to David (2 Sam 7:14), Zion theology envisions Mount Zion as the site of the messianic king's enthronement. Some exilic and postexilic texts specify the king as One of Davidic origin (Ezek 17:22–24; 34:23–31); some specify Yahweh himself as the king (Zech 14:8–11; Isa 24:23; 52:7); and some portray Yahweh reigning with a king of David's line (Ezek 20:33, 40; 43:7; Mic 4:7 with 5:2–4). In these texts the separate traditions of messianism and Zion theology converge in "the vision of eschatological Zion as the mountain of enthronement."[81]

The ἐξουσία which Jesus declares now to be given over to him recalls the Son of humanity reference in Daniel 7:14 where, in the LXX, ἐδόθη αὐτῷ ἐξουσία occurs. If this were the only parallel between Matthew 28:17–20 and Daniel 7:13–18, the notion that Matthew's theology echoes Daniel's Son of humanity tradition would be doubtful, but πάντα τὰ ἔθνη occurs in both texts as well. Matthew's accen-

---

[80]Donaldson, *Jesus on the Mountain*, 175–76.
[81]Ibid., 47.

tuation of both the messianic royalty traditions and the eschatological role of the Son of humanity—here Matthew has six texts lacking in Mark[82]—aligns his theology with that of 4 Esdras 13 and the 1 Enoch texts cited above where royal kingship and Son of humanity merge into one common eschatological portrait. In Matthew these two streams merge to certify Jesus' post-resurrection authority as Son of God, for upon Jesus as both Son of humanity and Son of God the Father bestows all authority in heaven and on earth.[83]

Psalm 2:7–8 is also background for this Matthean text. Once God declares the crowned king on Mount Zion divine Son, he invites the Son to "Ask of me, and I will [give] (not NRSV "make," LXX δώσω) the nations (ἔθνη) [to you as] your heritage" (v. 8). As Donaldson puts it, "Here, in a manner similar to Mt 28.18b, δίδωμι is used, with God as agent, to express the bestowal of world-wide sovereignty on God's royal Son, a bestowal taking place on Zion, God's holy mountain."[84]

b. Fulfillment of the Commission. The instruction of the commission specifies a means by which Zion's eschatological vision of gathering together God's people, including the nations (τὰ ἔθνη), on the mountain of the Lord (Isa 2:2ff.; 51:11; etc.) is to be fulfilled. The gathering is under the authority of the Son who directs his disciples to "make disciples of all nations" (μαθητεύσατε πάντα τὰ ἔθνη). The emphasis falls not upon "Go" but upon "make disciples." The going is a circumstantial participle, attending the finite imperative verb "make disciples."[85] Baptizing and teaching are modal participles, specifying the essential manner of accomplishing the task of making disciples. Both the baptizing and the teaching are further specified: baptizing is in the name (which represents the authority of the person) of the Father, Son and Holy Spirit; the content of the teaching is specifically those things which Jesus commanded (recall here the five discourses).

Both the Zion vision (Isa 2:2ff., 24:23; 25:6–10a; 56:6–8; Mic 4:1f.; Zech 8:20–23) and the Danielic vision of the Son of humanity

---

[82]These Son of man eschatological sayings are: 10:23; 13:41; 16:28; 19:28; 24:30; 25:31 (Kingsbury, *Matthew,* 114).

[83]It is striking to see that Luke uses the same terminology of "giving all authority," δώσω τὴν ἐξουσίαν ταύτην ἅπασαν (4:6), to describe Satan's offer to Jesus in the kingdoms of the world temptation. Satan indicates that the authority was given over to him. This echoes the *Test. of Job* 8:2–3 (Charlesworth, *OTP* 1.842) where Satan asks for authority to test Job.

[84]Donaldson, *Jesus on the Mountain,* 181. Donaldson also notes Rev 2:26ff. which utilizes Ps 2:8 with similar emphasis.

[85]J. H. Yoder, *As You Go* (Scottdale, Penn.: Herald, 1961).

receiving authority, dominion, and an everlasting kingdom embrace
the τὰ πάντα ἔθνη, with restored Israel, as co-recipients of God's
eschatological blessings. The πάντα τὰ ἔθνη are specifically welcomed
at the eschatological banquet, the feast of fat things on God's holy
mountain (Isa 25:6–10a). They also come to learn Torah, the law
which goes out from the holy mountain. Eating at God's table and
learning God's Torah are here fulfilled in the baptizing—which initiates one into the Eucharist—and in the teaching of that which
the Son-Lord has commanded. While much of the Zion theology is
centripetal (the nations come to Zion), this Isaianic vision is also
centrifugal: the Torah goes out to the nations, empowering people to
beat swords into plowshares. Indeed, Zion's reign is a rule of peace
(Isa 52:7) which, Jesus declares, marks his followers as God's children
who participate in Jesus' own Sonship (5:9, 45). Jesus commands this
word to be shared with all nations.

The teachings of Jesus in Matthew, as well as in the Zion
tradition, emphasize God's justice—the greater righteousness—, humility and trust in God, true piety and freedom from wealth's and
power's seductions.[86] These are the teachings the royal Son orders
(ἐντέλλω in 28:20) and gives (chs. 5–7) on the mountains. This climactic mountain scene brings into focus not only the messianic royalty
aspect of the Zion tradition, but also its moral, didactic content which
measures David's Son by God's Son. Truly, the baptism is not in the
name of David, or royalty per se,[87] but in the name of the crucified,
resurrected and now enthroned royal Son of God, with the Father and
the Spirit. The "Zion symbolism [of] human subordination and humility before the kingship of God"[88] has now been incarnated in Jesus,
the humble obedient Son of God. Zion's universal rule is thus established anew in King Jesus, installed Son of God forever. God's people
are now no longer confined to any one nation, but consist of those
who humbly accept and trust in the rule of God's crucified and
resurrected Messiah, Jesus the royal Son.

For Matthew, Christ becomes "Zion as the centre of eschatological fulfillment."[89] Christ, not the mountain, is the gathering point,

[86]See Ollenburger's excellent description of the moral dimension of
the Zion theology (*Zion*, 160–62 esp.).
[87]Ollenburger sums up Zion's theological bearing on kingship: "In
summary, the monarchical language of Zion does not legitimate 'imperial
monarchy', it prohibits it" (*Zion*, 161).
[88]Ollenburger, *Zion*, 160.
[89]Donaldson, *Jesus on the Mountain*, 184. Donaldson says Christ

though the mountain motif in the Gospel plays a narrative role that discloses Jesus as God's Son consummating the Zion vision to peaceably establish God's sovereignty. Matthew's narrative anticipates this climactic mountain scene, gathering to go in the name of Jesus, when Jesus promises that wherever two or three gather in his name he will be present (18:18–20). Jesus' presence gives the authority to bind and loose, and to petition God, with the assurance that prayers will be heard. Still earlier in the story, the nations' kings bring gifts to the Christ-Child, fulfilling Zion's vision of earth's royalty coming to pay homage (2:2, 11 echoes Isa 60:6; Ps 72:10, 15; perhaps also Isa 39:1–2).[90]

    c. Jesus' abiding presence. Jesus promises his followers his abiding presence: "Lo, I am with you (μεθ' ὑμῶν) always, to the close of the age." This promise fulfills the Zion vision of God's dwelling in Zion with restored Israel and the ingathering of believers from the nations. That Zion is the place where God will dwell with his people— indeed will be *with* them—is strongly attested in the Zion traditions (Pss 43:3; 48:1–2, 14; 68:16; 74:2; 76:2; 132:13–14; 135:21; Isa 8:18; Joel 3:17, 21).[91] After examining this theme in its many expressions in Israel's history, R. E. Clements says, "Throughout the pages of the Old Testament we can see that this conviction of Yahweh's dwelling in the midst of Israel forms a unifying theme."[92] Donaldson notes that Yahweh frequently promises to be *with* his people, both individually and corporately, for comfort, strength, and defense. The long-standing "Fear not, for I am with you" and Yahweh's defense of Zion are strong traditions in which the Lord God pledges his abiding presence.

    Within the context of the exile, Israel voices hope for Yahweh to return and abide with them on Mount Zion. Ezekiel's vision of the Lord God's regathering of the scattered sheep culminates with such a *with* text: "And they shall know that I, the Lord their God, am with them, and that they, the house of Israel, are my people" (34:30). Furthermore, when Gentiles hear that the Lord of hosts is *with* Israel, "ten from the nations of every tongue shall take hold of the robe of a Jew, saying, 'Let us go with you, for we have heard that God is with

---

replaces Zion, but this misses half the point. Rather, Christ becomes Zion.

    [90]Ibid., 185. Nolan argues that Isa 39:1–2 is the most adequate allusion. He notes five common terms and three equivalent terms. This parallel puts into a new light the issue of the referent of the child to be born in Isa 7:14: Hezekiah or Jesus Christ? See Nolan, *Royal Son of God*, 206–9.

    [91]Donaldson, *Jesus on the Mountain*, 186, gives some of these references.

    [92]Clements, *God and Temple*, 135.

you' " (RSV, Zech 8:23). Similar texts occur in later Jewish literature also (Jub. 1:17f.; *Vita Adam and Eve* 29:7), and the grand vision of Revelation climaxes with God's dwelling with humanity (21:3).[93]

In Matthew this stream of emphasis on the Zion tradition finds its consummation in Jesus' final words of promise, "I am with you always, to the end of the age." God's royal Son Jesus—indeed God's own self, Emmanuel—promises to be *with* his disciples who receive his authority to make disciples of all people. Indeed, as David R. Bauer suggests, God's vow to be with humanity through his royal Son forms an *inclusio* for Matthew's Gospel, promised first at Jesus' birth (1:23) and affirmed as the Gospel's closing word (28:20). Herein is the gathering of Zion, paradoxically in the going that enables the gathering of people from all nations into the authority of a common baptism and teaching: the εἰρήνη-making children of God, in obedience to the crucified royal Messiah, Son of God, manifesting the *šālôm* of Zion.

LUKE

1. Content of the Narrative

Luke's passion narrative differs significantly from those of Matthew and Mark, containing both more and less content. It lacks Mary's anointing at Bethany,[94] Jesus' second and third times of prayer and going to his disciples in Gethsemane, the false accusation about destroying and rebuilding the temple and later temple mockery, material on Barabbas (see 23:18b), the soldiers' mockery following the Sanhedrin trial (but see 22:63–64 for a partial par.), and the cry, "My God, my God, why have you forsaken me" (but see Jesus' two other words from the cross in 23:43, 46). It lacks as well most of Matthew's content not found in Mark. Of the twenty-eight pericopes in the passion narrative, fourteen are unique to Luke (see Table IV, pp. 250–51).

Clearly, with this amount of difference, Luke's passion and resurrection narrative merits its own structural analysis. Luke's special emphases suggest the following segmental structure, with interpretive titles:

---

[93]For these texts I am indebted to Donaldson, *Jesus on the Mountain*, 187. Indeed, the tabernacle *miškan* tradition is also part of the *with* theme.

[94]Luke 7:36–50 has been regarded by some to be a reworked parallel, but its actual content is altogether different. The only two common points are the name Simon and the act of anointing with oil. But Luke has the oil put on the feet, not the head. Only in John is the woman named Mary (12:3).

I. Satan's Moves; Jesus' Countermoves (22:1–34)

II. Jesus' Moves; Opponents' Countermoves (22:35–23:2)

III. Pilate (and Herod), Unwitting Accomplices (23:3–38)

IV. Jesus and God: Victors (23:39–24:12)

V. Jesus Explains and Fulfills the Drama (24:13–53)

It is beyond the scope of this study to work in detail with all the theological elements of this narrative. But several comments, to justify this outline and provide context for the following commentary on the royalty theme, are appropriate. Luke highlights Satan's role in relation to both Judas' betrayal and Peter's denial. While the chief priests and scribes conspire, it is Judas, controlled by Satan, who enables the leaders to implement their evil intentions. Again, in Peter's denial and desertion of Jesus, Satan is the influencing power, which Jesus limits by his own intercession. That Jesus does not similarly forestall Judas' action (or Peter's denial) corresponds to the divine necessity that permeates the total narrative (22:15, 22, 37; 24:7, 26, 46). Jesus' countermoves consist of planting the seeds of victory in the midst of the swelling storm, by giving explicit teaching about the kingdom of God (22:16, 29b–30) and the disciples' kingdom conduct and authority (22:24–30). In segment II Jesus dramatically prepares the disciples for the bitter events ahead in both the call for and dismissal of swords. Jesus' decisive "No more of this" when the sword is used, after which he heals the severed ear, indicates that the use of the sword is on the side of "the power of darkness" (22:53d), a phrase parallel to "your hour," the hour when the chief priests, temple officers, and elders, coming with swords and clubs, shall have their way. In this segment, the Jewish leadership of Jerusalem, allied with the power of darkness, has its time of victory.

In segment III Rome, with its rule of Palestine personified in Pilate and Herod, falls unwillingly (Pilate) and unwittingly (Herod) under the culpability of acting under the power of darkness in implementing the death of "the Christ of God, his Chosen One" (23:35d; cf. Acts 4:27).

In segment IV Jesus' welcome of the repentant criminal into Paradise (23:43) and his dying words, "Father, into your hands I commend my spirit" (23:46), signal God's and Jesus' victory. The centurion's glorifying of God, together with his confession, "Truly this man was righteous" (own trans., 23:47), functions as an antiphonal response to Jesus' words of victory. In Luke, Jesus dies under a hallelujah halo. God accomplishes his will and purpose, openly manifest by the empty tomb and the words of two men in dazzling apparel: "He is not here, but has risen" (24:5).

Segment V, in three major scenes, reinforces God's triumph by showing that what has been accomplished *is* God's willed action in fulfillment of all Scripture.

2. Kingship in Luke's Passion Narrative

The most pertinent difference for this study between Luke's passion narrative and Matthew's and Mark's is in their varying portrayal of Jesus as God's royal Son. Luke's centurion does not acclaim Jesus as "Son of God." Instead, the centurion says, "Indeed, this man was righteous" (δίκαιος) (23:47).[95] A proper assessment of Luke's intentions in this rendering of the centurion's declaration is essential to understanding Luke's Christology, specifically his emphasis on Jesus' royalty. This feature, together with the accompanying comment that the centurion glorified (ἐδόξασαν) God, occupies a crucial place in the narrative. Other christological emphases in Luke's Gospel must tally with this highly significant narrative feature. In light of the scholarly legacy that has assigned to Luke the literary purpose of "political apologetic," the question presses upon us: Did Luke silence the tradition that a Roman confessed Jesus as Son of God, i.e., King, in order to comport with and advance his overall purpose of showing that Christianity is not a threat to Rome, that it is politically benign, or even supportive of the Empire?[96] After examining the Lukan christological portrait in the passion narrative, with brief forays into the whole of the Gospel for related emphases, we will return to this question.

Based upon the logical progression in 22:67–71, Luke clearly regards the title "Son of God" as part of the royal messianic tradition. Further, Luke's designation of Jesus as *Savior* (σωτήρ) two times (Luke 2:11; Acts 5:31) and his prevalent use of the title *Lord* (κύριος) belong

---

[95]The RSV and NRSV rendering of δίκαιος as *innocent* is lamentable, for it misses Luke's larger use of the term δίκαιος to denote those *righteous* and also those who feign righteousness (see ch. 4, 137–38). The translation *innocent* is motivated by the fallacious notion that ch. 23 more broadly declares Jesus' *innocence*. But this common view should be put to rest. In all Pilate's statements in ch. 23, no Greek term for *innocence* occurs. But Luke does use δίκαιος elsewhere with crucial significance; it is a primary feature of Luke's Christology.

[96]The essays in *Political Issues in Luke–Acts*, ed. Cassidy and Scharper, address this issue from a variety of viewpoints. See my summary of Conzelmann on this matter, as well as Cassidy's opposing view: Swartley, "Politics and Peace," 19–22.

to this same tradition. Distinguished from this dominant pluriform set of royalty traditions, another stream of emphasis, appearing less frequently but at strategic places, portrays Jesus as the Mosaic Prophet and Righteous One; here belongs also Luke's designation of Jesus as *servant* (παῖς), which occurs four times (Acts 3:13, 26; 4:27, 30). The ensuing study examines both emphases, with the passion narrative at the center, and then describes the interrelationship between these sets of christological affirmations in the Lukan narrative.

    a. Messiah-Christ, King (kingdom of God), Son of David, Son of God, Savior, Lord (Son of humanity).[97] Luke's portrayal of Jesus' royalty is so massive, with heavy concentration in the passion account, that Danker rightly refers to Luke's passion story as "the clash of kings."[98] Indeed, in Luke's presentation of Jesus' royalty, the comparison between the reign of the kings of the earth and Jesus' kingship may be epitomized: "So long as Rome endures" versus "the reign of Jesus the Great, who will rule forever" universally.[99]

    (1) Jesus as Christ (Messiah), King and kingdom, Son of God. In the passion narrative Luke uses *Christ* four times (22:67; 23:2, 35, 39), which is the same as Matthew and twice as often as Mark. But then Luke uses Christ three additional times in this resurrection narrative.[100] Also like Matthew, but half as often as Mark, the phrase, "King of the Jews," appears three times (23:3, 37, 38). The first two uses of Χριστός occur during the trial before the Jewish council, followed immediately by a list of charges which are presented to Pilate. This list, unique to Luke, presented by "the whole company" (presumably the chief priests, elders, scribes, and the council of the Sanhedrin in 22:66), accuses Jesus of "perverting our nation, and forbidding us to give tribute to Caesar, and saying that he himself is Christ a king" (23:2). This last charge arises directly from the trial before the council,

---

[97]The key sources on Christology and Jesus' royalty in Luke are A. George, "La royauté de Jesus," *Etudes sur l'oeuvre de Luc* (Sources Biblique; Paris: Gabalda, 1978), 257–82; three essays by D. L. Jones: "The Title *Christos* in Luke–Acts," *CBQ* 32 (1970), 69–76; "The Title *Kyrios* in Luke–Acts," *SBL 1974 Seminar Papers*, ed. G. Macrae (Missoula, Mont.: Scholars, 1974), 2.85–101; "The Title 'Servant' in Luke–Acts," *Luke–Acts: New Perspectives from the SBL Seminar*, ed. C. H. Talbert (New York: Crossroads, 1984), 148–65; F. J. Foakes-Jackson and K. Lake, "Christology," *The Beginnings of Christianity* (London: Macmillan, 1920), 1.345–418; Danker, *Luke*, 60–81.

[98]Danker, *Luke*, 13.

[99]Ibid., 63.

[100]Luke lacks the phrase, "King of Israel," which occurs in both Matthew and Mark.

for there the lead question is, "If you are the Messiah, tell us." Jesus evades the query with a note of reprimand, "If I tell you, you will not believe; and if I question you, you will not answer" (22:67b–68). Jesus continues with his Son of humanity declaration, "But from now on the Son of Man will be seated at the right hand of the power of God" (v. 69). They ask, "Are you then the Son of God?" Jesus answers, "You say that I am" ('Υμεῖς λέγετε ὅτι ἐγώ εἰμι). In Luke they do not then accuse Jesus of blasphemy, but simply say, "What further testimony do we need? We have heard it ourselves from his own lips." By getting assent to the Son of God question, they conclude also that he is saying *yes* to the first question: "Are you the Christ?" This then is the basis of the third charge they put to Pilate.

Luke's third use of *Christ* comes in the scoffing mockery by the Jewish rulers as Jesus hangs on the cross, "He saved others; let him save himself, if he is the Christ of God, his Chosen One!" (RSV, 23:35b). Luke's fourth use of *Christ* is on the lips of the unrepentant criminal, again as sarcasm, "Are you not the Christ? Save yourself and us" (RSV, 23:39). The third mockery, wedged between these two, is by the Roman soldiers, "If you are the King of the Jews, save yourself!" Similarly, the inscription over him on the cross reads, "This is the King of the Jews" (23:38b). These uses of *Christ* and *King of the Jews* in the mockeries shift Jesus' Messiahship into an ironic key. They assume the declarations false, but the reader knows them to be true.

With this full portrayal of Jesus as Christ and King of the Jews, Luke is more explicit than either Matthew or Mark that Jesus was condemned and crucified on the charge of claiming messianic kingship. But the narrative is also more explicit in portraying Pilate as trying to avert the sentence of death (23:4, 14, 22). In Pilate's first response, he implies that even if Jesus claims to be "The King of the Jews," he finds nothing here worthy of death. In the second case, Pilate mentions the specific charge "of perverting the people" (23:13) and then says that he finds Jesus not "guilty of any of your charges against him." This appears to contradict the first response or makes Pilate understand Jesus' "So *you* say" as a denial of the charge, a denial he accepts. Pilate's third response restates the first line of defense, "I have found in him no ground for the sentence of death" (v. 22b). Thus Luke's Pilate either disbelieves Jesus' alleged kingship, regarding it as inconsequential (hardly possible), or knows it as truth but refuses to accept it. Whichever the case, Pilate finally gives "his verdict that their [the Jewish leaders'] demand should be granted" (v. 24). Luke's presentation of Pilate is astounding. Pilate not only declares Jesus' innocent, but, even more strikingly, Pilate is a hostage to both the truth of and the Jewish leaders' denial of Jesus' messiahship.

The resurrection narrative resumes, in clear didactic form, Luke's designation of Jesus as Messiah. Twice Jesus says, to the Emmaus couple and to the eleven, "Was it not necessary that the Messiah should suffer . . . ?" (24:26, 46). These statements orient the title *Christ* to a kingship and rule that explodes all prevailing Jewish messianic expectations, for they make clear the necessary role of suffering in the divine purpose of the Messiah's work. Thus, the messianic dimension of Jesus' identity is affirmed but safeguarded against political, militant messianism.

Luke's use of *Christ* elsewhere in Luke–Acts occurs in two crucial texts, Luke 2:11 and Acts 2:36 (see also 10:36). By embedding the declaration of Jesus as the *Christ* in the angel's announcement of Jesus' birth and in Peter's Pentecost speech, Luke allows no doubt of its importance.[101] Other distinctive Lukan uses occur in Luke 2:26 where Simeon speaks, by the Holy Spirit's revelation, of seeing the "Lord's Messiah"[102] before his death; in 3:15 in reference to whether John is the *Christ*; and in 4:41 where Jesus hushes the demons because "they knew that he was the Messiah." Luke's use in 9:20 (Peter's confession) and 20:41 (David's Son) are traditional to the Synoptics. This total of twelve uses in Luke is complemented by twenty-nine uses in Acts, though some of these are in the designation *Jesus Christ* or *Christ Jesus* which, as Dahl argues, never loses its messianic reference. Further, the meaning of this name/title has been shaped more by the person and work of Jesus as the Messiah-Christ than by all preceding Jewish conceptions.[103] George notes the various settings of use: when Paul preaches to Jews, he presents Jesus as the Christ descended from David (Acts 13:16–41), but when addressing Gentiles he refers to Jesus as Christ the Lord (10:36; 11:20).[104] In 2:11 Luke links the

---

[101] Danker, *Luke*, 74.

[102] Jones argues that Luke wrote χριστός κυρίου in both 2:26 and 2:11, since the Syriac has this reading in 2:11 also, rather than Lord as nominative (χριστός κύριος). He believes that a Christian scribe changed 2:11 to κύριος, but Luke in both places speaks of the Christ-child as the Christ/Messiah *of* the Lord ("The Title *Christos*," 75–76). Compare Luke's "Christ of God" in 9:20; 23:25 and the "anointed of God" in Acts 4:27.

[103] Dahl, *Crucified Messiah*, 24–25.

[104] A. George, "La royauté de Jesus," 260–61, 280. For 11:20 George is following Western text witness. Χριστόν is supported here only by D, apparently 33 (Alexandrian), a few other MSS, an Old Latin MS w, and a fourth–fifth century, Middle Egyptian MS.

"Savior born this day" to David, "born in the city of David" and identifies him as Lord "Χριστός κύριος."

The significance of Jesus' identity as Christ is double-sided: the Sanhedrin use it to connote a temporal kingship in adversarial relation to Caesar's (23:2); but they and certainly the Christian believers reading Luke–Acts also connect it with Jesus' identity as God's Son (22:70; Acts 9:20, 22; cf. Luke 4:41). Further, Luke also connects Jesus' identity as Son of God with the royal coronation in Psalm 2 (Luke 3:22; Acts 13:33; 4:25–26—with Ps 2:2). Hence, Christian readers see in the title *Christ* the enthronement of Jesus as King (so Acts 2:36). Luke's use of the term *King* to identify Jesus is similarly double-sided. In 23:2 and Acts 17:7 it denotes adversarial relation to Caesar, but in Luke 19:38, at Jesus' triumphal entry, its use incorporates the conception of the Messiah's enthronement as God's royal Son. Indeed, the Messiah of the Lord, i.e., God, inherits a kingdom to which Pilate's, Herod's, and Caesar's cannot compare.

Correlatively, Luke's emphasis on *the kingdom of God* within the passion narrative is striking. In the first segment (22:1–34), it accounts in large part for Luke's distinctive units (nos. 4 and 7 in Table IV) and the royalty emphases of the segment. The problem of Luke's double institution of the cup pales when one grasps Luke's theological purpose. Before the actual celebration of the Lord's Supper (22:19–20) Luke sets forth the "eating this Passover" and "dividing this cup" as proleptic participation in the fulfillment and/or establishment of the kingdom of God (vv. 14–18). Hence the traditional kingdom of God saying moves to the front of the institution ceremony and conjoins with Luke's portrayal of Jesus' consummating the inauguration of the kingdom of God (initiated already in Jesus' Galilean ministry, but especially in the mission of the Seventy, ch. 10). This combination of eating the Lord's Supper and consummating the kingdom is anticipated by Luke's introduction to the parable of the great banquet: "Blessed is anyone who will eat bread in the kingdom of God" (14:15). That parable is also proleptic of the kingdom theology to be worked out in Acts: that the Gentiles are invited to the banquet of the kingdom.

When Jesus says of the Passover meal, "I will not eat it until it is fulfilled in the kingdom of God,"[105] in the context of having just said, "I have eagerly desired to eat this Passover with you before I suffer," it is clear that Jesus regards his suffering—and this meal

---

[105] According to the Nestle-Aland and RSV reading which omits the οὐκέτι of several MSS.

commemorating his suffering—as a participation in and an anticipation of the consummated kingdom of God.[106] The same point reappears in verses 28–30 where Jesus links "those who have stood by me in my trials" with conferring on the disciples what the Father "has conferred on me, a kingdom." He then declares, "so that you may eat and drink at my table in my kingdom." While this pericope begins with the disciples sharing "in my trials," it ends with the disciples sitting "on thrones judging the twelve tribes of Israel." This, in turn, is set in the context of Luke's unique placement of the disciple's dispute on greatness (22:24–27). Jesus speaks of "the kings of the Gentiles [who] lord it over them; and those in authority over them [who] are called benefactors"—usually older wealthy patrons. But Jesus says it shall not be so among them. The greatest shall become as the youngest, and the leader as one who serves. He then identifies himself as one among them who serves and calls them to follow his example. Hence, in order for the disciples to participate in the banquet of the kingdom, their values must undergo major transformation:

Chief Benefactor (a term Luke's readers understood)	=	Most Willing Servant
Host for the Kingdom Banquet	=	Suffering Journeyer, Rejected Prophet
Messiah	=	Suffering Son of humanity, lowly Savior

Indeed, Luke dips his diversity of christological portraits in the sweat of service and the blood of suffering.

Jesus again appears as kingdom heir in the repentant criminal's plea, "Jesus, remember me when you come into your kingdom" (23:42). Jesus replies by declaring "today you will be with me in Paradise." Luke describes Joseph of Arimathea, like the pious righteous ones in chapters 1–2, as a "good and righteous man . . . [who] was waiting expectantly for the kingdom of God" (23:50b–51; cf. the description of Anna who spoke of Jesus "to all who were looking for the redemption of Jerusalem" [2:38] and the Emmaus couple's statement, "But we had hoped that he was the one to redeem Israel" [24:21]). These hopes for the kingdom are not in vain, for Jesus' victory through suffering establishes the kingdom (see 24:49 and Acts 1:3–8; 8:12; 14:22; 20:25; 28:23–31), as Gabriel announced to Mary:

---

[106] Little wonder then that Jesus' identity in his resurrection form is later disclosed, in the Emmaus narrative, in the eating together with his disciples, and that table fellowship remains a prominent feature in Acts.

"He will be great, and will be called
the Son of the Most High;
and the Lord God will give to him
the throne of his ancestor David,
He will reign over the house of Jacob forever;
and of his kingdom there will be no end" (1:32–33).

(2) Jesus as Son of David, Savior and Lord (Son of humanity).
Luke frequently identifies Jesus with Davidic royalty (1:27, 32, 69; 2:4,
11; 3:22 and, in triple tradition, 18:38–39; 20:41–44; through Acts
also), thus accentuating the fulfillment of God's promise to David
(2 Sam 7:14). But Luke also qualifies this tradition: by associating it
with *Lord* (2:11; Acts 2:36; 10:36), thus universalizing royalty for
Gentile ears; by anchoring Jesus' Davidic certification and authority
to reign in Jesus' resurrection and heavenly exaltation at the right
hand of God (Acts 2:33–36); and by omitting the kings descended
from David in the genealogy (3:27–31; cf. Matt 1:6–12).[107] The passion narrative and the triumphal entry make no mention of the
Davidic connection. This too suggests that Luke seeks to universalize
Jesus' royal authority.

This is especially evident in his use of *Savior* and *Lord*. While
Luke designates Jesus as Savior (σωτήρ) only twice (2:11; Acts 5:31),
his pervasive emphasis on the verb *to save* (σῴζω) and related terms
(σωτηρία, διασῴζω) indicates his extensive interest in this portrait of
Jesus, as Marshall notes.[108] Mary begins her Magnificat by rejoicing
in God her *Savior* (1:47). Zechariah's Benedictus exudes praise that
the Lord God of Israel is now bringing *salvation* to his people (1:69,
71, 77). John the Baptist's proclamation of the dawning new age ends
its Isaianic burst with, "all flesh shall see the *salvation* of God" (3:6).
And Zacchaeus rejoices to hear Jesus' word, "Today *salvation* has come
to this house" (19:9). While the verb is used often for healings (6:9;
7:50; 18:42), as in Matthew and Mark, it also means yielding one's life
to God (9:24; 13:23; 17:33) and restored relation with God (19:10;
through Acts). In the passion narrative, the rulers of Israel, the soldiers,
and the unrepentant criminal mock Jesus' power to save (23:35–39).
The title, Savior, and the task of bringing salvation are the Messiah's
work, but here again Luke's use of this vocabulary transforms its

[107] George has an extended treatment of this theme, "La royauté de
Jesus," 264–65.
[108] I. H. Marshall, *Luke: Historian and Theologian* (Grand Rapids:
Zondervan, 1971), 77–215.

meaning. Josephine Ford contrasts Luke 1–2, depicting a Maccabean militant view of salvation from enemies, to the rest of the Gospel, a pacifism that makes the enemy the guest. Though this contrast is too sharp[109] and open to question,[110] the Lukan perspective indeed disowns violence and crushing the enemy in the name of either liberation or peace. The transformed understanding of Messiah and God's kingdom also means transformed views of salvation and peace.

Because the Greco-Roman world knew of both divine liberators and protectors (Zeus, Athena, etc.) and political Saviors (the Ptolemies, Seleucids, Pompey, Augustus Caesar, etc.), Luke's terminology connects to Gentile experience. To meet the challenge of portraying Jesus' royalty and role as Savior (and even Benefactor), Luke used a variety of interrelated royal images to communicate his gospel view clearly and securely. His preponderant use of "Lord" puts Jesus' royalty in competition with what people in the Greco-Roman world assign to the Emperors, first to Augustus in 12 B.C. (cf. Festus' reference to Nero as his Lord, Acts 25:26).[111]

But *Lord* also has a long tradition in the Hebrew Scriptures, with the LXX rendering the sacred Tetragrammaton as κύριος. Not only does Luke use *Lord* to refer often to God (33 times in Luke; 51 in Acts, according to Schneider's lists),[112] but he alone of the Synoptics frequently uses *Lord* to refer to Jesus (42 times in Luke; 50 in Acts). Of those in Luke, 16 occur in narrative, 18 in direct address (κύριε), and 8 in direct address referring to Jesus, e.g., "mother of my Lord."[113] Of these 42 uses, 7 occur in the passion narrative. In 22:33 Peter addresses Jesus as Lord and in 22:61 Luke twice identifies Jesus as Lord in his story of Peter's denial. In 22:39 and 49 the disciples, in dialogue with

---

[109] J. M. Ford, *My Enemy Is My Guest: Jesus and Violence in Luke* (Maryknoll, N.Y.: Orbis, 1984), 1–36 and the contrasting portrait of Jesus on pp. 53ff. John the Baptist represents a transitional stance (37–51); he "prepares for the nonviolent ministry of Jesus."

[110] It is hard to believe that Luke uses the terms *peace* in 1:79; 2:14, 29 and *salvation/Savior* in 1:47, 69, 71, 77; 2:14 with different meanings here than in the rest of the Gospel and Acts. See Swartley, "Politics and Peace," 26–28.

[111] D. Jones, "*Kyrios,*" 85. Robert C. Tannehill's essay, "Israel in Luke–Acts: A Tragic Story," *JBL* 104 (1985), 69–85, argues that the Jewish political hope stirred by this language in Luke–Acts was not fulfilled, and therefore it is a tragic story. In my judgment, the text seeks to transform both the language and the hopes, as this study seeks to show.

[112] G. Schneider, *Lukas, Theologie der Heilsgeschichte: Aufsätze zum lukanischen Doppelwerk* (BBB 59; Bonn: Peter Hanstein, 1985), 214–15. This is from his 1980 essay, "Gott und Christus als *kyrios* nach der Apostelgeschichte."

[113] Ibid., 216–17. The counts of Schneider's lists are mine.

Jesus about the sword and its use, address Jesus as Lord. In 24:3 the women at the tomb ask about the body of the "Lord Jesus" (in some MSS), and in 24:34 the Emmaus two report to the disciples, "The Lord has risen indeed." Schneider contends that *Lord* was a self-understood title for God and Jesus among the people to whom Luke wrote, and thus Luke readily uses it. Nonetheless, by his many special usages, Luke accentuates this dimension of Jesus' identity. For Luke, *Lord* establishes Jesus' identity and role as *Savior-Ruler* in universal categories. Jesus the Messiah's Lordship is analogous to God's (some MSS report the disciples worshipping Jesus in 24:52).[114]

Luke's use of "Son of humanity" is also plentiful. In the passion narrative distinctive uses, associated with suffering, appear in 22:48 and 24:7 (cf. the traditional synoptic use in 22:22). The most significant use, highlighting Jesus' royalty, is Jesus' final word to the Sanhedrin: "But from now on the Son of Man will be seated at the right hand of the power of God" (22:69). Luke stresses that Jesus' enthroned position with God as Ruler takes effect now in the events of the passion. Seated at the right hand of God as Son of humanity, Jesus assumes the prerogative of Lordship, which believers behind and within the Gospel already attribute to him.

b. *Prophet, Righteous One (and Martyr), (Παῖς/'ebed of Yahweh and Ἀρχηγός).* While titles and images of royalty predominate in Luke 1–4 and the passion narrative, the Galilean and journey sections—indeed the bulk of the Gospel—make scant use of these titles, except for "Lord" (occurring sometimes in the sense of *Sir* and often as *Lord* of the disciples) and "Son of humanity" (occurring in mostly traditional uses). Conversely, the designation of Jesus as Prophet or Righteous One is scant in chapters 1–4 and 22–24. In his narrative of Jesus' ministry Luke develops a portrait of Jesus and a set of titles to temper and interpret the royalty set. Hence, in the centurion's confession Luke differs from Mark and Matthew, designating Jesus as the *righteous one* instead of Son of God. Also, Jesus' dying word (23:46) comes not from a royal Psalm, but from one of the classic psalms of the righteous sufferer (31:5).[115]

(1) *Jesus as Prophet.* Within the passion and resurrection narratives Jesus is designated a prophet only once. The Emmaus two speak to their guest about "Jesus of Nazareth who was a prophet

---

[114]Ibid., 225.

[115]L. Ruppert has shown how the Righteous Sufferer tradition, even in Pss 18 and 22, is determinative for Luke's view (*Jesus als der leidende Gerechte?* [Stuttgart: KBW, 1972], 21–37).

mighty in deed and word before God and all the people" (24:19b). After speaking about their "chief priests and rulers [who] handed him over to be condemned to death and crucified him," they say, "But we had hoped that he was the one to redeem Israel" (vv. 20–21). This use of *prophet* is strategic, for in linking it to "the one to redeem Israel" Luke has the term echo the function of Moses as prophet, in his role as Prophet-Redeemer for the Israelites.

Jesus' identity as a prophet emerges first in 4:24. On the one side of the text, he takes up the mantle of prophet Isaiah (v. 17) who, anointed by the Spirit, proclaims the gospel of liberation to the poor, captives, blind, and oppressed, and thus inaugurates Jubilee; on the other side Jesus identifies himself with prophets Elijah and Elisha. The narrative also identifies him with the fate of the prophets, rejection. In chapter 7 the recognition of Jesus as a prophet by the people is the leitmotif of the narrative. In chapter 9 some say Jesus is "one of the prophets" risen from the dead, and then he appears with Moses and Elijah. Most striking is Jesus' self-identification as a rejected prophet in 13:33, in discourse directed to Herod who seeks to kill him; "it is impossible that a prophet should be killed outside of Jerusalem." Jesus then continues a dirge to those following him on his journey: " 'Jerusalem, Jerusalem, the city that kills the prophets and stones those who are sent to it' " (v. 34).

Peter's first post-Pentecost sermon to the people of Jerusalem clinches this identification. Peter not only specifies that the Jesus events fulfill what God "had foretold through all the prophets . . . all the prophets, as many as have spoken, from Samuel and those after him" (Acts 3:18, 24), but also designates Jesus as the long-awaited Moses-*redivivus* prophet, "The Lord your God will raise up for you . . . a prophet like me" (v. 22).

(2) Jesus as the suffering Righteous One. Luke complements his portrayal of Jesus as prophet with that of Jesus as the suffering Righteous One. L. Ruppert examines the trajectory of the suffering Righteous One in the Old Testament and intertestamental literature.[116] He shows how this tradition identifies the "poor" with the righteous sufferer and how the Righteous One suffers as martyr for the people[117] whom God vindicates. Both themes, that of the poor and

---

[116] Ruppert, *Jesus*, 1–38; see also Wis 2:12–22; 5:1–5.

[117] Oscar Cullmann says that this never included forgiveness of sins (*Christology of the New Testament*, 17). This is likely correct, but 4 Macc. does specify atoning efficacy for the people. See ch. 4, n. 55.

the righteous martyr, permeate Luke–Acts. Luke specifically identifies Jesus as "the (Holy and) Righteous One" (Acts 3:14; 7:52; 22:14).

As already noted, Luke boldly departs from the other Synoptics in saying that the centurion *glorified* God and then declared, "This man was righteous" (or, a righteous one). In light of Luke's clear intention to identify and portray Jesus as the Righteous One in Acts (three times), the centurion's confession must be rendered similarly, "the Righteous One." The anarthrous grammatical form matches that of υἱὸς θεοῦ in Mark and Matthew, except that δίκαιος could be either a predicate adjective or predicate nominative. The titular designation in Acts calls for the latter, since here at this climactic point in the Gospel's narrative Jesus' identity concurs with Luke's consistent portrayal of Jesus.

Another Lukan narrative strategy confirms this interpretation. Three times earlier Luke portrays Jesus' opponents as thinking themselves to be or feigning righteous identity (cf. also 10:29 where the lawyer who asked what he must do to inherit eternal life seeks to justify [δικαιῶσαι] himself). He designates the Pharisees, judged by Jesus to be "lovers of money," as those who think themselves to be righteous (οἱ δικαιοῦντες; 16:15). Then again, following his parable of the unrighteous judge (ὁ κριτὴς τῆς ἀδικίας), Jesus tells another parable, The Pharisee and the Tax Collector, to "some who trusted in themselves that they were righteous (δίκαιοι) and despised others" (18:9). Third, Luke introduces those who came to entrap Jesus on the tax question, not as "Pharisees together with the Herodians" as do Matthew (22:15–16) and Mark (12:13), but as those who were watching him and sent spies who pretended (ὑποκρινομένους, 20:20) themselves to be righteous (ἑαυτοὺς δικαίους εἶναι). These spies, and most likely those who sent them, are also motivated by "harmful deceit" (τὴν πανουργίαν, 20:23).

Each of these representations of Jesus' opponents as *pretending to be righteous* is distinctly Lukan. In light of this narrative feature, the centurion's confession sets the record straight. This man, an outsider, a Gentile, declares who *truly* is the Righteous One. Hence, in Luke's continuing narrative, Jesus is the Righteous One, the One who trusts humbly in God, obeys the divine will, and whom God vindicates from trouble (a frequent refrain in the Psalms where God's righteous one(s) will not be put to shame, but will surely be vindicated by "the God of my right").[118]

---

[118]See Pss 5, 25, 26, 31, 43, 54, 64, 71, 94, 109, 140, 142.

This strategically placed declaration by the centurion matches Luke's general portrayal of Jesus : born within the circle of righteous, devout, and humble folk (1:6, 38; 2:7–20, 25, 36–38), advocate of the righteous poor whom God will vindicate (note 18:1–8 as well as the announcing of blessing upon the poor), and friend of those made outcasts by the supposedly righteous (see 5:32 in context). Further, just as Luke arranges an antiphonal chorus singing "peace" (εἰρήνη) at Jesus' birth and entry into Jerusalem, so he also places antiphonal acclamations of "glory to God" at Jesus' birth (2:14, 20; cf. 2:9) and death (the centurion's glorifying of God upon *seeing* what had taken place, 23:47),[119] thus fulfilling the Isaianic hope, "the glory of the Lord shall be revealed, and all people shall see it together" (only in Luke 3:5, but with the first strophe present only as metaleptic echo). Between these first and last bursts of worship, moreover, Luke's emphatic depiction of humans glorifying God in the face of Jesus' deeds of compassion and justice is not lost in the narrative (5:25–26; 7:16; 13:13; 17:15, 18; 18:43; 19:38).[120] Clearly, Luke's portrayal of Jesus as the Righteous One, interacting strategically in the narrative with Jesus' royalty, discloses an important christological Lukan conviction: Jesus' royalty rises gloriously from the common landscape of mangers, shepherds, fisher-folk, widows, rejected prophets, and, most significantly, the humble, suffering righteous ones whose lives God upholds. For such ones, God is a God of help, salvation, and resurrection power, exalting the Righteous One to the right hand of Power, as Christ and Lord. No other royalty does Luke know.

(3) Jesus as Ἀρχηγός *and* Παῖς/*'ebed.* That Luke links to his designation of Jesus as the Righteous One the term Ἀρχηγός, meaning Author, Guide, Head, Leader,[121] whom "you killed [and] God raised from the dead" (3:15), stresses God's vindication of the rejected Righteous One. Luke's use of παῖς to designate Jesus (Acts 3:13, 26; 4:27, 30), drawing on the Isaiah *'ebed Yâhweh* tradition, makes the

---

[119]D. D. Sylvan relates this point to his proposal that Luke seeks to portray Jesus' death as participating in the piety and worship of the temple. The rent temple veil precedes Jesus' prayer, "Father, into Your hands I commit my spirit." Then the centurion glorifies God ("The Temple Curtain and Jesus' Death in Luke," *JBL* 105 (1986), 239–50.

[120]The refrain continues in Acts, especially on Gentiles' lips (4:21; 11:18; 13:48; 21:20). Luke also stresses Jesus' participation in divine glory (9:31, 32; 24:26; Acts 3:13).

[121]George, *Etudes*, 270.

same point. God glorifies his "servant" (παῖς) whom "you handed over and rejected in the presence of Pilate" (Acts 3:13).

In light of this larger Lukan use of tradition which stresses the suffering and vindication of "God's elect," Luke's twofold identification of Jesus with the righteous sufferer (in the centurion's confession and the last cry) must be seen as a conscious effort to transform the very heart of the royalty tradition. It is not a matter of choosing one over the other but rather of recognizing that both dwell together in the Lukan Gospel's Christology. Jesus is Messiah-King, royal Son of God, and Lord, as well as rejected Prophet and suffering Righteous One (who is also the *'ebed Yâhweh* in Acts).[122] The centurion's confession thus displays the Lukan prism which Jesus' royalty refracts. In the light of Jesus' humble royalty, the centurion rightly glorifies God, thereby joining the lowly shepherds (2:20) to form a "glorifying inclusio" framing Jesus' earthly life in this world.

3. Correlation of the Two Streams of Tradition

The two streams of tradition in sections a and b above are firmly linked by Luke. In the baptismal declaration, the voice from heaven joins the quotation from the royal Psalm 2 with a line from Isaiah 42:1, a servant song. The beloved (a Gen 22 echo) royal Son of God and the One in Whom I delight (the *'ebed Yâhweh*) dwell together in Jesus. Again, at the transfiguration, the royal Son of God, my Chosen One (the *'ebed*) and the Mosaic Prophet, in "listen to him" (Luke 9:35c//Deut 18:15b), dwell together in Jesus.

Second, Jesus own depiction of his ministry under the umbrella of the Isaiah 61:1–3 reading (4:16–19) links together the Spirit's anointing of the Prophet-King with the servant-*'ebed* ("me" designates the servant of Isa 40–55 in Luke's way of reading Isaiah as one whole). Further, the Jewish rulers, who should understand, but only scoff at, the truth, mock Jesus as royal Messiah, God's Chosen One (23:35), blending Psalm 2 and Isaiah 42:1. Finally, the believers, who have come to know the truth through sharing in Jesus' trials, designate Jesus as "servant" (*'ebed*) and combine it with Messiah and anointed one (Acts 4:25–27 quotes Ps 2:2).[123]

---

[122] In this respect Luke's theology anticipates John's, as shown by W. Meeks, *Prophet-King.*

[123] I do not agree with Jones who says that Luke uses παῖς interchangeably with "Son of God" and "Christ." Nor does Jones substantiate his argument

Third, Luke's use of Psalm 31, which contains a rich array of royalty titles, in two strategic placements in the passion narrative clinches the joining of the two tradition streams. Jesus' final words, "Father, into your hands I commend my spirit," and the centurion's pronouncement, "Certainly this man was righteous," wrap the royal Christ again in the common stuff of the lowly righteous. Even after resurrection and Pentecost, Luke's royal-servant Christology continues (Luke 24:26, 46; Acts 3:13–4:30).

In light of the above sketch of Luke's Christology, with its strong emphasis on Jesus' royalty flowering in the passion narrative, it is impossible to hold that Luke has produced a political apologetic.[124] Pilate's conduct, when analyzed in its narrative role, does not prove Jesus' innocence, but it shows that Pilate cannot comprehend the nature and scope of Jesus' royalty. The role of the Jewish leaders epitomizes truth denied. The political charges against Jesus are neither sustained nor resolved. Rather, Luke's two volumes narrate boldly that Jesus is Messiah-King, Savior, and Lord, who as rejected prophet, righteous one, and dying servant receives a never-ending kingdom conferred to him by his Father.[125]

KINGSHIP TRADITIONS: CONTINUITY AND TRANSFORMATION

Each Gospel writer has his own way of showing the royalty tradition focused and fulfilled in Jesus, but each also significantly transforms those traditions in the process of narrating the Jesus story. While Mark's portrait of Jesus' kingship emerges almost entirely in the sections of Jesus' Jerusalem ministry, bulging in the passion narrative,

---

textually ("Servant," 154–55). This text is the closest evidence, but this is a joining of traditions and not an easy interchange of titles.

[124]E. J. Via argues for a modification of both Conzelmann's and Cassidy's positions ("According to Luke, Who Put Jesus to Death?" in *Political Issues in Luke–Acts*, ed. R. J. Cassidy and P. J. Scharper, 139–40).

[125]I agree that other purposes are at work in the narrative also, such as scriptural apologetic (see Daryl Schmidt, "Luke's 'Innocent' Jesus: A Scriptural Apologetic" in *Political Issues in Luke–Acts*, ed. R. J. Cassidy and P. J. Scharper, 111–21) and parenetic encouragement for Christians called to suffer persecution (see E. Buck, "The Function of the Pericope 'Jesus Before Herod' in the Passion Narrative of Luke," in W. Haubeck and M. Bachmann, eds., *Wort in der Zeit: Festschrift für K. H. Rengstorf* [Leiden: E. J. Brill, 1980], 165–78).

both Matthew and Luke concentrate their kingship emphases in both the birth-preparation and passion narratives. In all three Gospels the Galilean ministry and journey sections (until Jesus arrives at Jericho) contain virtually no kingship designations. The outcries of the demons that Jesus is Son of God stand as one exception, but these, as voices from the outside to the human story world, have a proleptic function, pointing to the latter parts of the Gospels. Heaven's voice at Jesus' baptism and transfiguration functions similarly in the narrative. The declaration of Jesus' Sonship at his baptism and Jesus' heralding the dawning of God's kingdom prepare for a Galilean ministry oriented to the kingdom of God. But Jesus' royal identity remains muted during the Galilean and journey sections of the Gospels.

While Peter's confession of Jesus as Messiah initiates the kingship theme, Jesus hushes the disclosure so that it does not control the focus of the narrative in the prepassion section. Rather, Jesus as the suffering Son of humanity emerges onto center narrative stage.[126] The declaration of Jesus' Sonship at the transfiguration appears on a mountain, set above the plain of Jesus' ministry, for both before and after this mountain experience Jesus speaks of the sufferings of the Son of humanity. Granted, the birth narratives function as overtures to the royal Christology to be developed in the passion narrative. In Matthew and Luke the overture is so strong that one hears already the full range of the movements.

In all three passion stories kingship imagery shows strong continuity with the royal tradition. With full resonance we hear echoes of Psalm 2, 110, and 2 Samuel 7:14. Jesus' Son of humanity declaration before the Sanhedrin, "seated at the right hand of Power," links Jesus' self-identification with the royal authority of the king in Psalm 110:1. Bonnard suggests that Psalm 72, with its ideal portrait of the king, has also likely influenced Luke's portrait of Jesus.[127] Bonnard shows that five thematic accents of the Psalm are significant themes in Luke: (1) defense of the poor; (2) salvation of human life; (3) judgment according to justice; (4) deliverance from the might of the oppressor; and (5) redemption of the people.[128] In this light, the work of Yahweh's ideal king is precisely that which Jesus' Nazareth address highlights and that which also marks his entire ministry. Nonetheless,

---

[126] These comments assume that "Son of humanity" as Jesus' self-designation does not of itself convey messianic meaning.

[127] P. E. Bonnard, "Le Psaume 72: Ses relectures ses traces dans l'oeuvre de Luc?," *RSR* 69 (1981), 259–78.

[128] Ibid., 274–77.

the Synoptics do not develop the royal identification of Jesus until Mark 11/Matthew 21/Luke 19.

One might counter that both the repeated identification of Jesus as *Lord* in Luke and Matthew throughout Jesus' ministry and his prevailing proclamation of the *kingdom of God* in all three Gospels are evidence that the royalty theme lies at the center of the entire narrative. While this is true in that the latter is planted as seed in the narrative, certain to bear fruit, the narrative characters do not see or understand the seed's royal significance. In Luke and Matthew the narrative feature is two-sided. By addressing Jesus as Lord the disciples reflect the standpoint of the first readers of the narrative; but by not focusing on nor comprehending Jesus' royalty they reflect the Markan depiction that Jesus' royal identity was not grasped by humans until after Jesus' resurrection. In each story, the narrative strategy saves the disclosure and riddle of Jesus' royalty for the Jerusalem section, especially the passion narratives.

Each of the Gospels has its own strategy for extensively transforming the kingship traditions, though all bear common witness to the transformation in the combined royal, servant, and Mosaic-Prophet elements in the baptismal and transfiguration pronouncements. But beyond this, each has its own literary means of safeguarding Jesus' royalty portrait from the oppressive, violent, and exclusivistic strands in the messianic legacy. Mark tones his story with secrecy, which acts as a control against indiscriminate broadcasting of Jesus' identity. Furthermore, he uses statements of the Son of humanity's suffering to set up a creative tension between messianic disclosure and the divine necessity (δεῖ) of the Messiah's suffering. Climactically, he allows the only fully approved human confession of Jesus' royalty, that Jesus is God's true Son, to be spoken under the cross, facing a crucified Messiah, and by a Gentile, thus ensuring the victory of the inclusivistic strand of the royal messianic traditions.

Matthew's strategy consists of introducing into the narrative from the outset a mountain typology which places Jesus amid the Sinai and Zion traditions. Exclusivistic elements in the earlier story are converted by the command to love the enemy, coupled with a relentless critique of narrow Pharisaic interpretation of Torah traditions. As the narrative unfolds, the Zion mountain traditions come more squarely into focus, climaxing in Jesus' claim to all authority in heaven and on earth, which is appropriated not for rule over the enemies or the weak, but for bringing the blessing of the gospel to all nations. God's sovereignty in Father, Son and Spirit relativizes all human authority (23:8) and calls people everywhere to be disciples whose identifying mark is love even for the enemy (5:43–48). Thus, Matthew's story of Jesus fulfills Israel's Scriptural traditions of making Zion, God's royal presence in the Son, the prophetic critique and control of all Davidic royalty.

Luke's strategy accentuates the liberating, compassionate, and healing aspects of Jesus' ministry, thus functioning as a Rosetta Stone for the disclosure of Jesus' royalty at both the beginning and end of his Gospel's narrative. Presenting Jesus' ministry under the twin motifs of Jubilee and rejected prophet, the full-orbed royalty portrait is one of a King who defends God's vindication of the poor and oppressed and who himself, in his suffering and rejection, humbly trusts in God (e.g., his death cry of Ps 31:5) for his vindication over the powers incited against him (hence Acts 4:25–26 quotes Ps 2:2). Thus with integrity Jesus' royal mission promises salvation for all people, where relationships of greatest enmity (Jews and Samaritans) are transformed by the gospel of peace. As Lord of the Banquet, Jesus the Christ-King, Savior-Lord, Prophet and Righteous One welcomes *all* to the feast of the kingdom conferred to him by his Father in his sufferings as Servant of the Lord (*'ebed Yâhweh*).[129]

TABLE IV: PARALLEL AND DISTINCTIVE MATERIAL IN LUKE'S PASSION NARRATIVE

In order to show both parallel and distinctive material, I list the content by thematic unit, noting whether it has a parallel or is distinctively Lukan. A distinctive paragraph, or a parallel with distinctive content, that contains anything on the royalty theme, is italicized.

Descriptive Title of Paragraph	Has Parr	Distinctive
1. Conspiracy Against Jesus (22:1–2)	x	
2. Satan Incites Judas Against Jesus (22:3–6)	x	
3. Jesus Prepares for the Passover (22:7–13)	x	
4. *Preamble to Lord's Supper (22:14–17)*		x
5. Institution of the Lord's Supper (22:18–23)[130]	x	

---

[129]Numerous scholars contend that Luke does not appreciably utilize the Isaianic servant of the Lord tradition. This conclusion rests on the unwarranted restriction of evidence to explicit reference to Isa 52:13—53:12. See p. 114, n. 55, for further comments on this matter.

[130]Here I follow the Nestle-Aland text in the longer reading, which has by far the stronger MS support. It is one of the most significant of Luke's so-called Western non-interpolations, a concept that should be dispensed with.

Descriptive Title of Paragraph	Has Parr	Distinctive
6. Jesus Foretells His Betrayal (22:21–23)	x	
7. *Dispute About Greatness* (22:24–30)		x[131]
8. Peter's Sifting by Satan (22:31–32)		x
9. Peter's Denial Foretold (22:33–34)	x	
10. *The Two Swords Text and Healing* (22:35–38, 51)		x
11. Jesus in Gethsemane (22:39–46)[132]	x	
12. Betrayal and Arrest of Jesus (22:47–53)	x	
13. Peter's Denial of Jesus (22:54–62)	x	
14. Mocking and Beating of Jesus (22:63–65)	x	
15. *Jesus' Trial Before the Council* (22:66–71)	x	
16. *Charges Against Jesus Before Pilate* (23:1–2)		x
17. Pilate's Trial of Jesus (23:3–5)	x	
18. Jesus Before Herod (23:6–12)		x
19. *Pilate Tries to Save Jesus,* But Gives Sentence of Death (23:13–25)	x	x
20. *Weep, Daughters of Jerusalem* (23:27–31)		x
21. *The Crucifixion of Jesus* (23:26, 32–43)	x	
22. *Jesus' Final Words and Death* (23:44–49)		x
23. The Burial of Jesus (23:50–56)	x	
24. The Women and the Word of Resurrection (24:1–11)		x
25. Jesus' Appearance to Peter (24:12)[133]		x
26. *The Emmaus Narrative* (24:13–35)		x
27. *Jesus' Appearance to the Disciples* (24:36–49)		x
28. *Jesus' Ascension* (24:50–53)		x

---

[131] I consider this distinctive because it is placed in the passion narrative, unlike Matthew and Mark, and has a significant shift in word choices as well as two significant additions, to be commented on later.

[132] Here I include vv. 43–44 on the basis of strong Alexandrian ℵ*² L Δ 892* 1241), Western (D it^e syr^c), and Caesarean (f¹ 565 700 syr^p).

[133] The textual support is strong (P⁷⁵ ℵ B K L Δ Θ f¹ f¹³ 28 33 et al. and v. 34 of the narrative assumes it; thus my decision to include it.

7

STORY SHAPING STORY: STRUCTURE, THEOLOGY, AND FUNCTION OF THE SYNOPTICS

In formulating a synthesis, explanation, and statement of significance for the findings of this study, I consider it important to note what this contribution does not attempt or claim to do. First, it does not answer *why* each Gospel modified the synoptic pattern in its distinctive way. This is an appropriate and important task that would entail proposals for life-settings for each of the Gospels. Such a study would need to use additional methodologies to those of narrative and tradition-history analyses which were the primary foci of this study. This would require social world analyses as well as the more traditional historical and cultural investigations of the communities and environments in which the Gospels functioned.[1] While some might wish to read narratives only in light of such data, this investigation has approached the task first from the other side. It has assumed the text itself to be the primary source of information for the reconstruction of the world of the text. The findings of this study may thus contribute to such subsequent endeavors.

Second, though this study often shows transformation of the older story by the newer story, it must be acknowledged that parallel developments were at work in first-century and later Judaism as well. To acknowledge this is also to avoid making Christian Scripture a "trump" over Judaism. I believe it offers a distinctive transformation, but similar efforts were part and parcel of the rabbinic midrashic tradition as well. Again, a comparison between rabbinic and Christian

---

[1] To illustrate, see J. A. Overman, *Matthew's Gospel and Formative Judaism: The Social World of the Matthean Community* (Minneapolis: Augsburg/Fortress, 1990).

appropriation of Israel's canonical narratives calls for another volume of study. It may well be that Christian interpretation sometimes borrowed from rabbinic sources,[2] but again parallels do not prove use.[3] Furthermore, dating the origin of documents or the traditions therein is always a thorny issue. Most significant in this regard, the very thesis of this study suggests that we do not separate the Synoptic phenomenon *from Judaism.* It is essentially part of the ongoing trajectory of Hebrew Scripture; early Christian identity and self-understanding were essentially intertwined with and nurtured by the Hebrew Scriptures. Granted, from this arises the agonizing problem of dual peoples' claims, a fact that must be respected and even treasured from both sides. On this Will Herberg's provocative suggestion that we regard the relation of Judaism and Christianity as one in which "the Jew fulfills his vocation by 'staying with God,' while the Christian can fulfill his only by 'going out' to conquer the world for God" (related as root and vine) continues to nourish and empower the ongoing relationship of the synagogue and church.[4]

Having delimited the intended scope of this contribution, I identify now the considerations of this final chapter. First, this chapter summarizes and synthesizes the above findings and assesses their strengths, noting areas of weakness as well. Second, it examines the hermeneutical manner in which the Synoptics used OT faith traditions as well as how they transformed them through their use. Noting also similarities and divergences among the Synoptics, the discussion describes the extent to which each Gospel demonstrates the influence of Israel's four faith traditions. In this I do not take up the *why* question

---

[2] See here the helpful work of S. T. Lachs, *A Rabbinic Commentary on the New Testament: The Gospels of Matthew, Mark, and Luke* (Hoboken, N.J.: KTAV, 1987); H. Strack and P. Billerbeck, *Kommentar zum Neuen Testament aus Talmud und Midrasch,* 6 vols. (Munich, 1922); D. Flusser, *Die rabbinischen Gleichnisse und der Gleichniserzähler Jesus* (Bern: Peter Lang, 1981); R. Bultmann, *The History of the Synoptic Tradition,* trans. J. Marsh (rev. ed., reprint Peabody: Hendrickson, 1993 [1963]). Since Bultmann finds some rabbinic or hellenistic parallel to almost all the individual pericopes of the Synoptics, it is incredible that in his thirty pages of analysis of the composition and editing of the Synoptic Gospels (337–67), he nowhere considers OT literary influences!

[3] S. Sandmel, "Parallelomania," *JBL* 81 (1962), 1–14, esp. 4, 7.

[4] W. Herberg, *Faith Enacted as History: Essays in Biblical Theology* (Philadelphia: Westminster, 1976), 53–54. See also the stimulating collection of essays in *Jewish Perspectives on Christianity,* ed. F. A. Rothchild (New York: Crossroad, 1990). For a helpful summary and analysis of understandings of this relationship, see J. Pawlikowski, *Jesus and the Theology of Israel* (Wilmington, Del.: Michael Glazier, 1989), 9–47.

(see above), but only *that* it occurred. Third, it probes into the significance of the pattern that has emerged, asking the *why* question: why does the synoptic pattern show such extensive use of OT faith traditions? Further, what is the significance of the distinctive Synoptic structure in light of this use? Fourth, the chapter makes some tentative proposals to explain the origin and function of this Gospel pattern in the early church.

SYNTHESIS OF FINDINGS IN CHAPTERS 3–6: SUMMARIZING AND CLARIFYING

This narrative-compositional study of each Synoptic Gospel has shown a significant sequential use of the exodus, conquest, temple, and kingship traditions within the structure and emphases of the Gospels' respective sections, as follows:

Israel's exodus-Sinai traditions influenced the structural design and the theological emphases of the Synoptics' stories of Jesus' Galilean ministry. In Mark's structure, the narrator correlates a topographical sequence of sea, mountain, and wilderness with his development of the discipleship theme. The sea and wilderness motifs also recur throughout the narrative as settings for various events. Both Mark and Luke strongly echo the exodus tradition by accentuating liberational themes as the core of Jesus' Galilean ministry. Luke specifically mentions *exodus* in the transfiguration narrative, placed in the Galilean section, to link the character of Jesus' ministry with its consummation in his departure. In Matthew the Messiah's ministry thus fulfills this exodus refrain. Jesus' mighty works and wonders lead all to know that the Lord God is indeed truly God. The narrative also contains the Sermon on the Mount, echoing Sinai and Zion, in which the surpassing righteousness of Jesus' person and teachings fulfills the covenant-law of Mount Sinai and thus provides the charter for a new community that both begins and prefigures the eschatological community of Zion.

Israel's way-conquest traditions significantly influenced the structure and emphases of the Synoptics' journey narrative, particularly in Mark and Luke. The conquest aspect of the journey to the promised land is radically transformed by the path-blazing suffering Son of humanity's teachings that lead the way into the kingdom of God. In Mark, the "way" (ὁδός), which frames the narrative, is marked by the path of discipleship with its stations of cross, child, and servant— the way of entrance into the promised kingdom of God. Matthew shows no way-conquest motifs from the older story but programmatically emphasizes victory over evil and prevention of sin from entering and strangling the life of the believers. In Luke, with Deuteronomy as a literary prototype, Jesus is portrayed as a journeying Guest and rejected Prophet. He brings the peace and justice of God's kingdom, and thereby triumphs over evil, saving those who accept and judging those who reject. The narrative prepares for the feast of rejoicing before the Lord. Invitations to the banquet of the kingdom include those formerly barred from Israel's feasts. The older story's call to destroy the enemy in the land is transformed, even reversed, in the portraits of the enemy Samaritans. The "Good Samaritan" epitomizes the neighborly love of the double commandment, and the Samaritan leper models gratitude for God's mercy and healing power in Jesus.

Israel's temple traditions provide a focus and foil for the Synoptics' stories of Jesus' pre-passion ministry in Jerusalem. In Matthew and Mark, temple traditions are not only reformed, but set within the paradox of continuity in discontinuity. For the temple as God's sanctuary falls under judgment for its exclusivity and hierarchically restricted access into God's presence. In Mark, the resurrected Jesus, appearing in Galilee, is the new ναός for the nations, so that mission and eschatological hope are the context of worship. In Matthew, Jesus-in-the-church is the new entity of meaning, the "thing greater" than the temple. Believers meet in the name of Jesus to do temple business, to "bind and loose" from sin. In Luke, the temple renders itself up to Jesus' and his followers' mission: to glorify God and make the whole world the field into which the seed of the kingdom's εὐαγγελίζεσθαι is planted in order to release people from Satan's tyranny.

Israel's traditions of kingship permeate the Synoptics' stories of Jesus' passion. In this function, these traditions are significantly transformed, vindicating similar strands of kingship—against others—already in Israel's traditions. As in the Psalms, human kingship bows to divine kingship. Jesus manifests a servant kingship that the rulers of this world could not comprehend; thus they crucify him. Jesus was crucified under the identity, "King of the Jews," but his death evoked an enduring confession of his true royal identity, surprisingly and ironically disclosed by a Gentile soldier co-opted into the passion drama: true Son of God (Matthew and Mark) and faithful Righteous One (Luke). Vindicated by resurrection, the servant-king sits at the right hand of Power, with all authority given him to commission his followers to disciple all nations into the reign of the Father, Son, and Holy Spirit (Matthew).

This study has correlated four sequential OT faith traditions with four sequential sections in each of the Synoptics. However, it has also observed that the four traditions are in some ways only two traditions and that these traditions are not restricted in their influence to one matching section of each Gospel. Thus, while the findings demonstrate a remarkable degree of sequential correlation, they also note that exodus themes are not fully separable from journey-conquest themes, in either the older or newer stories. Further, the exodus motif reappears in the Lord's Supper and in the passion narrative constructed primarily around the kingship theme. Also, the exodus theme extends throughout the Lukan narrative, a point which some have argued regarding Mark as well.[5] But when the exodus theme is defined in terms of freedom from bondage, of receiving bread from heaven in the wilderness, journeying and rejoicing at the feasts, countering unbelief, and of testing generally, the exodus tradition clearly predominates in the Galilean and journey sections of Jesus' ministry in all three Gospels. While the wilderness locale for narrative events is restricted to the Galilean section, these thematic emphases, including liberation, continue into the journey narratives and combine with the way-conquest traditions, especially in Luke's lengthened journey narrative. While stories of liberation occur in Luke's journey section and serve also the way-conquest emphasis, the clear narrative markers of way-conquest imagery in both Luke's and Mark's journey sections distinguish the section from the exodus tradition and the markers that belong to it (such as sea, wilderness, manna). As noted, however, Jesus' transfiguration on the mountain, with its different sectional placement, reflects the overlap of the exodus and way-conquest traditions in both the older and newer stories.

The kingdom of God motif permeates the entire Gospel story. But even in this, the *issue* of Jesus' royal identity is not addressed in the Galilean narratives (except perhaps by the demonic outcries which for the reader have only the effect of "putting it on hold"), even though Matthew and Luke accent Jesus' kingship already in their birth and preparation narratives. This contrasts with John's story of Jesus, which highlights Jesus' identity as king in a Galilean narrative (John 6:1–15).[6] In the Synoptics, Jesus' royal identity and the related motif of Jesus' action and teaching in the temple are focused in the prepassion and passion narratives. The temple theme dominates the prepassion

---

[5] See the discussion in chapter 1 above, especially the references to the views of E. C. Hobbs, O. Piper, and J. Bowman.

[6] There are actually relatively few Galilean narratives in John compared to the Synoptics. Strikingly, John has Jesus' messiahship disclosed already in ch. 4 in *Samaria* by/to a Samaritan woman. How divergent this is from the Synoptic treatment of the kingship theme in Jesus' public ministry!

section, and the kingship theme controls the passion narratives. In John, however, the temple theme is handled quite differently (in chs. 2 and 4). That the Synoptics and John treat the temple theme so differently discloses the theological significance of their unique literary designs. The fact that the prepassion narratives in each of the Synoptics are so closely correlated with the temple bears witness not simply to geographical location—for John here has Jesus in the upper room!—but to a quite specific and distinctive structural design. In their birth and preparation narratives Matthew and Luke introduce Jesus' royal identity as developed in their prepassion and passion narratives. To a limited extent, Luke also uses this technique for the temple theme, since Luke's story begins and ends in the temple (1:5ff. and 24:48–50). But these features do not subvert the Galilean and journey sections devoted to exodus and way-conquest themes, nor do they detract from the respective temple and kingship foci in the Jerusalem sections of the Synoptics.

All these variations occur within the prevailing pattern; none results in a deviation from or muting of the sequential pattern. In none of the twelve Gospel sections (the four sections in each of the three Gospels) is the designated theme from the older story absent. Conversely tested, attempting to analyze a given section with one of the other themes simply does not work, apart from the overlapping phenomena of exodus with way-conquest and temple with kingship. Even in these sections into which an earlier theme is extended, its presence there makes sense only because it is narratively developed in the other section which is its home. In short, a differing sequential pattern cannot be demonstrated. The Galilean sections of the Synoptics do not contain the narrative markers and plot coherence that identify the way-conquest traditions in the journey narratives. Further, even though the prepassion narratives contain some significant kingship markers and plot development, these sections anticipate, in that particular respect, the passion narratives. They prepare for the King of the passion narratives. One might argue that the passion-resurrection narrative could be understood through the conquest tradition. However, the passion narrative does not contain "markers" of the OT way-conquest tradition, such as are present in the journey section. Hence, it would be more appropriate, from the standpoint of OT tradition influence, to interpret the conquest aspect of the passion narrative as already anticipated in the journey narrative. The journey narrative, with its passion-resurrection predictions framed by imagery of the way-conquest tradition, provides the conceptual and theological categories by which to understand the conquest of the passion narrative. Mark 10:45 (par. Matt 20:28), in speaking of the Son of humanity who gives his life a ransom for many, provides a specific example of this point. In Luke, the overthrow of Satan, the disarming of hostilities between Jews and Samaritans, and the gift of God's εἰρήνη as power over evil are also concrete examples.

Granting the strength of this evidence, the Synoptics' sequential use of exodus, way-conquest, temple, and kingship motifs, however, is not to be construed so as to preclude the vitality of story. The plot of each narrative does indeed unfold in order to highlight each theme in each respective section, but hints and signals of the other themes punctuate the entire narrative in each Gospel. Such literary design does not disempower the creativity of an unfolding plot in which given thematic concentrations are prepared for or echoed later in the narrative. Indeed, a structural model does not preclude artistic excellence. Further, the case argued here does not mean that these writers thought of tradition-history in the same way that modern biblical critics do, as discrete phases that can only follow each other chronologically. Isaiah's joining of the exodus and Zion traditions witnesses otherwise. Rather, we must see these traditions as part of a story which faith treasures and which allows for subtle interweaving of themes and reconfigurations. Observing such in the Synoptics' narrative need not negate the findings of this study. Both can and must dwell together in our conception of the Synoptics' story to the degree that the narrative itself bears witness to both. This study contends that the Synoptics contain a story structure significantly correlated with the form of an older story, a story that the Gospel-makers heard in the liturgy of the synagogue and in the nurture of the home as well. Not only is the full sequential utilization of exodus, way-conquest, temple, and kingship themes present in each Synoptic, but conversely the absence of narrative "markers" belonging to other motif-traditions corroborates the thesis.

To both summarize and assess the research data, the following table indicates the degree to which the respective motif of OT theological tradition is present in the various Gospel sections, based on the analysis in chapters 3–6. On a 1–3 grid, with 1 high and 3 low, the strength and clarity of the respective traditions of Israel's faith in the various Gospel sections is weighted as follows:

Traditions	Matthew	Mark	Luke
Exodus and (Sinai) in Galilean Section	2 (1)	1	1
Conquest-Journey in journey Section	2	1	1
Temple in Prepassion Section	1	1	2
Kingship in Passion Section	1	1	1

Of the twelve sections, ten (including Sinai for Matthew) receive the highest rating. Specific narrative features in each of these ten sections show the influence of the respective faith tradition from the older story to be unmistakable. Were that thematic emphasis removed from that section completely, the story would collapse; the narrative plot would lose coherence.

The rationale for deviations from the highest rating is as follows: (1) in Matthew's Galilean section explicit exodus-deliverance imagery and themes are scant while Sinai imagery and emphases are distinctly present; (2) though Matthew has strong victory and triumph imagery in his Galilee-to-Jerusalem section, the imagery is not significantly linked to any explicit Deuteronomic way-conquest motifs, indicating a major transposition of conquest motifs into a new thought-structure and making the link to the older story somewhat tenuous; and (3) even though Luke in both his volumes gives major attention to the temple, his prepassion narrative, at those places where the temple is under sharp attack in Matthew and Mark, pedals softly the temple theme. This phenomenon, together with positive temple emphasis elsewhere, has the effect of muting its significance in this section where the temple is under judgment.

THE SYNOPTICS' HERMENEUTICAL USE AND TRANSFORMATION OF OLD TESTAMENT TRADITIONS

This study has also examined the degree of continuity, discontinuity, and transformation in the four streams of OT traditions as they are utilized in the shaping of the Synoptic stories of Jesus. The very use of these four streams of tradition witnesses to continuity. This witness exemplifies well Douglas Knight's opening comments in his introductory essay in *Tradition and Theology in the Old Testament*: tradition provides "meaning-content and conveys meaning-structures"; it also "provides us with the very structures for understanding and communicating." [7] Accordingly, it should be no surprise that the early Christians would comprehend and narrate the story of Jesus within a narrative framework developed within the earlier story of God's presence in act and word. Israel's cultic legacy witnesses clearly to the prominent role that these four streams of tradition had within the

---

[7] D. Knight, "Tradition and Theology," in *Tradition and Theology in the Old Testament*, 1. See also his "Canon and the History of Tradition," *HBT* 2 (1980), 127–49.

worshipping community, even at an early date (see ch. 2). That this framework should be carried over into the story of Jesus is thus an expected phenomenon, since tradition provides the handles by which humans perceive and communicate.

But not all the OT traditions are prominent in the Gospels. In chapter 5 it was noted that some elements of the temple traditions plays no significant role in the narratives, i.e., sacrifice, priesthood, and festivals. The sabbath traditions are present, but in dispute: what actions and conduct are lawful on the sabbath? Certain holiness and purity traditions, as interpreted and observed by the Pharisees, approximate discontinuity in Jesus' own actions and conduct. Though imagery of the natural world abounds in both the so-called Q sayings and the parables, OT creation theology as such is not significantly present in the Synoptic corpus (though Jesus' appeal to God's creation of *adam* as male and female in Mark 10 and parallels may be cited). The wisdom traditions are more visible, especially in Matthew, but even these play a minor role in the shape of the Gospel story. But absence of structural influence does not mean discontinuity with those traditions. Those traditions, while appearing on occasion in the Synoptics' narratives, did not exert appreciable influence upon the structural design of the Synoptics' story of Jesus, as did the exodus, way-conquest, temple, and kingship traditions.

The most significant factor in this analysis of traditions' influence upon the Synoptics' narratives is the extensive, creative, and profound transformation discernible in these four major streams of tradition, as they served and shaped the new story. In examining this transformation, the hermeneutics of the Synoptic writers are discernible. In a somewhat analogous study to this one, *Echoes of Scripture in the Letters of Paul*, Richard Hays demonstrates the major role of Israel's Scripture in Paul's letters.[8] Borrowing his terms, the *echoes* of

---

[8] Hays, *Echoes of Scripture*. Hays's ch. 1 (1–33) provides a hermeneutical setting for his study of Paul's use of Israel's Scripture. In this he considers, among other matters, current hermeneutical theories regarding where or when intertextual fusion takes place: in the author's mind, in the mind of the original readers, in the text itself, in my act of reading, or in the community of interpretation (26–27). Hays opts to choose no one single theory but wishes to hold them together, with all theories contributing to the hermeneutical event. In his study and mine, however, we are talking about an intertextual fusion that takes place before the original reader or we as contemporary readers participate in the hermeneutical event. Hence, it is important to distinguish between canonical intertextuality, on which our studies focus, and the hermeneutical event generally, even though the hermeneutical theories of "reader response" criti-

Israel's Scripture in the structure of the Synoptics' story are strong and clear, witnessing to the thunder of *intertextual resonance*. Three types of use are evident in the Synoptics; each type contributes to varying degrees of continuity and transformation. First, there is the use of an image or motif, such as *exodus* itself in Luke 9, or the mountain in Matthew, or the wilderness and way in Mark. Second, at times some type of structural parallel may be employed, as in Mark's sequential use of several exodus motifs, sea (1:16–20), mountain (3:13–19) and wilderness (6:7–13, 29ff.), correlated with the theme of his narrative plot on discipleship so that each of these motifs is linked to the beginning of a new major section in the Galilean division of the Gospel. Another structural parallel is Luke's use of Deuteronomy for his journey narrative. A third type of use of the older traditions is thematic, in which the younger story is analogically related to the older by thematic emphasis. Matthew's journey section exemplifies this type. Of course, more than one type of use may be evident in a given section, in which case the influence of the older tradition is more evident and decisive for our analysis. The following discussion has two foci: identifying for each tradition in each Gospel the particular type(s) of hermeneutical use present, and assessing the nature and degree of the transformation of the tradition.

 1. Exodus traditions. In the Synoptics' use of the exodus and Sinai traditions, the type of hermeneutical use differs considerably. Mark employs all three types of use, as follows:

 Type 1: Mark employs the exodus *motifs* of sea, mountain, and wilderness and sets Jesus' deeds and words within those motifs. The wilderness and sea recur throughout chs. 1–8 to set an overall new exodus tone for the Galilean section of the Gospel.

 Type 2: Additionally, Mark uses motifs for structural effect, so they provide the sequential structural design for the Galilean narrative.

---

cism and deconstruction would argue otherwise. Theories of "hermeneutical event" may be used in either analyzing intertextuality within Scripture or the act of readers interpreting Scripture. While the theoretical process may be discerned to be similar, statements which describe the process from the reader's standpoint, in relation to the text, do not sensibly apply to the process of a past intertextual hermeneutical event. While indeed the role of the first reader or present day readers may be deemed to be part of the hermeneutical event, the original act of Scripture's intertextual fusion cannot be explained by its happening in the first or present readers' minds, a process occurring subsequent to the original writing. For a helpful survey and discerning critique of recent critical literary theories and methods, see Moore's *Literary Criticism.*

Type 3: Mark demonstrates type three use also, in relation to type one and two. In 1:20–3:6 and 4:35–6:6 strong *themes* of liberation appear, and in 3:13–35 and 4:1–34 *both* the Sinai mountain *motif* and the *theme* of Jesus as *word*-teacher appear. In 6:7–8:27 again, both *motifs* from the older story, wilderness and miraculous bread, and a *theme,* unbelief of God's people (7:1–24; 8:10–12), are present.

Within the context of these continuities between the two stories—Israel's faith story and the church's Jesus story—significant transformations also appear. Liberation is not from Egyptian bondage, but from the bondages of illness, demonization, socio-purity taboos and ostracisms, and death itself. Not the Egyptians, either as people or as a political or idolatrous entity, but Satan and his hosts of demons, are portrayed as the enemy, from whose oppressive powers, manifest also in the religious and political leaders, Jesus liberates. The definition for the new covenant peoplehood is not those saved from Egypt, but those who do the will of God (3:31–35). Most significant, those most receptive to and benefiting from the new liberation are those outside the previous boundaries of the people of God, specifically Gentiles (5:1–20; 7:24–30; also those fed in the second bread miracle, 8:1–9). While these transformations might appear to be so deep that the tradition itself is substantially changed, thus a paradigm shift (to use Thomas Kuhn's model of analysis), it must be remembered that the exodus tradition journeyed through significant changes and transformations prior to the Jesus story, especially in Isaiah 40–55. From a Christian point of view, though, this vision was proleptic of the Jesus event.

Like Mark, Matthew employs all three types of use of the older story, in his use of the Sinai tradition. By locating the Great Sermon and a summary of the Galilean section (15:29–31) on mountains and there incorporating the Feeding of the 4,000 (15:32–39), he juxtaposes Jesus' word and deeds, placing both under the interpretive light of Sinai. Since, as Donaldson suggests, these two mountain events function as structural inclusios, Matthew uses the older story not only for motifs, but for structural purposes as well. Further, since Matthew's five great discourses reflect the *theme* of revelation to the community—and three are in the Galilean section—Matthew employs the older story in the third hermeneutical pattern as well. Jesus' teachings, identified as *fulfillment* of Torah, are divine revelation to the Jesus community just as the Sinai revelation was given through Moses to Israel as God's covenant community.

In the six antitheses of the Sermon, however, Jesus' authoritative reinterpretation of the Torah transforms the tradition, as well as maintains continuity with it.[9] Both the Missionary (ch. 10) and the Parables Discourses (ch. 13) presuppose a substantive new dimension; the *newness* is the rationale for the mission to the "lost sheep of the house of Israel" and for the scope and intensity of teaching in the parables of the kingdom.

The function of Matthew's emphasis in the Galilean section upon Gentile receptivity to Jesus' deeds should be understood as an echo fulfilling the Exodus refrain, "in order that they may know that I am the Lord." In Matthew, the Gentiles praise the God of Israel. In this context, the ten miracles also recall the plague narrative of the exodus. In both motifs—and both are woven into the structure—Matthew again shows Jesus greatly transforming the tradition. For unlike the plagues which afflicted and destroyed the opponent, Jesus heals, saves, and liberates victims of oppression. Here the transformation takes an ironic twist. Matthew's parallel to the plague recipients is not the recipients of the ten miracles, but those who refuse Jesus' prophetic words, i.e., the Pharisees. A "Great Reversal" takes place: ironically, the liberation of Jesus' salvation benefits primarily not "God's own" but those outside the boundaries set up by "God's own" in order to keep themselves "pure" for God. This reversal theme is the greatest force bearing upon the transformation of the tradition; it is concretized in Jesus' command to "love your enemies and pray for those who persecute you" (5:43–48). This command, set within the Sinai mountain frame of the Sermon and contrasting to the exodus treatment of the enemy, again transforms the tradition to the point of showing discontinuity. Strikingly, however, the same OT corpus provides the source for Jesus' twofold summary of the Torah, love of God (Deut 6:4) and neighbor (Lev 19:18), appearing in a later section of Matthew (22:37–39; cf. Luke 10:25ff.). The insights of this analysis concur with larger streams of interpretation in Matthean scholarship: both strong continuity—Verhey puts it well, "the law holds"[10]—and transformation occur side by side in Matthew's story of Jesus.

In Luke, the influence of the exodus' liberation tradition appears strongest in his analogical use of the tradition, filtered through Second (Third) Isaiah's earlier use. Luke connects the deliverance-liberation theme of the exodus to the liberation of the Jubilee vision. He then uses this double-pronged tradition of liberation, merged

---

[9]W. Schrage, *The Ethics of the New Testament,* trans. D. E. Green (Philadelphia: Fortress, 1988), 145–50.

[10]A. Verhey, *Great Reversal,* 82–91.

already in Isaiah, to present Jesus' Galilean ministry as the good news (εὐαγγελίσασθαι) that liberates from all forms of oppression. Jesus replaces the religious ostracism of tax collectors and sinners with table fellowship, proclaims blessing to the poor, welcomes women into God's work of redemption, and overcomes the Jewish-Gentile wall of separation. At the very heart of this liberation from socio-religious, economic and gender-based oppressions, Jesus' gospel breaks the power of Satan, freeing people from alienation and enmity. Luke thus transforms the exodus theme of liberation by contextualizing it within Jesus' and his own social worlds.

In addition to this new contextualized exodus theme, Luke also employs a limited but significant use of explicit exodus motifs. The word "exodus" is woven into the transfiguration narrative which Luke places in the Galilean section, and the transfiguration echoes the Sinai event. Just as significant, in chapter 7 Luke begins his distinctive use of the Mosaic prophet motif. These features firmly link Luke's Galilean section to the exodus-Sinai tradition, but his use of the exodus-liberation theme shows also a freedom—and perhaps distance in communal identity—from the older story. While it is essential that continuity between Israel and the Jesus movement, extended into Luke's Christian community, be maintained, it is just as important that the distinctive character of Jesus' freedom from bondage be celebrated and lived anew in the εὐαγγελίζεσθαι mission of the church.

2. *Way-Conquest Traditions.* Mark's journey section strategically employs way-conquest motifs and images. His patterned use of ὁδός to frame the section, as well as his distinctive ὁδός introduction of the Gospel in 1:2–3, beg to be heard as echoes of Israel's *way* to the promised land (Exod 23:20); his use of the phrase, "to enter into the kingdom of God" in 9:41–10:29 (cf. 9:1), similarly echoes the Deuteronomic phrase, "to enter into the land." The numerous parallel motifs between Jesus' transfiguration and Moses' Mount Sinai experience (Exod 24) increase the resonance of the echo.[11]

In assessing the hermeneutical strategy by which Mark links the Jesus story to Israel's story, A. Suhl has designated this as a καθώς hermeneutic, a "just as" relationship, in which the past is shown by

---

[11]In Mark and Matthew the Transfiguration is placed within the journey narrative, in parallel to its placement in Exod 24 after the "way" to the land is announced. In Luke it is in the Galilean section. In terms of Israel's tradition history Sinai participates in both the exodus and the "way"-land entrance traditions. The Synoptics' variation maintains the same fluidity.

the author/narrator to re-present itself in Jesus' present.[12] This view of the relationship between the OT past and the Jesus-Gospel present testifies to strong continuity in the tradition. But some aspects of the tradition do not continue in a "just as" relationship. While humble, trustful dependence upon the Conqueror is present in both the older and younger stories, the necessity of suffering, cross-bearing, and renunciation of power, prestige, and position are distinctive to the new story. Ὁδός has become a didactic strategy by which Mark teaches the way of discipleship, in which the images of cross, child, and servant function paradigmatically. Further, the Warrior tradition has also undergone transformation in that the Conqueror has now become the Servant who gives his own life as a ransom for many. So while Mark shows strong links of continuity, he also crucially transforms the motifs and emphases of the older story, so that the degree of transformation is so heightened as to accent discontinuity as well as continuity. In this section the Son of humanity sayings disclose the necessity and certainty of a crucified Messiah, a unique feature of the younger story of faith.

Matthew, in contrast to both Mark and Luke, shows no hermeneutical use of the older story in either specific motifs or structural parallels. The one exception is his heightened Sinai imagery in the transfiguration. At the level of thematic analogy, however, Matthew develops clearly the theme of conquest of evil and sin so that the Jesus community maintains its victory in Christ. His portrait of Jesus as calling the community to "bind and loose" and to avoid offenses that cause one to stumble represents a categorical transformation from the emphases of the older way-conquest tradition. Though analogical thought-structures are discernible in the concept of overcoming the adversary, the evident discontinuity makes it nearly impossible to see connections between the two stories. Hence, the tradition has been so thoroughly contextualized that narrative markers connecting the two stories are lacking. The reason for this may be that Matthew's Galilean section draws more heavily on the Sinai traditions than those of the exodus. While the exodus traditions are sometimes fused with the way-conquest traditions in Mark's and Luke's journey narratives, Matthew's journey section has no explicit exodus or way-conquest motifs or structural analogies. In the transfiguration, however, Matthew accentuates the connection between the Jesus story and the Sinai tradition, thus extending the dominant emphasis of his Galilean section.

[12]A. Suhl, Die Funktion, 96, 130–37, 157–59, 167.

In his extended journey narrative Luke clearly uses both motifs and structure from Israel's story. Numerous thematic connections occur as part of his structural correspondences to Deuteronomy. In these connections significant transformation occurs in the means of treating the enemy, and in Jesus' effort to convert the disciples' perception of who is neighbor and enemy. Samaritans are no longer the enemy, but the neighbor. Satan is the foe to be overcome. Luke's "gospel of peace" (chs. 10 and 19 as inclusios) represents also a major transformation in the way-conquest tradition, but his portrayal of God's justice and call of humans to true justice shows striking continuity with the older story. Similarly, Luke's recurring portrait of Jesus banqueting during his journey echoes the Deuteronomic theme of feasting and rejoicing before the Lord. Luke connects *rejoicing* specifically with Jesus' eating with sinners and tax collectors. In this is continuity in motif and theme, but discontinuity in the manner and conditions of feasting. Rather than restricting the feasting to "the place where God will choose," Jesus violates the purity boundaries of the tradition. The strongest continuity is evident in Luke's emphasis on Jesus as rejected Prophet. Here Jesus *re*-presents the Moses tradition; the new continues the accent of the old.

In short, Luke crafts a narrative that both maintains strong lines of continuity and simultaneously transforms the tradition at crucial points, producing strong elements of discontinuity.

3. Temple traditions. For all three Synoptics, temple traditions are crucially important. In all three a combination of the hermeneutical uses of motif and theme occur. The temple motif, both ἱερόν and ναός, echoes Israel's rich literary temple traditions (through both the Nebiim and the Kethubim, and also in the Torah in the Tabernacle as precursor). Numerous specific quotations from Israel's temple texts clinch the point: all three Gospels quote parts of Psalm 118:25–26 as the praise accorded Jesus in his triumphal entry; all three quote from two Nebiim temple texts (Isa 56:7 and Jer 7:11) to interpret Jesus' cleansing of the temple; all three quote again Psalm 118:22 as the climax of the parable of the Wicked Tenants ("The stone that the builders rejected . . . "); and all three use the Zion Psalm 110:1 to pose the issue of the identity of the Messiah as David's son and Lord. Even the image of the "desolating sacrilege" in Matthew and Mark (Luke: Jerusalem) connects to the earlier Kethubim use in Daniel 9:27; 11:31; 12:11. The temple motif and theme in the prepassion section of the Synoptics, together with emphases on divine visitation, invitation, and judgment, draw explicitly from the older story in order to explicate the significance of the new story.

Luke punctuates his entire two-volume work with temple emphases, whereas Mark and Matthew focus their narrative treatment of the temple tradition in their prepassion sections, with continuing impact on the passion story. For both Mark and Matthew the tension between the new story and certain streams of the temple tradition in the older story is so severe that the literal temple is replaced by Christ himself as the new temple (Mark) and/or the new people of God (the church in Matthew). In both cases, however, the functions assigned to the temple in the eschatological age are now carried forward by Christ and believers who gather in Jesus' name. Both blessing to the Gentiles and a place of true worship are now mediated from God into human experience. Indeed "something greater than the temple" (Matt 12:6) has come and, as the scribe rightly put it in Mark, it "is much more important than all whole burnt offerings and sacrifices" (12:33b; cf. Matt 13:9). These sacrifices, intended to renew peace between humans and between humans and God, are now consummated by the new temple's functions of worship and mission, fulfilling true love for God and the neighbor. Thus, in both Mark and Matthew a major transformation in Israel's temple traditions occurs. Galilee, not Jerusalem, becomes the symbolic center from which to fulfill Mount Zion's blessings to the nations. Luke takes a different course on the temple traditions. Once purified by Jesus' cleansing, the temple serves Jesus' mission to call Israel to renewal as God's people. The Jesus story is cradled and consummated by God's people humbly and joyously praising God in the temple (chs. 1 and 24:50–53), and so the story continues in the early church (Acts 2–4). But the holy city and its people are under judgment for rejecting their Messiah, because they spurned the time of their visitation from God (Luke 19:40–44). For this reason the temple falls under the doom of God's judgment, already come to pass by Luke's Gospel time (ch. 21). Further, the exclusivity of the temple's function incurs sharp critique from the church's first martyr (Acts 6:8–15; 7:47–52), which for Luke and his readers legitimates the temple's fall that has already occurred. Its function as a sphere of blessing ends not because of its inadequacy for the church's worship and praise, but through its destruction because of God's judgment upon the city[13] and its people in rejecting Jesus as

---

[13]J. B. Tyson suggests a Lukan distinction between the city and the temple, holding that the atmosphere of conflict surrounding the temple in Luke 19–21 and Acts 2–4 arises from the Jewish leaders' refusal of the Messiah and his community: *The Death of Jesus in Luke–Acts* (Columbia, S.C.: University of South Carolina, 1986), 90–91, 96–109.

the Christ of God sent to them. Throughout Luke's Gospel and the narrative of Acts, Israel's temple traditions appear in the new story largely in continuity with emphases of the old story. The temple and its functions of worship and mediation of worldwide blessing assist God's fulfillment of Israel's eschatological hopes. Theologically, Zion endures for the sake of Israel and the nations.

4. *Kingship traditions.* Israel's kingship traditions are prominent in the passion narratives of all three Gospels. In this case the hermeneutical uses of motif and theme appear so explicitly and recur so frequently that they are unmistakable. The titles used for Jesus, especially Messiah-Christ and Son of God, as treated in chapter 6, are rooted in OT kingship traditions. The narrative is toned by the recurring use of "King of the Jews" and "King of Israel." If Bonnard's thesis that Psalm 72 influenced the thought of Luke's presentation of Jesus is accepted, a degree of structural parallel is present as well. While the passion narrative draws heavily upon Israel's kingship in both motif and theme, it also puts that tradition in tension with other traditions of Israel's faith story.

In all three Gospels the divine voice at Jesus' baptism and transfiguration identifies Jesus as God's royal Son and immediately joins the royal tradition to the motif of Yahweh's servant of justice to the nations by its use of Isaiah 42:1. At the transfiguration the same heavenly voice links Jesus' royal identity to the Prophetic tradition by citing Deuteronomy 18:15. In all three Gospels the suffering Son of humanity sayings function also to qualify and interpret Jesus' messianic identity. In the triumphal entry Jesus' kingship is qualified by the Zechariah 9:9–10 portrait of a lowly king whose universal peace ends war. Further, in the trial narratives in all three Synoptics, Jesus' kingship discloses its divine dimension through mockeries, the cross, and the irony of unexpected confession. Only through eyes that see Jesus "seated at the right hand of power" and the tongue that names him Son of God/Righteous One can his kingship truly be grasped.

Beyond these features common to all three Gospels, each Gospel has its own pattern of further qualifying the kingship tradition, thus transforming the militaristic, imperious, and nationalistic strands in Israel's messianic kingship traditions. Mark does it by employing secrecy, through which he allows Jesus' royalty as Son of God to be humanly declared only in the face of "the crucified Messiah," and by a Gentile, thus precluding once and for all any nationalistic interpretation of Jesus' kingship. Matthew does it in his birth narrative by deliberately setting Jesus' kingship, in all its weakness and vulnerability, in contrast to Herod's, by combining humble kingship and wisdom traditions in 11:25–30, and by transferring Jesus' claim of cosmic authority from Mount Zion in Jerusalem to a nameless mountain in Galilee, from which the reign of God will permeate all nations, extending baptism in the name of the Father, Son, and Spirit to all people. Luke does it by announcing that the Savior-King's birth means peace for *all people* who shall see the salvation of the Lord, by portraying Jesus as a journeying Prophet whose reign of peace is offered to enemy Samaritans, and by showing that Jesus in his rejection and death is the suffering Righteous One par excellence, blessed and exalted by God into glory, seated at the right hand of Power.

Hence, each of the Synoptics uses the royalty tradition of the older story as a leitmotif for the new story. Each in its own way discloses with narrative art and theological profundity a new genus of royal politics and peace, one in which "lording it over others" gives way to humble servanthood, childlike trust in God, and love for God, neighbor, and enemy. Liberation, conquest, temple and kingship are from God and for God in Jesus, the true Son of Israel.

DISCERNING THE MEANING OF THE PATTERN

Until now this chapter has summarized, assessed, and analyzed hermeneutically the influence of four of Israel's major faith traditions upon the structural shape and the thematic emphases of the Synoptics' stories. It has also observed significant dimensions of continuity and transformation, and some discontinuity in this story to story relationship. It now takes up the question of the story's theological significance in relationship to the Synoptics' distinctive structure of Galilee, journey, Jerusalem, and return to Galilee (in Matthew and Mark).

1. The Significance of the Galilee-Jerusalem Structure

As an essential component in the influence of Israel's faith-story upon the shape of the Synoptics, the distinctive synoptic structural feature of construing the story of Jesus around a bi–polar geographical axis, Galilee-Jerusalem, calls now for fresh examination. Indeed, the Galilee-Jerusalem structure is an important feature of the view that Matthew, Mark, and Luke are *syn-optic*, presenting the story of Jesus from a common perspective. Granted, there are variations among the three Gospels in the geographical outline,[14] especially in

---

[14]Luke 4:44 presents a special case, in that this note that "Jesus continued proclaiming the message in the synagogues of Judea" has been taken

the beginnings and endings. But the common features are pervasive, and they have led to the long-standing search for the literary, historical, and theological significance of the Galilee-Jerusalem structure (see ch. 2).

Since the above evidence demonstrates a significant degree of influence from Israel's faith traditions upon the content of the Synoptics in motifs, structural correspondences, and thematic analogies, I propose that the Synoptics' use of these OT traditions shaped the synoptic pattern into its bi–polar Galilee-Jerusalem structure. Although Israel's faith traditions were shared by the north (Israel) and south (Judah), the temple and kingship traditions "belonged," in the sense of origin and home, to the south, specifically Jerusalem (witness the Zion Psalms, the Isaiah traditions, and the Primary History which locates kingship and temple in Jerusalem). Further, the exodus and conquest traditions were first owned and developed in the north (witness the testimony of the Pentateuch, the Primary History, and Hosea's exodus imagery).[15] Certainly, these traditions were also owned by the south and even blended with southern traditions (witness Isa 40–55). Yet they were identified with Israel's experience prior to the Jerusalem monarchy. Chronologically, they developed prior to David's capture of the Jebusite stronghold, and thus had earlier cultic connections to northern shrines such as Gilgal, Shechem, and Shiloh.[16] This northern faith experience celebrated Yahweh as Warrior and Defender, generating the persistent criticism of kingship and temple traditions as they developed in the south. Such criticism was not, however, a matter of northern versus southern loyalties. As noted in chapter 2, the voice of criticism came also from southern prophets, and chiefly from the southern Zion theology itself. Further, in some cases northern traditions were used to complement and qualify southern emphases, and vice versa. These observations advanced by Levenson, however, assume the validity of distinctive northern and southern traditions.

---

by some to indicate that Jesus has here already concluded his Galilean ministry. But this cannot be the case in light of the very next verse, 5:1, which locates Jesus by the lake of Gennesaret. In 23:5 *Judea* refers to all Israel (cf. also 1:5; 7:17), and this surely must be the denotation here. The MS variants also witness to the difficulty perceived by scribes who thus attempted to resolve the problem. See Freyne, *Galilee*, 90–91, for treatment of the issue.

[15]The fact that the Samaritans, located in the northern sector, closed their canon with the Pentateuch, bears witness also to the fact that exodus and conquest (in Deut) traditions had their theological identity with the north.

[16]See Cross, "Divine Warrior."

Because of the earlier exile of the north, the south continued to own and utilize the earlier traditions, blending them with their own later traditions. As reflected in the Zion psalms, these northern traditions were often subsumed in a celebration of kingship (both Yahweh's and David's) and worship on God's holy hill.[17] Thus in Israel's ongoing history the southern traditions, especially those associated with the messianic hope, attained a significant degree of hegemony. In the developing strands of eschatological hope, Jerusalem became, as it were, "the navel of the earth." God's salvation will come to Israel in and through Jerusalem. However, Zion theology, though headquartered in Jerusalem, frequently embraced in its vision the whole world.

In view of the imprint of Israel's distinctive northern and southern traditions upon the respective sections of the Synoptic Gospels, I propose that *the Synoptic Gospels, in their bi–polar structure of Galilee and Jerusalem, reflect the northern and southern settings of the origins and development of Israel's major faith traditions. A direct correlation of emphases is evident in the Synoptic narrative pattern: the Galilean and journey sections develop Israel's northern traditions of exodus-liberation, Torah-instruction, and way-conquest; the prepassion and passion narratives located in Jerusalem develop Israel's southern traditions of temple and kingship.*

Thus, Israel's northern setting as the home and nourisher of the exodus-Sinai and way-conquest traditions provided the shapers of the synoptic story of Jesus with a theological-geographical prototype for Jesus' own ministry. Hence, the Synoptics tell their story of Jesus with distinct northern components, locating the Galilean and journey section in Israel's northern regions.

Similarly, Israel's southern setting as the home and nourisher of the temple and kingship traditions provided the shapers of the synoptic story of Jesus a theological-geographical prototype for Jesus' later ministry. Hence, the Synoptics tell their story of Jesus with

---

[17]Psalm 78 consists largely of the earlier traditions, but it consummates with Mount Zion, the sanctuary and Davidic kingship (vv. 68–70); Jer 31 is similar. Psalm 89 celebrates Yahweh's covenant with David but echoes exodus and conquest (vv. 10b, 13). Some psalms are oriented entirely to the earlier traditions of exodus and conquest (105, 106, 114) while others are oriented to temple and kingship traditions (2, 48, 72). Psalm 50 incorporates elements of both sets of traditions and Pss 18 and 118 in their more generalized language of conflict and triumph could catch up experience from both sets, though their endings are clearly identified with the Zion tradition. The imagery in 18:1–2 comes largely from the exodus and conquest traditions but has Zion overtones.

distinct southern components, locating the prepassion and passion narratives in Jerusalem.

Further, the grouping of events and teachings of Jesus into an itinerary that proceeds from Galilee to Jerusalem via one great journey (contra John) reflects Israel's faith memories and celebrations of its story within the sequential cycle of annual festivals celebrating its faith traditions.

Although this study makes its proposal on the basis of narrative analysis, questions of historical continuity with Jesus and the influence of Jewish and early Jewish Christian liturgy upon the development of this pattern also merit analysis. But these can be only minimally addressed here.

Although the shapers of the common synoptic Galilee-Jerusalem structure cannot be identified, some outline of the story must have existed prior to Mark, Matthew and Luke.[18] At least elements of this developing structure must certainly go back behind the Gospels and may reflect the way in which the early church understood and began to communicate the gospel story. Indeed, Jesus himself may have conducted aspects of his ministry in such a way as to suggest this structure. But the structure in its Gospel form cannot be reduced to a Jesus of history inquiry. John's differing structure witnesses against this.

Certainly the first Synoptic author is to be credited with valuing and developing the form in its Gospel wholeness and significance, contributing the theological significance of the Galilee-Jerusalem symbolic polarity. If Mark wrote first, then certainly he is to be credited with a significant share of this contribution. If the case is made for Matthean or Lukan priority, then that respective Gospel writer receives the significant share of credit. Because the literary presentation of these symbolic roles dominates the entire corpus of Mark's selected content, on the one hand, and these symbolic roles are to some extent blunted in Matthew and Luke by including large sections of content not controlled directly by the symbolic contrast,

---

[18]We should consider here the role of early Christian prophets, as suggested by M. E. Boring in his chapter, "The Prophet as Hermeneut," *Sayings of the Risen Jesus: Christian Prophecy in the Synoptic Tradition* (London et al.: Cambridge University, 1982), 95–110. Note: "C. H. Dodd has shown that, without denying that New Testament theology has a substantial Hellenistic element, its substructure is built upon the Old Testament and the conviction that what is written there is now being fulfilled in the ministry of Jesus and the life of the church. His thesis is that whoever explained the Scriptures to the early church was the real architect of New Testament theology" (*Sayings of the Risen Jesus*, 97).

STRUCTURE, THEOLOGY, AND FUNCTION OF THE SYNOPTICS 273

on the other hand, this aspect of the study's findings tilts toward Markan priority. Sean Freyne's treatment of the literary role of Galilee in each Gospel assumes this order, and his portrait of the function of Galilee (and Jerusalem) in the three Gospels tends to confirm it.

Of course, it could be argued that the most artistically crafted presentation of the symbolic role relations of Galilee-Jerusalem *developed* within the chronology of Synoptic Gospel origins, and thus came last. In that case the order would be Luke, Matthew, Mark. Or, it might be argued that Matthew's OT citation, "Galilee of the nations," suggested to Mark his skillful and extensive symbolic enterprise—hence Matthew, Mark, Luke. But the purpose of this study is not to make a new proposal for one or another theory of Gospel origins. These issues may be debated by others, taking these findings into consideration.

Within the context of the northern and southern locations for the origins of four of Israel's major faith traditions, the Galilee-Jerusalem structure for the story of Jesus and the symbolic roles of each in the Gospels' stories take on new significance. That Galilee and the journey function as the home for the exodus-Sinai and conquest emphases in Jesus' ministry witnesses to continuity in tradition; that Jerusalem functions as the home for the temple and kingship components of Jesus' ministry also witnesses to continuity in tradition. That Galilee, however, and not Jerusalem, becomes the radiating axis of the proclamation and reception of the kingdom of God, both in Jesus' initial ministry and in his post-resurrection commission in Mark and Matthew, witnesses to transformation, even reversal or inversion of the tradition. That which was devalued in the older story, even later disparaged as a land and people of inferior religious status—in which Galileans had come to be viewed by observant Jews as second class religious covenant members[19]—becomes now the celebrated theater of God's eschatological salvation. This is a matter of no small account. Indeed, God has exalted the lowly, in the very structure of the narrative.

2. Sean Freyne's Confirmation Regarding Galilee-Jerusalem

Sean Freyne has come to a similar view of the Galilee-Jerusalem relationship from quite a different angle of study, the correlation between the socio-religious factors of Galilean life—as perceived by

---

[19]That the designation "Galilean" is used disparagingly or even pejoratively, see Mark 14:70 par. and John 7:15, 45–52. Josephus (*War* 2:237) and rabbinic sources are even sharper in their denigration of Galileans. See Freyne, *Galilee*, 1–2, 123–24.

southern testimonies—and the literary role of Galilee in the Gospels. In his literary analysis Freyne notes that in Mark the symbolic role of Galilee is "disclosure and revelation" (chs. 1–8). Though Galilee is Jewish in overall ethos, its location enables easy contact with the surrounding regions and enough similarity in the social situation between Jews and Gentiles to open conversation on religious issues.[20] This concurs with the portrait in Mark, where Jesus as a Jew heals Gentiles in accord with his own charismatic powers as God's prophet and royal Son, yet to be disclosed to humans in the narrative. Further, the "promise of seeing Jesus in Galilee [14:28; 16:7] is highly significant because of the manner in which sight and blindness are woven into the narrative in terms of understanding events and sayings."[21] Conversely, the author/narrator portrays Jerusalem as the place of conflict, where Jesus' clashes with the Jerusalem scribes in Galilee come to denouement. But in his portrait of Jesus, "the author has prepared for the ironic enthronement of Jesus as king in the trial and crucifixion scenes."[22] Freyne's conclusions complement the thesis of this study:

> Insofar as all those narratives use Galilee as a symbol of the periphery becoming the new, non-localized centre of divine presence, and portray a Galilean charismatic and his retinue replacing the established religious leaders of Judaism, there is a highly paradoxical, even comic, character to the story. The pilgrim from Galilee subverts the place of pilgrimage even as he goes there; his journey becomes the new way that replaces the torah-symbol for those who follow him; their journey is to lead them, not to the centre where their Jewish faith has told them God can be encountered, but to bear witness to a new mode of encounter outside the land.[23]

Within the context of this study's influence of Israel's faith traditions upon the synoptic structure, another insight joins Freyne's claim that Galilee subverts Jerusalem in their respective roles in fulfilling messianic hopes. The traditions of exodus and conquest, contextualized and transformed by the new story, come to Jerusalem to liberate and conquer those notions of temple and kingship which mitigate, obfuscate, and defy the reign of God. True, temple and kingship continue, but specifically in relation to the reign of Jesus, Jerusalem's rejected Messiah, and from the locale of "Galilee of the Gentiles."

---

[20]Freyne, *Galilee*, 36, 40, 50.
[21]Ibid., 52–53.
[22]Ibid., 52.
[23]Ibid., 271–72.

These theses apply to the narrative character of Matthew and Mark, but not to Luke, at least not with the same force. Luke does not accomplish such a reversal via the triumph of Galilee over Jerusalem, in their symbolic narrative roles. Jesus and the disciples do not regather in Galilee; the gospel story continues in Jerusalem. But Luke has other ways of holding to the primacy of the exodus and conquest traditions in his continuing narrative. Israel's exodus-conquest story is noted repeatedly in the sermons in Acts. The gospel's liberation from oppression and triumph over Satan's powers—even in economic-political dimensions and scope—continues in the stories of Acts.[24] In this way Luke also has the theology of the "Galilee" traditions temper, and to some extent govern, the "Jerusalem" traditions. The journeying Prophet becomes the Lord of the Banquet, and the Lord-King of the Banquet continues to be identified as the journeying, rejected Prophet, both in the Emmaus story (24:19) and more generally in descriptions of Jesus in Acts (2:22; 3:22; 10:34–38).

This creative utilization of northern and southern traditions may also mean that the Synoptics bear witness to rather deep divergent theological positions within early Jewish Christianity. Several scholarly contributions have identified elements of "northern" tradition in conjunction with "Samaritan" and/or Hellenistic leaning, evident in Acts 6, the Gospel of John, and Luke's journey narrative.[25] While this connection is plausible, it is difficult to document due to the paucity of writings identifying and representing these positions. The Synoptic phenomenon bears witness, however, to both a correlation of Galilee with northern traditions and a critical theological perspective that renders up the strong southern traditions of temple and Zion for the service of the kingdom's proclamation, with its distinctive form of liberation and conquest, to all the world from Galilee.

3. Return to Galilee: Congruence with the Royalty Tradition

The return to Galilee in Matthew and Mark might on first blush appear to jeopardize the parallel between the OT northern-southern traditions and the Synoptics' Galilee-Jerusalem structure. Because the OT has no precedent for celebrating the ascendency of the

---

[24]Antioch plays a role in relation to Jerusalem that carries some of the symbolic significance of Galilee in Matthew and Mark.

[25]See here C. H. H. Scobie, "North and South: Tensions in Biblical History," *Biblical Studies, Festschrift W. Barclay*, ed. J. R. McKay and J. F. Miller (Philadelphia: Westminster, 1976), 87–98; Moessner, *Banquet*, 317–22.

north over the south,[26] the return to Galilee in the Gospels appears to go beyond the OT traditions. But the OT vision is not exhausted by the restoration and flourishing of Jerusalem's Zion. Isaiah's vision that God calls Israel to be a light to the nations (42:6; 49:6) provides the connection between Israel's tradition and the Gospels' return to Galilee. As argued above, the return to Galilee functions symbolically as the headquartering and mandating of God's mission in Jesus into all the world. Thus a strong link of continuity exists between Israel's traditions and the structure of Matthew and Mark on this significant point. This study has subsumed the return to Galilee under the royalty tradition, and thus the question must be raised whether this is consistent with the model in the older story.

Can Isaiah 40–55, the corpus in which Israel's mission to the nations is most clearly articulated, be considered a part of Israel's royal tradition? Normally, these traditions are connected with the servant, the servant of justice for the nations. Without doubt, the welfare of the nations is at the heart of this tradition, and that through God's servant Israel.[27] But are these kingship traditions? The answer is a decisive "yes," for at least three reasons. First, the servant accomplishes his mission as the one upon whom Yahweh puts his Spirit (42:1–4); the servant is the anointed one (cf. 61:1). The abiding of the Spirit upon the servant, as anointing for vocation, suggests the kingly, messianic tradition, combined perhaps with the prophetic tradition.[28] The royal servant's mission is to establish justice—occurring eleven times in chapters 40–55 (cf. royal Ps 72 and Isa 11)—and to include the Gentiles in the blessings of this justice. Second, the role of the servant

---

[26]Some of the prophecies of return to the land include the north, but always as a united Israel with Jerusalem as the center of God's rule. The British Israelite twist is a different story!

[27]See M. C. Lind, "Monotheism, Power, and Justice: A Study in Isaiah 40–55," *CBQ* 46 (1984), 432–46.

[28]C. Westermann takes this view, that the anointed servant reunites the earlier separated traditions of the royal and the prophetic (*Isaiah 40–66: A Commentary*, trans. D. M. H. Stalker [London: SCM, 1969], 97). It is difficult to document from the OT clear instances, however, where the act of anointing was used for the prophetic vocation. Psalm 105:15, speaking of the patriarchs as "anointed" and as "prophets," suggests this connection, but the phrase, "my anointed ones," may denote a royal standing of the patriarchs as well. The Spirit entering or falling upon a prophet (Ezek 2:2; 11:5) or passing from one person to another (1 Kgs 19:16) is not the same as the anointing of the king. The royal anointing is a vocational, inaugurational, and empowering event that is acknowledged as such by the community. The anointing of the servant, therefore, cannot be understood as only prophetic; royal status is clearly intended.

is derived from and dependent upon Yahweh's kingship. As Philip Harner has shown, Yahweh's self-identification, "I Am the Lord," occurring thirty times in Second Isaiah, resembles the self-identification of kings in the ancient Near East.[29] Third, Yahweh reigns in Zion (40:9; 52:7–10). From Yahweh's reign in Zion the gospel of peace and salvation streams forth to the ends of the earth.[30] Further, when it is recalled that the Targum translated both " 'Behold your God' " in Isa 40:9 and " 'Your God reigns' " in Isa 52:7 as " 'The kingdom of your God is revealed,' "[31] the OT royalty tradition is clearly present in Isaiah 40–55.

Although this study has referred to the Synoptics' structure as Galilee-Jerusalem, for Matthew and Mark it is Galilee-Jerusalem-Galilee. The final scene in Galilee, anticipated by Mark and actualized by Matthew, climaxes the royalty theme. It no longer is linked to human kingship but identifies Jesus' mission clearly with the Lord God's kingship, heralding the gospel of salvation to all nations. The same theological point holds for Luke, but his narrative makes the point by linking together the gospel-as-verb (εὐαγγελίζω) with peace (εἰρήνη) and the spread of the kingdom from Jerusalem to Rome. What Matthew and Mark achieve symbolically in the return to "Galilee," Luke narrates as story in a second volume. Both patterns consummate the Isaianic vision in and through Jesus, risen Son of God: "The Lord God reigns!"

EXPLAINING THE ORIGIN AND FUNCTION
OF THE SYNOPTIC DESIGN

While it is beyond the scope of this study to undertake investigation into the vast array of primary Jewish and Greco-Roman literature that might provide clues to the meaning of this literary

---

[29]P. B. Harner, *Grace and Law in Second Isaiah: "I Am the Lord"* (ANETS 2; Lewiston, N.Y./Queenston, Ont.: Edwin Mellen, 1988).

[30]This theme permeates Isa 40–55: 40:5; 42:1–6; 49:1–6; 51:4–5; 52:7–10. Even Cyrus is anointed by the Lord to assist in restoring Zion, but ultimately so that through Israel God's name might be known from the rising to the setting of the sun (44:28–45:6). Richard Hays's exegesis of Romans shows a parallel thought structure in Paul's use of Israel's Scripture, i.e., allusion to Isa 51:4–5 in Rom 1:16–17 and especially the catena of scripture citations in Rom 15:7–13 (Ps 18:50; Deut 32:43; Ps 117:1; Isa 11:10) to show God's purpose to include Gentiles (Hays, *Echoes of Scripture*, 58–62, 112–18).

[31]See B. Chilton, "REGNUM DEI," 103. See also p. 82 n. 96.

design in its contemporary world, several considerations merit mention here and further analysis in subsequent studies.

1. Contemporary Jewish and Jewish Christian Literature

While this study has resisted the common method of seeking to establish validity of insight by citing parallel phenomena from other earlier or contemporary sources—because such would compete with a narrative-compositional methodology—it is useful to consider some similar literary phenomena in roughly contemporary documents. In a general way the echoes of Israel's major faith traditions in OT apocryphal and pseudepigraphal, rabbinic, and other New Testament literature are commonplace. Unless such show some elements akin to the structure or themes observed in this study, they lie outside the scope of significance here.

But several merit notice. The second-century B.C. recital of Israel's history in *Sirach* includes each of the four major faith traditions present in the Synoptics: Moses – exodus, Joshua – land conquest, David and Solomon – kingship and temple (chs. 45–47). Similarly, The *Testament (Assumption) of Moses*, written in the first century A.D., contemporary to the Synoptics, recites Israel's history in such a way as to include each of these main faith traditions: exodus (ch. 1); land, leaders, and princes (2:1–3); building of the temple, its misuse through idolatry, and its fall (2:4–3:1); and after long times of oppression by the nations the appearance of a heavenly ruler and kingdom (ch. 10).[32] Similarly, another first-century writing, *Pseudo-Philo*, includes the themes of exodus and law (chs. 9–10), division of the land (20:1–10), and kingship in Saul and David (chs. 56–59). Exodus and kingship traditions also permeate the Gospel of John (see Appendix I). The sermons in Acts 7 and 13:16b–23 include these themes also (though ch. 7 mutes kingship by using only the phrase "the time of David"; ch. 13 lacks reference to the temple). In lesser ways, these features of similarity and parallelism are ubiquitous,[33] but they cannot be adduced to explain the Synoptic phenomenon which consists of a specific structural framework by which these traditions are utilized: Galilee, journey, Jerusalem. Indeed the evidence from these

---

[32]Charlesworth, *OTP* 1.927–32.

[33]See esp. H.-R. Weber's stimulating study, *Power: Focus for a Biblical Theology* (Geneva: WCC Publications, 1989) in which he shows how six OT faith traditions punctuate NT writings generally. In addition to the four of this study, he includes *wisdom* and *the poor*.

sources establishes beyond all doubt that Jewish faith-memories accented the four traditions noted in our study. But there are also crucial differences in the way these traditions are cited and utilized. Except for John and Acts, each of these sources recites only these particular features from the older story, but with no messianic fulfillment. Thus, while these parallels cannot be adduced to establish literary dependence or use by the Synoptics,[34] they do attest to the fact that this type of faith reflection and hermeneutical process was in the air, part of the *Zeitgeist.*

To analyze thoroughly these differences and similarities in this and other literature (see Josephus as well)[35] requires another study and volume. Further, the thesis of this study assumes a Synoptic structural distinctiveness, indeed uniqueness, in which Israel's faith traditions were correlated with a distinctive structure: Galilee, journey, Jerusalem, and return to Galilee in Matthew and Mark. None of these comparative uses of Israel's faith traditions shows such a feature.

2. The Liturgical Influence of Israel's Festivals

The four major streams of tradition that have informed this study are also rooted in Israel's festal celebrations. The four synoptic sections can be correlated, to a significant degree, with Israel's annual feasts, as follows:

Passover in Nisan	Galilean Section
Feast of Firstfruits	Jesus makes Twelve (Mark 3:13ff.)
Law/Pentecost	Sermon on Mount (Matt 5–7/Luke 6)
Tabernacles in Tishri	Wilderness Feedings
New Year and	Journey of Way-Conquest with
Day of Atonement	Passion Predictions/Transfiguration
Feast of Dedication	Temple Section
Lead-up to Passover	Kingship in Passion and
and Coronation of King	Resurrection Narrative
in religious New Year	

---

[34]See n. 3 above.

[35]Though Josephus' first eleven books in *Ant.* recount the history of Israel from creation to exile, they do not manifest the selection of events and themes noted in this study. The τέλος of his narrative is the Jewish revolt, not the messianic fulfillment.

The correlation of the annual feasts with the Torah and Haftarah readings is a key point in Goulder's proposal (see ch. 2). This argues for an annual cycle of readings, as opposed to the triennial cycle proposed earlier by Büchler.[36] Both the *Jewish Encyclopedia* (1901–6) and *Encyclopedia Judaica* (1971) hold to Büchler's triennial proposal, though the latter states that in Babylon an annual cycle (Tishri to Tishri) was followed in the first century.[37] Both Goulder's thesis and the Synoptics' structure, however, argue for an annual cycle, beginning in Nisan.[38]

The second strand of collaborative evidence from this study for the lectionary thesis is the design of the Lukan journey narrative. By accepting a textual parallel between Luke's journey narrative and Deuteronomy, this study supports Goulder's lectionary schedule of Torah and Lukan readings for the months Tebeth, week 2, through Shebat and Adar (middle December through February).

How shall this matter be assessed? It was not the aim of this study to vindicate the lectionary theory as the basis of the Synoptics' origins,[39] nor is it here the aim to deny that possibility. The prominence of these four major traditions in Israel's worship book, the Psalms (especially exodus and kingship; see also the recitals in Pss 78, 135, 136) should alert us to consider similar purposes for the Gospels,

---

[36] A. Büchler, "The Reading of the Law and the Prophets in a Triennial Cycle," *JQR* 5 (1893), 420–68, 6 (1894), 1–73. See Goulder, *Calendar*, notes on pp. 20–21 for literature assessing this and other theories.

[37] Since the twelfth century the annual cycle has been universally accepted by Judaism (*EncylJud*, 1971, 15.1386).

[38] Goulder, *Calendar*, regards Mark as only a half year lectionary; hence its early unpopularity. But as P. Carrington has shown, the earliest extant MS evidence we have for any lectionary is Vaticanus (Codex B, fourth century) for the Gospel of Mark, for forty-eight readings (*The Primitive Christian Calendar* [Cambridge: Cambridge University, 1952] and *According to Mark* [Cambridge: Cambridge University, 1960]. For several objections to Carrington, see Swartley, "Markan Structure," 216, n. 23, and C. T. Ruddick, "Behold, I Send My Messenger," *JBL* 88 [1969], 381–417). The correlation between the festivals and the Synoptic structure is clearer, in my judgment, in Mark than in either Matthew and Luke (Swartley, "Markan Structure," 217ff., though both Drury (*Tradition*, p. 141) and Goulder (*Calendar*, pp. x, 21–35, 49) have suggested a correlation between Matthew's five discourses and Israel's five annual festivals).

[39] Having arrived at this point, one cannot avoid the suggestion that if there is anything to the lectionary theory, the reason for *three* Synoptic Gospels may be seen in a new light. Scholars agree that the triennial cycle was followed in the east, Palestine, and Egypt, in first-century Judaism. It is a small step of logic to see the need for *three* Gospels; one for each year in the triennial cycle.

especially when the structure of Israel's confessions appears, as shown above, in the Synoptics' structure. Also, one of the earliest texts witnessing to the presence of all four themes is the Song of Moses (Exod 15). Further, as Kapelrud and others have shown,[40] the Psalms, and the cultic life of Israel generally, were the "melting pot" of the diverse histories of north and south and the traditions of faith arising from those histories and communities. In light of this study's evidence that four of Israel's major streams of tradition shaped the Synoptics and the appearance of these traditions in Israel's festivals and Psalmic worship, it is difficult to resist the conclusion that the origins of the Synoptic Gospels are to be linked at least to the lection and worship needs of the early church.

To propose a lectionary theory, however, whether Goulder's or Carrington's, goes considerably beyond the evidence. Moreover, to explain the origin of the Synoptic Gospels as solely for lection purposes does not account sufficiently for the theological and apologetic features so predominantly present. Certainly, the Gospels were written to serve the needs of the church, but not all those needs were lectional or liturgical in nature. Structuring Jesus' story around Israel's major faith-traditions could serve apologetic purposes as well.[41] While we might regard the apologetic and lectional or liturgical functions as competing explanations, the blending of the two may be one of the genial accomplishments of the gospel tradition, evidenced especially by the Synoptics' replete use of the psalms. For in the Synoptics' use of Psalms 2, 22, 31, 110, 118, Jesus' person and work are vindicated by Israel's traditions, but linked also at the same time with the language of praise and outcry to God. Further, it is virtually certain that the Gospel writers expected these books to be read in the gathered congregations, for both instruction and worship.

Hence, the early Jewish Christian festal celebrations and the writing of literature that could be read in congregational settings converge as two interrelated forces that lead to the conclusion that the distinctive structure of the Synoptics supports a lection—and perhaps lectionary—function as *one* motivating factor in the production of the Synoptic Gospels. For there appears to be some evidence that the Synoptic writers wished to tell the story of Jesus in such a way as to

---

[40]See ch. 2, pp. 33–37.

[41]See, e.g., Barnabas Lindars's view, held quite widely by scholars, that the purpose of providing apologetic for Christian beliefs from Israel's Scriptures was a primary motivation in the writing of the Gospels (Lindars, *New Testament Apologetic*, esp. 285–86).

correlate its plot development with the cycle of festivals, thereby providing Christian readings to extend the celebrations of Israel's faith.

3. Other Factors Motivating the Origin of the Synoptic Gospels

The contributions of C. H. Dodd, Barnabas Lindars, and Donald Juel in showing specific lines of OT influence upon the Synoptics may be viewed as complementary to the work of Nils Dahl (see ch. 2). On the one hand, the Synoptic writers utilized the OT to express early Christian self-understanding of its identity (Dahl and Juel), but at the same time they used the Scripture also for both apologetic and missional purposes (Lindars). Identity, apologetic, and mission converge (this is implicit in Dodd's contribution). This study's findings support these views, complementing the contributions of these writers.

The utilization of Israel's faith traditions in the shaping of the Synoptics' structure and theology witnesses directly to the distinctive identity of the early Christians. They saw themselves as heirs to God's salvation activity for and through Israel. The Gospels portray Jesus as God's true Son and Righteous Sufferer. Jesus' disciples, whom Matthew identifies as the church, are co-heirs of Israel's sonship and vocational mission through their following of Jesus and their continuation of his story (the Gospels' endings and Acts). Jesus' story is told within the structure and language of Israel's faith story. Israel's story shapes Jesus' story, as presented in the Synoptics. Indeed, the OT is a precondition for the Synoptics' story of Jesus.

The story of Jesus, because of its distinctive nature as fulfillment of God's covenant promises to Israel, carries intrinsically the dimensions of mission and apologetic. In each Gospel (including John) the mission of Jesus embraces the Gentiles. In Mark this is accomplished by sea crossings and the events that occur on the east side (especially the exorcism of the Gerasene with the command in 5:19 and the feeding of the 4,000) and the ἔθνη emphasis in chapters 11–15. In Matthew it is accomplished by the presence of Gentiles in the crowds, their choric refrain of praise, and the concluding Great Commission to all ἔθνη. In Luke the narrative breathes both universalism ("all flesh") and inclusion of the socially marginalized (especially in many parables), prefiguring the inclusion of Gentiles into the church in Acts (cf. John 12:20–23 where the arrival of the Greeks to see Jesus triggers the "coming of Jesus' hour").

Because the story of Jesus is thus toned so thoroughly with mission, the character of the apologetic is two-sided. On the one side, the Synoptics often use the OT to vindicate Jesus and his followers against exclusive Jewish claims. The narrative is toned by controversy with Jewish leaders, and these leaders are the antagonists of the narrative plot. They connive, plot, trap, and arrest Jesus; they cry for his crucifixion. Similarly, many parables vindicate the rights of the religiously marginal or outsiders to God's grace and blessing. These permeating emphases *defend* Jesus, his followers, and the Christian communities of faith against Judaism's exclusivity and refusal to acknowledge Jesus as the Messiah. Hence the strong language of judgment upon the Jewish leaders in the Gospels. The Synoptics put Judaism in deep tension with Jesus as Messiah, who not only completes a mission defined as one of restoring Israel but who presents liberation, conquest, mediation of the sacred, and kingship in non-exclusive, universal dimensions and claims.

From the other side, the story is presented as an apologetic for the Gentiles. In this mode it portrays Jesus as bringer of God's kingdom and salvation for all people. As such it is the *confession* side of apologetic, epitomized by the word of the soldier at the cross. In the narrative Gentiles are regularly portrayed as those receptive to Jesus' gospel,[42] and thus are models for reader-identification.[43]

Arising from this side of the apologetic nature of the Synoptics, another significant factor must be considered among those claiming a place in the origin of the Synoptic Gospels. To what extent do these Gospels utilize genre and literary techniques especially appropriate and appealing to the Greco-Roman world? Numerous scholarly proposals have been advanced to identify the Gospels with existing types of Greco-Roman literary genre (contra Bultmann who argued for distinctiveness in genre on the basis that the Gospel was an expansion of the early Christian kerygma calling for its own form). In view of the culminating role of Jesus' kingship in each Synoptic narrative, Talbert's proposal that the Synoptic Gospels resemble the Greek biographical genre gains credence, since one type in this genre (his Type B) serves the function of dispelling false images of the leader, a ruler, or philosopher, and setting forth an accurate portrayal.[44] However, Talbert classifies Luke and Matthew as different types of the biographical genre. He regards Luke–Acts as the type (his D) that locates the source and nature of the true tradition rooted in

---

[42]Though Mark 10:42 might be seen as an exception of significant proportion, the accent here falls on *kings* of the Gentiles, not Gentiles *per se*.

[43]This is true of most women in the narrative. See pp. 213–14, n. 47.

[44]C. H. Talbert, *What Is a Gospel? The Genre of the Canonical Gospels* (Philadelphia: Fortress, 1977), 77–79, 133–34.

the life of the founder and shows it carried forward by his successors, while Matthew represents his Type E which legitimates the founder's teaching-legislation and provides "a hermeneutical key to its meaning."[45] While this study has observed elements in all three Gospels that relate to these respective emphases, the essential character of the Gospels is not biography, but a story that is shaped by Israel's faith traditions. The dimensions of festal celebration, lection readings, and two-sided apologetic put a strain on the thesis of biography (*bios*) genre,[46] though Burridge argues anew, on the basis of numerous generic features, for this view.[47]

Some recent and specific Gospel studies propose other connections between the Greco-Roman literary genres and the Synoptics.[48] Refining Talbert's study of the *bios* type, Shuler has proposed that Matthew fits the biographical type intended to praise or persuade. He regards Matthew as an "encomium biography" in that it employs τόποι, techniques, and purposes that correspond to hellenistic encomiums.[49] Tolbert's effort to find a genre home for Mark in the hellenistic literature proposes that it is closest to the "historical/biographical type of ancient novel."[50] Unfortunately, since this novel type is not extant—only the erotic type exists—it is impossible to postulate that Mark belongs to this genre, though Tolbert has convincingly shown numerous parallel features. Equally persuasive, Bilezikian has demonstrated many parallel narrative features between Mark and Greek tragedies, arguing that while Mark did not intend to write a Greek tragedy, his story contains many features that would

---

[45]Talbert, *Genre*, 134.

[46]For other critical issues see P. L. Shuler, *A Genre for the Gospels: The Biographical Character of Matthew* (Philadelphia: Fortress, 1982), 21–22.

[47]R. A. Burridge, *What Are the Gospels? A Comparison with Greco-Roman Biography* (SNTSMS 70; Cambridge: Cambridge University, 1992), esp. 191–219.

[48]For an overall survey see D. Dormeyer and H. Frankemölle, "Evangelium als literarische Gattung und als theologischer Begriff . . . ," *ANRW* II.25.2; ed. W. Haase (Berlin/New York: W. de Gruyter, 1984), 1543–1704, and D. L. Tiede, "Religious Propaganda and the Gospel Literature of the Early Christian Mission," *ANRW* II, 25, 2, (idem), 1705–29.

[49]Shuler, *Biographical Character*, 92–109.

[50]Tolbert, *Sowing*, 63–65. D. R. Edwards identifies similarities in social function, i.e., how marginal people cope and flourish when caught in a 'web of power,' between Acts and the Roman Chariton's historical romance ("Acts of the Apostles and the Greco-Roman World: Narrative Communication in Social Contexts," *SBL 1989 Seminar Papers* (Atlanta: Scholars, 1989), 362–77. Here the connection is on function, not genre per se.

make it appealing to readers of Greek tragedy.[51] For Luke, several recent proposals have argued for classifying it as Greco-Roman history, given the crucial distinction between the nature of ancient history and modern critical history. Sterling identifies Luke–Acts as apologetic history, akin to Josephus's *History* and earlier Hellenistic Jewish historians (Demetrius, Artapanus, an anonymous Samaritan, and Eupolemus). This type of history matches in content, form and function what we find in Luke.[52] Balch identifies similarities between Luke–Acts and the Roman Dionysius' political history in which stories are narrated for rhetorical effect in accord with political function. Both writers "narrate history in three epochs: ancestors, Founder(s), and successors."[53]

While these analyses suggest some significant analogies,[54] as do Robbins's contributions on rhetorical techniques,[55] Sigal's perceptions on this topic are most apropos. After noting the variety of genres represented in the Gospels themselves and their likely dependence on OT models, especially Deuteronomy—"which includes history, biography, a lack of exact chronology, anecdotes, teachings, vicissitudes of the hero (Moses) and his mysterious departure"—and the Elijah-Elisha cycle of stories, Sigal rightly argues against the notion that the Gospels should be regarded as aretalogies[56] and says that though they contain fragments of liturgy they "were not seen as liturgies, such as aretalogies were designed to be," but they were rather teaching media. "Like the Old Testament, the Gospels were included in worship celebrations as lection readings but were not in themselves considered " 'liturgies.' "[57] Sigal then identifies the Gospel content and function

---

[51]On this, see G. Bilezikian, *The Liberated Gospel: A Comparison of the Gospel of Mark and Greek Tragedy* (Grand Rapids: Baker, 1977), esp. 100–109.

[52]G. F. Sterling, "Luke–Acts and Apologetic History," *SBL 1989 Seminar Papers* (Atlanta: Scholars, 1989), 332–42.

[53]D. L. Balch, "Comments on the Genre and a Political Theme of Luke–Acts: A Preliminary Comparison of Two Hellenistic Historians," *SBL 1989 Seminar Papers* (Atlanta: Scholars, 1989), 360.

[54]C. B. Puskas provocatively argues that Mark and John resemble the Greco-Roman tragic drama; Matthew, biography; and Luke, history (*An Introduction to the New Testament* [Peabody, Mass.: Hendrickson, 1989], 109–38). For scholarly literature on these three genres, see notes on pages 4, 16, 27.

[55]Robbins, *Jesus the Teacher.*

[56]So M. Hadas and M. Smith, *Heroes and Gods* (New York: Harper & Row, 1965).

[57]P. Sigal, "Manifestations of Hellenistic Historiography in Select Judaic Literature," *SBL 1984 Seminar Papers* (Chico, Calif.: Scholars, 1984), 176–77. Similarly, R. Pervo calls attention to Greek Bible precedents for history

with the designation of Papias and Justin as "memoirs" or "remembrances"; these were of both theological and biographical nature patterned after OT models and functioned as lections for biographical and historical recall, but were not lectionaries.

These notions appear to be along the right lines, though this study would privilege the faith-confessional function and the missional apologetic functions over that of historical recall per se. This is not to argue for Bultmann's kerygmatic thesis for Gospel origins, but to characterize the function even more broadly in confessional terms, enumerated in part 2 above.

4. John Mark's Role and the Ethnic Composition of the Early Christian Churches

Although this study did not assume Markan priority, the manner in which each Gospel treats the common structural pattern and the symbolic roles of Galilee and Jerusalem raises anew whether Mark is the creator of the synoptic design in its literary form. This is not to deny preMarkan oral precursors or even sections of this design in preMarkan literary form. But for either we can tender only hypotheses.

Despite scholarly skepticism that the John Mark named in Acts is the author of the second Gospel, this is still the most plausible view, in my judgment. John Mark's role in the church's early history uniquely qualifies him for this task of producing the first Gospel. Four converging considerations support this view.

a. Mark's distinctive use of the word "gospel" (εὐαγγέλιον) in its noun form shows affinity to Paul's use of the same term in his letters, undoubtedly reflective of Paul's missionary preaching, in which John Mark likely assisted as the official ὑπηρέτης on the first missionary journey (Acts 13:5–13). The connections between Paul's use of εὐαγγέλιον/εὐαγγελίζομαι and Mark's (and Luke's) use are argued persuasively by Peter Stuhlmacher.[58] Further, Stuhlmacher demonstrates that the roots of this use by NT writers are to be found in several key OT texts, namely Isaiah 52:7 and 61:1–3, passages which,

---

in Acts: 1–4 Kgdms., 1–2 Esd., 1–2 Macc. ("Must Luke and Acts Belong to the Same Genre?," *SBL 1989 Seminar Papers* [Atlanta: Scholars, 1989], 315).

[58] *Das paulinische Evangelium, I. Vorgeschichte* (Göttingen: Vandenhoeck & Ruprecht, 1968), esp. 234–44. See also Stuhlmacher's two essays in *The Gospel and the Gospels*, ed. idem (Grand Rapids: Eerdmans, 1991), 1–25 and 149–74.

from another dimension of consideration, contributed evidence for the thesis of this study.

b. John Mark is a crucial link between Peter's and Paul's leadership roles in the early church. Trained by Peter to be an official oral reciter[59] of the traditions of Jesus,[60] he accompanies Barnabas and Paul on the first missionary journey as a certified ὑπηρέτης to recount the teachings and deeds of Jesus in the synagogues where the missionary team goes. John Mark's leaving at Pamphylia to return home is a major loss for Paul and Barnabas since it cuts the mission team's ties to the Jerusalem church, and thus its historical continuity to Jesus of Nazareth. Mark's "desertion" is for theological reasons, to keep the support for the Jerusalem church behind Paul's missionary work as he moves into the Gentile world and, in keeping with his vocational call, invites Gentiles into the faith community as Gentiles. The resultant Jerusalem conference is related to Mark's effort to keep Peter and Paul united in mission to the Gentiles. The unity of these two leaders in this mission is attested further in Acts by the prior position of Paul's call (ch. 9), on the one hand, and the priority of Peter's action (chs. 10–11), on the other hand. The notion that John Mark composed his Gospel in the joint service of Peter, whose witness

---

[59]Cf. here B. Gerhardsson's essay, "The Path of the Gospel Tradition," in *The Gospel and the Gospels*, ed. P. Stuhlmacher (Grand Rapids: Eerdmans, 1991), 75–96, for the role of oral tradition and recognized transmitters in the community. See also his earlier *Memory and Manuscript* (Lund: C. W. K. Gleerup, Uppsala, 1961), 108–19, 243–44, and H. Riesenfeld, *The Gospel Tradition* (Philadelphia: Fortress, 1970), 16–19, 54–55. See Luke's pairing of the term ὑπηρέται with "eyewitness" in Luke 1:2.

[60]Here I agree with M. Hengel in assigning the Papias traditions significant value in considering John Mark to be the author of the Gospel. Hengel makes a strong case for Mark's dependence on Peter, contending that earlier objections to this view are no longer persuasive ("Literary, Theological, and Historical Problems in the Gospel of Mark," in *The Gospel and the Gospels*, ed. P. Stuhlmacher, 202–51, esp. 232–46). Hengel also addresses the issue of the origin of Mark's use of the term εὐαγγελίζω, since the term is not associated with Peter in the speeches in Acts. Even though Hengel concedes that the use of εὐαγγέλιον in Mark 13:10 and 14:9 have a Pauline-sounding ring, he proposes that Mark's use of the term is derived from a general tradition which regarded the great events of exodus and reception of the law at Mt. Sinai as saving events, i.e., gospel (247–49). The proper solution to this conundrum, in my judgment, is to combine the theses of Stuhlmacher and Hengel and posit John Mark's significant dependence on both Peter and Paul. It is precisely this unique, and vulnerable, dual affiliation that theologically and vocationally qualifies him to write the first Gospel and thus lay the foundation for the invaluable contribution of the Synoptics.

to Jesus he interpreted as a Gospel ὑπηρέτης, and Paul, whose call to take the gospel to the nations he also shared, explains early Christian origins, perhaps including Coptic traditions (Acts 15:39—Cyprus was possibly the first stop of a larger journey to Egypt). Paul's later valuing of John Mark (Col 4:11; 2 Tim 4:11) as well as Peter's mention of him as his dear son (1 Pet 5:13) shows early traditional support for linking John Mark to both Paul and Peter. Paul's touchiness about Peter's authority (Gal 1:15—2:14) explains his stubbornness in not wanting to take along John Mark as the ὑπηρέτης on his second journey (Acts 15:38–39).

c. John Mark is present at crucial moments in the gospel story historically, not only at the time of Paul's first journey, but even earlier: as witness to the gatherings of the apostles and wider circle of disciples in his mother Mary's home (Acts 12:12). If this meeting place is the same as the "upper room" of Acts 1:14 and the location of the Last Supper in the Synoptics, then John Mark is a primary witness to early church history in Jerusalem over the period of 29–45 A.D.,[61] spanning Jesus' own last days in Jerusalem and the birth of the early Christian community.[62]

d. John Mark is considered to have strong roots in the Jewish faith, like other devout Israelites of Jerusalem, and to have been nurtured in its traditions. Thus he shared with the apostles and Jesus himself an understanding that appealed in fundamental ways to Jewish faith to explicate the story of Jesus. Further, Hengel is likely correct in saying that "Mark was a Greek-speaking Jewish Christian who also understood Aramaic."[63] Moreover, Mark's early theological orientation was likely similar to Paul's, in that he was a "Hebrew of the Hebrews." [64] But Mark also underwent "conversion" on this matter so

---

[61] It is also possible that John Mark was the young man in Mark 14:13 who carried the jug of water on his head and who prepared the upper room, the young man in the garden who ran away naked (14:50–51), and even the young man in the tomb on Easter morning (16:5). The latter two points are stronger on the basis of narrative analysis than is the former one, though the former is more historically plausible, especially in light of continuity with the story in Acts 1:14 and 12:12. See my consideration of these matters in *Mark*, 34–36 and notes 6–8 on pp. 214–15.

[62] Counting against this reconstruction is the fact that Luke wrote the Acts narrative, and not Mark. But indeed, Luke has not only a historical account in view, but also a rich interplay of theological, ecclesial, and missional purposes in composing the Acts narrative.

[63] Hengel, "Problems in the Gospel of Mark," 230.

[64] J. H. Farmer, "Mark," *ISBE*, 2d ed., 3.1987.

that his gospel story of Jesus challenges Judaism in fundamental ways, for its messianic claims for Jesus invite Gentiles to be co-heirs of the covenant blessings consummated in Jesus' own covenant making (Mark 14:26–30; 13:10; 15:39).

Not only is it essential to rethink John Mark's role in the origin of the Synoptic Gospels and their structural design, but the question of the ethnic composition of the early churches merits attention as well. If the above theses are valid, it is dubious that the first communities of hearers (or readers) of either of the first three Gospels were predominantly Gentile. Each of the three Gospels must have been written to churches that were predominantly composed of Jewish Christians located in the Hellenistic world and culture. Explanations of Aramaic words regarding Jewish customs are one face of this reality—the presence of Gentile hearers. But the many scriptural citations, allusions, and echoes from the Hebrew Scriptures, as demonstrated by this study, witness to the other face of compositional reality—that the Hellenistic Jewish Christians constituted a significant core of those early Christian communities. Indeed, in the Gospels, the Gentiles sit at Abraham's table! They learn, treasure, and communicate the story of Jesus in categories of faith that are inherently Jewish. In this respect, Israel's story of faith and the Gospel's story of Jesus are inseparable, for Israel and Jesus are one story of God's salvation for all people.

SUMMARY: THE SYNOPTICS' DISTINCTIVE ACHIEVEMENT

Nurtured on the traditions of the Hebrew Scriptures, the early followers of Jesus first perceived and then narrated the story of Jesus' life and work in a structure that echoed and reflected major streams of Israel's traditions: exodus-Sinai, way-conquest, temple, and kingship. Quite naturally, but not unreflectively, the new story, in deference to the older story with its northern and southern components, developed around the dual axis of Galilee and Jerusalem. This distinctive feature of the Synoptics' story of Jesus witnesses to both continuity with and significant transformation in Israel's major faith traditions.

In at least three fundamental dimensions the Synoptics represent a distinctive literary and theological achievement.

1. *Form.* Even though the first three canonical Gospels cannot be regarded as exactly the same in genre and form, since the three authors denote the narratives differently—Mark an εὐαγγέλιον, Mat-

thew a βίβλος, and Luke a διηγήσις—the common structural design and reflection of OT faith traditions manifest a truly distinctive literary genre. The numerous attempts to identify the genre of these books by comparison to Jewish or hellenistic prototypes have been severely stymied by the diversity of proposals. Even more significantly, none comes to grips with the several distinctive features that this study brings into focus. Of these numerous features, two are substantial. The patterning of the essentially *new* Jesus story in accord with the structure, motifs, and themes of Israel's earlier faith story finds no parallel in other literature. Second, the symbolic narrative role of Galilee, with all its theological and missional import, is of such a nature as to set it off completely from other writings. While John's Gospel attests to this latter feature in part, it nonetheless consists of a completely different structure. Further, the noncanonical Gospels are lacking on both counts (see Appendix I).

2. *Transformation of Traditions.* We have observed major transformations in Israel's exodus, way-conquest, temple, and kingship traditions as they served the synoptic structure and its narration in three Gospels, thus producing this distinctive synoptic form of comprehending and communicating the story of Jesus. What we have witnessed is what Childs has called a "massive construal" effected by the New Testament's use of tradition: "At the heart of the process lay a dialectical move in which the tradents of the developing New Testament were themselves being shaped by the content of the material which they in turn were transmitting, selecting, and forming into a scriptural norm."[65]

Drawn by his respondents into the issue of how OT Scripture affected the formation of the NT, Childs suggests an answer similar to that proposed by this study: "the synagogue liturgy of the daily services and the special festivals in which large portions of Scripture were read" were significant factors bearing upon the NT use of OT Scripture. Further, both Jews and Christians had a "wholistic understanding of the canonical collection."[66]

This view explains two factors important to the shaping of the synoptic structure. First, the four streams of tradition are present wholistically, in basic conception and theological significance. They are utilized not woodenly but at the deep subconscious—though not unconscious—level of ritual and, to a significant extent, by the inten-

---

[65]Childs, *Canon*, 21.
[66]B. S. Childs, "A Response," *HBT* 2 (1980), 203.

tion of the authors as well.[67] In this way the older story provides categories of thought by which the new story can be grasped and communicated. Functioning in such a way as to provide a shaping *gestalt* for the story of Jesus, the specific original referents of the traditions in the older story give way to new referents and appropriations. Both contextualization and transformation occur. Second, to varying degrees the authors/narrators cite specific OT texts to document the authority of the tradition.[68] The tradition lives by the Scripture, and citation therefrom conveys authoritative word in the presentation of the narrative.[69] On both levels, in the wholistic grasp dependent upon large sections of canonical testimony and in specific citations, the Synoptics narrate a new story with the words of the OT witness, drawn from Scripture and the traditions which Scripture nourishes, from generation to generation.[70]

3. *Function in early church.* This study proposes that the origin and purpose of the Synoptic Gospels relate to four dimensions of life: transformation of the traditions by which the early church understood itself; lections for reading in the communities of faith, thus serving the nurturing and worshipping needs of believers; an apology of defense against Jewish exclusivist claims regarding covenant peoplehood; and a confessional apology that opened the door of God's kingdom salvation through Jesus to all nations.

---

[67]Both dimensions are at work here, though it is impossible to say where one, the subconscious, and the other, the conscious intention, begins. As R. Hays notes in comparing Paul's use of the OT with Hollander's tracing of intertextual echoes in English poetry, this phenomenon of intertextual echo in biblical literature is similar to that in other types of literature as well (*Echoes of Scripture*, 200, n. 75). See also his comments on the possibility of recovering authorial intention (201, n. 90).

[68]Though this study did not pursue the more usual task of examining specific OT quotations, it is striking that virtually all the OT quotations in the temple section are from the prophets whose writings interact with the temple reality in Israel. Similarly, the quotations in the passion narrative draw upon psalms associated with royalty. There are many fewer quotations in the Galilean and journey sections. While some of these come from the respective OT sections, as per this thesis, not all do.

[69]For Matthew, often as a prooftext, see Stendahl, *School of St. Matthew.*

[70]Note here a similar statement by Childs in discussing the NT's use of the OT: "Aber—und hier liegt der wichtigste Punkt—das Neue Testament erzählt seine neue Geschichte mit den Worten des alttestamentlichen Zeugnisses." In "Biblische Theologie und Christliche Kanon," *Jahrbuch für Biblische Theologie* 3 (1988), 22.

At this point reductionism is to be avoided. The complexity and multi–faceted character of the literature attests to numerous interacting and complementary purposes and functions. But this much is clear: clarifying identity, aiding worship and nurture, and serving an apologetic function in both defense and mission are essential factors in the Gospel-making, Gospel-using, and canon-preserving process.

Further, these functions instruct us today in our use of the Gospels. The life of believing communities can be evaluated against these emphases and Gospel functions. To illustrate: does the nurture and worship of a congregation utilize in its regular task of "equipping the saints" significant emphasis on liberation from bondages of all kinds, the gospel way of triumph over evil and sin, the inclusive mediation of the holy for its own life and for the world, and an understanding of royalty that knows the cross and thereby critiques all oppressive forms of power? Are the worship, nurture, and community life of Christian congregations faithful to and worthy of the crucified Messiah?

In short, does the Synoptic story of Jesus, shaped by an earlier faith story, exert formative influence upon the story of Jesus that we today proclaim, teach, and live? If so, we will transmit from generation to generation a most important biblical hermeneutical paradigm.

EPILOGUE

Let us live truly the Jesus story

    liberated from bondage and oppression
        freed

    to think and act as obedient followers on the way
        faithful

    through unhindered and unhindering worship
        fulfilled

    of the cross-formed royalty, God-in-Jesus exalted

Praise and glory be to God

APPENDIX I: THE BEARING OF THIS STUDY UPON JOHN'S GOSPEL AND THE NONCANONICAL GOSPELS

These remarks will focus on observations on John's Gospel and the noncanonical gospels from the viewpoint of accents and learnings derived from this study; they will not speak to questions of chronology in origins or interdependence.

JOHN

1. *Galilee and Jerusalem in John.* John's Gospel differs from the Synoptics in locating Jesus' ministry primarily in Jerusalem, with several excursions north into Galilee and, on one occasion, Samaria. The points of transition are:

To Galilee (1:43); Cana (2:1–11); Capernaum (2:12)

To Jerusalem (2:13)

Into Judea (Aenon, near Salim) (3:23)

To Galilee, through Samaria (4:3–4), arriving at Cana (4:46)

To Jerusalem (5:1)

In Galilee, by the Sea of Galilee (6:1); in Capernaum (6:59)

To Jerusalem (7:1–10)

Appearance in Galilee (ch. 21)

In chapters 7–20 Jesus' ministry is based in Jerusalem and surrounding villages, notably Bethany (11:1ff.: 12:1ff.), with a period of retreat across the Jordan where John first baptized (10:40). Though it is customary to speak of Jesus' journeys to Jerusalem, such language results from imposing the Synoptics' framework upon John. From the perspective of John's scheme, we should speak of Jesus' three journeys north. In each of these journeys, only one major event is noted: the wedding sign at Cana, healing the Capernaum official's son (see Matt 8:5–13; Luke 7:1–10), and the feeding of the 5,000 (with parr. in each Synoptic).

Both Sean Freyne in his recent study of Galilee in the Gospels and Wayne Meeks in his earlier study of Jesus as Prophet-King in John have advanced the view that Galilee carries positive symbolic meaning in John. This conclusion is based on the positive response of Galileans to Jesus' first miracle at Cana (2:11), the contrast in 4:43–45 between Judea/Jerusalem and Galilee in the receptivity of the people, the exemplary faith of the Capernaum centurion (4:46–54), the favorable response to the feeding miracle (6:14–15), and the narrative role of the Greeks from Bethsaida who seek out Jesus in Jerusalem (12:20–23).

However, as Freyne notes in his observations on the ensuing controversy in John 6 between Jesus and Galileans, the Jews in Galilee can be as unbelieving as those of Jerusalem (6:41ff.). Upon hearing his "hard saying," some Galilean disciples leave him (vv. 60, 66).[1] Conversely, many in Jerusalem also believe (2:23; cf. Nicodemus in ch. 3). Further, the most positive declarations of Jesus' identity come from people in Samaria (ch. 4) and Bethany (chs. 11–12). Hence, it is not possible to align only Galilee with positive response and Jerusalem with unbelieving negative response. But such a clean polarity does not exist in the Synoptics either. We need only recall the cycle of conflict stories (Mark 2:1–3:6 and parr.) and Jesus' rejection at Nazareth, which in Luke is a scene of hostility threatening Jesus' life. Nevertheless, the overall portrait in the Synoptics, and in John also, is one of Galilee showing greater receptivity and Jerusalem greater rejection, a hostility that leads to Jesus' death (see Luke 13:31–35).

Galileans are typified as sympathetic to Jesus in 7:52, where chief priests and Pharisees in Jerusalem make a "Galilean" insinuation against Nicodemus for suggesting that Jesus be given a hearing before speaking words of condemnation. The narrative portrays this as southern religious arrogance against Galileans, thus heightening the Jeru-

---

[1] On this matter I agree with Freyne, *Galilee*, 120–25. I underscore Freyne's concluding remark: "We saw that Galileans could in the author's view espouse a superficial attitude to Jesus' deeds that was as blinding to the true realities as was Pharisaic legalism" (132).

salem-Galilee polarity as an attitude of the respective peoples, at least
the south against the north. Meeks rightly focuses on 4:44–45 as the
strongest narrative evidence of contrast between the symbolic roles of
Judea/Jerusalem and Galilee. Here the saying, "a prophet has no
honor in the prophet's own country (ἐν τῇ πατρίδι)" must, in context,
refer to Jerusalem. As Meeks points out, "the πατρίς is not Jesus' *native*
land, but his *own* land."[2] While in his own land he is not received, he
is warmly welcomed in Galilee, his native land. John's use of "his own"
here likely connects back to the narrative theme of 1:11, "he came
unto his own (τὰ ἴδια), and his own (οἱ ἴδιοι) did not receive him."[3]
Meeks sum up the contrast well:

> The journeys to Jerusalem in John symbolize the coming of the re-
> deemer to "his own" and his rejection by them, while the emphasized
> movement from Judaea to Galilee (esp. 4:43–45) symbolizes the re-
> deemer's acceptance by others, who thereby become truly "children of
> God," the real Israel.[4]

Further, an inferred positive symbolism for Galilee arises
from the narrative role of Nathaniel, a Galilean who emerges as "an
Israelite in whom is no guile" (1:45; cf. 21:2). His confession that Jesus
is "the Son of God, the King of Israel" discloses true Christology
(1:49),[5] though even it must be supplemented by John's distinctive
view of Jesus as One with heavenly origin (1:50–51). Andrew's designation of Jesus as Messiah-Christ (1:41) also plays a supportive role
in this positive portrait of Galileans. But these narrative roles of
Nathaniel and Andrew are tenuous for ascribing a positive function
to Galilee in John; they are not denoted as Galileans by the narrative
in connection with their response, though such can be inferred.[6]

Two additional features should be cited in John's "typing" of
the narrative roles of Galilee and Jerusalem. First is the contrasting
portrait in chapter 2, which to a great extent plays out the Synoptics'
Galilee-Jerusalem theological significance. Galilee is the wedding locale, where the wine of the kingdom appears as divine creation and is

---

[2]Meeks, *Prophet-King,* 40.
[3]Ibid.
[4]Ibid., 41.
[5]It appears that John takes up where Mark ended in matters of
Christology. Mark's goal was to disclose Jesus' kingship as suffering, dying Son
of God (15:39). The suffering component comes later in John; it is not apparent
in ch. 1, except, perhaps by inference, in the title "Lamb of God" in 1:29.
[6]At the time of Andrew's confession of Jesus as One who must be the
Messiah, the narrative has not yet even located Jesus in Galilee (1:35–43).

served to the wedding guests; in contrast, Jerusalem is the locale of judgment upon distorted priorities of Jewish religion. Wedding time has come; the old institutions must be purified and reformed, or alternatively face their destruction. Little rationale is given for Jesus' bold actions so early in the narrative, thus heightening the symbolic role of each, and setting a tone for the later Galilee-Jerusalem depictions (4:44–54 esp.), even though the narrative notes that, as a consequence of both acts, many believed, both in Galilee and in Jerusalem.

The second important feature is the arrival of the Greeks, presumably from Bethsaida or its environs since they contact Philip, to see Jesus. This episode has more significance in the narrative than is normally given, for it "rings the alarm" on Jesus' "hour-clock," a most important narrative marker for John's Gospel (see 2:4; 7:6). Immediately when Jesus hears that Greeks, i.e., Gentiles, have come to see him, he exclaims, "The hour has come for the Son of humanity to be glorified" (12:23). From this moment onward the narrative sweeps to its denouement, the glorification of the Son of humanity by being lifted up onto the cross to draw all people to himself (12:32).

We have observed in our study of the Synoptics that the inclusion of Gentiles into the benefits of Jesus' messianic mission was an essential feature of the narrative. The same can be said for John, though his narrative technique for doing this is quite subtle and readily overlooked. But the jolting logic of the narrative should arrest even the sleepy reader's attention, not to speak of the ideal reader. When Jesus is told that the Gentiles are here to see him, he says, "Okay, the time is here," and pronto, he outlines in staccato fashion the events of the passion (note how subsequent uses of "the hour" now carry forward the passion narrative, in 13:1; 17:1). Quite clearly, John joins the Synoptics, but in his own unique narrative way, to declare that the gospel of Jesus is no gospel at all unless it is for everyone. The effect of this theological conviction and narrative technique is to highlight the positive role of Galilee in the narrative. But even more important, Galilee is cast positively because it is the place where Gentiles intermingle with Jews. Jesus' sole healing miracle located in Galilee was for a centurion's son, on behalf of a Gentile who had great faith. Hence, the positive significance of Galilee in John is due in great part to the fact that it is the land of Gentiles as well as Jews. The bearing of John's much used "whosoever" (actually πᾶς, meaning "all") on this point should not be missed.

2. *John's even deeper "typing."* While Galilee emerges in a positive narrative role, in contrast to Jerusalem, an even deeper and more theologically profound "typing" occurs in John. Those who

emerge in positive portrait are those who, regardless of their origin, confess Jesus' true identity, as One sent from above (1:49; 4:25, 29, 42; 11:27; 19:9). This oppositional polarity transcends that of Galilee and Jerusalem. While believers are not "typed" Galileans (except for the hint in 7:52), those who do not believe, and therefore become Jesus' opponents, are typified as "Jews" (Ἰουδαῖοι).[7]Meeks's discussion of the controversy in 7:40–52, whether the Christ can come from Galilee, points toward the true Johannine polarity: those who perceive that Jesus' true origin is from above versus those blinded from seeing that truth. This point transcends the Galilee-Bethlehem argument and the Christ-Prophet designations as well.[8] Hence, "the significant question is not whether Jesus is from Galilee or Judaea, but that he is from *God*."[9] Further, while the trial narrative heightens the intensity and irony of Jesus' kingship even over any of the Synoptics, Jesus is nowhere called χριστός, as in the Synoptics.[10] Nor is he called "King of Israel" in the trial narrative. The alleged identity of Jesus as "King of the Jews" is the pivotal movement in the dramatic action of the narrative,[11] culminating in the ironic exchange (18:39; 19:12, 14–16, 20–22):

Pilate: "Do you want me to release for you the King of the Jews?"

[Later]

The Jews: "everyone who claims to be a king sets himself against the emperor."

---

[7]Freyne rightly uses this word as contrasting to "Israelites, Judeans, and Galileans." Even Jesus' brothers fall finally on the side of the Ἰουδαῖοι; they do not appear at the cross, and are not given the care of Jesus' mother (*Galilee*, 131).

[8]In v. 41 the title "Christ" is distinguished from that of "Prophet," but in v. 52 they appear to be indirectly correlated as referring to one and the same. This point is significant in relation to Meeks's thesis that John portrays Jesus as Prophet-King, based on the correlation in 6:14–15. But he stresses the discontinuity between Christ and Prophet (using this 7:41 text), since he argues that "Christ" for John is subservient to kingship, a broader category of thought which can be based on different Jewish traditions, not necessarily Davidic messianic.

[9]Meeks, *Prophet-King*, 38.

[10]Ibid., 60, 81.

[11]The Jews' charge that Jesus called himself "Son of God" (19:7) really doesn't go anywhere in John's narrative. The Jewish trial mentions only questioning about his teaching (18:19); there is no accusation of blasphemy nor any temple charge. When handing Jesus over to Pilate, the Jews feebly explain that he does evil (κακὸν ποιῶν, 18:30).

Pilate: "Here is your King" . . . "Shall I crucify your King?"

The Jews: "We have no king but the emperor."

The chief priests to Pilate, about the title over the cross written in Hebrew, Latin, and Greek!:

"Do not write, 'The King of the Jews,' but, 'This man said, "I am King of the Jews." ' "

Pilate's answer: "What I have written I have written."

All this must be understood in light of 18:36ff., where Jesus answers Pilate's query about his alleged kingship of the Jews: "My kingship is not of this world; if my kingship were of this world, my servants would fight, that I might not be handed over to the Jews; but my kingship is not from the world" (RSV). Further, Jesus' next response continues the point, "You say that I am a king. For this I was born, and for this I came into the world, to testify to the truth."

This christological issue, the nature of Jesus' kingship,[12] emerges as the nexus of the belief-unbelief polarity developed throughout the Gospel. The narrative implores the reader to see what no one in the narrative said explicitly: Jesus' kingship is from God! Meeks correctly links this kingship with the prophet identification, as they are interconnected in 6:14–15, and thus stresses the distance John puts between kingship and the Davidic royalty identity, conveyed by Christ or Davidic lineage, a point unresolved in 7:42ff. But rather than conclude that *Christ* must be understood via analysis of Jesus' kingship, not vice versa,[13] it is more essential to say that all references to Jesus' royalty—"King of Israel" (1:49), Jesus as Prophet-King (6:14–15), Christ from Galilee or Bethlehem (7:41–52) or King of the Jews (trial narrative)—must be understood against the central opposition: from above or of this world (see 1:50–51; 3:3–12, 31; 6:33, 51; 8:42; 18:36–37). Meeks's own later work, "The Man From Heaven in Johannine Sectarianism," points in this direction.[14]

---

[12]For an excellent narrative analysis of this theme in the passion narrative and its theological significance see D. Hill, "My Kingdom Is Not of This World," *IrishBibStud* 9 (1987), 54–62; D. Rensburger, "Jesus' Kingship in John's Trial Narrative," *JBL* 103 (1984), 395–411 (appearing in similar form as ch. 5 in *Community and Liberation in John's Gospel* (Philadelphia: Westminster, 1988).

[13]Meeks, *Prophet-King*, 81.

[14]W. A. Meeks, "The Man from Heaven in Johannine Sectarianism," *JBL* 91 (1972), 44–72.

3. *John and the Synoptics.* The differences between John and the Synoptics are fundamental, as can now be seen and succinctly stated:

a. Though Galilee and Jerusalem carry similar theological significance, in their symbolic narrative roles, the Galilee-Jerusalem geographical pattern is quite different. The Johannine Gospel is not characterized by a distinct northern section that precedes a distinct southern section. John has nothing analogous to the extended journey narrative of Mark 8:27–10:52 and parallels. Rather, Jerusalem is the "center of the earth" in John, and Galilee is outlying territory, a conception quite different from that in the Synoptics. The symbolism of Galilee as the land of reception and Jerusalem as the locus of rejection is indeed present but is also transcended by the "true Israelite-Ἰουδαῖος" polarity. People from any land can belong to either side of the belief-unbelief polarity.

b. The fundamental polarity consists of an "above" versus a "below" christological conception. Kingship is to be understood not in the messianic tradition of Davidic royalty, but in a Mosaic Prophet-King model which insists that the manna comes from above, that Jesus' words and signs are those of a true prophet, sent from above. Hence, while exodus and royalty motifs permeate the Johannine narrative, they reflect a different orientation to Israel's traditions, drawing on portraits, as Meeks shows, from conceptual developments at home in Philo's, Josephus', rabbinic, Samaritan, and Mandean sources.[15] While the Synoptics locate Jesus' royal identity in Israel's earlier messianic traditions, John explicates Jesus' kingship via a later world of diverse Jewish traditions. John's theological goal, however, is akin to that of the Synoptics: to save Jesus' kingship from exclusivistic and nationalistic interpretations.

c. Unlike the Synoptics, John lacks any structural pattern of developing a sequential emphasis of exodus, journey-conquest, temple, and kingship traditions. John 6 and the passion narrative are the closest parallels. Jesus' cleansing of the temple is placed in chapter 2 and temple traditions play no role in the passion narrative.[16] Replac-

---

[15]Meeks, *Prophet-King,* 100–285.

[16]In John's report of Jesus' cleansing of the temple, Jesus makes the statement, "Destroy this temple and in three days I will raise it up" (2:19). Who destroys the temple? Here the subject is "you." In the Synoptics' report the alleged claim is that Jesus said *he* will destroy it. John's account makes clear his reference as "the temple of his body" (2:21). Hence, the cleansing and this saying do not form an ongoing temple polemic in John; they play no role in the charges at Jesus' trial.

ing the Synoptics' temple section is Jesus' "upper room" farewell discourse, a location and atmosphere of comparative triumph compared to controversies in the temple court. Here Jesus is already the comforter-teacher of the disciples, and the promised Holy Spirit will continue his role. Luke's pattern of tempering and qualifying Jesus' Davidic royalty by the prophet and Righteous One may be prototypically related to John's christological strategy,[17] but the differences are more impressive than the similarities. This similarity between Luke and John may suggest a christological trend, a trend that strongly affirms Jesus' kingship but shows its transcendence over and judgment upon earthly empires.

Summary. The distinctiveness of John's Gospel, in both its geographical structure and christological emphases, testifies to the theses of this study: that a major unique feature of the Synoptics' narrative(s) is one that correlates a unique Galilee-Jerusalem structure with its utilization of four of Israel's major streams of tradition (exodus-Sinai, way-conquest, temple, and kingship), in a basic sequential pattern, in order to explicate the nature of Jesus' work and the identity of his person.

THE NONCANONICAL GOSPELS

The purpose of these brief comments is not to take up an analysis of noncanonical gospels in any comparative way to the Synoptics, but simply to make a few observations about the differences between the Synoptics, emerging from this study, and the noncanonical gospels. Schneemelcher's classification of the noncanonical gospels into three types is helpful in relation to these remarks. His first type is those "closely connected with the canonical Gospels," showing dependence on a common tradition or the canonical Gospels. Among others (P. Oxyr. 840 and 2), he includes here the Jewish-Christian Gospels which are, unfortunately, available only in fragments, mostly from citations in the Fathers. His second type are the Gnostic-type gospels in which Jesus is no longer the historical Jesus but an "exalted Revealer" mediating γνῶσις, secret truth to "enlighten" the πνευματικοί. The third type are those which seek to supplement some aspect of the canonical Gospels, e.g., the Infancy Gospels.[18]

---

[17]See Meeks's summary of Luke's use of "prophet" for Jesus (*Prophet-King*, 28, n. 1)

[18]W. Schneemelcher, ed., in E. Hennecke, *New Testament Apocrypha* (Philadelphia: Westminster, 1963), 1.82–84.

Of these types, only the first and third bear potential affinity to the canonical Gospels in reflecting a narrative structure. Type two consists primarily of sayings, revealed γνῶσις, and lacks a "history-appearing" narrative form. Only in and by a narrative framework could a gospel utilize Israel's streams of tradition as interpretive categories for Jesus' ministry, as we have witnessed in the Synoptics. The narrative itself is that which anchors the story in a particular tradition-bearing history.[19] The gospels of the third type develop only a small slice of the narrative, undercutting the history-face of the whole story. Vignettes, such as Jesus' boyhood or Pilate's character, are embellished into Novelle or moral apologetic type tales.

Only type one, therefore, reflects a narrative character that embodies "history-appearing" events, to use Hans Frei's term. Both the Gospel of the Nazareans and that of the Ebionites are so fragmentary that no judgment can be made, though it is clear that the former is an expanded version of Matthew.[20] Though the fragments include variant or expanded readings from all the four sections of Matthew's Gospel studied above, none mention Galilee. Two OT citations appear from Matthew 2 and a short note from the temptation scene has Satan showing Jesus "Jerusalem," rather than "the holy city."[21] The Gospel of Peter, paralleling the canonical passion-resurrection narratives, identifies Jesus twice as "King of Israel" and once as "Son of God," all in mockeries (3:7–11). The Gospel goes beyond the canonical witness in showing the scribes, Pharisees and elders "beating their breasts" after they perceived the evil they did, and saying, "behold, how righteous he was!" (cf. 8:28; Luke 23:47). But nowhere do we find any sustained portrait of Israel's traditions shaping the story. Except for the Gospel of the Nazareans, which may reflect the narrative structure of Matthew, Cameron's statement about the Apocryphon of James most likely applies to all the noncanonical Gospels, "Unlike the four gospels that came to be included in the New Testament, the body of the Apocryphon of James has no narrative structure."[22]

---

[19]See here H. Frei's important work which establishes the narrative as the bearer of history-like events: *The Eclipse of Biblical Narrative* (New Haven/London: Yale University, 1974). Eighteenth- and nineteenth-century rational exegesis was not the first to supplant the narrative witness; the Gnostic Gospels did it their own way much earlier.

[20]R. Cameron, ed., *The Other Gospels: Non-Canonical Texts* (Philadelphia: Westminster, 1982).

[21]Ibid., 99.

[22]Ibid., 55.

The significance of this for our purposes is twofold: (1) the narrative form as a tradition-bearing medium of history-like events may well be a distinguishing mark of the canonical Gospels, and even a factor in canonicity, and (2) the distinctiveness of the Synoptics' narrative, reflecting the shaping influence of Israel's story, remains unique. The grounding of the story of Jesus within the conceptual and cultic categories of Israel's story may well mark off the canonical Gospels from all other Gospels.[23] Further, the Galilee-Jerusalem structures of the Synoptics and John, different though they be, are also without parallel in the noncanonical gospels. This historical-geographical structure anchors the canonical gospels, not only in the history of Jesus and the church, but most significantly in Jesus' and the church's historical struggle to extend God's covenant promises with and through Israel to the Gentiles.[24]

---

[23]In his treatment of Gospel origins, in which canonical and non-canonical developments are viewed interactively, H. Koester overlooks these distinctive features of the canonical Gospels (*Ancient Christian Gospels: Their History and Development* [Philadelphia: Trinity International, 1990]).

[24]In addition to these two factors influencing canon formation, intrinsic to the literature itself, William R. Farmer's proposal that the interplay between the persecutions of the early church and the valuing of certain books, saving them at the risk of life, provides a third pillar that connects the canonical process to historical struggle. According to this view, those books which made it into the canon did so because they nurtured and empowered Christians amid suffering. It is striking how prominent that theme is in virtually all the New Testament writings. See Farmer, *Jesus and the Gospel*, 177–221. Farmer, after showing the correlation between emerging lists of books and persecution, concludes: "That the reality of Christian martyrdom in the early church and the selection of Christian writings for the New Testament canon stand in some vital relationship to one another is as certain as anything that can be conjectured on this complex historical question" (221). See also Farmer and Farkasfalvy, *Formation of the New Testament Canon*, 7–95. See p. 115 above, n. 59, for related discussion.

APPENDIX II: SECONDARY LEVELS OF TESTING THE THESIS: Correlation of Findings with the Distinctive Content of the Synoptic Gospels

The Synoptics contain two distinctive structural features: the Galilee-Jerusalem design and the function of Peter's confession as the watershed of the narrative, shifting the setting from Galilee to the journey to Jerusalem.[1] In addition, six themes are distinctive to the Synoptics: the kingdom of God, exorcisms, tax collectors and sinners,[2] parables, a prepassion narrative oriented to the temple setting with the Olivet discourse, and the institution of the Lord's Supper extending Passover symbolism. None of these occurs in John, though elements of some do appear in a few of the noncanonical gospels.[3] But the pattern and extent of their occurrence in the Synoptics is distinctive.

---

[1] Luke places the Transfiguration before the shift in setting and thus modifies this design. John's parallel, if it be so considered, occurs in 6:68–69.

[2] John 4 and 8:1–12 would seem to indicate that the same theme is present in John and therefore cannot be said to be only synoptic. For purposes of thematic theological construction, this may be true. But John nowhere uses the phrase, "tax collectors and sinners," and he does not identify either the woman of Samaria or the one taken in adultery as "sinner." As we shall see in the following discussion, the term "tax collectors and sinners" carried special social connotation.

[3] While "kingdom of God" appears in the Gospel of Thomas, it lacks theological tone and depth. The Synoptics' contribution, unlike all the noncanonical Gospels, sets Jesus' proclamation of the kingdom of God within the context of Israel's eschatological hopes and theological vision. Numerous noncanonical gospels contain varying amounts of the passion narrative. Most notable is the Gospel of Peter. In examining this gospel in comparison to the canonical gospels, J. D. Crossan proposes the existence of a more primary *Cross Gospel* as a source behind all these (see J. D. Crossan, *The Cross that Spoke: The Origins of the Passion Narrative* [San Francisco: Harper & Row, 1988]).

Each of the Synoptics privileges the kingdom of God theme: Mark's keynote summary in 1:14–15; Matthew's declaration of Jesus' mission in 4:17; and Luke's anticipation of the theme in 1:33 with a definitive statement of the purpose of Jesus' mission in 4:43, "to proclaim the good news of the kingdom."[4]

Each of the Synoptics contains exorcisms, but John contains none.[5] As noted in ch. 3 above, the exorcisms show forth Jesus' and God's power over the forces of evil. In the Synoptics the proclamation of the gospel (εὐαγγελίζω in Luke; εὐαγγέλιον in Mark and Matthew), is accompanied by exorcisms and healings. These mark the advance of God's kingdom power through Jesus.

In extending table fellowship to tax collectors and sinners, Jesus not only violates the purity laws of Pharisaic Judaism, but he mediates to them God's holy presence and blessing. Luke accents this theme most strongly, but it is present in all three Synoptics.[6]

---

[4]B. Chilton has brought together numerous scholarly expositions of the meaning and significance of the kingdom of God in the teaching of Jesus. These essays helpfully explicate the significance of Jesus' kingdom ministry. For R. Otto, Jesus' bringing of God's kingdom expels the kingdom of Satan. W. G. Kümmel seeks to show that the kingdom is both present and future. M. Lattke locates the meaning of the concept "kingdom of God" in the Jewish background of God as King and One who reigns. N. Perrin proposes that the term "kingdom of God" functions as a tensive symbol that allows for expansive meaning. Most important, Chilton stresses that it signifies a dynamic reality of God's coming in strength to liberate and defend his people. See B. Chilton, ed., *The Kingdom of God in the Teaching of Jesus* (Philadelphia and London: Fortress and SPCK, 1984).

[5]In John two structurally strategic statements declare Jesus' victory over evil: "Now shall the ruler of this world be *cast out* (ἐκβληθήσεται)" at the end of Jesus' public ministry (RSV, 12:31) and "It is finished" at the climax of Jesus' dying (19:30), which in John is also "lifting up" to glory. This portrayal of Jesus' fight against and victory over the power of darkness, profound as it is, deviates significantly from the Synoptics' portrait of Jesus' attack on and victory over the evil powers.

[6]While the issue of authenticity is not at stake in this study devoted to the narrative depictions of the Synoptics, the arguments set forth by Walker and Horsley to challenge the historical reliability of this emphasis as part of a reconstruction of the historical Jesus are weak. They do not account for the rise of the tradition apart from Jesus' own actions. W. O. Walker, "Jesus and the Tax Collectors," *JBL* 97 (1978), 221–38, and Horsley, *Spiral of Violence*, 212–23.

Norman Perrin has argued that Jesus' table fellowship with sinners and tax collectors could have precipitated his death, since fellowship with tax collectors was viewed by the main Jewish political parties as an act broaching treason. Tax collectors were "Jews who made themselves Gentiles," so said Josephus (*Rediscovering the Teaching of Jesus* [New York: Harper & Row, 1967],

The Synoptics also share the common feature of presenting Jesus as a teacher who used many parables. John records no parables of Jesus. In some of the noncanonical Gospels a few parables occur, mostly in Thomas, but with different settings and functions than those in the Synoptics. In the Synoptics the parables are inherently linked to Jesus' proclamation of the kingdom of God and its demands.[7] In the prepassion section of Jesus' Jerusalem ministry each of the Synoptics develops Jesus' relationship to the temple. In Mark all the segments are *located* in relation to the temple, a feature present in Matthew and Luke in significant degree also. In contrast, John has none of this,[8] not even the temple cleansing, in his prepassion section, chs. 12—17. John advances the temple cleansing to chapter 2 and does not even mention the temple in the story of Jesus' triumphal entry (12:12–18). Nor are there any parallels to be found in the noncanonical Gospels to this distinctive structural-thematic feature of the Synoptics.

In the passion narrative more similarities occur between the Synoptics and John's Gospel than in any other section of the gospel story. A most striking difference, however, occurs in relation to the Lord's Supper and its connection with Passover. John's Gospel has no Lord's Supper, although a profound theology of it appears in John 6:53–57—one of John's short snippets of Jesus' ministry *in Galilee!* For each of the Synoptics, however, the Last Supper marks the solemn

---

93–103). J. Donahue assesses Norman Perrin's claim and concludes, on the basis of Galilee's independence from direct Roman control until A.D. 44, that such a judgment would have been possible only in Jerusalem, as his Galilean conduct was assessed there, and during later periods when these traditions were used ("Tax Collectors and Sinners: An Attempt at Identification," *CBQ* 33 [1971], 39–61, esp. 59–60).

For a persuasive portrait of Jesus that handles this feature well, see M. Borg, *Conflict*, 52–82; also *Jesus: A New Vision*, 87–92, 131–37. See also the excellent narrative study by Joanna Dewey, *Markan Public Debate: Literary Technique, Concentric Structure, and Theology in Mark 2:1–3:6* (SBLDS 48; Chico, Calif.: Scholars, 1980), 138ff.

[7] J. Jeremias has suggested nine themes (*The Parables of Jesus* [New York: Scribner's, rev. ed. 1963], 115–226); J. W. Miller groups them under three major main headings (*Step By Step Through the Parables* [New York: Paulist, 1981], v–vii); R. H. Stein discusses their message under four major themes (*An Introduction to the Parables* [Philadelphia: Westminster, 1981], 82–148); M. C. Connick has classified them under seven headings (*Jesus: The Man, The Message, and The Mission* [Englewood Cliffs: Prentice-Hall, 2d ed. 1974), ch. 14.

[8] The temple referent in John 18:20, similar to Mark 14:49 and parr., is actually to events in the first half of the Gospel, quite different from the Synoptics' sequential place-scheme.

(re)making of God's covenant with his followers through Jesus' body and blood. Incorporation into this covenant is through partaking of the bread and the cup, which respectively signify Jesus' body and blood.

In the Synoptics this meal and event are explicitly specified as Passover events. This covenant (in Luke, a *new* one) is described by the awesome phrase, referring to Jesus' own imminent death, " 'this [cup] is my blood of the covenant, which is poured out for many (Matt 26:28; Mark 14:22) for the forgiveness of sins' " (Matt). Luke reads, " 'This cup that is poured out for you is the new covenant in my blood' " (22:20). The solemnity and historic, all-time significance of this event are intensified by the Markan and Lukan introduction which notes that this was the time ("the first day of Unleavened Bread") when "the passover lamb had to be sacrificed" (Luke's reading, 22:7). While the Synoptics use the Passover lamb's body and blood to signify Jesus' own body and blood, to be broken and shed the next day, John makes Jesus the slain Lamb whose death is the Preparation for the Passover (19:31), presumably to occur that evening.[9]

These six thematic features should correlate in some way with the theses set forth in this study. For, if both sets of features are distinctive to the Synoptics, then indeed some degree of correlation should exist. Of these six themes, two, *viz.* the kingdom of God and the parables—more a literary type than a theme—characterize the Synoptic corpus as a whole. Accordingly, all four emphases of Israel's theological traditions are connected to the kingdom of God theme. In the Galilean section, the kingdom of God is linked to the liberating power of the gospel. The good news that sets people free is the gospel of the kingdom of God. Further, the kingdom is inclusive, breaking racial, economic, and gender boundaries. In the Journey section, "entering the kingdom of God" is through costly discipleship. In the temple section, judgment falls upon the covenant children of the kingdom for their abuse of the temple and the mediatorial function it represents. In the crucial parable of the vineyard, the kingdom is taken from the vineyard's temple tenants and given to others. In the

---

[9] The difference involves calendar: the Synoptics put Jesus' crucifixion on 15 Nisan, the day after Passover; John puts it on 14 Nisan, the day of the Passover. For the most thorough scholarly effort to resolve this difference, see A. Jaubert, *The Date of the Last Supper*, trans. I. Rafferty (New York: Alba, 1965). D. G. Dix has also given extensive attention to this issue in *The Shape of the Liturgy* (London, 1945; rep. New York: P. Marshall, 1982). I. H. Marshall helpfully reviews and assesses numerous attempts to resolve this discrepancy (*Last Supper and Lord's Supper* [Grand Rapids: Eerdmans, 1980], 67–75).

passion narrative the kingdom of God motif occurs in all three Gospels in connection with the Lord's Supper. While the covenant-making may appear to echo the exodus motif, rather than the kingship motif which this study accented in the passion narrative, we must observe that the covenant is of the Zion-Davidic unconditional type, and not the conditional Mosaic type.[10] Hence even though the terminology, "the blood of the covenant" harks back to Exodus 24 and the Mosaic covenant-making ceremony, the terms of the covenant echo the Davidic-kingship covenant of 2 Sam 7:13–16; Pss 89 and 132. Hence at the crucial point at which the kingdom of God theme emerges in the passion narrative, the event itself echoes the kingship tradition and the Davidic covenant. The climactic emphasis, "drinking it new in the kingdom of God," likely echoes also Isaiah's royal Zion imagery of the feast of fat things at the messianic banquet (25:6). The kingdom of God theme then is directly correlated with each of the four theological traditions that have influenced the structure and theology of the Synoptics.

Jesus' parables appear in six of the twelve sections (four tradition-shaped sections in three Gospels). In Mark 4 the parables describe the nature of the kingdom community which Jesus is beginning (4:13–34). In 12:1–12 the parable of the Vineyard not only echoes temple imagery, but also typifies the response of the religious leaders, the temple tenants. Luke's parables, concentrated in the Journey narrative, depict emphatically the key themes developed in the way-conquest narrative as a whole: God's love for, grace to, and inclusion of the marginalized, even the enemy. In Matthew the parables of the kingdom (ch. 13) accent the challenge and cost of the kingdom for both the first and the last, thus echoing the Sinaitic motif of covenant-law expectations. The parables in Matthew's transitional section portray attitudes and actions necessary to maintain the life of victory over sin and evil. In the temple section Matthew's early set of parables (chs. 21—22) correlates directly with the temple theme, speaking judgment upon the temple tenants. In the latter set (chs. 24—25), the parables are hooked to the temple theme only indirectly:

---

[10]For this distinction, see D. N. Freedman, "Divine Commitment and Human Obligation," *Int* 18 (1964), 425f. The nature of the Abrahamic covenant, as outlined here by Freedman, is extended in the Davidic covenant. Precisely because the Mosaic conditional covenant put such a heavy obligation upon the human partner, Second Isaiah, according to B. W. Anderson, did not invoke the Sinai covenant tradition amid his extensive Exodus traditions ("Exodus and Covenant in Second Isaiah," 349–57).

the judgment that befell the temple tenants now stands at the door of Matthew's community and calls for faithful, watchful, and compassionate response.

Of the remaining features distinctive to the Synoptics, Jesus' exorcisms and his association with tax collectors and sinners are readily correlated with the thematic emphases in those sections in which they occur, mostly in the Galilean section and some in the Journey narrative. Both features highlight precisely those emphases, liberation and conquest, which belong to these sections, as shown in this study. The exorcisms demonstrate Jesus' liberating power from Satan's bondage. Jesus' fellowship with sinners and tax collectors shows Jesus' liberation ending barriers erected by religious and socioeconomic differences. Hence these two themes correlate directly with the findings of this study.

The correlation of the temple theme with the temple emphasis is tautological, and thus self-evident.

For the final distinctive feature, the connection of the Lord's Supper with the Passover meal, earlier discussion has shown the convergence of the exodus and kingship themes in the institution of the Lord's Supper (pp. 211–12, 238–39, 256 and n. 5.)

Hence none of the distinctive thematic features of the Synoptics fights against the findings of this study. Rather, they all support the findings, and are to a significant extent instruments by which the four OT theological traditions exert their impact within the narrative. This test of this study's hypothesis and findings thus shows that the influence of the OT story with its main theological traditions is an intrinsic part of those features commonly recognized as distinctive to the Synoptics. The influence of the OT traditions, therefore, is not, as it were, a luxury add-on, but an essential feature of the construction of the Synoptic Gospels. It lies at the heart of the structural design; it belongs to the synoptic blueprint. Without the impact of these traditions upon the thought of Jesus, the early church, and the Gospel writers, it is unlikely that the phenomenon we know as the synoptic pattern, with its distinctive features, could have come into existence.

BIBLIOGRAPHY

Aalen, S. " 'Reign' and 'House' in the Kingdom of God in the Gospels." *NTS* 8 (1962) 215–40.

Ambrozic, A. M. *The Hidden Kingdom.* CBQMS 2. Washington, D.C.: CBA of America, 1972.

Anderson, B. W. "Exodus and Covenant Theology in Second Isaiah and Prophetic Tradition." In *Magnalia Dei: The Mighty Acts of God.* Edited by F. M. Cross, Jr., W. E. Lemke, and P. D. Miller. Pages 339–60. New York: Doubleday, 1976.

_____. "Exodus Typology in Second Isaiah." In *Israel's Prophetic Heritage: Essays in Honor of J. Muilenberg.* Edited by B. W. Anderson and W. Harrelson. Pages 177–95. New York: Harper & Row, 1962.

_____. "The Messiah as Son of God: Peter's Confession in Traditio-historical Perspective." In *Christological Perspectives: Essays in Honor of Harvey K. McArthur.* Edited by R. F. Berkey and S. A. Edwards. Pages 157–69. New York: Pilgrim, 1982.

_____. Review of *König und Tempel im Glaubenszeugnis des Alten Testaments,* by N. Poulssen. In *CBQ* 31 (1969), 450–52.

_____., ed. *The Old Testament and the Christian Faith: A Theological Discussion.* New York: Harper & Row, 1963.

Bachmann, M. *Jerusalem und der Tempel: Die geographisch-theologischen Elemente in der lukanischen Sicht des jüdischen Kultzentrums.* BWANT 109. Stuttgart et al.: W. Kohlhammer, 1980.

Bailey, K. E. *Poet and Peasant: A Literary-Cultural Approach to the Parables in Luke.* Grand Rapids: Eerdmans, 1976.

Bal, M. *Narratology: Introduction to the Theory of Narrative.* Toronto: University of Toronto, 1985.

Balch, D. L. "Comments on the Genre and a Political Theme of Luke–Acts: A Preliminary Comparison of Two Hellenistic Historians." *SBL 1989 Seminar Papers.* Pages 343–61. Atlanta: Scholars, 1989.

Baltzer, K. *The Covenant Formulary.* Philadelphia: Fortress, 1971.

_____. "The Meaning of the Temple in the Lukan Writings." *HTR* 58 (1965), 263–77.

Barr, J. *Holy Scripture: Canon, Authority, Criticism.* Philadelphia: Westminster, 1983.

_____. *Old and New in Interpretation: A Study of the Two Testaments.* New York: Harper & Row, 1966.

Barrett, C. K. "The Interpretation of the Old Testament in the New." In *The Authoritative Word: Essays on the Nature of Scripture.* Edited by D. McKim. Pages 37–58. Grand Rapids: Eerdmans, 1983.

Bartsch, H. W. "Die Bedeutung des Sterbens Jesu nach den Synoptikern." *TZ* 20 (1964), 87–102.

Basser, Herbert W. "Derrett's 'Binding' Reopened." *JBL* 104 (1985), 297–300.

_____. "Marcus' 'Gates': A Response," *CBQ* 52 (1990), 307–8.

Bassler, J. "The Parable of the Loaves." *JR* 66 (1986),157–72.

Beardslee, W. A. "The Wisdom Tradition and the Synoptic Gospels." *JAAR* 35 (1967), 231–40.

Bender, P. D. "The Holy War Trajectory in the Synoptic Gospels and the Pauline Writings." M.A. Thesis, Associated Mennonite Biblical Seminaries, 1987.

Berger, K. "Die königlichen Messiastradition des Neuen Testaments." *NTS* 20 (1973), 1–44.

_____. "Zum Problem der Messianität Jesu." *ZTK* 71 (1974), 1–30.

Best, E. "Discipleship in Mark: Mark viii.22–x.52." *SJT* 23 (1970), 323–37.

_____. *Following Jesus: Discipleship in the Gospel of Mark.* JSNTSS 4. Sheffield: University of Sheffield, 1981.

Betz, H. D. *Christology and a Modern Pilgrimage: A Discussion with Norman Perrin.* Claremont, Calif.: The New Testament Colloquium, 1971.

_____. "The Sermon on the Mount: In Defense of an Hypothesis." *BibRes* 36 (1991), 74–80.

Bilezikian, G. *The Liberated Gospel: A Comparison of the Gospel of Mark and Greek Tragedy.* Grand Rapids: Baker, 1977.

Birch, B. "Tradition, Canon and Biblical Authority." *HBT* 2 (1980), 113–25.

Black, C. C. *The Disciples according to Mark: Markan Redaction in Current Debate.* JSNTSS 27. Sheffield: Sheffield Academic, 1989.

Blosser, D. "Jesus and Jubilee, Luke 4:16–30: The Year of Jubilee and Its Significance in Luke." Ph.D. diss., St. Andrews University, 1979.

Bonnard, P. E. "Le Psaume 72: Ses relectures ses traces dans l'oeuvre de Luc?" *RSR* 69 (1981), 259–78.

Boobyer, G. H. "Galilee and Galileans in St. Mark's Gospel." *BJRL* 35 (1952–53), 334–38.

Boomershine, T. *Story Journey: An Invitation to the Gospel as Story-telling.* Nashville: Abingdon, 1988.

Booth, W. C. *The Rhetoric of Fiction.* 2d ed. Chicago: University of Chicago, 1983.

Borg, M. J. *Conflict, Holiness and Politics in the Teachings of Jesus.* New York: Edwin Mellen, 1984.

————. *Jesus, A New Vision: Spirit, Culture and the Life of Discipleship.* San Francisco: Harper & Row, 1987.

Boring, M. E. "The Prophet as Hermeneut." In *Sayings of the Risen Jesus: Christian Prophecy in The Synoptic Tradition.* Pages 95–110. London et al.: Cambridge University, 1982.

————. *Sayings of the Risen Jesus: Christian Prophecy in the Synoptic Tradition.* London, et al.: Cambridge University, 1982.

Bovon, F. *Luke the Theologian: Thirty-three Years of Research [1950–1983].* Translated by K. McKinney. Allison Park, Penn.: Pickwick, 1978.

————. "Studies in Luke–Acts: Retrospect and Prospect." *HTR* 85 (1992), 175–96.

Bowman, J. *The Gospel of Mark: The New Christian Jewish Passover Haggadah.* SPB 8. Leiden: E. J. Brill, 1965.

Bowman, J. W. *Which Jesus?.* New York: Macmillan, 1970.

Brettler, M. Z. *God Is King: Understanding an Israelite Metaphor.* JSOTSS 76. Sheffield: JSOT, 1989.

Brownlee, W. "From Holy War to Holy Martyrdom." In *The Quest for the Kingdom of God.* Edited by H. B. Huffman, F. A. Spina, and A. R. W. Green. Pages 281–92. Winona Lake, Ind.: Eisenbrauns, 1983.

Bruce, F. F. *This is That: The New Testament Development of Some Old Testament Themes.* Exeter: Paternoster, 1978.

Büchler, A. "The Reading of the Law and the Prophets in a Triennial Cycle." *JQR* 5 (1893), 420–68; 6 (1894), 1–73.

Buck, E. "The Function of the Pericope 'Jesus Before Herod' in the Passion Narrative of Luke." In *Wort in der Zeit: Festschrift für*

K. H. Rengstorf. Edited by W. Haubeck and M. Bachmann. Pages 165–78. Leiden: E. J. Brill, 1980.

Bultmann, R. *The History of the Synoptic Tradition.* Translated by J. Marsh. Reprinted Peabody: Hendrickson, 1993, rev. ed.

_____. *Das Verhaltnis der urchristlichen Christusbotschaft zum historischen Jesus.* Sitzungsberichte der Heidelberger. Akademie der Wissenschaftes, 1960; Heidelberg: C. Winter, 1962.

Burger, C. *Jesus als Davidssohn: Eine traditionsgeschichtliche Untersuchung.* FRLANT 98. Göttingen: Vandenhoeck & Ruprecht, 1970.

Burkill, T. A. "Galilee and Jerusalem." In *Mysterious Revelation: An Examination of the Philosophy of St. Mark's Gospel.* Ithaca, N.Y.: Cornell University, 1963.

_____. *Mysterious Revelation: An Examination of the Philosophy of St. Mark's Gospel.* Ithaca, N.Y.: Cornell University, 1963.

Burnett, F. *The Testament of Jesus-Sophia: A Redaction-Critical Study of the Eschatological Discourse in Matthew.* Lanham/New York/London: University Press of America, 1981.

Burridge, R. *What Are the Gospels? A Comparison with Graeco-Roman Biography.* SNTSMS 70. Cambridge: Cambridge University, 1992.

Cameron, R., ed. *The Other Gospels: Non-Canonical Texts.* Philadelphia: Westminster, 1982.

Cargal, T. B. " 'His Blood be upon Us and upon Our Children': A Matthean Double Entendre." Paper read at the 1988 Annual SBL Meeting (*1988 Abstracts,* §153. Page 363).

Carrington, P. *According to Mark.* Cambridge: Cambridge University, 1960.

_____. *The Primitive Christian Calendar.* Cambridge: Cambridge University, 1952.

Cassidy, R. J. "Luke's Audience, the Chief Priests, and the Motive for Jesus' Death." In *Political Issues in Luke–Acts.* Edited by R. J. Cassidy and P. J. Scharper. Pages 146–67. Maryknoll, N.Y.: Orbis Books, 1983.

Cassidy, R. J. and P. J. Scharper, eds. *Political Issues in Luke–Acts.* Maryknoll, N.Y. Orbis Books, 1983.

Chance, J. B. *Jerusalem, the Temple, and the New Age in Luke–Acts.* Macon, Ga.: Mercer University, 1988.

Chatman, S. *Story and Discourse: Narrative Structure in Fiction and Film.* Ithaca, N.Y.: Cornell University, 1980.

Childs, B. S. *Biblical Theology of the Old and New Testaments: Theological Reflection on the Christian Bible.* Minneapolis: Augsburg/Fortress, 1992.

_____. "Biblische Theologie und Christliche Kanon." *Jahrbuch für Biblische Theologie* 3 (1988), 13–27.

_____. *Exodus: A Commentary*. London: SCM, 1974.

_____. *The New Testament As Canon: An Introduction*. Philadelphia: Fortress, 1984.

_____. "A Response." *HBT* 2 (1980), 203.

_____. Review of *Holy Scripture: Canon, Authority, Criticism*, by James Barr. *Int* 38 (1984), 66–70.

Chilton, B. *A Galilean Rabbi and His Bible: Jesus' Use of the Interpreted Scripture of His Time*. Wilmington, Del.: M. Glazier, 1984.

_____. ed. *The Kingdom of God in the Teaching of Jesus*. Philadelphia and London: Fortress and SPCK, 1984.

_____. "REGNUM DEI DEUS EST." *SJT* 31 (1978), 261–70.

_____. *Targumic Approaches to the Gospels: Essays in the Mutual Definition of Judaism and Christianity*. Lanham-New York-London: University Press of America, 1986.

Clements, R. E. *God and Temple*. Oxford: Blackwell, 1965.

Coats, G. W. *Rebellion in the Wilderness: The Murmuring Motif in the Wilderness Tradition of the Old Testament*. Nashville: Abingdon, 1968.

Comblin, J. "La Paix dans la Théologie de saint Luc." *ETL* 32 (1956), 439–60.

Connick, M. C. *Jesus: The Man, The Message, and The Mission*. 2d ed. Englewood Cliffs: Prentice-Hall, 1974.

Conrad, E. W. *Fear Not Warrior: A Study of 'al tira' Pericopes in the Hebrew Scriptures*. BJS 75. Chico, Calif.: Scholars, 1985.

Conzelmann, H. *The Theology of St. Luke*. Translated by G. Buswell. New York: Harper & Row, 1961.

Cook, G. "The Israelite King as Son of God." *ZAW* 73 (1961), 202–25.

Cook, M. *Mark's Treatment of the Jewish Leaders*. Leiden: E. J. Brill, 1978.

Cope, O. L. *Matthew: A Scribe Trained for the Kingdom of Heaven*. CBQMS 5. Washington, D.C.: CBA of America, 1976.

Craigie, P. C. "Yahweh Is a Man of War." *SJT* (1969), 183–88.

Croatto, J. S. *Exodus: A Hermeneutics of Freedom*, trans. S. Attanasio. Maryknoll, N.Y.: Orbis Books, 1981.

Crockett, L. C. "Luke 4:25–27 and Jewish-Gentile Relations in Luke–Acts." *JBL* (1969), 177–83.

Crosby, M. H. *House of Disciples: Church, Economics and Justice in Matthew*. Maryknoll, N.Y.: Orbis Books, 1989.

Cross, F. M., Jr. "The Divine Warrior in Israel's Early Cult." In *Biblical Motifs: Origins and Transformations*. Edited by A. Altmann. Pages 11–30. Cambridge, Mass.: Harvard University, 1966.

Crossan, J. D. *The Cross That Spoke: The Origins of the Passion Narrative*. San Francisco: Harper & Row, 1988.

Cullmann, O. *The Christology of the New Testament*. London: SCM, 1959.

_____. *Salvation in History*. New York: Harper & Row, 1967.

Culpepper, R. A. *Anatomy of the Fourth Gospel*. Philadelphia: Fortress, 1983.

Dahl, N. A. *The Crucified Messiah and Other Essays*. Minneapolis: Augsburg, 1974.

_____. *Das Volk Gottes: Eine Untersuchung zum Kirchenbewusstsein des Urchristentums*. Oslo: I Kommisjon hos Jacob Dybwad, 1941.

Dahood, M. *Psalms*. AB. Garden City, N.Y.: Doubleday, 1966.

Danker, F. W. *Luke*. Proclamation Commentaries. Philadelphia: Fortress, 1987.

_____. Review of *The Gospel According to Luke I–IX* (Anchor Bible), by Joseph Fitzmyer. *Int* 37 (1983), 297–99.

Daube, D. "The Earliest Structure of the Gospels." *NTS* 5 (1958), 174–87.

Davies, J. G. "The Prefigurement of the Ascension in the Third Gospel." *JTS* n.s. 6 (1955), 229–33.

Davies, J. H. "The Purpose of the Central Section of St. Luke's Gospel." In *Studia Evangelica*, II (TU 87). Edited by F. L. Cross. Pages 164–69. Berlin: Akademie-Verlag, 1964.

Davies, W. D. *The Setting of the Sermon on the Mount*. Cambridge: Cambridge University, 1964.

de Jonge, M. "The Earliest Use of *Christos*, Some Suggestions." *NTS* 32 (1986), 321–43.

Derrett, J. D. M. "Binding and Loosing (Matt 16:19; 18:18; John 20:23)." *JBL* 102 (1983), 112–17.

_____. *The Making of Mark: The Scriptural Bases of the Earliest Gospel*. Shipston-on-Stout: Drinkwater, 1985.

Deutsch, C. "Wisdom in Matthew: Transformation of a Symbol." *NovT* 32 (1990), 13–47.

Dewey, J. *Markan Public Debate: Literary Technique, Concentric Structure, and Theology in Mark 2:1–3:6*. SBLDS 48. Chico, Calif.: Scholars, 1980.

Dibelius, M. *From Tradition to Gospel*. Translated by B. L. Woolf. New York: Scribner's, n.d.

Dix, G. *The Shape of the Liturgy.* London, 1945; reprint New York: P. Marshall, 1982.

Dodd, C. H. *According to the Scriptures: The Substructure of New Testament Theology.* London: Nisbet, 1952.

_____. "The Framework of the Gospel Narrative." *ExpTim* 43 (1932), 396–400; reprint *NTS* 1 (1953), 1–11.

Donahue, J. R. *Are You the Christ? The Trial Narrative in the Gospel of Mark.* SBLDS 10. Society of Biblical Literature, 1973.

_____. "The Good News of Peace." *The Way* 22 (1982), 88–89.

_____. *The Gospel in Parable: Metaphor, Narrative, and Theology in the Synoptic Gospels.* Philadelphia: Fortress, 1988.

_____. "Tax Collectors and Sinners: An Attempt at Identification." *CBQ* 33 (1971), 39–61.

_____. "Temple, Trial, and Royal Christology. In *The Passion in Mark.* Edited by W. H. Kelber. Philadelphia: Fortress, 1976.

_____. *The Theology and Setting of Discipleship in the Gospel of Mark.* Milwaukee, Wis.: Marquette University, 1983.

_____. "Who Is My Enemy? The Parable of the Good Samaritan and the Love of Enemies." In *The Love of Enemy and Nonretaliation in the New Testament.* Edited by W. M. Swartley. Pages 137–56. Louisville: Westminster/John Knox, 1992.

Donaldson, T. L. *Jesus on the Mountain: A Study in Matthean Theology.* JSNTSS 8. Sheffield: JSOT, 1985.

Dormeyer, D. and Frankemölle, H. "Evangelium als literarische Gattung und als theologischer Begriff . . . " *ANRW* II. 25. 2. Edited by W. Haase (Berlin/New York: W. de Gruyter, 1984). Pages 1543–704

Dowd, S. E. *Prayer, Power, and the Problem of Suffering.* SBLDS 105. Atlanta, Ga.: Scholars, 1988.

Dowda, R. E. "The Cleansing of the Temple in the Synoptic Gospels." Ph.D. diss., Duke University, 1972.

Drury, J. *Tradition and Design in Luke's Gospel.* Atlanta: John Knox, 1976.

Duling, D. C. "Binding and Loosing: Matthew 16:19; Matthew 18:18; John 20:23." *Forum* 3 (4, 1987), 3–31.

_____. "Solomon, Exorcism, and the Son of David." *HTR* 68 (1975), 235–52.

Eaton, J. H. *Kingship and the Psalms.* 2d ed. The Biblical Seminar 3. Sheffield: JSOT, 1986.

Edwards, D. R. "Acts of the Apostles and the Greco-Roman World: Narrative Communication in Social Contexts." *SBL 1989 Seminar Papers.* Pages 362–77. Atlanta: Scholars, 1989).

Elias, J. "The Beginning of Jesus' Ministry in the Gospel of Luke." Th.D. diss., Toronto School of Theology, 1978.

Elliott-Binns, L. E. *Galilean Christianity.* SBT 16. London: SCM, 1956.

Ellis, E. E. "How the New Testament Uses the Old." In *Prophecy and Hermeneutic in Early Christianity.* Pages 147–72. Grand Rapids: Eerdmans, 1978.

_____. "The Old Testament Canon in the Early Church." In *Mikra: Text, Translation, Reading and Interpretation.* Edited by M. J. Mulder and H. Sysling. Philadelphia: Fortress, 1988.

_____. *The Old Testament in Early Christianity.* Grand Rapids: Baker, 1992.

_____. *Paul's Use of the Old Testament.* Edinburgh: Oliver and Boyd, 1957. Reprinted Grand Rapids: Baker, 1981.

Ellis, P. F. *Matthew: His Mind and His Message.* Collegeville, Minn.: Liturgical, 1974.

Encyclopedia Judaica. vol.15. Jerusalem: Keter Publishing House, 1971.

Esler, P. F. *Community and Gospel in Luke–Acts: The Social and Political Motivations of Lucan Theology.* Cambridge/New York et al.: Cambridge University, 1987.

Evans, C. F. "The Central Section of Luke's Gospel." In *Studies in the Gospels.* Edited by D. E. Nineham. Pages 37–53. Oxford: Blackwell, 1955, 1967.

_____. *Saint Luke.* TPINTC. London: SCM and Philadelphia: Trinity, 1990.

_____. "I Will Go Before You Into Galilee." *JTS* n.s. 5 (1954), 3–18.

Farmer, J. H. "Mark." *ISBE* 3, 1987.

Farmer, W. R. *Jesus and the Gospel: Tradition, Scripture and Canon.* Philadelphia: Fortress, 1982.

Farmer, W. R. and Denis M. Farkasfalvy. *The Formation of the New Testament Canon: An Ecumenical Approach.* New York/Ramsey/Toronto: Paulist, 1985.

Farrer, A. *St. Matthew and St. Mark.* 2d ed. Philadelphia: Westminster, 1966.

Fawcett, T. *Hebrew Myth and Christian Gospel.* London: SCM, 1973.

Finger, T. N. *Christian Theology: An Eschatological Approach.* vol. 1. Scottdale, Penn.: Herald, 1985.

Fischer, K. M. and U. C. von Walde. "The Miracles of Mark 4:35–5:43: Their Meaning and Function in the Gospel Framework." *BTB* 11 (1981), 13–16.

Fishbane, M. "The 'Exodus' Motif: The Paradigm of Historical Renewal." In *Text and Texture: Close Readings of Selected Biblical Texts*. Pages 121–40. New York: Schocken, 1979.

_____. "Exodus 1–4: The Prologue to the Exodus Cycle." In *Text and Texture: Close Readings of Selected Biblical Texts*. Pages 63–76. New York: Schocken, 1979.

Fitzmyer, J. A. *The Gospel According to Luke I–IX, vol. 1*. AB 28. Garden City, N.Y.: Doubleday, 1981.

Flender, H. *St. Luke, Theologian of Redemptive History*. Translated by R. H. and I. Fuller. London: SPCK, 1967.

Flusser, D. *Die rabbinschen Gleichnisse und der Gleichniserzähler Jesus*. Bern: Peter Lang, 1981.

Foakes-Jackson, F. J. and K. Lake. "Christology." In *The Beginnings of Christianity*. Volume 1. Edited by F. J. Foakes-Jackson and K. Lake. London: Macmillan, 1920.

Ford, J. M. *My Enemy Is My Guest: Jesus and Violence in Luke*. Maryknoll, N.Y.: Orbis Books, 1984.

Forsyth, N. *The Old Enemy: Satan and the Combat Myth*. Princeton, N.J.: Princeton University, 1987.

Fowler, R. *Loaves and Fishes*. Chico, Calif.: Scholars, 1981.

France, R. T. *Jesus and the Old Testament: His Application of Old Testament Passages to Himself and His Mission*. Downers Grove, Ill. InterVarsity, 1971.

Freedman, D. N. "Divine Commitment and Human Obligation." *Int* 18 (1964), 419–31.

Frei, H. *The Eclipse of Biblical Narrative*. New Haven, Conn./London: Yale University, 1974.

Freyne, S. *Galilee, Jesus and the Gospels: Literary Approaches and Historical Investigations*. Philadelphia: Fortress, 1988.

Frye, N. *The Great Code: The Bible and Literature*. New York/London: Harcourt Brace Jovanovich, 1982.

Frye, R. M. "The Jesus of the Gospels: Approaches Through Narrative Structure." In *From Faith to Faith: Essays in Honor of Donald G. Miller*. PMS 31. Edited by D. Y. Hadidian. Pages 75–89. Pittsburgh: Pickwick, 1979.

Garland, D. E. *The Intention of Matthew 23*. NovTSup 52. Leiden: E. J. Brill, 1979.

Garrett, S. R. *The Demise of the Devil: Magic and the Demonic in Luke–Acts*. Minneapolis: Augsburg/Fortress, 1989.

_____. "Exodus from Bondage: Luke 9:31 and Acts 12:1–24." *CBQ* 52 (1990), 656–80.

Gaston, L. "The Messiah of Israel as Teacher of the Gentiles: The Setting of Matthew's Gospel." In *Interpreting the Gospels*. Edited by J. L. Mays. Pages 78–96. Philadelphia: Fortress, 1981.

_____. *No Stone Upon Another: Studies in the Significance of the Fall of Jerusalem in the Synoptic Gospels*. NovTSup 23. Leiden: E. J. Brill, 1970.

George, A. *Etudes sur l'oeuvre de Luc*. Sources Biblique. Paris: Gabalda, 1978.

_____. "La royauté de Jesus." In *Etudes sur l'oeuvre de Luc*. Pages 257–82. Sources Biblique. Paris: Gabalda, 1978.

Gerbrandt, G. E. *Kingship According to the Deuteronomic History*. SBLDS 87. Atlanta: Scholars, 1986.

Gerhardsson, B. *Memory and Manuscript*. Lund: C. W. K. Gleerup, Upsala, 1961.

_____. "The Path of the Gospel Tradition." In *The Gospel and the Gospels*. Edited by P. Stuhlmacher. Pages 75–96. Grand Rapids: Eerdmans, 1991.

Gese, H. *Essays on Biblical Theology*. Translated by K. Crim. Minneapolis: Augsburg, 1981.

_____. "Tradition and Biblical Theology." In *Tradition and Theology in the Old Testament*. Edited by D. Knight. Pages 301–26. Philadelphia: Fortress, 1977.

_____. *Vom Sinai zum Zion*. Munich: Chr. Kaiser, 1974.

Gill, D. "Observations on the Lukan Travel Narrative and Some Related Passages." *HTR* 63 (1970), 199–221.

Goergen, D. *The Mission and Ministry of Jesus*. Vol. 1. Wilmington, Del.: Michael Glazier, 1986.

Goppelt, L. *Theology of the New Testament*. vol. 1. Grand Rapids: Eerdmans, 1981.

Goulder, M. D. "The Chiastic Structure of the Lucan Journey." In *Studia Evangelica*. Vol. 2. Edited by F. L. Cross. Pages 195–202. Berlin: Akademie-Verlag, 1964.

_____. *The Evangelists' Calendar: A Lectionary Explanation of the Development of Scripture*. London: SPCK, 1978.

_____. *Midrash and Lection in Matthew*. London: SPCK, 1974.

Grassi, J. A. *The Hidden Heroes of the Gospels: Female Counterparts of Jesus*. Collegeville, Minn.: Liturgical, 1989.

Gray, S. W. *The Least of My Brothers, Matthew 25:31–46. A History of Interpretation*. Atlanta: Scholars, 1989.

Greene, T. M. *The Light in Troy: Imitation and Discovery in Renaissance Poetry*. New Haven, Conn.: Yale University, 1982.

Greenspoon, L. J. "The Origin of the Idea of Resurrection." In *Traditions in Transformation: Turning Points in Biblical Faith*. Edited by B. Halpern and J. D. Levenson. Pages 247–321. Winona Lake: Eisenbrauns, 1981.

Guelich, R. " 'The Beginning of the Gospel': Mark 1:1–15." *BR* 27 (1982), 5–15.

Gundry, R. H. *Matthew: A Commentary on His Literary And Theological Art*. Grand Rapids: Eerdmans, 1982.

————. *The Use of the Old Testament in St. Matthew's Gospel*. NovTSup 18. Leiden: E. J. Brill, 1967.

Hadas, M. and Smith, M. *Heroes and Gods*. New York: Harper & Row, 1965.

Haenchen, E. *Der Weg Jesu: Eine Erklärung des Markus-Evangeliums und der kanonischen Parallelen*. Berlin: Walter de Gruyter, 1968.

Hahn, F. *Mission in the New Testament*. SBT 47. London: SCM, 1965.

Harner, P. B. *Grace and Law in Second Isaiah: "I Am the Lord."* Ancient Near Eastern Texts and Studies 2. Lewiston, N.Y./Queenston, Ont.: Edwin Mellen, 1988.

Harris, R. *Testimonies I and II*. Cambridge: Cambridge University, 1916 and 1920.

Hauerwas, S. *The Peaceable Kingdom*. Notre Dame and London: Notre Dame University, 1983.

Hay, D. M. *Glory at the Right Hand: Psalm 110 in Early Christianity*. SBLMS 18. Nashville/New York: Abingdon, 1973.

Hays, R. B. *Echoes of Scripture in the Letters of Paul*. New Haven, Conn.: Yale University, 1989.

Hedrick, C. W. "What Is A Gospel? Geography, Time, and Narrative Structure." *Persp Rel Stud* 10 (March 1983), 255–68.

Heine, S. *Women and Early Christianity: A Reappraisal*. Minneapolis: Augsburg, 1988.

Held, H. J. "Matthew as Interpreter of the Miracle Stories." In *Tradition and Interpretation in Matthew*. Edited by G. Bornkamm, G. Barth, and H. J. Held. Pages 165–299. Philadelphia: Westminster, 1963.

Hengel, M. "Literary, Theological, and Historical Problems in the Gospel of Mark." In *The Gospel and the Gospels*. Edited by P. Stuhlmacher. Pages 202–51. Grand Rapids: Eerdmans, 1991.

Hennecke, E. *New Testament Apocrypha*. Vol. 1. Philadelphia: Westminster, 1963.

Herberg, W. *Faith Enacted As History: Essays in Biblical Theology*. Philadelphia: Westminster, 1976.

Hiers, R. H. " 'Binding and Loosing': The Matthean Authorizations."
    JBL 104 (1985), 233–50.

Hill, D. *The Gospel of Matthew.* NCB. London: Oliphants, 1972.

_____. "My Kingdom Is Not of This World." *IrishBibStud* 9 (1987),
    54–62.

Hobbs, E. C. "The Gospel of Mark and the Exodus." Ph.D. diss.,
    University of Chicago, 1958.

Hollander, J. *The Figure of Echo: A Mode of Allusion in Milton and
    After.* Berkeley: University of California, 1981.

Hooker, M. *The Son of Man in Mark.* Montreal: McGill University,
    1967.

Horsley, R. A. "Ethics and Exegesis: 'Love Your Enemies' and the
    Doctrine of Non-Violence." *JAAR* 54 (1986). Pages 3–31. Article
    also in *The Love of Enemy and Nonretaliation in the New Testa-
    ment.* Edited by W. M. Swartley. Pages 72–101. Louisville: West-
    minster/John Knox, 1992.

_____. *Jesus and the Spiral of Violence: Popular Jewish Resistance in
    Roman Palestine.* San Francisco: Harper & Row, 1987.

Hunter, A. M. *A Pattern for Life: An Exposition of the Sermon on the
    Mount, Its Making, Its Exegesis, and Its Meaning.* Rev. ed. Phila-
    delphia: Westminster, 1962.

Janzen, W. *Still in the Image: Essays in Biblical Theology and Anthro-
    pology.* Newton, Kans.: Faith and Life, 1982.

Jaubert, A. *The Date of the Last Supper.* Translated by I. Rafferty. New
    York: Alba House, 1965.

Jenkins, A. K. "Young Man or Angel." *ExpTim* 97 (1983), 237–40.

Jeremias, J. *Jerusalem in the Time of Jesus.* Translated by F. H. and C.
    H. Cave. Philadelphia: Fortress, 1969.

_____. *New Testament Theology: The Proclamation of Jesus.* Trans-
    lated by J. Bowden. New York: Scribner's, 1971.

_____. *The Parables of Jesus.* rev. ed. New York: Scribner's, 1963.

Johnson, L. T. *The Writings of the New Testament: An Interpretation.*
    Philadelphia: Fortress, 1986.

Johnson, S. E. "The Davidic-Royal Motif in the Gospels." *JBL* 87
    (1968), 136–50.

Jones, D. L. "The Title κύριος in Luke–Acts." In *SBL 1974 Seminar
    Papers,* vol. 2. Edited by G. MacRae. Pages 85–101. Missoula,
    Mont.: Scholars, 1974.

_____. "The Title χριστός in Luke–Acts." *CBQ* 32 (1970), 69–76.

_____. "The Title 'Servant' in Luke–Acts." In *Luke–Acts: New Per-
    spectives from the SBL Seminar.* Edited by C. H. Talbert. Pages
    148–65. New York: Crossroads, 1984.

Juel, D. *Messiah and Temple: The Trial of Jesus in the Gospel of Mark.* Missoula, Mont.: Scholars, 1977.

_____. *Messianic Exegesis: Christological Interpretation of the Old Testament in Early Christianity.* Philadelphia: Fortress, 1988.

Kähler, M. *The So-called Historical Jesus and the Historic Biblical Christ.* Translated by C. E. Braaten. Philadelphia: Fortress, 1963.

Kapelrud, A. S. "Tradition and Worship: The Role of the Cult in Tradition Formation and Transmission." In *Tradition and Theology in the Old Testament.* Edited by D. Knight. Pages 101–24. Philadelphia: Fortress, 1977.

Keck, L. E. "Christological Motifs im Mark 14:1–42: A Preliminary, Tentative, Series of Observations." Unpublished SBL paper, 1971.

Kee, H. C. *Community of the New Age: Studies in Mark's Gospel.* Philadelphia: Westminster, 1977.

_____. *Miracle in the Early Christian World.* New Haven and London: Yale University, 1983.

_____. "The Terminology of Mark's Exorcism Stories." *NTS* 14 (1968–69), 232–46.

Kelber, W. H. "Conclusion: From Passion Narrative to Gospel." In *The Passion in Mark: Studies on Mark 14–16.* Edited by W. Kelber. Pages 153–80. Philadelphia: Fortress, 1976.

_____. "Kingdom and Parousia in the Gospel of Mark." Ph.D. diss., University of Chicago, 1970.

_____. *The Kingdom in Mark: A New Place and New Time.* Philadelphia: Fortress, 1974.

_____. *Mark's Story of Jesus.* Philadelphia: Fortress, 1979.

_____. "Narrative as Interpretation and Interpretation of Narrative: Hermeneutical Reflections on the Gospels." *Semeia* 39 (1987), 107–33.

Keller, E. and M.-L. *Miracles in Dispute.* Philadelphia: Fortress, 1968.

Kermode, F. *The Genesis of Secrecy: On the Interpretation of Narrative.* Cambridge, Mass.: Harvard University, 1979.

Kingsbury, J. D. *The Christology of Mark's Gospel.* Philadelphia: Fortress, 1983.

_____. "The Composition and Christology of Matt. 28:16–20." *JBL* 93 (1974), 573–84.

_____. *Matthew: Structure, Christology, Kingdom.* Philadelphia: Fortress, 1975.

Kittel, G. ed. *Theological Dictionary of the New Testament.* Translated by G. Bromiley. Grand Rapids and London: Eerdmans, 1964.

Klassen, W. "The God of Peace: New Testament Perspectives on God." In *Towards a Theology of Peace*. Edited by S. Tunnicliffe. London: European Nuclear Disarmament, 1989.

_____. "The Novel Element in the Love Commandment of Jesus." In *The New Way of Jesus*. Edited by W. Klassen. Newton, Kans.: Faith and Life, 1980.

_____. *Love of Enemies*. Philadelphia: Fortress, 1984.

_____, ed. *The New Way of Jesus*. Newton, Kans.: Faith and Life, 1980.

Knight, D. "Canon and the History of Tradition." *HBT* 2 (1980), 127–49.

Knight, D. "Tradition and Theology." In *Tradition and Theology in the Old Testament*. Edited by D. Knight. Pages 1–8. Philadelphia: Fortress, 1977.

Knight, D., ed. *Tradition and Theology in the Old Testament*. Philadelphia: Fortress, 1977.

Koester, H. *Ancient Christian Gospels: Their History and Development*. Philadelphia: Trinity Press International, 1990.

Kort, W. A. *Story, Text, and Scripture: Literary Interests in Biblical Narrative*. University Park, Penn./London: Pennsylvania State University, 1988.

Kümmel, W. G. *The Theology of the New Testament*. Translated by J. E. Steely. Nashville/New York: Abingdon, 1973.

Lachs, S. T. *A Rabbinic Commentary on the New Testament: The Gospels of Matthew, Mark, and Luke*. Hoboken, N.J.: KTAV, 1987.

Ladd, G. E. *A Theology of the New Testament*. Part I. Grand Rapids: Eerdmans, 1974.

Lane, W. L. *Commentary on the Gospel of Mark*. NICNT. Grand Rapids: Eerdmans, 1974.

Lapide, P. *The Sermon on the Mount: Utopia or Program for Action?* Trans. A. Swidler. Maryknoll, N.Y.: Orbis Books, 1986.

Levenson, J. D. *Creation and the Persistence of Evil*. San Francisco: Harper & Row, 1988.

_____. *Sinai and Zion: An Entry into the Jewish Bible*. San Francisco: Harper & Row, 1985.

Liefeld, W. L. "Theological Motifs in the Transfiguration Narrative." In *New Dimensions in New Testament Study*. Edited by R. N. Longenecker and M. Tenney. Pages 162–79. Grand Rapids: Zondervan, 1974.

Lightfoot, R. H. *The Gospel Message of St. Mark*. Oxford: Oxford University, 1950.

_____. *Locality and Doctrine in the Gospels.* London: Hodder & Stoughton, 1938.

Lind, M. C. "Monotheism, Power, and Justice: A Study in Isaiah 40–55." *CBQ* 46 (1984), 432–46.

_____. "Transformation of Justice: From Moses to Jesus." In *Monotheism, Power, and Justice: Collected Old Testament Essays.* TR 3. Pages 82–103. Elkhart, Ind.: Institute of Mennonite Studies, 1990.

_____. *Yahweh Is A Warrior.* Scottdale, Penn.: Herald, 1980.

Lindars, B. *Jesus, Son of Man: A Fresh Examination of the Son of Man Sayings in the Gospels.* Grand Rapids: Eerdmans, 1983.

_____. *New Testament Apologetic.* London: SCM, 1961.

Lindbeck, G. A. *The Nature of Doctrine: Religion and Theology in a Postliberal Age.* Philadelphia: Westminster, 1984.

Lohfink, G. *Die Sammlung Israels: Eine Untersuchung zur lukanische Ekklesiologie.* Munich: Kösel-Verlag, 1975.

Lohmeyer, E. *Galiläa und Jerusalem.* Göttingen: Vandenhoeck & Ruprecht, 1936. Translated by L.E. Elliott-Binns in his book, *Galilean Christianity.* SBT 16. London: SCM, 1956.

_____. "Das Gleichnis von den bosen Weingartern (Mark 12:1–2)." In *Urchristliche Mystik: Neutestamentliche Studien.* 2d ed. Pages 159–81. Darmstadt: H. Gertner, 1958.

_____. *Lord of the Temple: A Study of the Relation Between Cult and Gospel.* Translated by S. Todd. Edinburgh and London: Oliver and Boyd, 1962.

_____. *Urchristliche Mystik: Neutestamentliche Studien.* 2d ed. Darmstadt: H. Gertner, 1958.

Longenecker, R. *Biblical Exegesis in the Apostolic Period* (Grand Rapids: Eerdmans, 1975).

Luz, U. "Das Geheimnismotiv und die Markinische Christologie." *ZNW* 56 (1965), 9–30.

Maddox, R. *The Purpose of Luke–Acts.* Edinburgh: T. & T. Clark, 1982.

Malbon, E. S. "Fallible Followers: Women and Men in the Gospel of Mark." *Semeia* 28. Edited by M. A. Tolbert. Pages 29–48. Chico, Calif.: Scholars, 1983.

_____. "Galilee and Jerusalem: History and Literature in Marcan Interpretation." *CBQ* 44/2 (1982), 242–55.

_____. "The Jesus of Mark and the Sea of Galilee." *JBL* 103 (1984), 363–77.

_____. *Narrative Space and Mythic Meaning in Mark.* San Francisco: Harper & Row, 1986.

_____. "Structuralism, Hermeneutics, and Contextual Meaning." *JBL* 51/2 (1983), 207–20.

Mānek, Jindrick. "The New Exodus in the Books of Luke." *NovT* 2 (1958): 8–23.

Manson, T. W. *The Servant-Messiah.* Cambridge: Cambridge University, 1953.

Marcus, J. "The Gates of Hades and the Keys of the Kingdom (Matt 16:18–19)." *CBQ* 50 (1988), 443–55.

_____. *The Way of the Lord: Christological Exegesis of the Old Testament in the Gospel of Mark.* Louisville, Ky.: Westminster/John Knox, 1992.

Marshall, C. D. *Faith as a Theme in Mark's Narrative.* SNTSMS 64. Cambridge: Cambridge University, 1989.

Marshall, I. H. *Last Supper and Lord's Supper.* Grand Rapids: Eerdmans, 1980.

_____. *Luke: Historian and Theologian.* Grand Rapids: Zondervan, 1971.

Martin, R. P. "A Gospel in Search of a Life-Setting." *ExpTim* 80 (1969), 361–64.

Marxsen, W. *Mark the Evangelist: Studies on the Redaction History of the Gospel.* Translated by R. A. Harrisville, et al. Nashville and New York: Abingdon, 1969.

Masuda, S. "The Good News of the Miracle of the Bread: The Tradition and Its Markan Redaction." *NTS* 28 (April 1982), 191–219.

Matera, F. J. *The Kingship of Jesus: Composition and Theology in Mark 15.* SBLDS 66. Chico, Calif.: Scholars, 1982.

_____. *Passion Narratives and Gospel Theologies.* Maryknoll, N.Y.: Paulist, 1986.

Mattill, J. A., Jr. *Luke and the Last Things.* Dillsboro, N.C.: Western North Carolina, 1979.

Mauser, U. *Christ in the Wilderness: The Wilderness Theme in the Second Gospel and its Basis in the Biblical Tradition.* London: SCM, 1963.

_____. *The Gospel of Peace.* SPS 1. Louisville: Westminster/John Knox, 1992.

Mays, J. L. "What is Written: A Response to Brevard Childs." *HBT* 2 (1980), 151–63.

McCarthy, D. J. *Treaty and Covenant.* 2d ed. AnBib 21A. Rome: Pontifical Institute, 1978.

McCasland, V. "The Way." *JBL* 77 (1958), 222–30.

McCown, C. C. "The Geography of Luke's Central Section." *JBL* 57 (1938), 53–66.

McCurley, F. R. *Ancient Myths and Biblical Faith: Scriptural Transformations.* Philadelphia: Fortress, 1983.

McKelvey, R. J. *The New Temple: The Church in the New Testament.* London: Oxford University, 1969.

McNeil, B. "The Son of Man and the Messiah: A Footnote." *NTS* 26 (1980), 419–21.

Meeks, W. A. "The Man from Heaven in Johannine Sectarianism." *JBL* 91 (1972), 44–72.

_____. *The Prophet-King: Moses Traditions and the Johannine Christology.* NovTSup n.s. 14; Leiden: E. J. Brill, 1967.

Meier, J. P. *The Vision of Matthew: Christ, Church, and Morality in the First Gospel.* New York et al.: Paulist, 1979.

Mendenhall, G. E. "Ancient Oriental and Biblical Law." *BA* 17 (1954), 26–46.

_____. "Covenant Forms in Israelite Tradition." *BA* 17 (1954), 50–76.

Mettinger, T. N. D. *The Dethronement of the Sabaoth: Studies in the Shem and Kabod Theologies.* Lund: C. W. K. Gleerup, 1982.

_____. *King and Messiah.* Lund: C. W. K. Gleerup, 1976.

_____. "Fighting the Powers of Chaos and Hell—Towards a Biblical Portrait of God." *ST* 39 (1985), 21–38.

Meye, R. *Jesus and the Twelve.* Grand Rapids: Eerdmans, 1968.

Miller, J. W. *Step By Step Through the Parables.* New York: Paulist, 1981.

Miller, P. D., Jr. *The Divine Warrior in Early Israel.* HSM 5. Cambridge, Mass.: Harvard University, 1975.

_____. "God the Warrior." *Int* 19 (Jan 1965), 35–46.

Minear, P. *The Eyes of Faith: A Study in the Biblical Point of View.* Philadelphia: Westminster, 1946.

_____. *The God of the Gospels.* Atlanta: John Knox, 1988.

_____. *To Heal and To Reveal: The Prophetic Vocation According to Luke.* New York: Seabury, 1976.

_____. *Saint Mark.* LBC. London: SCM and Nashville: Abingdon, 1962.

Moessner, D. P. *Lord of the Banquet: The Literary and Theological Significance of the Lukan Travel Narrative.* Minneapolis: Augsburg/Fortress, 1989.

_____. "Luke 9:1–50: Luke's Preview of the Journey of the Prophet Like Moses of Deuteronomy." *JBL* 102 (1983), 575–605.

Moo, D. J. *The Old Testament in the Gospel Passion Narratives.* Sheffield: Almond, 1983.

Moore, S. D. *Literary Criticism and the Gospels: The Theoretical Challenge.* New Haven, Conn.: Yale University, 1989.

Morgan, R. with J. Barton. *Biblical Interpretation of the Bible*. New York: Oxford University, 1988.

Mowery, R. L. "God the Father in the Gospel of Matthew." Speech and handout at the Boston SBL meeting, 1987.

_____. "God, Lord and Father: The Theology of the Gospel of Matthew." *BR* 33 (April 1988), 24–33.

Munck, J. *Christ and Israel: An Interpretation of Romans 9–11*. Translated by I. Nixon. Philadelphia: Fortress, 1967.

Nebe, G. *Prophetisch Züge im Bild Jesu bei Lukas*. BWANT 7/7. Stuttgart/Berlin/Köln: W. Kohlhammer, 1989.

Neirynck, F. *Duality in Mark: Contributions to the Study of the Markan Redaction*. Louvain: Leuven University, 1972.

Neusner, J. *From Politics to Piety: The Emergence of Pharisaic Judaism*. Englewood Cliffs, N.J.: Prentice-Hall, 1973.

Niedner, F. A. Jr., "Re-reading Matthew on Jerusalem and Judaism." Paper read at the 1988 Annual SBL Meeting (*1988 Abstracts*, §38. Page 263).

Nolan, B. *The Royal Son of God: The Christology of Matthew 1–2 in the Setting of the Gospel*. OBO 23. Göttingen: Vandenhoeck & Ruprecht, 1979.

Noth, M. *Exodus: A Commentary*. OTL. Philadelphia: Fortress, 1962.

_____. *A History of Pentateuchal Traditions*. Translated by B. W. Anderson. Englewood Cliffs: Prentice-Hall, Inc., 1972.

Ollenburger, B. C. *Zion, the City of the Great King: A Theological Symbol of the Jerusalem Cult*. Sheffield: JSOT, 1987.

Osten-Sacken, P. von der. "Zur Christologie des lukanischen Reiseberichts." *EvT* 33 (1973), 476–96.

Overman, J. A. *Matthew's Gospel and Formative Judaism: The Social World of the Matthean Community*. Minneapolis: Fortress, 1990.

Patrick, D. *The Rendering of God in the Old Testament*. Philadelphia: Fortress, 1981.

Patte, D. *The Gospel According to Matthew: A Structural Commentary on Matthew's Faith*. Philadelphia: Fortress, 1987.

_____. *Paul's Faith and the Power of the Gospel: A Structural Introduction to the Pauline Letters*. Philadelphia: Fortress, 1983.

Pawlikowski, J. *Jesus and the Theology of Israel*. Wilmington, Del.: M. Glazier, 1989.

Peck, M. S. *People of the Lie: The Hope for Healing Human Evil*. New York: Simon and Schuster, 1983.

Perrin, N. *Christology and A Modern Pilgrimage: A Discussion with Norman Perrin*. Edited by H. D. Betz. Claremont, Calif.: The New Testament Colloquium, 1971.

————. "The Creative Use of the Son of Man Traditions by Mark." *USQR* 23 (1967–68), 357–65.

————. "The Literary Gattung 'Gospel'—Some Considerations." *ExpTim* 82 (Oct. 1970), 4–7.

————. *Rediscovering the Teaching of Jesus*. New York: Harper & Row, 1967.

Pervo, R. "Must Luke and Acts Belong to the Same Genre?" *SBL 1989 Seminar Papers*. Pages 309–16. Atlanta: Scholars, 1989.

Pesch, R. "The Markan Version of the Healing of the Gerasene Demoniac." *The Ecumenical Review* 23 (1971), 349–76.

————. *Naherwartungen: Tradition und Redaktion im Markus 13*. Düsseldorf: Patmos-Verlag, 1968.

Petersen, N. *Literary Criticism for New Testament Critics*. Philadelphia: Fortress, 1978.

Pilgrim, W. E. *Good News to the Poor: Wealth and Poverty in Luke–Acts*. Minneapolis: Augsburg, 1981.

Piper, O. A. "God's Good News: The Passion Story According to Mark." *Int* 9 (1955), 165–82.

————. "The Origin of the Gospel Pattern." *JBL* 78 (1959), 115–24.

————. "Unchanging Promises: Exodus in the New Testament." *Int* 11 (1957), 3–22.

Pobee, J. *Persecution and Martyrdom in the Theology of Paul*. JSNTSS 6. Sheffield: JSOT, 1985.

Poulssen, N. *König und Tempel im Glaubenszeugnis des Alten Testamentes*. SBM 3. Stuttgart: Katholisches Bibelwerk, 1967.

Puskas, C. B. *An Introduction to the New Testament*. Peabody, Mass.: Hendrickson, 1989.

Quesnell, Q. *The Mind of St. Mark: Interpretation and Method Through the Exegesis of Mark 6:52*. AnBib 38. Rome: Pontifical Biblical Institute, 1969.

Räisänen, H. *Das "Messiasgeheimnis" im Markusevangelium*. Schriften der Finnischen Exegetischen Gesellschaft 28. Helsinki: Länsi–Suomi, 1976.

Rast, W. E. *Tradition History and the Old Testament*. Philadelphia: Fortress, 1972.

Reicke, B. "Instruction and Discussion in the Travel Narrative." In *Studia Evangelica*, I (TU 73). Edited by K. Aland. Pages 206–16. Berlin: Akademie-Verlag, 1959.

————. *The Roots of the Synoptic Gospels*. Philadelphia: Fortress, 1986.

Reid, D. P. "Peace and Praise in Luke." In *Blessed Are the Peacemakers.* Edited by A. J. Tambasco. Pages 79–115. New York/Mahwah: Paulist, 1989.

————. *The Roots of the Synoptic Gospels.* Philadelphia: Fortress, 1986.

Reitzel, F. X. "St. Luke's Use of the Temple Image." *Review for Religious* 38 (1979), 520–539.

Rensburger, D. "Jesus' Kingship in John's Trial Narrative." *JBL* 103 (1984), 395–411.

Reploh, K.-G. *Markus—Lehrer der Gemeinde: Eine redaktionsgeschichtliche Studie zu den Jüngerperikopen des Markusevangeliums.* SBM 9. Stuttgart: Katholisches Bibelwerk, 1969.

Resseguie, J. L. "Interpretation of Luke's Central Section (Luke 9:51–19:44) Since 1856." *Studia Biblica et Theologica* 5/12 (1975), 3–36.

Reventlow, H. G. *Problems of Biblical Theology in the Twentieth Century,* trans. J. Bowden. Philadelphia: Fortress, 1986.

Rhoads, D. "Narrative Criticism and the Gospel of Mark." *JAAR* 50 (1982), 411–34.

Rhoads, D. and D. Michie. *Mark As Story: An Introduction to the Narrative of a Gospel.* Philadelphia: Fortress, 1982.

Richard, E. *Acts 6:1–8:4: The Author's Method of Composition.* SBLDS 41. Missoula, Mont.: Scholars, 1978.

————. "Luke—Writer, Theologian, Historian: Research and Orientation of the 1970's." *BTB* 13 (1983), 3–15.

Riesenfeld, H. *The Gospel Tradition.* Philadelphia: Fortress, 1970.

Ringe, S. H. *Jesus, Liberation, and the Biblical Jubilee.* Philadelphia: Fortress, 1985.

————. "Luke 9:28–36: The Beginning of An Exodus." In *The Bible and Feminist Hermeneutics,* Semeia 28. Edited by M. A. Tolbert. Pages 83–99. Chico, Calif.: Scholars, 1983.

Ringgren, H. *The Messiah in the Old Testament.* SBT. Chicago: Allenson, 1956.

Rivkin, E. *A Hidden Revolution: The Pharisees' Search for the Kingdom Within.* Nashville: Abingdon, 1978.

————. "Pharisees." In *IDB: Supplementary Volume.* Pages 657–63. Nashville: Abingdon, 1976.

Robbins, V. *Jesus the Teacher: A Socio-Rhetorical Interpretation of Mark.* Philadelphia: Fortress, 1984.

Robinson, J. M. "Jesus as Sophos and Sophia: Wisdom Tradition and the Gospels." In *Aspects of Wisdom in Judaism and Early Chris-*

tianity. Edited by R. L. Wilken. Pages 1–16. Notre Dame: Notre Dame, 1975.

————. *The Problem of History in Mark*. SBT 21. London: SCM, 1957.

Robinson, W. C., Jr. "The Theological Context for Interpreting Luke's Travel Narrative (9:51ff.)." *JBL* 79 (1960), 20–31.

————. *Der Weg des Herrn, Studien zur Geschichte und Eschatologie im Lukas-Evangelium*. Hamburg: Herbert Reich, 1964.

Roth, W. *Hebrew Gospel: Cracking the Code of Mark*. Oak Park, Ill.: Meyer-Stone, 1988.

Rothchild, F. A., ed. *Jewish Perspectives on Christianity*. New York: Crossroad, 1990.

Rost, L. "Sinaibund und Davidsbund." *TLZ* 72 (1947), 129–34.

Ruddick, C. T. "Behold, I Send My Messenger." *JBL* 88 (1969), 381–417.

Ruppert, L. *Jesus als der leidende Gerechte?* Stuttgart: KBW, 1972.

Saldarini, A. J. "Pharisees." *ABD* 5. New York: Doubleday, 1992.

Sanders, J. A. *Canon and Community: A Guide to Canonical Criticism*. Philadelphia: Fortress, 1984.

————. "Canonical Context and Canonical Criticism." *HBT* 2 (1980), 173–97.

————. *From Sacred Story to Sacred Text: Canon as Paradigm*. Philadelphia: Fortress, 1987.

Sandmel, S. "Parallelomania." *JBL* 81 (1962), 1–14.

Schmidt, D. "Luke's 'Innocent' Jesus: A Scriptural Apologetic." In *Political Issues in Luke–Acts*. Edited by R. J. Cassidy and P. J. Scharper. Pages 111–21. Maryknoll, N.Y.: Orbis Books, 1983.

Schnackenburg, R. *Matthäusevangelium 16,21–28,20*. Würzburg: Echter, 1987.

Schneider, G. *Lukas, Theologie der Heilsgeschichte: Aufsätze zum lukanischen Doppelwerk*. BBB 59. Bonn: Peter Hanstein, 1985.

Schneider, J. "Zur Analyse des lukanischen Reisenberichtes." In *Synoptischen Studien*. Edited by J. Schmid and A. Vögtle. Pages 207–29. Munich: Karl Zink, n.d. [1953].

Schnellbächer, E. L. "The Temple as Focus of Mark's Theology." *HBT* 5/2 (1983), 95–112.

————. "Q Bibliography: 1981–1989." In *SBL 1989 Seminar Papers*. Pages 23–37. Atlanta, Ga.: Scholars, 1989.

Schrage, W. *The Ethics of the New Testament*. Translated by D. E. Green. Philadelphia: Fortress, 1988.

Schreiber, J. *Theologie des Vertrauens: Eine redaktionsgeschicht-liche Untersuchung des Markusevangeliums.* Hamburg: Furche-Verlag, 1967.

Schweizer, E. *The Good News According to Mark.* Translated by D. H. Madvig. Richmond, Va.: John Knox, 1970.

Scobie, C. H. H. "North and South: Tensions in Biblical History." In *Biblical Studies.* FS W. Barclay. Edited by J. R. McKay and J. F. Miller. Pages 87–98. Philadelphia: Westminster, 1976.

Seitz, C. R. *Zion's Final Destiny: the Development of the Book of Isaiah: A Reassessment of Isaiah 36–39.* Minneapolis: Augsburg/Fortress, 1991.

Selvidge, M. J. *Daughters of Jerusalem.* Scottdale, Penn., and Kitchener, Ont.: Herald, 1987.

Shank, A. "Peace Themes in the *Psalms of Solomon.*" Unpublished paper. Elkhart, Ind.: Institute of Mennonite Studies, 1985.

Shuler, P. L. *A Genre for the Gospels: The Biographical Character of Matthew.* Philadelphia: Fortress, 1982.

Sigal, P. "Manifestations of Hellenistic Historiography in Select Judaic Literature." *SBL 1984 Seminar Papers.* Pages 161–83. Chico, Calif.: Scholars, 1984.

Sloan, R. B. *The Favorable Year of the Lord: A Study of Jubilary Theology in the Gospel of Luke.* Austin, Tex.: Schola, 1977.

Smith, D. E. "Table Fellowship as a Literary Motif in the Gospel of Luke." *JBL* 106 (1987), 613–38.

Smith, W. C. "Scripture as Form and Concept: Their Emergence for the Western World." In *Rethinking Scripture.* Edited by M. Levering. Pages 35–49. Albany, N.Y.: State University, 1989.

Stagg, E. and F. *Women in the World of Jesus.* Philadelphia: Westminster, 1978.

Steck, O. H. "Theological Streams of Tradition." In *Tradition and Theology in the Old Testament.* Edited by D. A. Knight. Pages 183–214. Philadelphia: Fortress, 1977.

Stegemann, W. and L. Schottroff. *Jesus and the Hope of the Poor.* Translated by M. J. O'Connell. Maryknoll, N.Y.: Orbis Books, 1986.

Stegner, W. R. *Narrative Theology in Early Jewish Christianity.* Louisville, Ky.: Westminster/John Knox, 1989.

Stein, R. H. *An Introduction to the Parables.* Philadelphia: Westminster, 1981.

Stendahl, K. *The School of St. Matthew and Its Use of the Old Testament.* 2d ed. Philadelphia: Fortress, 1968.

Sterling, G. F. "Luke–Acts and Apologetic History." *SBL 1989 Seminar Papers.* Pages 326–42. Atlanta: Scholars, 1989.

Stevens, B. A. "The Divine Warrior in the Gospel of Mark." *BZ* 31 (1987), 101–9.

Stock, A. *Call to Discipleship: A Literary Study of Mark's Gospel.* GNS 1. Wilmington, Del.: Michael Glazier, 1982.

————. "Hinge Transitions in Mark's Gospel." *BTB* XV, 1 (1985), 27–31.

Stott, J. R. W. *The Cross of Christ.* Downers Grove: InterVarsity, 1986.

Strack, H. and P. Billerbeck. *Kommentar zum Neuen Testament,* 6 vols. Munich, 1922.

Strecker, G. *Der Weg der Gerechtigkeit.* 3d ed. FRLANT 82. Göttingen: Vandenhoeck & Ruprecht, 1971.

Stuhlmacher, P. "Jesus as Reconciler. Reflections on the Problem of Portraying Jesus within the Framework of a Biblical Theology of the New Testament. In *Reconciliation, Law & Righteousness: Essays in Biblical Theology.* Translated by E. R. Kalin. Philadelphia: Fortress, 1986.

————. "The Pauline Gospel." In *The Gospel and the Gospels.* Edited by P. Stuhlmacher. Pages 149–74. Grand Rapids: Eerdmans, 1991.

————. *Das paulinische Evangelium, I. Vorgeschichte.* Göttingen: Vandenhoeck & Ruprecht, 1968.

————. "The Theme: The Gospel and the Gospels." In *The Gospel and the Gospels.* Edited by P. Stuhlmacher. Pages 1–25. Grand Rapids: Eerdmans, 1991.

Styler, G. M. "Stages in Christology in the Synoptic Gospels." *NTS* 10 (1964), 398–409.

Suggs, M. J. *Wisdom, Christology and Law in Matthew's Gospel.* Cambridge, Mass.: Harvard University, 1970.

Suhl, A. *Die Funktion der alttestamentlichen Zitate und Anspielungen im Markusevangeliums.* Gütersloh: Gütersloher Verlagshaus Gerd Mohn, 1965.

Swartley, W. M. "Beyond the Historical-Critical Method." In *Essays on Biblical Interpretation: Anabaptist-Mennonite Perspectives.* Edited by W. M. Swartley. Pages 237–64. Elkhart, Ind.: Institute of Mennonite Studies, 1984.

————. "The Christian and the Payment of Taxes Used for War." Elkhart, Ind. (P.O. Box 1245), New Call to Peacemaking, rev. 1985.

————, ed. *Essays on Spiritual Bondage and Deliverance.* OP 11. Elkhart, Ind.: Institute of Mennonite Studies, 1988.

_____. "Gentile Mission and Political Reversal: The 'Mystery of the Kingdom' in Mark 4." *SBL Abstracts 1985*. Page 187.

_____. "The Imitatio Christi in the Ignatian Letters." *VC* 27 (1973), 81–103.

_____, ed. *The Love of Enemy and Nonretaliation in the New Testament*. Louisville: Westminster/John Knox, 1992.

_____. *Mark: The Way for All Nations*. 2d ed. Scottdale, Penn.: Herald, 1981.

_____. "Politics and Peace (εἰρήνη) in Luke's Gospel." In *Political Issues in Luke–Acts*. Edited by R. J. Cassidy and P. J. Scharper. Pages 18–37. Maryknoll, N.Y.: Orbis Books, 1983.

_____. "The Role of Women in Mark's Gospel: A Narrative Analysis." *SBL Abstracts 1987*. Pages 283–84.

_____. *Slavery, Sabbath, War and Women: Case Studies in Biblical Interpretation*. Scottdale, Penn.: Herald, 1983.

_____. "The Structural Function of the Term 'Way' (ὁδός) in Mark's Gospel." In *The New Way of Jesus: FS Howard H. Charles*. Edited by W. Klassen. Pages 68–80. Newton, Kans.: Faith and Life, 1980.

_____. "A Study in Markan Structure: The Influence of Israel's Holy History Upon the Structure of the Gospel of Mark." Ph.D. diss., Princeton Theological Seminary, 1973.

_____. "Temple and Nations in Mark 11–16." Presented at the 1976 Annual Society of Biblical Literature. *SBL Abstracts*, §262. Missoula, Mont.: Scholars, 1976.

Swartz, H. L. "Fear and Amazement Responses: A Key to the Concept of Faith in the Gospel of Mark." Th.D. diss., Toronto School of Theology, 1988.

Sweetland, D. M. *Our Journey With Jesus: Discipleship According to Mark*. GNS 22. Wilmington, Del.: Michael Glazier, 1987.

Sylvan, D. D. "The Temple Curtain and Jesus' Death in Luke." *JBL* 105 (1986), 239–50.

Talbert, C. *Literary Patterns, Theological Themes, and the Genre of Luke–Acts*. Missoula, Mont.: Scholars, 1974.

_____. *What Is a Gospel? The Genre of the Canonical Gospels*. Philadelphia: Fortress, 1977.

Talley, T. J. *The Origins of the Liturgical Year*. New York: Pueblo Publishing Company, 1986.

Tannehill, R. C. "The Disciples in Mark: The Function of a Narrative Role." *JR* 57 (1977), 386–405.

_____. "The Gospel of Mark as Narrative Christology." In *Semeia* 16. Pages 57–96. Missoula, Mont.: Scholars, 1980.

————. "Israel in Luke–Acts: A Tragic Story." *JBL* 104 (1985), 69–85.

————. *The Narrative Unity of Luke–Acts: A Literary Interpretation.* Vol. 1. Philadelphia: Fortress, 1986.

Taylor, V. *The Atonement in New Testament Teaching.* London: Epworth, 1945.

Telford, W. R. *The Barren Temple and the Withered Tree.* JSNTSS 1. Sheffield: JSOT, 1980.

Theissen, G. *The Gospels in Contest: Social and Political History in the Synoptics.* Translated by L. M. Maloney. Minneapolis: Fortress, 1991.

Thissen, W. *Erzählung der Befreiung: Eine exegetische Untersuchung zu Mk 2,1–3,6.* Echter Verlag, 1976.

Tiede, D. L. *Prophecy and History in Luke–Acts.* Philadelphia: Fortress, 1980.

————. "Religious Propaganda and the Gospel Literature of the Early Christian Mission." *ANRW* II, 25, 2. Edited by W. Haase. Berlin/New York: W. de Gruyter, 1984. Pages 1705–29.

Toews, J. E. "Jesus Christ the Convenor of the Church." In *Jesus Christ and the Mission of the Church.* Edited by E. Waltner. Newton, Kans.: Faith and Life, 1990.

Tolbert, M. A. *Sowing the Gospel: Mark's World in Literary-Historical Perspective.* Minneapolis: Augsburg/Fortress, 1989.

Trocmé, E. *La formation de l'évangile selon Marc.* Paris: Universitaires de France, 1963.

Twelftree, G. H. *Christ Triumphant: Exorcism Then and Now.* London: Hodder and Stoughton, 1985.

Tyson, J. B. *The Death of Jesus in Luke–Acts.* Columbia, S.C.: University of South Carolina, 1986.

Ulansey, D. "The Heavenly Veil Torn: Mark's Cosmic Inclusio." *JBL* 110 (1991), 123–25.

van der Waal, C. "The Temple in the Gospel According to Luke." *Neot* 7 (1973), 49–59.

van Unnik, W. C. "The Death of Judas in Saint Matthew's Gospel." *ATR* Suppl. Series 3 (1974), 44–57.

Verhey, A. *The Great Reversal: Ethics and the New Testament.* Grand Rapids: Eerdmans, 1984.

Verseput, D. *The Rejection of the Humble Messianic King: A Study of the Composition of Matthew 11–12.* New York et al.: Peter Lang, 1986.

Via, D. O. Jr. *The Parables: Their Literary and Existential Dimensions.* Philadelphia: Fortress, 1967.

Via, E. J. "According to Luke, Who Put Jesus to Death?" In *Political Issues in Luke–Acts*. Edited by R. J. Cassidy and P. J. Scharper. Pages 122–45. Maryknoll, N.Y.: Orbis Books, 1983.

Vielhauer, P. "Erwägungen zur Christologie des Markusevangeliums." In *Aufsätze zum Neuen Testament*. TBü 31. Munich: Chr. Kaiser, 1965.

von Lips, H. *Weisheitliche Traditionen im Neuen Testament*. WMANT 64; Neukirchen-Vluyn: Neukirchener Verlag, 1990.

von Rad, G. *Old Testament Theology*. Vol. 1. Translated by D. Stalker. Edinburgh: Oliver and Boyd, 1962.

_____. *The Problem of the Hexateuch and other Essays*. Translated by E. W. T. Dicken. New York: McGraw Hill, 1966.

Walker, W. O. "Jesus and the Tax Collectors." *JBL* 97 (1978), 221–38.

Weaver, D. J. *Matthew's Missionary Discourse: A Literary-Critical Analysis*. JSNTSS 38. Sheffield: JSOT, 1990.

_____. "Transforming Nonresistance: From *Lex Talionis* to 'Do Not Resist the Evil One.' " In *The Love of Enemy and Nonretaliation in the New Testament*. Edited by W. M. Swartley. Pages 32–71. Louisville: Westminster/John Knox, 1992.

Weber, H.-R. *Power: Focus for a Biblical Theology*. Geneva: WCC Publications, 1989.

Weeden, T. J. Sr. "The Cross as Power in Weakness." In *The Passion in Mark*. Edited by W. H. Kelber. Pages 115–34. Philadelphia: Fortress, 1976.

_____. *Mark—Traditions in Conflict*. Philadelphia: Fortress, 1971.

Weinert, F. D. "The Meaning of the Temple in Luke–Acts." *BTB* 11 (1981), 85–89.

Weiss, K. "Ekklesiologie, Tradition, und Geschichte in der Jüngerunterweisung Mark viii:27–x:52." In *Der historische Jesu und der kerygmatische Christus*. Edited by H. Ristow and K. Matthiae. Pages 412–438. Berlin: Evangelische Verlagsanstalt, 1960.

Westermann, C. *Isaiah 40–66: A Commentary*. Translated by D. M. H. Stalker. London: SCM, 1969.

_____, ed. *Essays on Old Testament Hermeneutics*. Richmond, Va.: John Knox, 1963.

Wilder, A. *Early Christian Rhetoric: The Language of the Gospel*. New York: Harper & Row, 1964.

Will, J. E. *A Christology of Peace*. Louisville, Ky.: Westminster/John Knox, 1989.

Williams, S. K. *Jesus' Death As Saving Event: The Background and Origin of A Concept*. HTR Diss. 2. Chico, Calif.: Scholars, 1975.

Wilson, S. G. *Luke and the Law*. SNTMS 50. Cambridge et al.: Cambridge University, 1983.

Windisch, H. "Friedensbringer—Gottessöhne: Eine religionsgeschichtliche Interpretation der 7. Seligpreisung." *ZNW* 24 (1925), 240–60.

_____. "Die Sprüche vom Eingehen in das Reich Gottes." *ZNW* 27 (1928), 163–92.

Wink, W. "Counterresponse to Richard Horsley." In *The Love of Enemy and Nonretaliation in the New Testament*. Edited by W. M. Swartley. Pages 133–36. Louisville: Westminster/John Knox, 1992.

_____. "Neither Passivity nor Violence: Jesus' Third Way." *SBL 1988 Seminar Papers*. Atlanta: Scholars, 1988. Pages 210–24. Revised version in *The Love of Enemy and Nonretaliation in the New Testament*. Edited by W. M. Swartley. Pages 102–25. Louisville: Westminster/John Knox, 1992.

_____. *Unmasking the Powers: The Invisible Forces That Determine Human Existence*. Philadelphia: Fortress, 1986.

Witherington, B. III, *Women and the Genesis of Christianity*. Cambridge: Cambridge University, 1990.

Wright, G. E. *God Who Acts: Biblical Theology as Recital*. SBT 8. London: SCM, 1952.

_____. *The Old Testament and Theology*. New York: Harper & Row, 1969.

Yoder, J. H. *As You Go*. Scottdale, Penn.: Herald, 1961.

_____. "The Authority of the Canon." In *Essays on Biblical Interpretation: Anabaptist-Mennonite Perspectives*. Edited by W. M. Swartley. Pages 265–90. Elkhart, Ind.: Institute of Mennonite Studies, 1984.

_____. *The Politics of Jesus*. Grand Rapids: Eerdmans, 1972.

Ziesler, J. A. "The Transfiguration Story and the Markan Soteriology." *ExpTim* 81 (1970), 263–68.

INDEX OF MODERN AUTHORS

Greene, T. M., 139
Greenspoon, L. J., 97
Guelich, R., 108
Gundry, R. H., 10, 62, 70, 71, 120, 123, 171, 173, 174

Haase, W., 284
Hadas, M., 285
Hadidian, D. Y., 29
Haenchen, E., 108
Hahn, F., 169
Halpern, B., 97
Harner, P. B., 277
Harrelson, W., 38
Harris, R., 10
Haubeck, W., 247
Hauerwas, S., ix
Hay, D. M., 13, 199
Hays, R. B., x, 12, 260, 277, 291
Hedrick, C. W., 28
Heine, S., 80
Held, H. J., 1, 62, 64
Hengel, M., 287, 288
Hennecke, E., 302
Herberg, W., 253
Hiers, R. H., 121
Hill, D., 217, 300
Hobbs, E. C., 10, 13, 50, 103–6, 256
Hollander, J., 291
Hooker, M., 114
Horsley, R. A., 67, 68, 306
Hubbard, B., 228
Huffman, H. B., 148
Hummel, R., 224
Hunter, A. M., 72

Janzen, W., 95
Jaubert, A., 308
Jenkins, A. K., 216
Jeremias, J., 2, 228, 307
Johnson, L. T., 10
Johnson, S. E., 205, 213, 214
Jones, D. L., 235, 237, 241, 246
Juel, D., 10, 12, 13, 157–61, 165, 167, 179, 193, 195, 207–10, 282

Kähler, M., 198
Kapelrud, A. S., 33, 37, 281
Keck, L. E., 159
Kee, H. C., 51, 55

Kelber, W. H., 30, 40, 60, 93, 98, 104–6, 110, 157, 158, 163, 165, 166
Keller, E., 91
Keller, M.-L., 91
Kelsey, D., ix
Kermode, F., 28, 59
Kingsbury, J. D., 61, 66, 70, 99, 109, 118, 202, 203, 206, 207, 215, 217, 219, 220, 222–25, 227, 229
Kittel, G., 78, 159
Klassen, W., 69, 98, 148
Knight, D., 24, 259
Koester, H., 304
Kort, W. A., 28, 29
Kraus, H.-J., 15, 16
Kuhn, T., 262
Kümmel, W. G., 2

Lachs, S. T., 253
Ladd, G. E., 2
Lake, K., 235
Lane, W. L., 68
Lapide, P., 71
Lattke, M., 306
Levenson, J. D., 36, 37, 57, 58, 97, 154
Liefeld, W. L., 103, 105
Lightfoot, R. H., 41, 164, 169
Lind, M. C., x, 34, 56, 95, 139, 200, 276
Lindars, B., 10–13, 99, 281, 282
Lindbeck, G. A., 28
Lohfink, G., 188
Lohmeyer, E., 40, 157, 162, 166, 168
Lohse, E., 10
Longenecker, R. N., 10, 103
Luz, U., 105, 108, 111

McCarthy, D. J., 47
McCasland, V., 107
McCown, C. C., 127, 129
McCurley, F. R., 25, 55, 57, 157
McKay, J. R., 275
McKelvey, R. J., 156, 166, 194, 195
McKim, D., 10
McNeil, B., 202
MacRae, G., 235
Maddox, R., 191, 192
Malbon, E. S., 28, 40, 42, 43, 60, 101, 115, 158, 160, 165, 166, 214
Malina, B., 228
Mánek, J., 87

INDEX OF NAMES AND SUBJECTS

Jewish leaders
  elders, 103n21, 158n9, 162, 174,
    176n62, 178, 188, 218, 222, 233,
    235, 303
  high priests, 137, 158, 161–65,
    170, 174, 176n62, 178, 188, 203–
    23, 227, 233, 235, 243, 296, 300
  Pharisees, 52, 56, 72n75, 73–74,
    84, 134–37, 142, 150, 153, 162,
    171, 176–78, 181n72, 196, 223,
    244, 260, 263, 296, 303
  Sadducees, 73, 162, 176
  scribes, 137, 158, 161–63, 170–71,
    174, 176, 178, 180, 188, 202, 210,
    218, 222–23, 233, 235, 267, 274,
    303
John Mark (as author/priority), 3,
    45, 272–73, 286–89
Joseph of Arimathea, 204, 212, 216,
    239
Josephus, 273, 279, 285, 301, 306
Jubilee, 76–80, 87–88, 91, 97,
    189n97, 243, 250, 263
Judas, 178, 203–5, 216, 233, 250
Judea, 28n79, 41, 64, 105, 269n14,
    295–97
Judgment, 16, 34n9,64, 66, 72, 98,
    112, 119, 133–53 passim, 156,
    159–61, 163n26, 164, 170–79,
    183–85, 188–89, 192, 194, 196,
    207, 248, 255, 259, 267, 283, 286,
    298, 302–3, 308
Justice, 45n1, 66, 88, 114n55, 133–
    48 passim, 156, 175n61, 179n69,
    184, 200–201, 210, 230, 245, 248,
    255, 266, 268, 276
Justin, 286

Kingdom of God, 2, 6, 54, 77–83,
    89–91, 98n5, 104–5, 108,
    110n47, 113, 115n59, 132, 135–
    36, 141–42, 148n131, 151n135,
    157n6, 174–75, 179n68, 193,
    195, 198, 201, 204–5, 211–13,
    216, 223, 233, 235, 238–39, 248–
    49, 254–56, 264, 273, 305–10
King of the Jews, 12, 220n55,
    221n59, 222n60, 299–301
King(ship), 4n17, 6–7, 13, 15, 32–
    38, 44–47, 90n114, 95, 103n19,

109, 112n54, 118, 136, 143,
    150n134, 154–58, 163, 168, 172–
    75, 182–86, 190, 195–96, ch. 6
    passim, 254–60, 268–83, 289–90,
    296–303, 308–9

Land, Promised, 38n24, 59, 87, 96–
    97, 103–5, 108, 130, 134, 141,
    151, 254, 264
Lection/Lectionary, 4, 6, 17–18, 129,
    280–81, 284–86, 291
Liberation, 39n27, ch. 3 passim, 96,
    128, 132, 146, 241, 243, 254, 256,
    262–64, 269, 271, 275, 283, 292–
    93, 310
Liturgy(ical), 1, 6, 16–17, 38, 40, 45–
    46, 86, 128, 214n47, 258, 272,
    279–82, 285, 290
Lord, 10–13, 19, 32–33, 57, 66, 70–
    71, 76–79, 98, 103n21, 106–7,
    108n41, 110, 110n47, 111n48,
    113, 117–19, 123, 125, 131n101,
    132–38, 142–45, 148n131, 149,
    152–63, 166n36, 167n40,
    168n42, 170–84, 187, 191, 194–
    95, 202, 210, 220, 223–27, 229–
    31, 234–50, 254–56, 263, 266,
    269, 275, 277
Love (of) enemy, 67–70, 93, 140–41,
    141n121, 147–48, 263, 269

Martyr, 114n55, 115n59, 146–47,
    148n131, 187, 225, 242–43, 267
Mary (Jesus mother), 213, 239–40,
    288
Mary (sister of Martha/Lazurus),
    150, 168, 203, 205, 213–14, 232
Mary Magdalene, 86, 213
Messiah (Christos), 9, 101n13,
    102n16, 109–10, 112, 115–16, ch.
    6 passim, 256n6, 266, 268, 274,
    283
  crucified, 12–13, 203, 206n27,
    213, 237n103, 249, 265, 268, 292
  suffering, 97n3, 110
Messianic psalms, 11n5, 12, 211, 229
Military (ant), 58n41, 60, 96n2,
    112n54, 196, 216, 225, 241
Mission(al), 7, 9, 41–44, 55, 59–74
    passim, 80–87, 99, 110, 113,

INDEX OF ANCIENT SOURCES

25	244
26	244
29	182
31	12, 203, 244, 247, 281
31:5	242, 250
33	175
43	244
43:3	231
45	210
46	199
47	199
48	37, 155, 175, 182, 271
48:1–2	231
48:9	155
48:10	v
48:12–14	155
48:14	v, 231
46	37
50	37, 182, 271
54	244
64	244
65	175
68	34
68:8–9	34
68:16	231
68:18	34
68:19	11
69	12, 203
71	244
72	37, 201, 210, 248, 268, 271, 276
72:10	231
72:15	231
74	37, 156
74:2	231
75	37
76	37
76:2	231
76:5–6	57
77	37
78	37, 47, 59, 98, 270, 280
78:2	11
78:13–31	46
78:52	46
78:68–70	271
78:70–72	199
80	37
80:16	57
81	37
84	37, 155, 175
84:1–2	155
84:10	154
89	12, 13, 37, 271, 309
89:10b	271
89:13	271
93	199
94	244
95—99	199
96:5	53, 121
97	36, 37
99	37
101	37
104:7	57

105	37, 46, 47, 271
105:15	276
106	37, 39, 46, 98, 271
106:37	53, 121
109	244
110	13, 162, 199, 248, 281
110:1	11, 248, 266
114	37, 271
114:3	46
116	11
117:1	277
118	158, 175, 271, 281
118:22	11, 266
118:22–23	11, 162
118:25–26	173, 266
118:27	162
121—135	156
132	37, 155, 199, 309
132:13–14	231
135	280
135:21	231
136	37, 47, 280
140	244
142	244

Proverbs
| 1—9 | 182 |

Isaiah
1	156
1:2–3b	199
1:3	107
2:1–5	156
2:2	73, 160
2:2ff.	229
2:2–5	195
2:4	43
3	156
5	158
6:3	182
6:9f.	11
6:9–10	11
7—8	156
7:14	11, 224, 231
8:18	231
8:23—9:1	11
9	206
9:1–7	156
9:2–7	199
9:5	11
9:6–7	224
10	156
11	276
11:1	11
11:1–5	224
11:1–9	156
11:10	11, 277
14	112, 140
24:23	228
25:6–8	35, 136, 195
25:6–10a	229, 230
25:6–10	73
25:23	229
27:12–13	195

19:41–44	144, 186	22:35—23:2	233
19:42	136	22:37	233
19:42–44	190	22:39	241
19:43–44	143	22:39–46	251
19:44	126, 136	22:43–44	251
19:45	126	22:47	189
19:47	188	22:47–53	251
19:47–48	186	22:48	242
19:47—21:4	186	22:49	241
19:47—22:2	188	22:51	251
19:48	188	22:53d	233
20:1	81, 83, 84, 188	22:54–62	251
20:4	237	22:61	241
20:6	188	22:63–64	232
20:9	188	22:63–65	251
20:18	11	22:66	188, 235
20:19	188	22:66–71	251
20:20	138, 244	22:67	235
20:23	244	22:67–71	234
20:26	188	22:67b–68	236
20:41–44	240	22:69	236, 242
20:45	188	22:70	238
21	189, 267	23	234
21—23	186	23:1–2	162, 251
21:5–38	186	23:2	235, 238
21:6	189	23:3	235
21:23	189	23:3–5	251
21:24	189, 190	23:3–38	233
21:27	190	23:4	236
21:28	189, 190	23:5	188, 270
21:36	190	23:6–12	251
21:37–38	186–87	23:13	188, 236
21:38	188	23:13–25	251
22—24	242	23:14	188, 236
22:1–2	250	23:18b	232
22:1–34	238	23:18–23	188
22:1–54	233	23:22	236
22:2	188	23:22b	236
22:3–6	250	23:24	188, 236
22:6	189	23:25	237
22:7	308	23:27–31	251
22:7–13	250	23:32–43	251
22:7–27	133	23:35	188, 221, 235, 236
22:7–38	131	23:35b	236
22:7—23:16	94	23:35d	233
22:14–17	250	23:35–39	240
22:14–18	238	23:37	235
22:15	233	23:38	235
22:16	233	23:38b	236
22:18–23	250	23:39	221, 235, 236
22:19–20	238	23:39—24:12	233
22:20	308	23:42	239
22:21–23	251	23:43	232, 233
22:22	233, 242	23:44–49	251
22:24–27	239	23:45b	186
22:24–30	233, 251	23:46	232, 233, 242
22:28–30	239	23:47	138, 233, 234, 245, 303
22:29b–30	233		
22:30	187	23:50–56	251
22:31–32	251	23:50b–51	239
22:33	241	24	131
22:33–34	251	24:1–11	251
22:33–38	251	24:3	242

3:14	244	19:18–30	85
3:18	243	20:25	239
3:22	19, 89, 92, 128, 243, 275	21	186, 191
3:24	243	21—40	85
3:26	235, 245	21:20	245
4:21	245	22:4	194
4:25–26	250	22:14	244
4:25–27	246	24:21	195
4:27	233, 235, 237, 245	25:26	241
4:30	235, 245	26:18	85
5:1–11	79, 121	26:23–31	239
5:31	234, 240		
5:42	81	**Romans**	
6	275	1:4	105
6—7	186, 191	1:16–17	277
6:1—8:4	185, 187	9—11	190
6:8–15	267	15:7–13	277
6:13	194	16:20	150
7	50, 89, 98, 194, 278		
7:38	47	**1 Corinthians**	
7:44–50	192	2:6–8	115
7:47–52	267	10:6–22	53
7:52	244	11:15	114
8	85	15:25	11
8:4	81		
8:12	81, 239	**Galatians**	
8:23	77	1:15—2:14	288
8:25	81	6:16	15
8:40	81		
9	287	**Ephesians**	
9:2	194	1:22	11
9:20	238	2:11	167
9:22	238	2:17	81
10—11	287	4:8–11	11
10:34–38	275		
10:36	81, 237, 240	**Philippians**	
10:38	77	2:9–11	226, 228
11:18	245		
11:20	81, 237	**Colossians**	
12:1–24	87	2:11	167
12:12	288	4:11	288
13	85, 278		
13:5–13	286	**1 Thessalonians**	
13:16–41	237	1:6–7	115
13:16b–23	278		
13:32	81	**1 Timothy**	
13:33	238	2:6	114
13:48	245	3:16	228
14:7	81		
14:15	81	**2 Timothy**	
14:21	81	4:11	288
14:22	239		
15	191	**Hebrews**	
15:1–21	195	1:5–14	228
15:15–18	185, 187	2:5–8	11
15:25	81	3:1–6	179
15:38–39	288		
15:39	288	**1 Peter**	
16:10	81	3:19	121
17:7	238	5:13	288
17:18	81		
19	85, 87	**Revelation**	
		2:26ff.	229
		20—21	136